NOW IS THE
DAWNI...
OF THE
NEW AGE NEW WORLD ...RDER...

NEW AGE
Now — 21st Century

FRANCE
1789

RUSSIA
1917

Though there has been revolution after revolution (symbolized by spirals or whirlwinds) around the world for centuries, the New Age Revolution is the all-encompassing, largest one ever. All borders must come down; all religious barriers must be broken. One world; one government; one religion; one humanity, made up of humans with a collective consciousness and serving as "points of light" networking around the globe. The symbol of the red dragon is explained in Revelation 12:3-4. The colors depicted under the dragon symbolize the tri-vehicle of Economy-Ecology-Ecumenism upon which the dragon is riding as he ushers in the New Age New World Order by means of crises and various consciousness-changing processes. These will result in increased numbers joining inter-faith environmental ministries ("greening of religion") or even the re-emerging mythological Great Mother Earth/Goddess/Gaia movement, and in many more people believing, in desperation, the false promise to bring forth a Utopian world of health and happiness (wellness-wholeness), peace and prosperity, and harmony and unity — or as some have described it: the "Golden Dawn." Watch carefully plans and actions resulting from the U.N. Conference on Environment and Development (Brazil, 1992), and from the World Parliament of Religions (United States, 1993), especially the "Earth" section.

Dennis Laurence Cuddy has a Ph.D. in American History from the University of North Carolina at Chapel Hill, has taught in the public schools and at the university level, and has been a Senior Associate with the U.S. Department of Education, as well as a political analyst for an international consulting firm. He has four published books and articles in journals such as *The Lincoln Review* and *The Australian Journal of Politics and History*. Other articles of his have been printed mostly in major American daily newspapers about 500 times over the past decade. Two of these articles have won awards in the annual Amy Writing Awards, which promote biblical values in the secular press. Dr. Cuddy has also been a guest on radio talk shows in various parts of the nation, such as ABC-Radio in New York City. And he has also been a guest on the national television program "USA Today" and CBS' "Nightwatch."

NOW IS THE
DAWNING
OF THE
NEW AGE NEW WORLD ORDER

DENNIS LAURENCE CUDDY, Ph.D.

Hearthstone Publishing Ltd.
P.O. Box 815 · Oklahoma City, Ok 73101

A Division Of
Southwest Radio Church Of The Air

All scripture references are from the King James Version unless otherwise stated.

Printed in the United States of America

Published by:
Hearthstone Publishing
P.O. Box 815
Oklahoma City, OK 73101
(405) 235-5396 • WATS 1-800-652-1144
FAX (405) 236-4634

ISBN 1-879366-22-3

"Since I entered politics, I have chiefly had men's views confided to me privately. Some of the biggest men in the United States, in the field of commerce and manufacture, are afraid of somebody, are afraid of something. They know that there is a power somewhere so organized, so subtle, so watchful, so interlocked, so complete, so pervasive, that they had better not speak above their breath when they speak in condemnation of it."

— President Woodrow Wilson
The New Freedom (1913)

If schools teach dependence on one's self, *"they are more revolutionary than any conspiracy to overthrow the government."*

— H.J. Blackham (a founder of the four million-member International Humanist and Ethical Union) in *The Humanist*, September/October 1981

"Radical change is necessary now; you cannot escape it. . . . Strategies and behaviors must be changed because the dawning of this new age is far more significant than the transformation of the national and world economics taking place. . . ."

— Shirley McCune of the Mid-continent Regional Educational Laboratory (McRel)

"We have a new relationship with the Soviet Union. . . . It happened when we acted on the 'ancient knowledge' that strength and clarity lead to peace. . . . An election that is about ideas and values is also about philosophy. And I have one. At the bright center is the individual. And radiating out from him or hear . . . a brilliant diversity spread like stars, like a thousand points of light. . . . Property has a purpose. It is to allow us to pursue 'the better angels,' to give us time to think and grow. . . . For an endless enduring dream and a thousand points of light . . . that is my mission. And I will complete it."

— Vice-President George Bush's acceptance speech at the Republican National Convention, August 18, 1988

"The Master Mason [is] a divinized man. . . . The knowledge of this fact was with the wise ancients . . . the occult potentialities . . . the esoteric science. . . . That man radiates from himself an ethereal surround is testified to by haloes shown in works of art about persons of saintly character. . . . They 'shine as the stars.' . . . Over the cosmic system there presides the Great Architect and Most Worshipful Grand Master of all, whose officers are holy Angels. . . . The Junior Warden symbolizes the third great light . . . the balance-point. . . . God is not outside him, but within him. . . . It is the inextinguishable light of a Master Mason which, being immortal and eternal, continues to shine when everything temporal and mortal has disappeared. . . . Good and evil are realized as a unity or synthesis. . . . The Ancients anticipated the modern Hegelian proposition that thesis, antithesis, and synthesis are the essential ingredients of a given truth. . . . The Master Mason must ascend the 'winding staircase' of his inner nature. . . . The condition attained by the illumined candidate is spoken of as cosmic consciousness . . . the blissful concord of the Eternal . . . perceiving the unity of all in the Being of Deity."

— Past Provincial Grand Registrar W.L. Wilmshurst in *The Meaning of Masonry*

The World Goodwill Bulletin issued a special edition on the United Nations in July 1957, which contained an article entitled "Lodestone." We quote from its description of the Meditation Room: "The visitor will be totally unprepared for what he will see as he steps in the door for a moment of quiet. . . . Because of the converging walls and the dim light, *he will experience a peculiar spatial disorientation*, and dimension and perspective will seem difficult to establish. In the center of the room, he will see, illuminated by a single point of light from the ceiling, a rectangular mass. . . .

"The ore piece . . . is many millions of years old . . . one feels . . . as though one is in a repository for some *natural talisman of significant and noble importance* rather than in a chapel in the ordinary sense. . . . Those who are wedded to seeking communion in traditional settings may be somewhat ill at ease here. This is a sudden break with prior experience. One is thrown violently upon his [own] resources.

"The room and the concept do not seem indicative of the supplications or the dualistic concept of the mystic in which illumination is sought as a boon granted by Deity. Rather, seemingly inherent in the decoration of the room, in the pinpoint of light playing on the ore, is the concept of a personal concentration of forces, creating a focus that illumines the field of attention. . . .

"The pinpoint of light, the void of space, the illuminated crystalline ore — one feels projected into a setting of cosmological symbolism rather than one of planetary or even solar intent.

"It is interesting to speculate on what *the long-term influence of this 'new departure' will be on current religious thinking.* Ensconced here in the highest Hall of Man, it cannot be inconsiderable. Whatever interpretations one may attribute to the United Nations Meditation Room, it can be said with certainty that the words and the repercussions have only just begun." (Emphasis supplied.)

— Reprinted from *The Cult of the All-Seeing Eye* by R.K. Spenser

Note: the Baha'U'llah (of the Bahai's) was known as the "Point" or the "Unity"; and for the Babylonians and Egyptians, the east was the point of sunrise (light).

Table of Contents

Introduction

This volume is not a book in the usual sense of the word; neither is it fiction, nor is it for entertainment. It is, rather, a chronology evidencing the persistent strivings toward a New Age New World Order, which is being so openly and widely promoted today. But it is much more than that, for it will give the reader a broader, long-range view through the window of history than previously seen in one publication. It could be termed a reference book with focus on historical sequences of events and significant quotations by "makers of history," all gaining momentum through the decades and centuries and even accelerating in recent years, which they hoped would — though at first gradually — transform all the earth into the planned Utopian New Age New World Order. There are revealing connections and fascinating details described on a broader scale than, to my knowledge, are readily found anywhere else. It is my hope that the pulling together of voluminous evidence into this one volume of descriptions of earth-changing events and telling remarks in a chronological order will prove useful to all who truly care about helping preserve biblical values and national sovereignty. There are cited sources throughout, so that the reader can conduct further research.

Chapter One

Historical Background

In attempting to find the origins or basis of the New Age New World Order, it would be unwise to look for a single source. The primary goal of today's world planners is power and control, and they really have no exclusively liberal or conservative ideology. Over the years, they have networked through various secret societies to further their ambitions. Some of the leaders of one society, the Freemasons, which supposedly has secret oaths and rituals, have asserted that their organization had its origins in the "ancient mysteries." There is no solid evidence, however, that operative Masonry can trace its lineage generation through generation back to antiquity. On the other hand, one should not ignore certain historical facts and logic. Operative Masons (builders before the eighteenth century) through the years have been familiar with the basic architecture of ancient Egypt, Greece, and Rome, and it is therefore not illogical to assume that they also had some passing knowledge of the symbols, rituals, and oaths of the architects of those ancient civilizations. For example, the Abbey of Arbroath was founded in Scotland in 1178 (where the Scottish Declaration of Independence from England was issued on April 6, 1320), and the figures sculpted on the seal marked "initiation" there are strikingly similar to those described in Plutarch's *De Osiris*.

Further back in history, the Roman Colleges of Builders were established about 715 B.C. and involved far more than just the building associated with operative Masonry. They had a *magister*, or "master"; *decurions*, whose duties were like Masonic wardens; *scriba* or "secretary"; and *sacerdos*, or "chaplain" who provided religious services. The members of the Colleges called themselves *Fraters* and, according to Moses Redding's *The Illustrated History of Freemasonry* (1907), held *"secret meetings in which candidates were initiated, and craftsmen advanced to a higher grade and received esoteric instructions. . . . There were three grades of initiates — apprentices, fellow-workmen, and masters. Their meetings were opened by a religious ceremony — not sectarian, but recognizing Deity as the Grand Architect of the Universe.* [The earliest known reference to God the Creator as 'Architect of the Universe' is in Plato's *Timaeus*]. *The ritual comprised and taught certain religious ceremonies, a knowledge of the obligations and duties imposed upon the initiate, a knowledge of certain symbolism, and secret modes of recognition, and the oath of its inviolability. The fellow-craft was also instructed in the use of the implements of Masonry. . . . Subsequently, the Colleges were known as Guilds. . . . Between 312 and 285 B.C., the Appian Way was constructed by the Colleges, or Fraternities, as they were now often called. . . . They also erected in Paris two new temples, one to Isis, and one to Mithra. . . . In the first century A.D., particular attention was paid to teaching the Egyptian mysteries in the Colleges, which erected the Roman Colosseum beginning in A.D. 70."*

Therefore, while today's speculative Masonry

(modern Masonry beginning in the early eighteenth century) cannot legitimately say that it can trace its origins step-by-step backward through time, it is fair to say that certain of its symbols, rituals, and teachings are based upon a historical tradition that dates back to ancient times and the "ancient mystery religions" (e.g., religion of the Aryan race in the Vedas), in addition to Rosicrucianism and Gnosticism along with a fundamental belief in non-sectarianism.

Concerning historical references to descriptions of "world orders," the ancient Chinese believed that all are members of society, which belongs to everyone. In the West, Plato's *Republic* described an ideal society with no class struggle, while his work *The Laws* looked at a classless society. Aristotle's *Politics* recognized that there are social classes, but he said that *"the whole* [of society] *is more than the addition of its parts."* In more recent history, the two possibilities derived from the Platonic and Aristotelian views were the Utopian visions exemplified in Tommaso Campanella's *La Città del Sole* and Thomas More's *Utopia*, and the manipulative and ominous Machiavellian approach eventually resulting in a form of coercive order. For the purposes of this book, however, a convenient starting point for beginning the chronology toward the New Age New World Order being promoted today will be about one thousand years ago.

● ● ● ● ●

In the eleventh century A.D., Hasan-i Sabbah became first grand master of the Assassins. According to a famous Ismaili story, he had gone to school with Omar

Khayyam (see later where Fabians use his words), and later founded the Assassins who believed there is no absolute good or evil. In 1118, the Burgundian knight Hugues de Payens founded the Order of the Temple (meaning Temple of Solomon; they were also referred to as the Templars or Knights Templar) modeled after the Assassins (knights wore red crosses on a white ground similar in color to Assassin rafiqs, and wore red caps and belts and white tunics) and whose members knew of the esoteric doctrines of the East.

The "secret order" behind the Templars was the Priory (Order) of Sion, founded in 1090 by Godfroi de Bouillon nine years before the Crusaders conquered Jerusalem. The secret order came from the Merovingian (fifth through eighth century A.D. rulers of what is now France) bloodline which, according to a blasphemous and heretical belief, was descended from Jesus and Mary Magdalene. *Merovingian* comes from Merowig, the grandfather of Clovis I, the first Merovingian king. In the grave of Clovis' father, Childeric I, was found a crystal ball and three hundred gold bees. Crystal balls have been found in many Merovingian tombs. The headquarters of the Priory of Sion was in Notre Dame du Mont de Sion just south of Jerusalem. In R. Rohricht's *Regesta Regni Hierosolymitani* (1893), there is a charter dated May 2, 1125 with the name of Prior Arnaldus at Sion linked to Hugues de Payens, Templar first grand master. After a later Templar grand master, Gerard de Ridefort, lost Jerusalem to the Saracens in 1187, the Order of Sion separated from the Templars and chose its own grand master, Jean de Gisors, in 1188. Today, the most prominent descendants of the Merovingian bloodline are the members of the House of Habsburg-Lorraine, who have titles such as Duke of Lorraine and King of Jerusalem. Relevant to the fragmentation of the Catholic Church today is the fact that at the Council of Trent (1562), the Cardinal of Lorraine (Charles) attempted to decentralize the papacy giving greater authority to local bishops as there had been during the Merovingian dynasty. Later, in 1735, Francois, the Duke of Lorraine (an alchemist) married Maria Theresa of Austria linking the Houses of Habsburg and Lorraine. This was after John Desaguliers (the most prominent Mason of the early eighteenth century) initiated Francois into Freemasonry in 1731.

● ● ● ● ●

Returning briefly to the time of the Crusades (where Richard the Lionhearted fled from the Holy Land disguised as a Templar), the "Knights of the Occident" formed an association with the Hospitallers or Knights of St. John of Jerusalem, whose members later left the Orient to settle in the British Isles which, according to French historian Bernard Fay in *Revolution and Freemasonry — 1680-1800* (1935), *"became the abode of chivalrous Freemasonry. After several centuries they created the Scottish degrees."* There have been Templar graves dating back to the early fourteenth century discovered at Kilmartin, Scotland. This was the time of Robert Bruce of Scotland, who sought to restore a Celtic kingdom.

It was at this time in the early 1300s that Phillip IV of France discovered that the Templars were plotting against the Church as well as the thrones of Europe. (English king after king was in constant debt to the Templars, and mention will be made later of how the Houses of Orange and Rothschild used the indebtedness of sovereigns to those houses to control them). Therefore, King Phillip had many of them executed, including their grand master, Jacques de Molay, but not, according to Masonic leader Albert Pike, before he instituted what came to be known as the occult Hermetic or Scottish Masonry, the lodges of which were later established in Naples, Edinburgh, Stockholm, and Paris. According to the *Encyclopedia of Occultism and Parapsychology*, Jacques de Molay confessed that he had been guilty of denying Christ and spitting upon the cross. Just before he was executed, he retracted his confession, but there seems to be no retraction (even in a letter published after death) from any of the tens of thousands of other Knights Templar who survived condemnation. The encyclopedia also indicates that the Templars introduced Gnosticism into their rites, *"institutionalized homosexuality in their Order,"* and that candidates were compelled to take off part or all of their clothing during initiation.

Some of the Knights Templar were said to have remained together forming secret societies passing down through the centuries. A list of the grand masters of the Knights Templar from 1118 to 1838 is given in *The Illustrated History of Freemasonry* by Moses Redding. What may have happened was that from the beginning of the fourteenth century to the middle of the sixteenth century, the Templars perhaps merged with the Hospitallers, as there are references to the "Order of the Knights of St. John and the Temple." In J. Maidment's *Templaria* (1828-1830), there is a charter granted by King James IV of Scotland dated 1488, which refers to

"Fratribus Hospitalis Hierosolimitani, Militibus Templi Solomonis" and seems to indicate recognition of the continued existence of the Templars in some form.

The term "Freemason" was first recorded on official London records in 1376. In the 1425 *Old Charges* (rules of the Masons' assembly), Euclid is said to be the founder of Masonry, and the history of the craft is traced from the building of the Tower of Babel and of Solomon's Temple. The town of Roslin in Scotland was supposedly built by Masons (operative), and in Rosslyn Chapel built in the middle of the fifteenth century, there are a number of sculptures of the Celtic vegetation god known as "The Green Man," for which "Green Robin," or "Robin of Greenwood," or "Robin Hood" was named.

● ● ● ● ●

At this time in the late fifteenth century, Henry VII became the first Tudor king of England (1485-1509). The royal arms of Henry VII was the Tudor rose (his wife, Elizabeth Plantagenet's smaller white rose of the House of York within Henry's larger red rose of the House of Lancaster). In Col. A.G. Puttock's *Dictionary of Heraldry and Related Subjects* (1985), one reads, *"A rose is the difference for the seventh house."*

This reminds one of the first two lines of the song "Age of Aquarius" from the musical *Hair*, which are, *"When the moon is in the seventh house, and Jupiter aligns with Mars."* The "seventh house" is traditionally associated with marriage, and therefore the moon (the feminine, Elizabeth of York) is in the "seventh house" (the House of Henry VII). Jupiter (the higher physical nature) aligns with Mars (the animal instincts) to produce the dawning of the "age of Aquarius" (where supposedly chaos and conflict give way to peace and harmony, and where the allegedly old worn-out traditions give way to new ideas and ways of life). C. Wilfred Scott-Giles in *The Romance of Heraldry* (1929) astutely remarks: *"It is true that Henry mounted the throne with that Parliamentary sanction for which, viewed historically, the red rose stood, but having gained recognition as king in his own right, he wisely satisfied the claims of legitimism by marrying the heiress of the white rose, Elizabeth of York, thus ensuring that his descendants' title to the throne should be unquestionable."*

Note in chapter four of this book where a wizard supposedly gives Merlin the riddle, *". . . there is a little bit of moon in the rose . . ."* (a little bit of the feminine in authority, the white rose of Elizabeth in the red rose of Henry?). Henry VII incorporated the Tudor rose in a collar with a pendant of St. George and the dragon, which he made the insignia of the Order of the Garter. C. Wilfrid Scott-Giles indicates that the emblem had an ancient association with the eternal warfare between the sun and darkness, and *"taking an historical view, this innovation in our national heraldry in his* [Henry VII] *reign, the saint* [St. George] *appears to be the champion of ordered government striking down the monster of anarchy. Under the red rose, 'constitutional progress had outrun administrative order' . . . and the Tudor rose became the symbol of a strong personal rule. . . . Realizing that the maintenance by great lords of private armies of liveried retainers was a menace to the royal power and the peace of the realm, Henry VII vigorously prosecuted the policy,*

*vainly attempted by some of his predecessors, of sup-
pressing livery and maintenance. . . . At the same time,
Henry prohibited the use of family cries in battle. . . . But
his measures to secure internal peace could not be entirely
peaceful. He had to crush implacable Yorkists. . . ."*

In terms of today, one might say that President Bush
(a descendant from both the House of Lancaster and the
House of York) applies a strong personal rule to bring
"order out of chaos" (a Masonic slogan), or out of
conflict, establishing the New World Order. "Doonesbury"
cartoonist Garry Trudeau, who was tapped by the Yale
University secret society Skull and Bones, to which
George Bush had belonged, chose instead to belong to
another Yale secret society, Scroll and Key. Trudeau has
drawn cartoons regarding Skull and Bones. Several years
ago he drew a cartoon highlighting a red rose on a hotel
pillow that President Bush would use, and crowns on the
toiletries in the president's hotel room. And remember
several years earlier, David Morrell wrote a novel, *The
Brotherhood of the Rose* (1984), about a secret
international brotherhood, saying, *"The rose became a
symbol for silence and secrecy. In the Middle Ages, a rose
was customarily suspended from the ceiling of the council
chambers. The members of the council pledged themselves
not to reveal what they discussed in the room,* sub rosa,
under the rose."

Both King Henry VII and his granddaughter, Queen
Elizabeth I (Queen of England, 1558-1603), used the
"phoenix" as one of their badges. Queen Elizabeth I (to
whom President Bush is related) was also fascinated by
men's eyes. The seventeenth century English antiquary
John Aubrey wrote that Sir Francis Bacon (allegedly

Queen Elizabeth's son) had a *"delicate, lively eye. Dr. Harvey told me it was like the eye of a viper."* Favored servants of the queen signed their letters to her with symbolic eyes ("in the twinkling of an eye" can be a symbolic phrase), and John Dee (who headed the British espionage network) signed himself "007." Dee, an acquaintance of the queen's husband (the Earl of Leicester), was an alchemist, astrologer, psychic, and spy. According to *Mind Wars* (1984) by Ron McRae (former associate of columnist Jack Anderson), the basis for his "007" signature was: *"Each zero representing an eye and the seven being the sum of two eyes, four other senses, and last, mystical knowledge from 'the nine' spirits (muses) who spoke through Dee's crystal ball, the 'shew stone.' Dee credited the nine and his shew stone with uncovering a Spanish plot to burn the forests that provided wood for English shipbuilding. Whatever the source, the plot was real. Had it succeeded, the Spanish Armada might have sailed unopposed in 1588."*

Dee's disciple, Robert Fludd, was the chief proponent of Rosicrucianism in England, and Fludd along with Sir Francis Bacon and others were commissioned by King James I (King of England, 1603-1625) to produce an English translation of the Holy Bible.

In 1600, the Edinburgh Masonic Lodge was founded, allegedly handing down the "ancient mysteries." In 1609, Sir Francis Bacon wrote *The Wisdom of the Ancients.* In *Encyclopaedia Britannica,* one reads that Bacon *"claimed all knowledge as his province"* and developed *"a comprehensive plan to reorganize the sciences and to restore man to that mastery over nature that he was conceived to have lost by the fall of Adam."* In 1627,

Bacon's unfinished *New Atlantis*, about a Utopian society across the ocean from Europe, was published post-humously. Marie Bauer Hall writes about Bacon in *Collections of Emblems: Ancient and Moderne* (1987): *"He is the founder of Freemasonry . . . the guiding light of the Rosicrucian Order, the members of which kept the torch of true universal knowledge, the secret doctrine of the ages, alive during the dark night of the Middle Ages."*

According to thirty-third degree Mason Manly P. Hall in *The Secret Destiny of America* (1944), the Order of the Quest symbol is on the cover page of *New Atlantis*, and in his *America's Assignment with Destiny* (1951), one finds that Bacon *"threw the weight of his literary group with the English colonization plan for America."* Sir Walter Raleigh was already a member of what would be called the Baconian Circle when he began his expedition to the New World. In *The Secret Destiny of America*, Hall wrote that *"Bacon's secret society was set up in America before the middle of the seventeenth century."* Hall claimed that the secret society's membership was not limited to England, but was most powerful in Germany, France, and the Netherlands. He said: *"The mystic empire of the wise had no national boundaries. . . . The alchemists, cabalists, mystics, and Rosicrucians were the incisive instruments of Bacon's plan. Representatives of these groups migrated to the colonies at an early date and set up their organization in suitable places. One example would indicate the trend. About 1690, the German Pietist theologian, Magistar Johannes Kelpius, sailed for America with a group of followers, all of whom practiced mystical and esoteric rites. The Pietists settled in Pennsylvania . . . and brought with them the writings of the German mystic,*

Jacob Boehme, books on magic, astrology, alchemy, and the cabala."

•••••

The Mason Mark Twain and many others were convinced, according to William Still's *New World Order* (1990), that the works of the virtually illiterate William Shakespeare, who was only a groom in the employ of Bacon's alleged father, the Earl of Leicester (Robert Dudley, husband of Bacon's alleged mother, Queen Elizabeth I), were not written by him. Rather, it has been speculated that Sir Francis Bacon himself was the author of Shakespeare's works. And according to the Baconian Foundation (in Oregon, with activities in the tradition of the "mystery schools") today, Bacon's "Shakespeare" plays *"foster a lineage of illumination . . . overlighted by the Tenth Muse, Pallas Athena — Goddess of Wisdom, known as the 'Spear Shaker' and Maker of the Law. Her spear symbolizes a pen of literacy which destroys the serpent of ignorance."* Other evidence, however, suggests that perhaps the works of Shakespeare were written by the Earl of Oxford (Edward de Vere), or the Earl of Derby (William Stanley), or Christopher Marlowe, or Sir Walter Raleigh. But George Elliott Sweet in his *Shake-Speare: The Mystery* (1956) makes an excellent case that the works of Shakespeare were actually written by Queen Elizabeth I herself!

•••••

In 1614 in Germany, *Fama Fraternatis of the*

According to the Baconian Foundation (in Oregon, with activities in the tradition of the "mystery schools") today, Bacon's "Shakespeare" plays "foster a lineage of illumination . . . overlighted by the Tenth Muse, Pallas Athena — Goddess of Wisdom, known as the 'Spear Shaker' and Maker of the Law. Her spear symbolizes a pen of literacy which destroys the serpent of ignorance."

Meritorious Order of the Rosy Cross was published, probably by the Lutheran Johann Valentin Andrea and his circle of friends at the University of Tubingen in Wurttemberg. He was thus the founder of Rosicrucianism, a religious syncretist movement based on Gnosticism and a hermetic-cabalist view of man (the soul of man moves in a spiral upward through spheres of angelic hierarchies toward God). According to Norman MacKenzie's edited *Secret Societies* (1967), Andrea *"was an enthusiastic advocate of various unorthodox plans for Christian union, including one in the form of an ideal republic to be called the City of the Sun."* Some have suggested that there was no connection between the Rosicrucian's esoterica and the Masons, but Henry Adamson's 1638 poem, *The Muses Threnodie*, contains the well-known lines:

> *"For we be brethren of the Rosie Crosse;*
> *We have the Mason word, and second sight,*
> *Things for to come we can foretell aright. . . ."*

Another enthusiast for the hermetic tradition and the cabala was the Swiss alchemist Paracelsus (note later reference regarding L. Frank Baum who authored *The Wonderful Wizard of Oz*), who lived from 1493 to 1541 and provides a link between the Renaissance and the first period of Rosicrucianism. Italy was extremely important during the period of the Renaissance, and Catherine de Medici invited Nostradamus to her court, where he correctly predicted the death of her husband, Henri II, in 1559. (His predictions concerning the details of the French Revolution and Napoleonic era many years later proved very accurate.) Actually, if Nostradamus was an agent for the Houses of Guise and Lorraine, then King Henri's death may have been more planned than predicted. Cosimo de Medici's interest in esoterica had come largely from his frend Rene d'Anjou, the Duke of Lorraine. Also, Marie de Guise married James V, and via the Scots Guard and the earlier Templar influence, esotericism increased in Scotland.

Then in D.M. Lyon's *House of the Lodge of Edinburgh* (1900), one reads that John Mylne, *"Master of the Lodge at Scone, and at his Majesty's own desire, entered James VI (King James I of England) as 'frieman, meason, and fellow craft.'"* Also during this time, the famous architect Andrea Palladio (1518-1580) developed what has come to be called the Palladian style (Palladian likewise refers to Pallas Athena and supposedly wisdom or learning) known for its domes and arches (like Georgian-style and the style of many new buildings in the U.S. today). Two reasons many non-Masons would begin to join fraternal lodges were a growing interest in architecture and in obtaining some "hidden wisdom." Those financially able to make the Grand Tour of Europe at the time returned with an admiration for Palladian architecture, and this included Elias Ashmole who became a Freemason in 1646. According to Bernard Fay in *Revolution and Freemasonry — 1680-1800*, *"Many Scottish Masons of the seventeenth century have stated that the Restoration of 1660 was a Masonic feat, and we know for a fact that General Monk was a Mason, which lends a certain credibility to the story."*

● ● ● ● ●

In the last part of the seventeenth century, a

revolutionary change of mind was occurring in Europe. The Royal Society had been founded in 1660, and the views of Sir Isaac Newton were beginning to spread. He became a Fellow in the Royal Society in 1672, and though he was a Christian, his scientific theory concerning an unseen "force" (gravity) that controlled movement in the universe was used by English deists beginning in the late seventeenth century to prove the existence of God, "the Great Architect of the Universe." They did not believe in God through faith or revelation, but rather "reason" was to them supreme, and through "science" demonstrated that God had created certain natural laws which governed everything. On May 18, 1691, the famous architect and well-known Jacobite, Christopher Wren was initiated into Freemasonry, and served as an important link between operative and speculative Masonry.

Sir William Temple (a sort of John J. McCloy of the seventeenth century, and rumored to be the real father of Jonathan Swift) had negotiated the Triple Alliance of England, Sweden, and the Netherlands (against France) in 1668. And while in Holland, he began a lifelong friendship with William of Orange in 1677 helping arrange the marriage of William to Princess Mary (Protestant heir to the English throne). Temple argued that Britain should learn from Holland's toleration of those with different religious views, whereby they had created a rational, humane social order. (A number of his works are found in the Rothschild collection at Trinity College, Cambridge.) At about this same time, Thomas Wharton (a Hanoverian Protestant who organized the Whig Party between 1700 and 1715) was instigating the Revolution of 1688 to drive James II (a Stuart) from the throne of England, and replace him with William and Mary.

In 1689, William of Orange (Holland's House of Orange, which will be referred to again later), with his wife Mary, assumed the throne of England. At the same time, anti-Christian literature from Holland took root in England, and Protestant Huguenots fled from Catholic France to England. One of these Huguenots, John Theophilus Desaguliers (1683-1744), became the most influential individual in English Masonry for this entire period. Desaguliers hated Louis XIV, absolute government, Catholicism, and dogmatic Christianity. He, therefore, eagerly supported the Hanoverian rule of England beginning in 1714 (George I of the House of Guelph and Hanover). He hailed the Hanoverians as "philosopher kings" who believed in natural government which, like Newton's "natural laws" concerning equilibrium, meant that an equilibrium in government between the king and the people was desirable. The Grand Lodge of England was established in 1717, and in its "charges" was written: *"Yet 'tis now thought more expedient only to oblige them to that Religion which all Men agree."*

Previously, there had been invocations to the Trinity, but after 1717 there was no mention of the Trinity or Christ in Masonic rituals. According to Bernard Fay in *Revolution and Freemasonry — 1680-1800, "The new Masonry did not defend revelation, dogmas or faith. . . . In the place of a spiritual religion people were offered an intellectual religion. The new Masonry did not aim to destroy churches but, with the aid of progress in ideas, it prepared to replace them."*

In *Israel et l'Humanite'* (1961) by Rabbi Elie Benamozegh, the editors state, *"To those who may be surprised by the use of such an expression* [Masonic theology], *we should say that there is a Masonic theology in the sense that there exists in Freemasonry a secret, philosophic and religious doctrine, which was introduced by the Gnostic Rosicrucians at the time of their union with the Freemasons in 1717. This secret doctrine, or gnosis, belongs exclusively to the high, or philosophic, degrees of Freemasonry."*

Remember here that St. Paul in 1 Timothy 6:20 warned against the falsehood of gnosis or secret knowledge.

Desaguiliers became the third grand master in 1719, and would later initiate the Prince of Wales into the Grand Lodge. The sixth grand master in 1722 was Philip Wharton (Duke of Wharton, god-son of William of Orange, son of Thomas Wharton, and made a Knight of the Garter in 1741), who ordered that the *Constitutions of the Freemasons Containing the History, Charges, Regulations, Etc., of That Most Ancient and Right Worshipful Fraternity, for the Use of the Lodges* be prepared. Desaguiliers translated Jacques Ozanam's (1640-1717) work on sieges. And several generations later, the latter's descendant, Frederic Ozanam (1813-1853) wrote *Reflections on the Doctrine of Saint Simon* and *The Origins of Socialism*. Frederic was interested in the great mysteries of nature, India, and Buddhism, and he searched for the alleged bases of the ideas of primitive Christianity among the Chinese (Confucius), Egyptians, Persians (Zoroaster), Hindus, and Tibetans.

Desaguiliers also supervised the preparation of *The Constitutions* (published 1723) by a Reverend James Anderson. According to Paul Fisher in *Behind the*

Lodge Door: Church, State, and Freemasonry in America (1988), *"Many parts of [The Constitutions] were 'lifted' from the works of Jan Amos Komensky (Comenius), a seventeenth century bishop of the Moravian Church."* In Joseph Roucek's article, "Jan Amos Komensky," in *New Age* (the Masonic magazine), July 1944, he claims that Rev. Anderson's "Constitutions" changed English Masonry to *"a universal creed based upon the Fatherhood of God and the Brotherhood of Man,"* and that this fundamental ideology of Komensky appealed at once *"to freethinkers, to rationalists, and to lovers of magic and esoteric rites — to the love of mystery in myths, symbols, and ceremonies."* Comenius was an educational reformer (today's term is "restructuring") and Czech theologian, as well as an agent for the secret society, the Order of the Palm. John Cotter in *A Study in Syncretism: The Background and Apparatus of the Emerging One World Church* (1980) describes the ardent feminist Comenius as a religious syncretist who advocated a world parliament, a world ecumenical church, and one universal body of educators, which he called the "staff of *light.*" (In 1957, UNESCO hailed Comenius as its spiritual father and as the "Apostle of International Understanding.")

Three years after *The Constitutions* was written, Jonathan Swift (who worked for Sir William Temple) wrote *Gulliver's Travels* (1726). The Mason Swift was representative of the rationalism of the enlightenment, and many of his works were full of symbolism. Gulliver was *"in doubt to deem himself, a God, or Beast"* in his many travels, and in Lilliput (*lilli* meaning "arbitrary," so *Lilliput* means "arbitrarily put"), which represents England, he found the Lilliputians (narrow-minded, and small like L. Frank Baum's Munchkins) who were divided on religion. This was symbolic of the division between deists who believed in rationalism and reason, and the believers of traditional biblical values of faith and revelation. The Yahoos represented the concept of man as no better than an animal if he does not use his reason, and the Houyhnhnms represented the concept that *"Reason alone is sufficient to govern a* Rational *creature."* Swift is on the cover of the journal, *Knight Templar*, November 1987, vol. 33, no. 11.

• • • • •

Older Masonry was known as "operative" Masonry, but by 1735 the new or "speculative" Masonry was in full control, supporting free inquiry and tolerance. "Fraternity" or "brotherly love" and "good-fellowship" were substituted for Christian charity, and they transformed society. Instead of Christian spiritual freedom, Masonry spoke of civic liberty; and instead of equality of souls before God, Masonry emphasized political equality. Rationalism was in, and mystic thought was out. Historian Bernard Fay remarked about this period, *"Masonry, having thus ensured the political unity of England, started a new task: to try to unify political principles and customs throughout the world. . . . In a century when the conflicting religious denominations had reached a deadlock, the only way for humanity to achieve unity was through Freemasonry. The spirit of Masonry was thus placed above dogmas as a new kind of religion. . . ."*
    In France in the first half of the seventeenth century, Boulainvilliers and Montesquieu were both Masons and

philosophical forerunners of Rousseau and Voltaire. In Stephen Knight's *The Brotherhood: The Secret World of the Freemasons* (1983), one reads, *"Freemasonry, its undefined deism so close to that of Voltairian rationalism, was soon the rage among pre-revolutionary freethinkers in France. Ironically, it may have been planted there by Jacobite exiles around 1725."* Knight's book was followed in 1990 by Martin Short's *Inside the Brotherhood: Further Secrets of the Freemasons.*

In 1738, the Duc d'Antin became grand master in France, and in 1741 said, *"The whole world is only one Republic, of which every nation is a family, and every individual a child."* Here he was quoting from Andrew Michael Ramsay's March 20, 1737 "Oration." Ramsay had taken this particular statement from the liberal Catholic mystic Francois Fénelon, who was Ramsay's mentor. Ramsay further stated in his "Oration" that *"the interests of the Fraternity shall become those of the whole human race."*

The first volume of a French *Encyclopedia* was produced in 1751 under the editorship of Freemason Denis Diderot, with subsequent volumes written by "encyclopedists" Montesquieu, Rousseau, Voltaire, d'Holbach, and d'Alembert (they were called the "philosophers of the enlightenment"). The Grand Orient was created 1772-74 when the Duc d'Orleans was grand master, and the number of lodges quickly grew to include even one lodge composed completely of monks at a Benedictine monastery. In France, it was American Mason Benjamin Franklin who helped initiate Voltaire into Masonry. Voltaire has said: *"I am weary of hearing people repeat that twelve men have been sufficient to establish Christianity, and I will prove that one man may suffice to overthrow it.* " In a letter to fellow subversive Jean d'Alembert, Voltaire also said in code that *"the vine of truth is well cultivated,"* which translated means, "we make amazing progress against religion."

Concerning Freemasonry in other countries during this time, in Dr. Berthold Altmann's article, "Freemasonry and Political Parties in Germany," in the May 1955 issue of *New Age*, he mentions the influence of Freemasonry on the enlightenment of the eighteenth century. And regarding the "free thinkers" of Germany, one reads in Will and Ariel Durant's Pulitzer prizewinning book, *Rousseau and Revolution* (1967), *"Freemasonry shared in the movement. The first lodge of* Freimaurer *was founded at Hamburg in 1733; other lodges followed; members include Frederick the Great and Goethe. Generally these groups favored deism."*

Elsewhere, the Russian Lodge was organized in St. Petersburg in 1771, and Emperor Peter III served as grand master. In Leo Tolstoy's *War and Peace* (1869), about the Napoleanic era, the character "Phillip" joins the St. Petersburg Lodge and says, *"I myself thought like that, and do you know what saved me? Freemasonry. No, don't smile, Freemasonry is not a religious ceremonial sect, as I thought it was. Freemasonry is the best expression of the best, the eternal aspects of humanity."* Russian poet Alexander Pushkin (1799-1837) also writes of his membership in a Kishinev lodge which participated in the "Decembrist Plot" of 1825 that led to a ban of all lodges in the country.

Chapter Two

A Time of Revolution

Concerning the American Revolution, historian James Billington in *Fire in the Minds of Men* (1980) wrote, *"So great, indeed, was the impact of Masonry in the revolutionary era that some understanding of the Masonic milieu seems an essential starting point for any serious inquiry into the occult roots of the revolutionary tradition."*

In Bernard Fay's *Revolution And Freemasonry — 1680-1800*, he claims that organizations such as the Committees of Correspondence and the Sons of Liberty during the American Revolution were Masonic puppet societies. One of the leading individuals of the American Revolution was Benjamin Franklin who, in his youth, asserted there was no such thing as evil (because God created everything, and God cannot create anything evil), no heaven or hell, and no immortal soul or human responsibility. Franklin was a mystic who believed in cosmic spiritualism combined with ancient concepts from the Orient and Platonism. He became a Mason in 1731 at the age of twenty-five, and three years later was provisional grand master for all Masonry in Pennsylvania. According to Manly P. Hall, he was also a member of the Order of the Quest, and according to J. Gordon Melton's *The Encyclopedia Of American Religions*, vol. 2, he was a

Rosicrucian. In Bernard Fay's *Revolution and Free-masonry* — *1680-1800*, one finds that not only was the Boston Tea Party initiated from a tavern known as the "Green Dragon" or the "Arms of Freemasonry," but Benjamin Franklin garnered the aid of French Freemasons in the American Revolution after he became grand master of the Nine Muses Lodge in France. The "Indians" of the Boston Tea Party were led by Paul Revere, the junior warden of Boston's St. Andrew Lodge.

Also prominent in the American Revolution was George Washington, who became a Mason at the lodge in Fredericksburg, Virginia, on November 4, 1752, when he was only twenty years old. In the picture of Washington on the next page, he is shown at a Masonic ceremony. You will notice in the picture on page 27 that the interior of the Masonic ceremony room looks almost exactly like the interior of the remodeled Sacred Heart Cathedral in Raleigh, North Carolina (if one of the church's moveable candle stands is removed), after the church's traditional altar was discarded and the Holy Tabernacle was placed to the side and replaced at the center by the bishop's chair. One of the candlesticks is removed during a church funeral, and the three remaining candles are placed in the exact position in front of the center table, just like at a Masonic initiation ceremony. Another picture of Washington at a Masonic ceremony shows him wearing a smaller apron with a pouch that looks similar to the "belt packs" now being worn by trendy youth. One of the first things one hears from William A. Brown, curator of the George Washington Masonic National Memorial Library, when one enters the library is that Freemasonry was the catalyst of American independence, and the

George Washington became a Mason when he was twenty years old. Here he is shown at a Masonic ceremony. He was a member, but not a very active one. A similar illustration was undoubtedly used by the order to capitalize on what was only a nominal membership.

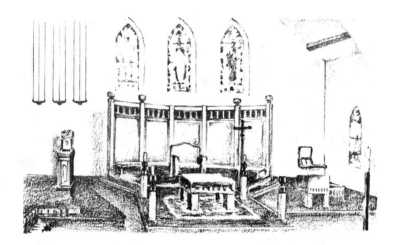

Interior of Masonic ceremony room looks very similar to remodeled Sacred Heart Cathedral in Raleigh, North Carolina.

Declaration of Independence itself is "Masonically worded." John Hancock and eight other signers of the Declaration of Independence were definitely Masons, and ten more signers were possibly Masons. An April 1940 editorial in *New Age* proclaimed regarding the American Revolution that *"it was Masons who brought on the war."* In the article "Freedom, Justice, Equality, and Fraternity Are the Four Cardinal Principles of Freemasonry" (*Education*, vol. 107, no. 4, 1987), former federal judge and Mason Jack Levitt reveals, *"Freemasons materially contributed to the conception, compromise, and ratification of the U.S. Constitution. They all insisted upon the federal system of the Masonic constitutions of 1723 being part of the fabric of the U.S. Constitution, and the federation established in the civil government is identical to the federalism of the system of Masonic government created in those Masonic constitutions."*

At least thirteen of the thirty-nine signers of the Constitution were master Masons.

Alexander Hamilton was also a Mason, and when he wrote a letter to George Washington (late September 1788) attempting to persuade him to seek the presidency, Hamilton said, *"The point of light in which you stand . . . will make an infinite difference."* Washington did not respond by asking what Hamilton meant by "point of light," because he knew exactly what was meant, and he replied in October 3, 1788, *"In taking survey of the subject in whatever point of light I have been able to place it. . . ."*

● ● ● ● ●

The Declaration of Independence was written in

1776. On May 1 of that year, the Bavarian Illuminati was founded by Adam Weishaupt who had adopted the principles of revolutionaries such as Jean Jacques Rousseau and the doctrines of the anti-Christian Manichaeans. Weishaupt was professor of canon law at Ingolstadt, and initially called his secret society Perfektibilisten. He was an ex-Jesuit, and according to the Durants' *Rousseau and Revolution*: *"He followed the model of the Society of Jesus, divided his associates into grades of initiation, and pledged them to obey their leaders in a campaign to 'unite all men capable of independent thought,' make man 'a masterpiece of reason, and thus attain the highest perfection in the art of government.' "*

Weishaupt said, *"Reason will be the only code of man. . . . When at last reason becomes the religion of man, so will the problem be solved."*

In *The* [New York] *World*, September 18, 1921, we find, *"An oath first used by the Paris Illuminati, as they were called in 1768 — the name being changed to Adepts in 1772 and Freemasons in 1778. . . . It was delivered in a cellar, back of a house in Rue Vaugirard in Paris, first in 1772, in a lodge attended by Jean Jacques Rousseau . . . Prince Louis Philippe . . . Jean Paul Marat . . . John Paul Jones, Emanuel Swedenborg, and other conspirators, and was dictated by the charlatan Cagliostro."*

In the *Memoirs Of Cagliostro*, this Sicilian count claimed to have been initiated into Freemasonry by Comte de Saint-Germain, a spy and mystic adventurer believed to be a Rosicrucian whom Cagliostro said founded Freemasonry in Germany.

Librarian of Congress James Billington in *Fire in*

the Minds of Men refers to Louis-Claude de Saint-Martin as *"the high priest of mysticism* [who] *discovered in the mysterious chaos of revolution the possibility of building a new Jerusalem by means of Pythagorean forms and numbers, and who said, 'A radiant sun has detached itself from the firmament and come to rest over Paris, from whence it spreads universal light.' The 'new man' can perceive that light by contemplating concentric circles that converge on a point within the flame of a lighted candle, thereby 'reintegrating' himself with the primal elements of air, earth, and water. As man moves toward pure spirit, revolutionary democracy will become 'deocracy.'"*

Another convert to Illuminism was Nicolas Bonneville who believed that global transformation could occur through "magic circles," and in his book *The Jesuits Drive from Freemasonry* (1788) and essay "The Numbers of Pythagoras" (1793), he claimed that "man is God" and will "become angelic" by broadening the social circle of universal brotherhood, and from that circle's center will *"emanate a **circle of light** which will uncover for us that which is hidden in the symbolic chaos of Masonic innovations."* Regarding Masonry, the teachings of Emanuel Swedenborg (1688-1772) not only influenced Freemasonry in Scandinavia, but can also be seen in the teachings and symbolism of the Masonic higher degrees today.

Concerning the Bavarian Illuminati, its founder Weishaupt said, *"We must win the common people in every corner. This will be obtained chiefly by means of the schools, and by open, hearty behavior, show, condescension, popularity, and toleration of their prejudices, which we shall at leisure root out and dispel."*

John Robison in *Proofs of a Conspiracy* (1798) reveals the contents of a Weishaupt letter: *"The great strength of our Order lies in its concealment; let it never appear in any place in its own name, but always covered by another name, and another occupation. None is fitter than the three lower degrees of Freemasonry."* In another letter, Weishaupt said: *"I have contrived an explanation which has every advantage; is inviting to Christians of every communion; gradually frees them from religious prejudices* [and] *cultivates the social virtues. . . . My means are effectual, and irresistible. Our secret Association works in a way that nothing can withstand."*

On the front page of the National Research Institute's *Trumpet* (October 1988), one reads, *"Toward the end of the ceremony of initiation into the 'Regents Degree of Illuminism,' according to a tract, 'a skeleton is pointed out to him* [the initiate], *at the feet of which are laid a crown and a sword. He is asked whether that is the skeleton of a king, a nobleman, or a beggar.' "*

According to Ron Rosenbaum in his article, "Last Secrets of Skull and Bones" (*Esquire*, September 1977), this statement is quite similar to the words (in German), *"Who was the fool, who was the wise man, beggar, or king? Whether poor or rich, all's the same in death,"* which appears above a painting of skulls encircled with Masonic symbols in room 322 of "Skull and Bones" (of which George Bush, nicknamed "Poppy," was a member in 1948, having been tapped in the spring of 1947) at Yale University. Rosenbaum also says, *"You could ask Averell Harriman whether he and young Henry Stimson and young Henry Luce lay down naked in a coffin and spilled the secrets of their adolescent sex life to fourteen fellow*

Bonesmen. . . . You could ask McGeorge Bundy if he wrestled naked in a mud pile as part of his initiation" (remember the Templar's initiation).

Similarly, in Steven M.L. Aronson's article, "George Bush's Biggest Secret" (*Fame*, August 1989), he relates that one woman who surreptitiously entered the Skull and Bones building said she saw *"a little Nazi shrine . . . [and] one room on the second floor has a bunch of swastikas, kind of an SS macho iconography. Somebody should ask President Bush about the swastikas in there."* Aronson indicated her story was confirmed by three other Yale University women who entered Skull and Bones' building and looked at its artifacts. And to demonstrate the power of "Bones," as the fraternal organization is called, Aronson begins his article with a dinner conversation in 1948, the year George Bush would be a member of the society (his senior year at Yale). F.O. Matthiessen was waiting to be called to testify before the House Committee on Un-American Activities, and he was dining at the apartment of Donald Ogden Stewart, *"who belonged to the left wing of the Screen Writers Guild."* Eileen Finletter was also at the dinner, and recalled: *"I very distinctly heard Matty say to Don Steward, 'As long as we have somebody from Bones who can bring pressure on the committee, I think we'll be all right.' "* Both men were members of Skull and Bones.

The Illuminati promoted the Freemason Johann Gottlieb Fichte in the late eighteenth century and early nineteenth century Germany as he developed the dialectical process (prior to Georg Wilhelm Friedrich Hegel), whereby through "conflict" of thesis and antithesis, a New World Order synthesis would emerge. (The motto for the thirty-third degree in Masonry is *Ordo ab Chao*, meaning "Order out of Chaos.") The French Revolution came shortly after the American Revolution, and according to William Still in *New World Order*, the Jacobins in France had *"vowed to destroy the monarchy, as well as other existing institutions* [the Church], *and sought to establish what they called a 'New World Order' or 'Universal Republic.' "*

Masons were clearly responsible for the French Revolution. When a Masonic congress met on July 16, 1889 in Paris to celebrate the principles of 1789, the speech by the Mason Colfavru included: *"In 1789, at the opening of the States-General, the great French Masonic family was in full development. It counted amongst its adepts the greatest minds of the day. It had received Voltaire into the famous Lodge of the Nine Sisters, under the respectful and fraternal patronage of Benjamin Franklin. Condorcet, Mirabeau, Danton, Robespierre, Camille Desmoulins were all Masons; the grand master was the Duke of Orleans."*

Mason Louis Amiable's speech at the same congress included: *"It is not an exaggeration to affirm that the Masonic reorganization of 1773 was the forerunner of the great Revolution of 1789. . . . The regime inaugurated by the French Grand Orient gave force and vigour to the truth which was to be formulated, sixteen years later, by the Declaration of the Rights of Man. . . . The French Freemasons of the eighteenth century made the Revolution. . . . They had elaborated its doctrines in advance so that these were not improvisations. . . . It was from Masonry that the nation took over the three words which form the motto of the French Republic: 'Liberty, Equality, Fraternity.' "*

In the "New World Order" or "Universal Republic" brought about by the French Revolution, the people would be ruled by "philosopher-kings." We read in *The City of Man: A Declaration on World Democracy*, by Herbert Agar et al (1941), *"Socrates, in the words of Plato, said that a perfect state will have the possibility of life and behold the light of day, that cities will finally have rest from their evils, 'when philosphers are kings, or the kings and princes of this world have the spirit and truth of philosophers, and political greatness and wisdom meet in one.' "*

The "philosopher-kings" of the French Revolution were "social engineers" like the Marquis de Sade (from whom the word "sadist" comes), who wrote in his *Philosophie dans le Boudoir* (1795) that induced abortions could be a means of controlling the population. The Marquis de Lafayette was involved in both the American and French Revolutions, and according to New Ager Marilyn Ferguson in her book *The Aquarian Conspiracy* (1980), George Washington initiated Lafayette into the Masonic order in the United States (there's some evidence that Lafayette had joined the Masons earlier in France). Today, in nearly every city hall in France, one will see a bust of "Marianne" (symbol of the French Revolution), and when one enters the bookstore of the Grand Orient's headquarters in Paris, one may be greeted by a clerk saying "Marianne."

According to *L'Express* (like *Time* in the U.S.), no fewer than a dozen cabinet ministers in France and one hundred members of the Chamber of Deputies and Senate are "initiates" into Masonry. The magazine stated that *"at the moment when the Fifth Republic is celebrating its thirtieth year, the Masons are emerging triumphant from the purgatory where Gen. de Gaulle had confined them. Because there is a veritable symbiosis between the socialists and Masonry"* (the government of President Francois Mitterand is socialist).

• • • • •

Music has also played a great part in Masonry. Franz Liszt (a Mason) met Ludwig von Beethoven (a Mason), who studied with Wolfgang Amadeus Mozart, who reached the heights of his ability at the time of the French Revolution. Mozart became a Mason in December 1784 when he was twenty-eight years old, and within a year of his initiation, both his father and Joseph Haydn, a friend and great musician also, became Freemasons. When Mozart was only eleven, he was introduced to the renowned hypnotist and Mason Franz Anton Mesmer (from whom the term "mesmerize" originates). When he was seventeen, he was asked by Freemason Tobias von Gebler to compose music for the latter's play, *Thamos, King of Egypt*, which included Masonic ritual and symbolism.

In "The Two Hundredth Anniversary of Mozart (1756-1791)" by Russell N. Cassel in *Education*, vol. 111, no. 3, 1991, one reads that Mozart's music *"has been described as . . . kind of mind altering; a quality earlier attributed to certain kinds of music by Plato. . . . Masonic member Otto von Gemmingen invited Mozart to write music for a melodrama on an Egyptian theme, based on Voltaire's play,* Semiramis. *. . . In the last year of his life, 1791, he made his greatest musical contribution,* The Magic Flute, *a musical filled with Masonic symbolism, verbal, visual (including a scene from a Masonic initiation* *ceremony), and musical taken directly from Masonic cere-monies. Goethe, after witnessing the playing of* The Magic Flute, *maintained that most people would be sure to enjoy the experience, but only the initiated Mason could really understand it."* For example, there is a stage set with two mountains, one containing a rushing waterfall and the other spitting out fire. In certain ancient Eastern religions, fire or the sun represented the male, while water or the moon represented the female, like Osiris and Isis (in Egyptian mythology) to which thanks are given at the play's end.

It might also be remembered here about Johann Wolfgang von Goethe that he wrote *Faust*, whose lead character sold his soul to the demon Mephistopheles for knowledge and power. In Manly P. Hall's *Secret Teachings of All Ages* (1928), on page CI there is a representation of Mephistopheles that looks remarkably like the character Yoda in *Return of the Jedi* of the "Star Wars" series. Returning to Cassel's *Education* article, he writes, *"After Mozart's death, his wife divulged finding his written personal plans to found a colony . . . based on the notions of Rousseau. There has been much speculation that his dream for that perfect colony was to involve the Masonic order, and that it may have been intended for organization in America."*

• • • • •

On July 4, 1812, retiring Harvard University president Joseph Willard claimed, *"There is sufficient evidence that a number of societies of the Illuminati have been established in this land. They are doubtless striving to secretly undermine all our ancient institutions, civil and sacred.*

. . . We live in an alarming period. The enemies of all order are seeking our ruin. Should infidelity generally prevail, our independence would fall, of course. Our republican government would be annihilated."

Such need for alarm is reinforced in Arthur M. Schlesinger, Jr.'s *History of U.S. Political Parties, vol. 1, 1789-1960* (1973), in which one reads the following statement by Mason W.F. Brainard made in 1825: *"What is Masonry now? It is powerful. . . . So powerful, indeed, is it at this time that it fears nothing from violence, either public or private, for it has every means to learn it in season, to counteract, to defeat, and punish it.*"

The murder of New York journalist William Morgan in 1826, after he had revealed the principal Masonic rituals of the period, caused a stir in America and anti-Masonic societies and publications began (note also Edgar Allen Poe's short story of this general time, *The Cask of Amontillado*, which is about Masonry and murder, and includes symbolism).

There were prominent individuals, including ex-Masons, who had been in American government and decided to sound the alarm about Masonry. Chief Justice of the U.S. Supreme Court John Marshall had been a Mason, but later said, *"The institution of Masonry ought to be abandoned as one capable of much evil, and incapable of producing any good which might not be effected by safe and open means.*"

In 1833 former President John Quincy Adams stated, *"I do conscientiously and sincerely believe that the Order of Freemasonry, if not the greatest, is one of the greatest moral and political evils under which the Union is now laboring. . . . I am prepared to complete the demonstration before God and man, that the Masonic oath, obligations, and penalties cannot by any possibility be reconciled to the laws of morality, of Christianity, or of the land."*

In 1835, according to Dee Strickland in "Masonry in Louisiana" (*New Age*, August 1962), Stephen Austin met in New Orleans *"with thirty-five prominent members of the local lodge of Freemasons, and planned the campaign which liberated Texas from Mexican rule."* Warning against Masonry, Millard Fillmore (U.S. President, 1850-53) cautioned, *"The Masonic fraternity tramples upon our rights, defeats the administration of justice, and bids defiance to every government it cannot control."*

Internationally, the concept of a New World Order or world federation was being promoted by Alfred Lord Tennyson, who wrote in *Morte de 'Arthur* (1842) that *"the old order changeth, yielding place to the new,"* and in *Locksley Hall* (1842) he wrote, *"For I dipped into the future, far as human eye could see, Saw the vision of the world, and all the wonder that would be. . . . Till the war-drum throbbed no longer, and the battle-flags were furled, In the Parliament of man, the Federation of the world. There the common sense of most shall hold a fretful realm in awe, And the kindly earth shall slumber, lapped in universal law."*

There was even an effort to establish a world government about this time. In the late 1840s, Ralph Waldo Emerson and select others traveled to the Midwest to discuss what the structure of such a government would be and where it would be located, though Emerson became disenchanted when the decision was made to place the headquarters of the world government in Constantinople, as he exclaimed, *"It's too far from Concord."*

A plan for world government was outlined in *The Science of Government Founded In Natural Law* (1841) by New York Assemblyman Clinton Roosevelt (ancestor of Franklin Roosevelt), who along with Horace Greeley participated in "Brook Farm" (1841-1847 experimental communist community in Massachusetts). In his book, Roosevelt also said: *"There is no God of justice to order things aright on earth; if there be a God, he is a malicious and vengeful being, who created us for misery,"* and he referred to other members of his "order" as "the enlightened ones."

The "order," according to William Still in *New World Order* was the Columbian Lodge of the Order of Illuminati, established in New York in 1785 with members Clinton Roosevelt, Horace Greeley, and Governor DeWitt Clinton. This was after a July 16, 1782 meeting of secret societies called the Congress of Wilhelmsbad in Europe, which formally joined Masonry and the Illuminati. DeWitt Clinton was the general grand high priest of the Royal Arch Masons; Horace Greeley was the founder and owner of the *New York Tribune*, which paid Karl Marx to be a special correspondent. When the Illuminati was broken by the Bavarian government in 1783, its members scattered from Germany, with some perhaps becoming members of the Parisian Outlaws League in France.

In 1948, the *New York Labor News* (publishing arm of the Socialist Labor Party) printed a hundredth anniversary edition of *The Communist Manifesto* by Karl Marx and Friedrich Engels. In the preface, Arnold Petersen wrote that the Communist League which Marx and Engels joined in 1846 *"sprang from what was known as the League of the Just. The latter, in turn, was an offshoot of the Parisian Outlaws League, founded by German refugees in that city. After a turbulent ten-year period, the League of the Just found its 'center of gravity' as Engels put it, in London where, he added, a new feature came to the fore: 'from being German, the League became international.' "*

Much of what Marx and Engels proposed came from French Utopian thinkers, such as Francois Babeuf. Known also as Gracchus Babeuf, he was asked in the winter of 1796, during the French Revolution, to lead a "conspiracy of equals" whom he would call the "Knights of the Order of the Equals," establishing a communist society in which all property would be communal and everyone would work according to his ability and receive according to his needs. The Italian Phillipe Michel Buonarroti was a disciple of Babeuf. According to James Billington in *Fire in the Minds of Men*, Buonarroti distilled his revolutionary plans from Babeuf, Masonry and the Bavarian Illuminists, and called his new organization the "Sublime Perfect Masters" and "Monde." In 1836, there was published an English translation of Buonarroti's history of *Babeuf's Conspiracy for Equality*. Karl Marx had a copy of Buonarroti's book, and Marx and Engels (the latter of whom had been converted to communism in 1842 by Moses Hess) planned a German edition of Buonarroti's book translated by Hess.

At the second congress of the Communist League, Marx and Engels were chosen to write the manifesto, and were told to have it ready by February 1, 1848, because many "spontaneous" revolutions were planned to occur throughout Europe and Russia immediately after that. In the 1848 revolution in France, Louis Blanc began a distinctly socialist trend of thought with the slogan, "la république sociale." Both he and Pierre Joseph Proudhon, perhaps the most renowned French socialist intellectual at the time, were Freemasons. Renowned nineteenth century Latin American revolutionaries like Simon Bolivar, Bernardo O'Higgins, and Benito Juarez were also Masons in the French Lodge.

• • • • •

In Italy in the 1860s, the Mason Garibaldi was conducting his revolution, having unified all of Italy except for Rome by 1861. Madame Helena Petrovna Blavatsky (born in Russia in 1831) was wounded fighting for him in 1866, after she had been initiated into the Carbonari (most Carbonari were Freemasons and vice versa) of Italy in 1856 by Masonic leader Giuseppe Mazzini. Grand master Lemmi, according to editor Norman MacKenzie's *Secret Societies*, said: *"We have applied the Chisel to the last refuge of superstition, and the Vatican will fall beneath our vivifying Mallet."* He urged Masons *"to scatter the stones of the Vatican, so as to build with them the Temple of the Emancipated Nation."*

Mazzini was associated with Karl Marx and Masonic leader Albert Pike, the latter of whom delivered a lecture to the Grand Lodge of Louisiana in 1858 titled, "The Meaning of Masonry," in which he stated, *"There is no . . . independent and self-existent Evil Principle in rebellion against God. . . . Evil is merely apparent; and all is in reality good and perfect."*

Pike was found guilty of treason in the United States

for his activities during the American Civil War, but by April 22, 1866, President Andrew Johnson (a Mason) pardoned him. President Johnson then received the fourth through the thirty-second degrees on June 20, 1867. While Pike was sovereign grand commander of the Scottish Rite, Southern Jurisdiction, he was also chief justice of the Ku Klux Klan, which was founded by a former Confederate general and Freemason, Nathan Bedford Forrest.

In 1868, a copy of the constitution of the Italian craft fell into the hands of an editor of a periodical in that country. He published the document in July of that year, and Article 6 reads, *"It* [Masonry] *proposes to itself as its first object to unite all free men in one vast family, which may and ought to take place in all Churches . . . thereby to constitute the true and only Church of Humanity."*

By 1871, the Italian Revolution was complete and the country was united. Mazzini, with Pike, developed a plan for three world wars so that eventually every nation would be willing to surrender its national sovereignty to a world government. The first war was to end the czarist regime in Russia, and the second war was to allow the Soviet Union to control Europe. The third world war was to be in the Middle East between Moslems and Jews and would result in Armageddon.

The same year, 1871, is the publication date of Pike's *Morals and Dogma*, about which Scottish Rite Sovereign Grand Commander C. Fred Kleinknecht wrote in *New Age* (January 1989), *"The apex of our teachings has been the rituals of our degrees and* Morals and Dogma, *written by Sovereign Grand Commander Albert Pike over a century ago."*

In *Morals and Dogma,* one reads, *"Masonry is a search after light: the search leads us directly back, as you see, to the Kabalah. . . . Kabalah alone consecrates the Alliance of the Universal Reason and the Divine Word. . . . Everything scientific and grand in the religious dreams of all the Illuminati, Jacob Boehme, Swedenborg, Saint-Martin, and others, is borrowed from the Kabalah; all the Masonic associations owe to it their Secrets and their Symbols. . . .Liberty of Thought, Equality of all men in the eye of God, universal Fraternity! A new doctrine, a new religion; the old Primitive Truth uttered once again! . . . For the Initiates, this* [the Devil] *is not a **Person**, but a **Force**, created for good, but which **may** serve for evil. It is the instrument of Liberty or Free Will. . . . Lucifer, the Son of the Morning! Is it **he** who bears the **Light**, and with its splendors intolerable, blinds feeble, sensual, or selfish Souls? Doubt it not! . . . Knowledge of Nature had for its symbolic key the gigantic form of that huge Sphinx. . . . Masonry is a worship. . . . Every Masonic lodge is a temple of religion; and its teachings are instruction in religion. . . . For six thousand years the Martyrs of Knowledge toil and die at the foot of this tree* [Tree of Knowledge], *that it may again become the Tree of Life. . . . The **Earth**, therefore, the great **Producer**, was always represented as a **female**, as the **Mother** — Great, Bounteous, Beneficient Mother Earth. . . . The Papacy and rival monarchies . . . are sold and bought in these days, become corrupt, and to-morrow, perhaps, will destroy each other. All that will become the heritage of the Temple: the World will soon come to us for its Sovereigns and Pontiffs. We shall constitute the equilibrium of the universe, and be rulers over the masters of the world."*

Some Masons point to Pike's emphasis upon "god" in *Morals and Dogma*, but one must ask, to what "god" is Pike referring? In that regard, Pike says, *"Masonry, around whose altars the Christian, the Hebrew, the Moslem, the Brahmin, the followers of Confucius and Zoroaster, can assemble as brethren and unite in prayer to the one God who is above **all** the Baalim."*

The dictionary defines "Baalim" (or Baal) as a fertility god, or a false god or idol. One such false god is Osiris. Pike states that *"Everything good in nature comes from **Osiris** — order, harmony, and the favorable temperature of the seasons and celestial periods."* Masonry also emphasizes "truth," but in *Morals And Dogma*, Pike says, *"The Blue degrees are but the outer court or portico of the Temple. Part of the symbols are displayed there to the Initiate, but he is intentionally misled by false interpretations. It is not intended that he shall understand them, but it is intended that he shall imagine he understands them."*

Robert Morey in *The Origins and Teachings of Freemasonry* (1990) indicates that A.E. Waite, Manly Hall, and certain other Masonic writers *"would have to be labeled as Luciferians,"* and he declares that Albert Pike (who in 1877 was named the provincial grand master by the Grand Lodge in Edinburgh, Scotland) plagiarized the writings of Eliphas Levi. Levi's real name was Alphonse Louis Constant, who was born in Paris in 1810 and was later cast out of a seminary and denied the priesthood because of his involvement in the occult and magic. He had written *The Key of the Mysteries* in 1861 and was a Mason, as well as a member of a secret occult society started in England by Bulmer Lytton.

In Pike's *Lectures of the Aryan* (1873), Pike expresses his belief in the concept of the "Aryan master race." Robert Morey states, *"Pike's Aryan racism supplies us with the reason why he used the Aryan symbol of the swastika as the Masonic symbol."* Morey's research also revealed that on July 6, 1875, Pike *"wrote a letter to one of the Brethren in Hawaii in which he stated that . . . Freemasonry was indeed a religion because it was the original religion of the Aryans as written in the Vedas."*

Thus, regarding Freemasonry today, Morey says, *"The craft has been filled with a mumbo-jumbo world of ancient mysteries, Isis worship, fertility cults, phallicism, ancient pagan deities, sorcery, magic, astrology, reincarnation, crystals, Aryan Hinduism, and other pagan religions."*

Pike's Morals and Dogma also contained such situation ethics and morally relative statements as *"all truths are truths of Period, and not truth for Eternity."* Perhaps this lack of moral absolutes is why, according to Stephen Knight in *Jack the Ripper — The Final Solution* (1986), the murder of five prostitutes in London in 1888 by Jack the Ripper were performed according to Masonic ritual, with the word "Juwes" (the three apprentice Masons who supposedly killed the fictional Hiram Abiff and who were the basis of Masonic ritual) written on the wall.

● ● ● ● ●

On October 10, 1875, Madame Helena Petrovna Blavatsky founded the Theosophical Society in New York, which synthesizes science, religion, and philosophy, using Hindu and Buddhist principles as its base. Another founder (and first librarian in 1876) of the Theosophical Society with Madame Blavatsky was Charles Sotheran of New York. He worked for *The* [New York] *World,* was a trustee of the New York Press Club, delegate to the district assembly of the Knights of Labor, and in 1896 spoke throughout New York under the auspices of the Democratic national and state committees. A biographer of Horace Greeley and Allesandro de Cagliostro, Sotheran was a prominent Mason and Sheikh of Kaaba, as well as assistant grand secretary general of the Supreme Council Ancient and Accepted Scottish Rite, and an initiate of the Rosy Cross. On January 11, 1877, he wrote to Madame Blavatsky that *"in the last century the United States was freed from the Tyranny of the Mother Country by the action of secret societies more than is commonly imagined."*

In that same year, Madame Blavatsky's *Isis Unveiled: A Master Key to the Mysteries of Ancient and Modern Science and Theology* was published, and on November 24, 1877 she was sent her Masonic certificate. In 1878, Thomas Edison joined the Theosophical Society and signed its secret pledge (as Pike did). In 1887, Madame Blavatsky started a Theosophical magazine, *Lucifer, The Light Bringer.* In 1888 her book, *The Secret Doctrine,* was published and later supposedly used by Adolf Hitler. (He learned the meaning of the swastika from her writings.)

The Statue of Liberty came to New York from France in 1882; it was the work of Masonic engineer Gustave Eiffel and Masonic sculptor Frederic Bartholdi. In January 1884, George Bernard Shaw and select others founded the Fabian Society (George Orwell's 1949 book entitled *1984* would be named for the centenary of the founding of the Fabian Society) whose purpose was to gradually move the world toward socialism through political synthesis or syncretism. In 1895, they established the London School of Economics (which Mick Jagger of the Rolling Stones would later attend). In 1904, another founder of the Fabian Society, Sidney Webb, became chairman of the Technical Education Board, which had been directing all higher education in England. In 1907, the Fabians began a weekly review called *New Age*. Their coat-of-arms is a wolf in sheep's clothing, and their motto is *"Remould it nearer to the heart's desire,"* which comes from Edward Fitzgerald's translation of Omar Khayyam:

> *"Dear Love, Couldst thou and I with fate conspire*
> *To grasp this sorry scheme of things entire,*
> *Would we not shatter it to bits, and then*
> *Remould it nearer to the heart's desire!"*

The Fabian window, originally at Beatrice Webb House, shows the Fabians arrogantly shaping the world with hammer blows, and it should be remembered they founded their society almost immediately after the death in 1883 of Karl Marx, who wrote *Oulanem* which states, *"If there is something which devours, I'll leap within it, though I bring the world to ruins — The world which bulks between me and the abyss I will smash to pieces with my enduring curses. I'll throw my arms around its harsh reality. Embracing me, the world will dumbly pass away, And then sink down to utter nothingness, Perished, with no existence — that would be really living."*

This sounds similar to a later statement by Teilhard de Chardin, *"We have only to believe, then little by little, we* *shall see the universal horror unbend, and then smile upon us, and then take us in its more than human arms. "*These all sound very much like Freud's "death wish" theory.

Four years after the Fabians founded the London School of Economics, Cecil Rhodes signed his seventh will on July 1, 1899. We read in *Behind the Lodge Door* by Paul Fisher: *"Cecil Rhodes . . . to accomplish his goal of world domination under English rule, drew up the first of six wills in which he stipulated that a secret society was to carry out his scheme. Later, he conceived of world domination in federation with the United States, using 'a secret society gradually absorbing the wealth of the world.' This plan is the 'meaning of his last will and the plan behind his scholarships.' That secret organization envisioned by Rhodes became the Round Table Group of England, the 'real founders of the Royal Institute of International Affairs . . . The Institute of Pacific Relations,' and the 'godfathers' of the Council on Foreign Relations."* Rhodes was a Mason. Fisher also provides extensive documentation that the Philippine Insurrection of 1896 (which was followed by the Spanish-American War of 1898) was orchestrated by Freemasonry.

During this same general period, Monsignor George Dillon, D.D., in 1885 wrote *Grand Orient Freemasonry Unmasked as the Secret Power Behind Communism*, in which he stated, *"In our day, if Masonry does not found Jacobite or other clubs, it originates and cherishes movements fully as satanic and as dangerous. Communism, just like Carbonarism, is but a form of the illuminated Masonry of Weishaupt."*

Similarly, Pope Leo XIII (Catholic pope, 1878-1903) wrote in *Humanum Genus* (1884), *"It is now Our intention to treat the Masonic society, of its whole teaching, of its aims, and of its manner of thinking and acting, in order to bring more and more into the light its power for evil, and to do what We can to arrest the contagion of this fatal plague. . . . If any members of Masonry are judged to have betrayed the doings of the sect or to have resisted commands given, punishment is inflicted on them not infrequently, and with so much audacity and dexterity that the assassin very often escapes the detection and penalty of his crime. . . . Their ultimate purpose, namely, the utter overthrow of that whole religious and political order of the world which the Christian teaching has produced, and the substitution of a new state of things in accordance with their ideas, of which the foundations and laws shall be drawn from mere 'Naturalism' . . . which states that human nature and human reason ought in all things to be mistress and guide. . . . In the education of youth nothing is to be taught in the matter of religion as of certain and fixed opinion. . . . With the greatest unanimity the sect of the Freemasons also endeavors to take to itself the education of youth. They think that they can easily mold to their opinions that soft and pliant age, and bend it whither they will; and that nothing can be more fitted than this to enable them to bring up the youth of the State after their own plan . . . and nothing which treats the most important and most holy duties of man to God shall be introduced into the instructions on morals. . . . This change and overthrow* [of nations] *is deliberately planned and put forward by many associations of* **communists** *and* **socialists***; and to their undertakings the sect of Free-masons is not hostile, but greatly favors their designs, and* *holds in common with them their chief opinions."*

Then on March 19, 1902, Pope Leo again spoke out against Freemasonry in his apostolic letter, "A Review of the Apostolate," declaring that the "Internationale" (Freemasonry) has as its objective *"the reversal of order, and for this it aims at exercising an occult suzerainty over the State, for the sole purpose of making war on God and His Church. . . . By bending rulers of States to its designs, sometimes by promises and sometimes by threats, it has succeeded in penetrating into all ranks of society. Thus it forms an invisible and irresponsible State within body corporate of the lawful State. . . . All this points, without a shadow of a doubt, to a concerted line of action and to the direction of all these activities by one central authority. These events are, in fact, but one phase in the development of a prearranged plan, which is being carried out over an ever-widening area, to multiply the ruins of which We have previously spoken. Thus Freemasonry is striving first to restrict and then to exclude completely religious instruction from the schools."*

The pope died not long after this, and in a June 18, 1984 *Time* article, one reads that *"there were the whispers about how poison killed Leo XIII in 1903."* The pope's concern seemed justified, as a number of years after his death, the Masonic *New Age* magazine printed an article in May 1918 that said, *"Before the insistent Liberty of today the Papal court stands condemned as practically the last autocracy left on earth. Before the world can be made safe for democracy, the autocratic Church must be cleared away."*

Reacting against Masonry more recently, the Orthodox Presbyterian Church in 1942 condemned Freemasonry; the Missouri Synod Lutheran Church in 1964 banned Masonic membership (as does the Catholic Church); the Christian Reformed Church in 1974 condemned Freemasonry; the Methodist Church of Great Britain in 1985 said Freemasons practice *"syncretism, an attempt to unite different religions in one, which Christians cannot accept"* (the Baptist Church of Britain also questioned whether their members should be Freemasons); and the Associated Press reported July 14, 1987 that *"Church of England leaders overwhelmingly endorsed a report yesterday that called Freemason rituals blasphemous. . . ."* Even Scotland Yard advised its twenty-seven thousand police officers in 1984 *"not to join or remain a member of the Freemasons because they risk raising doubts about their impartiality"* (*The London Times*, September 6, 1984).

In 1907, Albert Stevens wrote *The Cyclopedia of Fraternities* (second edition), and in it stated that the Masonic fraternity is *"the parent organization of all modern secret societies."* He traced the "germ" of political secret societies to the Loyal Orange institution (see later mention of the House of Orange), which "had Masonic antecedents."

● ● ● ● ●

Toward the end of the nineteenth century and beginning of the twentieth century, there was also the first concerted attempt to promote a one-world religion. According to the syncretistic Temple of Understanding magazine *Insight* (Spring 1977), the first World Parliament of Religions was held in Chicago for seventeen days in September 1893, with three thousand people in attendance. There were representatives from most of the world's major religions, including the three largest branches of Christianity. However, *"the Archbishop of Canterbury declined an invitation to Chicago saying that Christianity was the only true religion and that participation in such a conference implied that the other religions were equal to Christianity."*

Why Pope John Paul II would not have the same attitude regarding a similar meeting at Assisi in October 1986 isn't clear. On a visit to India, he allowed a priestess of Shiva to anoint his forehead, the rite of initiation into the worship of Shiva, the goddess of war and destruction. In Caryl Matrisciana's *Gods of the New Age* (1985), one reads that Shivites are *"recognizable by the three horizontal lines painted on their forehead. These disciples of the god Shiva consider madness, one of Shiva's attributes, to be one of the highest levels of spirituality! Many Hindus believe insanity to be a form of god-consciousness."*

In order for a syncretization of all religions to occur, though, religion would have to be redefined. In New Ager Marilyn Ferguson's *The Aquarian Conspiracy*, one reads, *"In 1902, William James, the great American psychologist, redefined religion not as dogma but as experience — the discovery of a new context, an unseen order with which the individual might achieve harmony."*

Alice Bailey wrote that a hierarchy of "ascended spiritual masters" had developed something called "the Plan" in 1900 whereby through "service to humanity" the outer form of a universal religion would take shape. Fabian Socialist H.G. Wells wrote that *"the coming World-State . . . will be based upon a common World Religion, very much simplified and universalized and better understood."* Perhaps not coincidentally, Wells wrote also in 1900 of a *New Republic* describing something called "the Plan" whereby socialism would gain control of the world.

Madame Blavatsky died in 1891, and in 1907 Fabian Annie Besant became president of the Theosophical Society, with the objectives of a world religion and a world government. In India, she would influence Ghandi, and beginning in 1910 she trained Jiddu Krishnamurti for the role of "messiah" or "world teacher." On February 19, 1922, an alliance was formed between her Co-Masonry and the Grand Orient of France. She also changed the name of *Lucifer* magazine (published by Lucifer Press) to *The Theosophist*. Lucifer Press or Lucifer Publishing Co. began in 1921; the name was changed to Lucis Trust in 1922. Lucis Trust publishes the works of occultist Alice Bailey and is now a non-governmental cooperating agency (NGO) with the United Nations, and has maintained the U.N.'s "meditation room."

In 1924, Hazrat Inayat Khan coined the term "planetary consciousness." He introduced Sufism to the West, which is based upon the concept that "God is everything, and everything is God." His wife was Ora Ray Baker, the sister of Mary Baker Eddy, the founder of Christian Science.

● ● ● ● ●

Foundations would also be a factor in the movement toward world government. In 1902, Daniel Coit Gilman (Skull and Bones, 1952), who had been influenced by Hegelian philosophy, became the first president of the Carnegie Institution. He had been the first president of the University of California and Johns Hopkins University where he introduced Wundtian experimental psychology.

Then in 1910, the Carnegie Endowment for International Peace was established, and according to Norman Dodd (research director for the U.S. House of Representatives' Reece Committee in the 1950s), records for the endowment trustees' early meetings showed that they hoped to involve the United States in a war which would lead to world government. Col. Edward Mandell House, who was President Woodrow Wilson's "alter ego," promoted *"socialism as dreamed of by Karl Marx"* in his book *Philip Dru: Administrator* (1912), and indicated how events could be manipulated to cause the U.S. to enter a world war, which America would do in 1917.

Relevant to Col. House's socialistic preferences, Arthur D. Howden Smith in *Mr. House of Texas* (1940) indicated House believed that *"the Constitution, product of eighteenth century minds and the quasiclassical, medieval conception of republics, was thoroughly outdated; that the country would be better off if the Constitution could be scrapped and rewritten. But as a realist he knew that this was impossible in the existing state of political education."*

Regarding Col. House being President Wilson's "alter ego," in Charles Seymour's edited volume, *The Intimate Papers of Colonel House* (1926), he quotes President Wilson as saying, *"Mr. House is my second personality. He is my independent self. His thoughts and mine are one. If I were in his place I would do just as he suggested. . . . If anyone thinks he is reflecting my opinion by whatever action he takes, they are welcome to that conclusion."*

Much of the legislation proposed by President Wilson was similar to that of "Philip Dru." In Arthur D. Howden Smith's *Mr. House of Texas*, one reads, " 'All that book

has said should be, comes about,'wrote Franklin K. Lane,
Wilson's secretary of the interior, in 1918 to a personal
friend. 'The president comes to Philip Dru in the end.' "

The First World War began August 1-4, 1914,
because of the assassination of Archduke Franz Ferdinand
on June 28 by the "Black Hand," which James Billington
in *Fire in the Minds of Men* claims was "a progeny of
Freemasonry." The assassin was Gavrilo Princep, and in
Mary Edith Durham's *The Sarajevo Crime* (1925), one
learns that Princep testified at his trial that his colleague,
Ciganovitch, *"told me he was a Freemason . . . [and] told*
me that the Heir Apparent (Franz Ferdinand) had been
condemned to death by a Freemason's lodge." John
Cotter in *A Study in Syncretism* suggests that *"the Baha'is*
[who are for a world government, a world system of
currency, and a syncretistic world religion] *were privy to*
the plans of the 'Black Hand,' or other secret societies to
cause World War I two years before it actually happened.!"
Cotter quotes Baha'i leader Douglas Martin as saying,
"Abdu'l-Baha predicted quite explicitly and repeatedly,
on public platforms and in newspaper interviews, the
world war. . . . See for example the Montreal Gazette,
September 11, 1912. On a number of occasions Abdu'l-
Baha stated that 'the time is less than two years hence'
when 'a tiny spark will set ablaze the world.' "

According to the *World Order* (American Baha'i,
October 1947), *"Baha' U'llah, the latest Manifestation,*
spoke of a United Nations of the World as early as 1860, a
time when such a thought was regarded as sheer fantasy."

Even though Archduke Franz Ferdinand had been
assassinated, world war could have been prevented if the
British had made it clear to the Germans that if the latter

joined with Austria, Britain would enter the fray. However, on July 20, 1914 British Secretary of State Sir Edward Grey told the German ambassador to England (Lichnowsky) that "[Grey] *hoped that the quarrel might be settled and localized, for the idea of war between the Great Powers of Europe must be repelled under all circumstances.*" Regarding the possibility of Austrian action against Serbia, Grey told the British chargé in Germany (Rumbold) that he *"had not heard anything recently,"* when the truth was that four days earlier the English ambassador to Austria (Bunsen) had informed Grey of a probable ultimatum. On July 29, when Lichnowsky asked Grey if England would intervene "under certain circumstances," Grey replied, *"I did not wish to say that, or to use anything that was like a threat or an attempt to apply pressure by saying that if things became worse, we should intervene."* (In other words, Grey misled the Germans just as Ambassador April Glaspie possibly misled Saddam Hussein.) Thus, the First World War began August 1-4, 1914 in part due to the German impression that England would not join the conflict, just as Saddam Hussein may have invaded Kuwait because he did not believe the United States would intervene militarily.

Winston Churchill had ordered a study of the political impact if Germany sank an ocean liner with Americans on board. And in *The Intimate Papers of Colonel House*, House states that about 10:30 a.m. on May 7, 1915, he and Grey *"spoke of the probability of an ocean liner being sunk and I told him if this were done, a flame of indignation would sweep across America, which would in itself probably carry us into war."* House wrote that it was "strange" that an hour later at Buckingham Palace, King George told him, *"Suppose Germany should sink the* Lusitania *with American passengers on board."* At 2:00 p.m., Germany sank the *Lusitania* (carrying munitions and 128 American passengers)!

In the same year of 1915, Col. William Simmons re-established the Ku Klux Klan in Georgia. He was a Mason and a Knight Templar, and most of the Klan leaders in the North and South were Freemasons. According to Paul Fisher in *Behind the Lodge Door*, there are strong indications that *"the Klan was a Masonic front group."*

In 1916, President Wilson was re-elected in large part because he had been able to keep the United States out of the world war. However, a number of people were advising him that if he wanted to be a part of the peace at the end of the war, he should think seriously about having the United States enter the conflict to help the Allies. And the U.S. did enter the war in 1917.

While the war was in progress, Kaiser Wilhelm II of Germany had the Gate of Ishtar removed from Babylon and brought to Berlin. The gate symbolized the Roman Empire, and on its right side was a dragon (which in the Holy Bible stands for Satan).

The Russian Revolution of 1917 was "inspired and operated" by Russian Masonic lodges, according to the February 1945 edition of *New Age*. In *Behind the Lodge Door*, one reads that in the early stages of the Second World War, the Craft believed a world government would be established. The *Empire State Mason* (New York) for February 1953 declared that if world Masonry ever came into existence, a great deal of credit would have to be given to the years Franklin Roosevelt was president.

Chapter Three

The Great Seals

President Franklin Delano Roosevelt, who was a thirty-second degree Knight Templar and member of the Mystic Shrine and Scottish Rite, nominated fellow Mason (and former Klan member) Hugo Black to the U.S. Supreme Court (confirmed by the U.S. Senate August 17, 1937). In 1935, F.D.R. had approved the placement of the Craft's pyramid in the Great Seal of the United States (created by Masons in 1782) on our dollar bill. In Arthur Schlesinger's *The Coming of the New Deal* (1958), he writes at some length of Mason Henry Wallace's (U.S. vice-president, 1941-1945) interest in the occult, saying, *"Though he remained non-committal about the extent of his own belief* [in the power of the occult]*, Wallace did induce the secretary of the treasury to put the Great Pyramid on the new dollar bill in 1935. He sold this to Secretary Morgenthau* [a Mason] *on the prosaic ground that 'Novus ordo' was Latin for New Deal, and for many years afterward Morgenthau was beset by people who assumed that the appearance of the Great Pyramid on the currency signified his own attachment to some esoteric fellowship."*

In *The Power of Myth* (an interview of Joseph Campbell by Bill Moyers, published by Doubleday), Campbell remarks regarding the seal, *"Look at the* pyramid on the left. A pyramid has four sides. These are the four points of the compass. . . . When you get up to the top, the points all come together, and there the eye of God opens."

In Mason Kenneth Mackenzie's *The Royal Masonic Encyclopedia* (1987), one learns that *"the eye was also the symbol of Osiris."* In his interview with Joseph Campbell, Bill Moyers then asks whether this is the "god of reason" of our eighteenth century Founding Fathers, and Campbell replies: *"Yes, these were eighteenth century deists. . . . That is not the God of the Bible. These men did not believe in a fall (but rather that) . . . the mind of man, cleansed of secondary and merely temporal concerns, beholds with the radiance of a cleansed mirror a reflection of the rational mind of God. . . . Now, back to the Great Seal. When you count the number of ranges on this pyramid, you find there are thirteen. The number thirteen is the number of transformation and rebirth. . . . These men were very conscious of the number thirteen as the number of resurrection and rebirth and new life. . . . If you look behind that pyramid, you see a desert. If you look before it, you see plants growing. The desert, the tumult of Europe, wars and wars and wars — we have pulled ourselves out of it and created a state in the name of reason, not in the name of power, and out of that will come the flowerings of the new life. . . . Now, what does the eagle represent? He represents what is indicated in the radiant sign above his head . . . thirteen stars. . . . This used to be Solomon's Seal. . . . They are Masonic signs. . . . The eighteenth century Enlightenment was a world of learned gentlemen. . . . These Founding Fathers who were Masons actually studied what they could of Egyptian lore. In Egypt, the pyramid represents the primordial hillock. After the annual flood of the Nile begins to sink down, the first hillock is symbolic of the reborn world. That's what this seal represents."*

Concerning Masonry and Egypt, G.A. Browne in "A Masonic Pilgrimage to the East" (*New Age*, June 1934) noted that the religious symbols, grips, and aprons on the walls and tombs of ancient Egypt would tend to make a Freemason *"almost believe he is witnessing a scene at a* [Masonic] *initiation."* And regarding the Great Seal of the United States, Prof. Charles Eliot Norton said, *"The device adopted by Congress is practically incapable of effective treatment; it can hardly (however artistically treated by the designer) look otherwise than as a dull emblem of a Masonic fraternity."* Furthermore, in the April 1960 issue of *New Age*, thirty-second degree Mason James B. Walker describes what he calls the Masonic symbols on the entire dollar bill: thirteen leaves in the olive branches, thirteen bars and stripes in the shield, thirteen feathers in the tail, thirteen arrows, thirteen letters in the *E Pluribus Unum* on the ribbon, thirteen stars in the green crest above, thirteen granite stones in the pyramid with the Masonic "all-seeing eye" completing it, thirteen letters in *Annuit Coeptis* ("God has prospered"), and thirty-two long feathers representing the thirty-second degree of Masonry.

A seal and symbol for the New World Order are also supposedly being developed. For more information regarding this, refer to the last chapter of this book.

Chapter Four

The Wonderful Wizard of Oz

Masons are supposed to be engaged in a search for "light" (Ahura-Mazda is the "spirit of light") with all of their "heart, mind, and strength." In L. Frank Baum's *The Wonderful Wizard of Oz*, the tin man wants a heart, the scarecrow a mind, and the lion wants strength or courage (the master Mason uses the "strong grip of the lion's paw"). In the occult, the heart represents the female (or emotion), the mind represents the male (or reason), and strength stands for action.

L. Frank Baum (possibly a Buddhist) was interested in Theosophy (which he and his wife joined in 1896), and *The Wonderful Wizard of Oz* is on page 36 of the Theosophical University Press 1989-90 catalogue, which features *"the principle source-writings of the modern Theosophical movement and seeks to provide a . . . comprehensive presentation of the ancient wisdom-tradition."*

Concerning Theosophy, Baum pronounced, *"God is Nature, and Nature God,"* and in the Aberdeen, South Dakota *Saturday Pioneer* (January 25, 1890), he wrote of *"an eager longing to penetrate the secrets of Nature — an aspiration for knowledge we have thought is forbidden."* The Theosophists are *"searchers for truth"* and *"admit the existence of God — not necessarily a personal God."* He believed in the theory of "elementals" (invisible, vapory beings) popularized in Madame Blavatsky's *Isis Unveiled* (1877), and like the Rosicrucians' belief in the combining of God and nature, and not unlike William Butler Yeats' (Mason and Fabian) search for a new mysticism.

Baum believed in reincarnation, in karma, that there was no Devil, and *"that man on earth was only one step on a ladder that passed through many states of consciousness, through many universes, to a final state of Enlightenment,"* according to Michael Patrick Hearn in his book, *The Annotated Wizard of Oz* (1973). Hearn is also quoted in *Children's Literature Review* (CLR), vol. 15, as saying: *"The author of* The Wonderful Wizard of Oz *was . . . well read in the occult sciences. . . . Paracelsus, the sixteenth century Swiss alchemist and physician, divided all spirits into four categories: Air, sylphs; Water, nymphs or undines; Earth, gnomes; Fire, salamanders. These could be expanded to the ancient idea of the four states of matter — gas, liquid, solid, and energy. . . . A quick glance at Baum's fairy tales reveals that he wrote about each Paracelsian classification of spirits. His sylphs are the 'winged fairies' (Lulea of* Queen Zixie of Ix; *Lurline of* The Tin Woodman of Oz*); the undines are the mermaids (Aquareine of* The Sea Fairies; *the water fairies of the first chapter of* The Scarecrow of Oz*); the gnomes are the Nomes (the Nome king of* The Life and Adventures of Santa Claus *and* Ozma of Oz*); and the salamanders are the fairies of energy (the Demon of Electricity of* The Master Key; *the Lovely Lady of Light of* Tik-Tok of Oz*). Baum seems to have created a highly sophisticated cosmology by interpreting this theory of spirits of 'elementals' in terms of traditional fairies. This is basically a religion of Nature. Modern science itself has its origin in* *the occult sciences, in the search for the secrets of nature.* . . . *It is not by mistake that the Shaggy Man in* The Patchwork Girl of Oz *refers to Oz as being a fairyland 'where magic is a science.' Both science and magic have the same ends."*

In many of Baum's works, there are revealing references. In *The Master Key*, a boy summons up the "Demon of Electricity," and *A Kidnapped Santa Claus* refers to a "Demon of Repentance." *The Tin Woodman of Oz* has a giantess skilled in transformations, and in *Dorothy and the Wizard Of Oz*, there is a climb up "Pyramid Mountain." Baum was a pacifist, and in *Ozma of Oz*, Dorothy is shipwrecked, and Princess Ozma (close friend of Glinda, "the greatest of sorceresses") is threatened by an attack from the Nome king, but he is powerless in the face of her faith and love as she states, *"No one has the right to destroy any living creatures, however evil they may be, or to hurt them or make them unhappy. I will not fight — even to save my kingdom."*

In the *Saturday Pioneer* (October 18, 1890), Baum wrote that *"the absurd and legendary devil is the enigma of the Church,"* and in the Oz books, he said there were both "good" and "bad" demons and witches. (Baum also wrote a play, *The Uplift of Lucifer, or Raising Hell* in 1915.) Remember when you read Revelation 4:3 (". . . *there was a rainbow round about the throne, in sight like unto an emerald"*), that in life Satan tries to imitate God. Could this be why Dorothy sings "Somewhere Over the Rainbow," while the rainbow looks green in some Oz books because green glasses are worn in the Emerald City where the Wizard is upon his throne?

Women were extremely influential upon Baum.

Osmond Beckwith points out in *CLR*, vol. 15, that *"in Oz, the principal boy always wears skirts,"* and *"true love is love between girls."* According to the *Dictionary of Literary Biography*, vol. 22, *"Baum complained of being grabbed by spirits when in bed asleep,"* and his wife, Maud, and his mother-in-law, the radical feminist Matilda Gage, had clairvoyants and seances in their home. Mrs. Gage was also interested in astronomy and palmistry. In 1890, because she felt mainstream suffragists were too conservative, she founded the Women's National Liberal Union dedicated to the separation of church and state.

Baum emphasized the need for "harmony of heart and mind," which sounds like today's New Agers' promotion of harmony through "right human relations" and Ted Turner's "Better World Society" (which also advocates population control). Dorothy in Oz is like the "Earth Mother" of mythology (*CLR*, vol. 15). There are "transformations" of character, and Ozma's magical belt transports people to Oz, where the Wizard has revealed that the "power" to accomplish important things individuals want already resides within themselves.

A similar message ("The Power Is Yours") is delivered today by Ted Turner's (1990 Humanist of the Year) "Captain Planet" cartoon program on television, where Gaia (the spirit of "Mother Earth") gives five "planeteers" separately the powers of fire, wind, earth, water, and heart (communicated telepathically). Captain Planet himself is actually a crystal in human form, and the five planeteers use the power of their occult magic rings (with crystals) working together (in harmony) to save "Mother Earth." An episode of ABC television's "MacGyver" recently had a similar segment where the four elements were used together to find "the eye of Osiris." Another two-part episode of "MacGyver" involved using the Mummer's rhyme "Ring Around the Rosie" in a search for the Holy Grail.

These all lead one to consider the possibility that Baum selected the word "Oz" because it sounded like "us" (Baum wrote a poem rhyming "Oz" with the word "was"), meaning that if the heart (tin man) and mind (scarecrow) work together with courage (lion) in "harmony" with "Mother Earth" (Dorothy), then "the power is yours" to be like "gods."

It is also possible that Baum chose the name "Oz" from the "O" in Oscar Wilde (famous author and Mason, born just two years before Baum and died in the year 1900, when the Oz books began) and from the "Z" in Zoroaster (founder of an ancient religion in Persia, now Iran). This is because in *Dorothy and the Wizard of Oz*, the Wizard said that his father named him Oscar Zoroaster Phadrig Isaac Norman Henkle Emmanuel Ambroise Diggs, which he shortened to O.Z. (the remaining initials spell "pinhead"). The Wizard was bald, and James Hastings has noted that Egyptian priests shaved their heads to retain their "supernatural power." The Wizard is called "Oz the Terrible" by those around him, and when one of them asks Dorothy, *"Are you really going to look upon the face of Oz the Terrible?"* the biblical symbolism seems clearly an attempt to portray Oz as Adonay (a judgmental God), whom Masons also find "terrible" in contrast to their view of Lucifer as the "Light of Illumination."

A third possibility for Baum's selection of the word "Oz" is that according to writer Jack Snow, Baum once wrote that he always enjoyed stories that caused the reader to exclaim with "Ohs" and "Ahs" of "wonder," thus the title *The Wonderful Wizard of Oz*. Another example of Baum's word-play and letter-play are that, according to Michael Patrick Hearn, "Ozma" may be Oz and Maud's (Baum's wife) name abbreviated, and the Rose Princess "Ozga" may be Oz and Maud's maiden name (Gage) abbreviated.

Baum dedicated *The Wonderful Wizard of Oz* (1900) to his wife, whom he called "my good friend and comrade." When Baum and his wife traveled to Europe in 1906, they also went on to Egypt, where Maud went up the Great Pyramid. In Baum's books, the land of Oz contains four triangular-shaped countries pointing inward (like a pyramid looks from above) toward the center of a square where the Emerald City is located (this shape is also like a Masonic rose croix, or Rosicrucian cross), and the name "Emerald" was possibly selected because that was Baum's birthstone. However, the emerald is also supposedly the stone of prophecy, and that leads to another interpretation of the journey to the Emerald City as a journey to the center of ourselves (to the center of "us," because the Emerald City was the center of "Oz," which Baum pronounced as "was"), to "the god within" where the Wizard said we would find the answer to what we are looking for. This is like the New Agers' search for "the god within."

The land of Oz, with its four countries, is rectangular in shape like the state of Kansas. In the city of Wichita in south central Kansas, about ten years ago a pyramid was built at 3100 North Hillside Street. It was sponsored by the philanthropist Olive Garvey, and designed by J. Phillip Callahan, author of *Ancient Mysteries, Modern Visions*. New Ager Buckminster Fuller (1969 Humanist of the Year) designed the domes near the pyramid, where today children are sold the comic book, *Knight of the White Light.* The first issue of the comic was called "The Tale of the Kingdom of Light," as the author (Pamela Wunder Myers) says: *"A paradigm* [referring to a cultural change] *shift occurs when a 'better way' becomes known and understood by the majority of people. . . . Such a shift is now occurring in our culture. Join Sir Cosmic on his adventures as he travels to other worlds to discover the New Order and a better way."*

In the first comic issue, Sir Cosmic searches for the Land of "Awes" where he finds the Wonderful Wizard who describes their "Divine Science of Nature" and gives a riddle to Merlin that says, *". . . there is a bit of moon in the rose. . . . "* Merlin says, *"that which was thought to be sin is but error,"* so there should be no guilt or blame. The king renames the Kingdom of White to the "Kingdom of Light" and says: *"The New Order is born . . . the Enlightenment of all and in the twinkling of an eye the world became unexpectedly divine!"* It should be remembered here that the "New Order" is what Hitler called his Nazi regime.

To reach the Emerald City in Baum's land of Oz, one has to follow the yellow brick road which snakes its way through a blue countryside. (The Masonic colors are blue and gold or yellow. Golden snakes and Osiris [sun god] are at the entrance of the "Temple of the Supreme Council of the Thirty-Third and Last Degree of the Ancient and Accepted Scottish Rite" in Washington, D.C. where there are many serpents upon the walls beneath a dark blue, starry domed ceiling.) On the road through the land of Oz, Dorothy and her acquaintances come upon a meadow of red poppies which causes them to sleep (Hearn says this is an allusion to opium).

Love and cooperation rule in Oz, and Masons seek light and harmony. Before meeting the Wizard in Oz, the cowardly lion says he will do what's necessary until the Wizard *"promises to give us what we desire"*; in Masonic initiation, the inidividual is asked, *"What do you most desire?"*

There is also a certain existentialist and gnostic (transcendental "self") aspect to *The Wonderful Wizard of Oz*. The Wizard in Oz tells Dorothy's companions that what they most desire is already within themselves, which is similar to M.L. Franz's analysis in Carl Jung's *Man and His Symbols* (1964) that *"the problem of an individual's imperfection can only be solved within himself."* Hearn says: *"Baum's concern is with the presentation of reality and worth and of the power of the Self. . . . In terms of the Rogerian* [Carl Rogers, 1964 Humanist of the Year] *method of treatment . . . a faith in the eventual cure of the individual must be established within himself before any treatment may begin."*

Just as in *The Wonderful Wizard of Oz* individuals are told they'll find the power to solve problems within themselves, the same is true in the more recent book and movie *Star Wars*. Similarly, just as the small, shaggy Toto helps Dorothy in Oz (where there are "Winkies"), Chewbacca (a large, shaggy "Wookie") helps the good side in *Star Wars*. "The Force" in *Star Wars* has a good and bad side, and in the motion picture *The Wonderful Wizard of Oz*, the struggle between the "good" white magic of the witches of the north and south and the "bad" black magic of the wicked witches of the east and west occurs in Dorothy's imagination.

What Masons say they desire most is "light," which is also very important in the Oz books. In *Tik-Tok of Oz*, there is the palace of the Queen of Light, and when Dorothy enters the Wizard's throne room in *The Wonderful Wizard of Oz*, "*in the center of the roof was a great light, as bright as the sun.*" Another wizard in *A New Wonderland* has a similar light, and these could be called "points of light." Regarding the Oz books and the more recent *Star Wars* and other similar books, remember that 2 Timothy 4:4 says, "*And they shall turn away their ears from the truth, and shall be turned unto fables.*"

Other children's stories that are full of symbolism are Lewis Carroll's (real name Charles Lutwidge Dodgson) *Alice in Wonderland* (1865) and *Through the Looking Glass* (1872). Carroll would use such terms as "my Muse." In Wonderland, the Queen of Hearts' gardener was painting white roses red. This could symbolize the fact that even though the white rose Yorks had won the mid-fifteenth century War of the Roses against the red rose Lancasters, a few years later Lancaster Henry VII defeated the Yorks. This same symbolism continues in *Through the Looking Glass,* where there are the strong red king, queen, and knight verses the weak white king, queen, and knight (the white knight represented Carroll himself befriending Alice). This story also includes Humpty Dumpty, who represents either the current political leader of the day or the power behind the leader. The symbolic characteristics are that he is precariously balanced upon a wall, yet he believes "*there's no chance of*" his falling; he believes that a word "*means just what I choose it to mean*"; and he feels "*the question is, which is to be master.*" The story also contains an episode with a lion and a unicorn. The lion ("ruddy beast") and the unicorn (white) are on the royal coat-of-arms of Great Britain, and represent the seventeenth century joining of Scotland (unicorn) and England (lion). The sketches in Carroll's book also make it clear that these figures also represent nineteenth century political leaders Benjamin Disraeli (unicorn) and William Ewart Gladstone (lion), the latter of whom the conservative Carroll did not like.

Remember that it was Disraeli (Lord Beaconsfield) who on July 14, 1856, said in the British House of Commons: *"I am told that a British minister has boasted — and a very unwise boast it was — that he had only to hold up his hand and he could raise a revolution in Italy tomorrow. . . . A great prince fell suddenly . . . solely and entirely by the action of secret societies. . . ."*

Chapter Five

The Masonic Connection

The term "point of light" is also used in Masonry and the occult, with "point" standing for the points on the Mason's compass, and "light" standing for "truth." "Light" also comes from the heavens, as the name "Blue Lodge" comes from Masons' *"ancient brethren who met under the starry canopy of heaven,"* according to Jim Shaw (former thirty-third degree Mason who became a Christian and rejected Masonry) in his book, *The Deadly Deception* (1988). According to the book's co-author, Tom McKenney, there were present at the presentation of the thirty-third degree to Shaw in 1966 Masons such as the King of Denmark, former U.S. President Harry Truman, Norman Vincent Peale, as well as an internationally prominent evangelist.

Perhaps coincidental is the fact that Mason Charles Willson Peale (born 1741) painted at least two portraits (including the first portrait ever painted) of George Washington with the latter's hand in his coat like Napolean. President Truman has been quoted as saying: *"Although I hold the highest civil honor in the world, I have always regarded my rank and title as a past grand master of Masons as the greatest honor that has ever come to me"* (*Empire State Mason*, February 1953). Noteworthy here is the fact that four Masons were appointed to the Supreme Court by Truman and F.D.R., so that a majority of the court from 1941 to 1971 were Masons, and it was during this time that the court ruled that a "wall of separation" existed between church and state, resulting in an increased secularization of American society, public life, and government.

J. Edgar Hoover actually presented the thirty-third degree Masonic certificate to Jim Shaw, according to *The Deadly Deception* co-author Tom McKenney, who also noted that Madame Blavatsky (founder of the Theosophical Society) and Albert Pike (leader of the Masons in the nineteenth century) were frequently seen arm-in-arm at Washington, D.C. social functions.

Symbolism is important in both the occult and Masonry. While the Christian rainbow has six colors, the occultic rainbow adds white as a seventh color because Lucifer was known as the "white spiritual ray of light" (in *The Wonderful Wizard of Oz*, the character Boq tells Dorothy that *"white is the witch color"*). The seven colors represent the seven levels or rays of initiation into the occult. According to former Mason Jim Shaw, the points of the compass stand for the male, and the square stands for the female. The compass represents the sun (Osiris, sun god) shining his light upon the earth (Isis, the moon goddess or fertility of "Mother Earth"). According to Mark Carnes in *Secret Ritual and Manhood in Victorian America* (1989), Albert Pike's symbolic drawing of the thirty-second degree was nearly identical to a 1613 etching by the Hermetic philosopher Valentinus, and Carnes states that *"Pike noted ancient and primitive peoples"* believed *"the male sun emanated points of light which were received by the female moon."*

In the exemplification of the thirty-first degree, Masonic candidates for that degree defend their lives before characters portraying Osiris and Isis, and they express their hope for better lives when reincarnated. In the thirty-second degree, they are told, "*You have reached the mountain peak of Masonic instruction, a peak covered by a mist, which* **you** *in search for further light can penetrate only by your own reflection . . . a consuming desire to pierce the pure white light of Masonic wisdom . . . in the Royal Secret, it is there that you may learn to find that light . . . in the Royal Secret. The true word-Man, born of a double nature (of what we call Good and what we call Evil; spiritual and earthly; mortal and immortal) finds the purpose of his being* **only when these two natures are in perfect harmony.** *Harmony, my brethren, Harmony, is the true word and the Royal Secret which makes possible the empire of true Masonic Brotherhood!*"

This brings to mind the Universal Brotherhood, which "*is to be the spiritual arm of U.N. world government,*" according to John Cotter in his book, *A Study in Syncretism: The Background and Apparatus of the Emerging One World Church.*

Chapter Six

Education, Literary Symbolism and One-World Socialism

Because of their desire for harmony, Masons do not say sectarian prayers to Jesus for example, because that would be "divisive." Perhaps this would explain why Horace Mann, a Mason who became known as "the father of American public education," felt that our public schools should be free from "sectarian religious influences." Mann became secretary to the Massachusetts State Board of Education in 1837 and established the first "normal" (public) school. His concept of "universal education" followed the European "Pestalozzi" schools, whose founder Johann Heinrich Pestalozzi (1746-1827) was a strong believer in Rousseau's permissive educational beliefs (as in the latter's book, *Emile*).

Rousseau was influenced by Johann Friedrich Herbart (1776-1841), who was influenced by the Freemason Fichte (promoted by the Illuminati). Preceding Mann was Fanny Wright (Madame Francoise d'Arusmont), who came to the U.S. in 1824 with the Marquis de Lafayette and then joined Robert Dale Owen in 1828 in an experiment in communism in New Harmony, Indiana. Wright was the favorite pupil of Jeremy Bentham (founder of Utopian welfare state utilitarianism) and developed a system she called, *"National, Rational, Republican Education, Free for All at the Expense of All, Conducted under the Guardianship of the State"* to be *"apart from the contaminating influence of parents."* She, Owen, and Orestes Brownson formed the Workingmen's Party in New York with the purpose of controlling political power in the state, so that they could establish a system of schools to destroy Christianity. (Karl Marx's first international was called the Workingmen's International Association.)

Brownson later converted to Christianity, and in *The Works of Orestes Brownson,* vol. 19, one reads: *"The great object was to get rid of Christianity, and to convert our churches into halls of science. The plan was not to make open attacks upon religion, although we might belabor the clergy and bring them into contempt where we could; but to establish a system of state — we said* **national** *— schools, from which all religion was to be excluded, in which nothing was to be taught but such knowledge as is verifiable by the senses, and to which all parents were to be compelled by law to send their children. Our complete plan was to take the children from their parents at the age of twelve or eighteen months, and to have them nursed, fed, clothed, and trained in these schools at the public expense; but at any rate, we were to have godless schools for all the children of the country. . . . The plan has been successfully pursued . . . and the whole action of the country on the subject has taken the direction we sought to give it. . . . One of the principal movers of the scheme had no mean share in organizing the Smithsonian Institute."*

This sounds somewhat like the 1930s congressional

testimony by Kenneth Goff, who said that he had been trained by the communists in "psychopolitics," which would link religion with mental illness in order to discredit religious beliefs.

It was Robert Dale Owen himself who, as a member of the U.S. Congress (1843-1847), introduced a bill establishing the Smithsonian Institute. After editing the *New Harmony Gazette* (name changed in 1829 to *Free Enquirer*, similar to the name of a twentieth century American Humanist Association periodical), Owen went to New York and founded the Association for Protection of Industry and for Promotion of National Education. After he left Congress, he wrote *Hints on Public Architecture* (1849), and from 1853 to 1858 he was chargé d'affaires in Italy (where the Masonic leader Mazzini initiated Madame Blavatsky into the Carbonari in 1856).

Beginning in 1837 in the U.S., Freemason Horace Mann was pushing non-sectarian education forward. In Paul Fisher's *Behind the Lodge Door: Church, State, and Freemasonry in America*, one reads that Mann was an enthusiastic advocate of a philosophy which was *"scientific, humanitarian, ethical, and naturalistic,"* and he believed in *"character education without 'creeds,' and in phrenology as a basis for 'scientific education.'"* He held that *"natural religion stands . . . preeminent over revealed religion. . . ."*

Mann believed in "humanizing" schools, as did the German philosopher Ludwig Andreas Feuerbach (1804-1872), who had studied under Hegel in Berlin for two years in the 1820s. According to Ted Byfield in "Again the Educators Have Used Our Children as Guinea Pigs," (*Western Report*, May 13, 1991), Feuerbach *"about one hundred fifty years ago . . . propounded the theory that since the highest known entity is the human self, then 'self-actualization' should be the ultimate goal of education"* (forerunner of the humanistic "self-actualization" theory of Abraham Maslow in twentieth century America). Feuerbach abandoned Hegelianism for naturalism and believed that God is merely the outward projection of man's inward nature.

These humanistic concepts greatly influenced Karl Marx, who wrote in his *Economic and Philosophic Manuscripts of 1844* that *"Communism begins from the outset with atheism. . . . Communism as fully developed naturalism, equals humanism."* Marx also offered to dedicate his book *Das Kapital* some years later to Charles Darwin, whose evolutionary theory explained in *The Origin of the Species by Means of Natural Selection, or the Preservation of Favored Races in the Struggle for Life* (1859) was to gain later acceptance in American public schools. Darwin further revealed his racist (and eugenic) attitudes in *The Descent of Man and Selection in Relation to Sex* (1871), in which he stated: *"At some future period, not very distant as measured by centuries, the civilized races of man will almost certainly exterminate, and replace, the savage races throughout the world. . . . The break between man and his nearest allies will then be wider, for it will intervene between man in a more civilized state, as we may hope, even than the Caucasian, and some ape as low as a baboon, instead of as now between the Negro or Australian and the gorilla."*

Not only would teachers contribute to the acceptance of Darwin's theory of evolution, but they would also contribute to the growth of Marx's communism, as Fyodor Dostoyevsky (1821-1881) predicted that *". . . men would gather together and exploit evil. Lawyers who will say there's no such thing as guilt will be on their side. Teachers who deny God will be on their side. They will not know it, but they will help evil conquer the world."*

Relevant here is the letter that the perceptive Lord Acton wrote to Richard Simpson on December 8, 1861, in which he characterized a cunning and treacherous group of people by saying, *"They saw 'no divine part of Christianity,' but divinified humanity, or humanized religion."* And in the same year, French statesman Adolphe Cremieux said, *"A new order will be substituted for the double empire of popes and emperors."*

Horace Mann's non-sectarian public schools were spreading far and wide in the second half of the nineteenth century, but questions were being raised. When the Hon. Zachary Montgomery was nominated for assistant attorney general, there were anti-Catholic attacks against him during his U.S. Senate confirmation hearings because of his views concerning public education.

In 1886, Montgomery published *Poison Drops in the Federal Senate: The School Question from a Parental and Non-Sectarian Standpoint*, stating that these attacks failed, and showing that after about two hundred years of public education in Massachusetts, the 1860 census figures showed that state to have one native white criminal to every 649 people, while Virginia, which always left the educational control of children to their parents, had only one criminal to every 6,566 inhabitants. Moreover, the aggregate figure for suicides in six northeastern states where the states controlled education was one to every 13,285, but in six mid-Atlantic and southern coastal states where parents controlled education, the aggregate for suicides was one to every 56,584. Why? Montgomery found that there were two causes — first, the loss of parental authority and home influence over children, through and by means of a state-controlled system of education; and second, a neglect of moral and religious education and training. After reading Montgomery's analysis, letters of support were sent to him by such individuals as John LeConte (president of the California State University) and George Washington (grand-nephew and nearest living relative to President Washington).

To demonstrate the attitude of those heading the public schools, Montgomery quoted from the 1864 biennial report of the California state superintendent of public instruction, John Swett, who wrote: *"The vulgar impression that parents have a legal right to dictate to teachers is entirely erroneous. . . . The only persons who have a legal right to give orders to the teacher are his employers, namely, the committee in some states and in others the directors or trustees. . . . If his conduct is approved of by his employers, the parents have no remedy against him or them."* How did this philosophical and psychological mindset come about?

●●●●●

It was during the first half of the nineteenth century that the French philosopher Auguste Comte (whose mentor was the French social philosopher and Mason Saint-Simon) founded positivism (which Comte called a "religion") and modern sociology. He was a social engineer who stated in his *System of Positive Polity* (1853), *"We must get rid of personality in every shape."*

He also stated, *"In the name of the past and of the future, the servants of humanity — both its philosophical and its practical servants come forward to claim as their due the general direction of this world."*

Keep in mind here that Lucis Publishing Co. would print a book, *Serving Humanity*, which would be a compilation from the writings of occultist Alice Bailey, who would write in her book *Education in the New Age*, published in 1954, that there is a need for "personality control" and that *"what is really taking place is the hastening of the process of light manifestation."*

In his excellent critical analysis of leading intellectuals in history, Paul Johnson wrote in *Intellectuals* (1988), concerning the social engineers, that *"social engineering is the creation of millenarian intellectuals who believe that they can re-fashion the universe by the light of their unaided reason. It is the birthright of the totalitarian tradition."*

The humanistic philosophy and sociology of social engineers such as Comte in the first half of the nineteenth century would be combined with the experimental psychology of the German physiologist and psychologist Wilhelm Wundt in the last half of the nineteenth century to have a revolutionary impact upon society in general and education in particular, beginning at the first half of the twentieth century. Wundt was influenced by Johann Herbart and was a professor at the University of Berlin in 1856, at the same time that Timothy Dwight was studying there. Dwight would become the twelfth president of Yale University, and was a member of Skull and Bones in 1849. Ironically, an ancestor of Dwight's by the same name was an earlier president of Yale University who had spoken out in 1798 against the French Revolution and the Illuminati.

Wundt's grandfather was a professor at Heidelburg and a member of the Illuminati with the code name "Raphael." Wundt's first American doctoral student in psychology at Leipzig was G. Stanley Hall. Some years earlier, Hall had studied philosophy at the University of Berlin with funds from Henry Sage, who was a member of Scroll and Key (the sister senior society to Skull and Bones at Yale University) and two of whose nephews were members of Skull and Bones. When Hall returned to the U.S. from Berlin, he became a professor at Antioch College, Ohio (where Horace Mann was president, 1853-1860), and spent an occasional Sunday there with Alphonso Taft (co-founder of Skull and Bones in 1832). After receiving his doctorate from Wundt at Leipzig, Hall was hired by Daniel Coit Gilman (member of Skull and Bones) to be a professor at Johns Hopkins University, where Hall became the mentor of John Dewey, the "father of progressive education."

At the beginning of the twentieth century, before John Dewey's "progressive" educational experimentation began to have its disastrous effects, illiteracy in the United States was becoming almost nonexistent. According to the census bureau, illiteracy among those ten to twenty years old went down from 7.6 percent in 1900 to only 4.7 percent in 1910. Dewey and his fellow progressive educators, like Edward Thorndike, James Russell, James Cattell, and Charles Judd, as well as Dewey disciples such as Harold Rugg, George Counts, and William H. Kilpatrick, would introduce a new type of education into American schools with the eventual results being the tragedy we see today.

Perhaps the best analysis of the "progressive educators" was written by Richard Weaver in the chapter,

"Gnostics of Education," in his book *Visions of Order* (1964). Weaver describes the "progressives" as a "revolutionary cabal" engaged in *"a systematic attempt to undermine society's traditions and beliefs."* When state education bureaucracies were created, he says, these "experts" required public school teachers to become indoctrinated in their philosophical premises and aims, which were that "change" is essential; children should follow their own desires; the teacher is not an evil "authority figure," but rather simply a "leader" cooperating with a group; grades are "undemocratic" because they demonstrate inequality; and discipline is bad because it has elements of fear and compulsion. Weaver compares the "progressives" with the anti-authoritarian gnostics of the first and second centuries A.D. who believed in divinized man who should do whatever he wants to do (e.g., if there is a "god within," then "if it feels good, do it").

This attitude was promoted by transcendentalists like Ralph Waldo Emerson, who believed that evil was illusory (so man could "do his own thing"), and because no moral absolutes exist, there is no ultimate basis for authority other than man himself. Because "superiority" was bad, the average condition of man was exalted and that meant "keeping down the standard of development and achievement." Knowledge was less important than methodology (e.g., "learn how to learn" via "critical thinking").

As John Dewey wrote in *The School and Society* (1899), *"The relegation of the merely symbolic and formal to a secondary position; the change in the moral school atmosphere . . . are not mere accidents, they are necessities of the larger social evolution."* This, according to Weaver, is *"a cant phrase standing for the political aims of the progressivists.* "The gnostic belief that man is divine also shows up in the progressives' "child-centered" education. Dewey in *The School and Society* approvingly quoted Friedrich Froebel that *"the primary root of all educative activity is in the instinctive, impulsive attitudes of children, and not in the presentation and application of external material, whether through the ideas of others or through the senses."*

This is like Rousseau's *Émile*, and Weaver points out that rather than "democracy" in the classroom, students actually need to be *made* to concentrate on what adults tell them they will need to know later in life. Weaver concludes by stating: *"The world for which the progressivists are conditioning their students is not the world espoused by general society, but by a rather small minority of radical doctrinaires and social faddists. . . . They have no equal as an agency of subversion. Their schemes are exactly fitted, if indeed they are not designed, to produce citizens for the secular communist state, which is the millennial dream of the modern gnostic."*

Because of the importance of Dewey's influence upon American society and especially education, it is worth looking at his background. Dewey entered the University of Vermont in 1875 and was tremendously influenced there by the writings of Thomas Huxley (known as "Darwin's Bulldog" because of his promotion of evolution). In 1881, he entered John Hopkins University for his doctoral work and became a Hegelian for a time. Hegel had developed a theory that in reality, everything (both good and bad) including man, is part of the Divine Spirit, or God, which is in the process of evolving (sounds similar to the beliefs of Teilhard de Chardin and leading Mason Albert Pike). In 1888, Dewey published his essay, "The Ethics of Democracy," emphasizing collectivism and that the individual is brought to reality in "the State" (a form of democratic socialism that is reminiscent of the French Revolution). He was probably greatly influenced in this by Edward Bellamy's *Looking Backward*, published in the same year (1888), in which the character, Julian West, falls asleep in 1887 and awakes in 2000 to find a bloodless, socialist revolution has occurred in which the government has nationalized everything. Madame Blavatsky wrote about *Looking Backward* in 1889 that it *"admirably represents the Theosophical idea of what should be the first step toward the full realization of universal brotherhood."*

In 1897, Dewey wrote *My Pedagogic Creed*, and in 1899, *The School and Society*, in which he spelled out how the schools should be the instrument to construct an American socialist society. In these schools, psychology would be used, and the academic basics would be de-emphasized. Dewey was teaching at the University of Chicago at the time, and he was on the first board of directors of Hull House, where Fabian socialist leaders Sidney and Beatrice Webb were staying after their arrival in the U.S. in April 1898. Dewey would then be one of the founders of the American branch of the Fabian Society called the Intercollegiate Socialist Society, later changed to the League for Industrial Democracy, with Dewey as president. He would also establish the Progressive Education Association, later named the American Education Fellowship.

● ● ● ● ●

The winds of revolution were in the air, and in Rev. Herman Kramer's *The Book of Destiny* (1955) one reads that *"in the prophets, winds represent revolutions"* (Dan. 7:2), *"a whirlwind signifies revolutions from nation to nation, invasions, and the overturning of kingdoms"* (Jer. 25:32), and *"For they have sown the wind, and they shall reap the whirlwind"* (Hos. 8:7). Percy Byssche Shelley (favorable toward the Assassins, Rosicrucians, and Illuminati) referred often to whirlwinds in his play, *Prometheus Unbound*, and in his "Introduction," he said, *"For my part I had rather be damned with Plato and Lord Bacon, than go to Heaven with Paley and Malthus."* Perhaps not coincidentally, L. Frank Baum in his 1900 *The Wonderful Wizard of Oz* used the wind of a tornado spiralling upward to symbolize revolutionary transformation in an imaginary land of the heart and mind.

A recent pamphlet by Lucis Trust states: *"The goal of the new world order is surely that every nation . . . should develop the realization that they are organic parts of one corporate whole and should consciously and selflessly contribute to that whole. This realization is already present in the hearts of countless numbers all over the world. . . . Spiritual values relate to the enlightenment, the freedom, and the creative growth of the human race. They promote the innate human tendency toward synthesis and wholeness. They expand rather than limit the horizons of human vision and capacity. They can be symbolized as an upward spiral of infinite potentiality."*

Not only is the "upward spiral," or "stairway to light" important in Masonry, but Nietzsche believed in "spiral progress," too. And in Debrah Rozman's *Meditating with Children: The Art of Concentration and Centering* (1975), one finds a drawing of "The Evolutionary Spiral: transpersonal transformation to the god within." The witch Starhawk, at Father Matthew Fox's college in California, says, *"We dance the spiral,"* and wrote a book, *The Spiral Dance* (1979).

In Robert Muller's *New Genesis: Shaping a Global Spirituality* (1982), he writes regarding Thanksgiving Square in Dallas: *"The most interesting and impressive symbol is the chapel built in the form of a spiral. Those who conceived Thanksgiving Square considered many ideas, including that of a Tree of Life. The concept finally retained was suggested by a monk, Brother David Steindl-Rast. He proposed the idea of a spiral. . . . As you stand inside, or under the chapel, you are taken by its spirit. In your mind you continue to draw the spiral and you visualize it expanding endlessly into the infinite, encompassing the entire universe! Such is the nature of a simple spiral."* Brother David Steindl-Rast networks with the Sufis. The spiral building in Dallas looks like a modern version of the spiral mosque of the Abbasid caliph al-Mutawakkil at Samarra in Iraq erected in A.D. 847.

In New Ager Marilyn Ferguson's *The Aquarian Conspiracy: Personal and Social Transformation in the 1980s* (1980), she quotes New Age hero Pierre Teilhard de Chardin speaking about man in an evolutionary "rising spiral," and Ferguson herself says: *"The crises of our time . . . are the necessary impetus for the revolution now under way. . . . Like the charting of a new star, naming and mapping the conspiracy only makes visible the light that has been present all along."*

Showing how the spiral is related to the New Age is Patricia Mische, who is co-author of *Toward a Human*

World Order (1977), co-founder of Global Education Associates in 1973, and editor of *The Whole Earth Papers.* At the November 9-11, 1984 symposium, "Toward a Global Society," Mische spoke on "The Spiral of Spiritual/Social Transformation," in which she pronounced: *"Traditional religion is failing to speak to problems in our society. The need for a New World Order is our greatest challenge and opportunity. . . . We see resistance to change — resistance to the New Age processes."* She closed her presentation by leading the audience in a five-minute centering meditation on the "sacred within."

The New Age movement is a pantheistic and monistic religious movement based upon Hindu, Buddhist, and other principles of Eastern mysticism (e.g., reincarnation). It's actually nothing "new" at all, but rather the "old" lie of Satan trying to take us back to the Garden of Eden, where he told Eve that if she and Adam ate of the forbidden fruit, *". . . Ye shall not surely die: For God doth know that in the day ye eat thereof, then your eyes shall be opened, and ye shall be as gods . . ."* (Gen. 3:4-5). Relevant here is the statement by Ruth Nanda Anshen in her introduction to William Irwin Thompson's *Evil and World Order* (1976) that *"Once the 'fruit of the Tree of Knowledge' has been eaten, the world is changed. The new world is dictated by the knowledge itself, not of course by an edict of God."* Similarly, Shakti Gawain in *Return to the Garden* (1989) wrote: *"Snake pointed to a certain tree known as the Tree of Knowledge. It had beautiful juicy-looking fruit. . . . Snake told Woman she must convince Man to eat some. . . . She knew she must do as advised. . . .* [Later] *men and women lived in harmony with the* [mother] *Earth. . . . Humankind had returned to the Garden.*"

It is also worth remembering that Satan and the New Age often imitate God, as in 2 Kings 2:11, by the power of God, ". . . *Elijah went up by a whirlwind into heaven.*" Jeremiah 23:19 states, "*Behold, a whirlwind of the Lord is gone forth in fury, even a grievous whirlwind: it shall fall grievously upon the head of the wicked.*" Dorothy is transported to Oz by a whirlwind (tornado), and her house falls upon the head of the wicked witch of the east (the wicked witch of the west is killed, melted away, when Dorothy pours, water on her — perhaps symbolic of baptism washing away sin). The whirlwinds of God are always of the north and south (Job 37:9; Ezek. 1:4; Zech. 9:14). Similarly, in Oz the "good" witches are of the north and south.

In NBC's movie of Baum's life (December 1990), Baum is shown to have changed the location of Dorothy's home from the Dakotas to Kansas, which is the absolute "heart" (middle) of continental America. The symbolism of the "rainbow" in the Oz books was picked up in D.H. Lawrence's *The Rainbow* (published in 1915 with a "phoenix" on the cover), where he not only uses language applicable to Dorothy of the Oz books, but also language used in occultist Alice Bailey's books which began publication a few years later. Lawrence writes, "*Rising to the light and the wind . . . she saw in the rainbow the earth's new architecture . . . the world built up in a living fabric of Truth.*" He speaks of her house and farm buildings that "*looked out to the road . . . [to] the magic land to her, where secrets were made known and desires fulfilled.*"

And language in *The Rainbow* similar to Bailey's are

references to "glamour," "Angel," *"state of oneness
. . . by obliterating his own individuality,"* and *"points
of light . . . the inner circle of light in which she lived
and moved. . . . Beyond our light and order there
is nothing, turning their faces always inward toward
the sinking fire of illuminating consciousness."* In
Bailey's *Initiation Human and Solar* (1922), she wrote
that *"the Lord of the World, the One Initiator, Who . . .
presides over the Lodge of Masters, and holds in his
hands the reins of government."* And in *A Treatise on the
Seven Rays: Esoteric Psychology* (1936 and 1942), she
described the goals and characteristics of what she calls
"the Illuminati of the world."

D.H. Lawrence also wrote *Fantasia of the Unconscious* (1922), and not too many years after his death,
Disney released its film *Fantasia* based upon pagan
mythology and occultism, including Mickey Mouse as
"The Sorcerer's Apprentice." Lawrence also hoped to
establish a Utopian community where elitists or "illumined
ones" would gather. It would be called Rananim, and he
hoped he would be joined there by Aldous Huxley
(author of *Brave New World* in 1932), Bertrand Russell,
and other Fabian socialists.

Another Fabian who looked to the future was
William Butler Yeats (a Mason). Iraq's Ministry of
Information and Culture recently put out a book titled,
*From Nebuchadnezzar to Saddam Hussein: Babylon
Rises Again*, which speaks of *"the phoenix of the new
time rising alive from the ashes of the past,"* and which
after Saddam's photos at the front includes a full-page
picture of a sculpted lion, the symbol of Iraq. Keep in
mind the lion and Saddam as you read Yeats' poem, "The

Second Coming" (written January 1919), in which he alludes to the coming of a false Messiah (the Antichrist) at the end of twenty centuries since the birth of Jesus:

> *"Surely some revelation is at hand,*
> *Surely the Second Coming is at hand.*
> *The Second Coming! Hardly are those words out*
> *When a vast image out of Spiritus Mundi*
> *Troubles my sight: somewhere in the sands of*
>   *the desert*
> *A shape with lion body and the head of a man*
> *A gaze blank and pitiless as the sun,*
> *Is moving its slow thighs, while all about it*
> *Reel shadows of the indignant desert birds.*
> *The darkness drops again; but now I know*
> *That twenty centuries of stony sleep*
> *Were vexed to nightmare by a rocking cradle,*
> *And what rough beast, its hour come round at*
>   *last,*
> *Slouches toward Bethlehem to be born."*

Not very long after Yeats' poem was published, British high commissioner Sir Percy Cox in late November 1922 drew up what became the Iraq-Kuwait border, which deliberately did not allow Iraq access to the sea, so that its influence in the Persian Gulf would be limited and it would remain dependent upon Great Britain. This would play an important part in Iraq's resentment toward the West and Kuwait, which helped to cause the recent conflict in the Middle East.

● ● ● ● ●

The year before Percy Cox's decision, and the same year Lucifer Publishing Co. began publishing Alice Bailey's works, Col. Edward Mandell House, in 1921, formed the Council on Foreign Relations. Col. House had earlier written a novel, *Philip Dru: Administrator*, in which he favorably described efforts to establish socialistic governments around the world with large spheres of influence. Much to House's dismay, however, the peace conference at the end of the First World War (1918) did not go as he desired. A primary component of the proposals offered at the peace conference was the League of Nations (the League's covenant was almost exclusively written by Col. House, not by President Wilson, and he was influenced by Fabian socialists' drafts of the League), but Congress for the second time voted against United States membership in the League on March 19, 1920, so in 1921 Col. House founded the Council on Foreign Relations to try to further his goals.

In *Fabian Freeway* (1968), author Rose Martin writes: *"To the ambitious young Fabians, British and American, who had flocked to the peace conference as economists and junior officials, it soon became evident that a New World Order was not about to be produced at Paris. . . . For them, Col. House arranged a dinner meeting at the Hotel Majestic on May 30, 1919, together with a select group of Fabian-certified Englishmen — notably, Arnold Toynbee, R.H. Tawney, and John Maynard Keynes (who would proclaim himself a Bolshevist). . . . They made a gentlemen's agreement to set up an organization, with branches in England and America. . . . As a result, two potent and closely related opinion-making bodies were founded, which only began their full growth in the 1940s, coincident with the formation of the Fabian International Bureau. The English branch was called the Royal Institute of International Affairs. The American branch, first known as the Institute of International Affairs, was reorganized in 1921 as the Council on Foreign Relations."*

In *Imperial Brain Trust* (1977), co-authors Laurence Shoup and William Minter indicate that the original conception of the scheme for the Anglo-American organization was primarily that of former South African colonial official Lionel Curtis, who *"for the previous nine years had been in charge of setting up a network of semi-secret organizations in the British dominions and the United States. These bodies, called the Round Table Groups, were established by Lord Milner . . . and his associates in 1908-1911. 'The original purpose of the groups was to seek to federate the English-speaking world along the lines laid down by Cecil Rhodes. . . .' Curtis and Philip Kerr were the two full-time activists in the scheme."*

President Woodrow Wilson's war aims planning body (called the Inquiry) under Col. House's direction included members of the United States Round Table Group such as Thomas J. Lamont of the J.P. Morgan banking house. Lamont's son, Corliss, would be author of *The Philosophy of Humanism* (1957), signer of the *Humanist Manifesto*, Humanist of the Year for 1977, head of Friends of Soviet Russia, and reportedly identified publicly as a communist by Louis Budenz, former editor of the *Daily Worker*.

In the CFR's *Foreign Affairs* (December 1922), Philip Kerr wrote, "From Empire to Commonwealth," in which one reads, *"Obviously there is going to be no peace or prosperity for mankind as long as* [earth] *remains divided into fifty or sixty independent states. . . . Equally obvious, there is going to be no steady progress in civilization . . . until some kind of international system is created which will put an end to the diplomatic struggles incident to the attempt of every nation to make itself secure. . . . The real problem today is world government. "*

In *Foreign Affairs* (June 1923), Col. House wrote "The Running Sands," in which he stated, *"Some two years ago in* La Revue de Genéve *I wrote: 'If war had not come in 1914 in fierce and exaggerated form, the idea of an association of nations would probably have remained dormant, for great reforms seldom materialize except during great human upheavals.' . . . If law and order are good within states, there can be no reason why they should not be good between states. "*

The same year, according to the October 27, 1923 issue of *New Statesman* (founded by the Fabians in 1913), Lloyd George of England was in America informing the Americans that they must save Germany financially. In Sister M. Margaret Patricia McCarran's *Fabianism in the Political Life of Britain, 1919-1931* (1954), one finds that *"economic discussions in the* New Statesman *indicate that Fabians followed Reginald McKenna and John Maynard Keynes,"* the latter of whom Prof. Ludwig von Mises linked with the Marxists.

Toward the end of 1915 and the beginning of 1916, Bertrand Russell introduced T.S. Eliot to the *New Statesman*, and Eliot would indicate that it was for this journal that he most enjoyed reviewing books. A few years later, Eliot wrote a poem, *The Hollow Men* (1925), which would end with the lines, *"This is the way the world ends/Not with a bang but a whimper."* This could be considered foreshadowing that the world would not end with a nuclear holocaust, but rather with enslavement by a socialist New Age New World Order. Eliot, Joseph Campbell, D.T. Suzuki, Lenin, Trotsky, Bakunin, Herman Hesse, Rudolf Steiner, Isadora Duncan, and others would go to the occultic center of Olga Froebe-Kapteyn at Ascona, Switzerland. It was financed largely by Pittsburgh philanthropists Paul and Mary Mellon (who were devotees of Carl Jung). Alice and Foster Bailey helped with sessions there beginning in 1931. The Bollingen Foundation would grow out of this effort. And lastly concerning T.S. Eliot, his *Old Possum's Book of Practical Cats* (1939) would later be the basis for the unusual modern musical, *Cats.*

• • • • •

At this time in the United States, socialism was being increasingly promoted. For example, it was strongly advocated by Arthur Calhoun in his three-volume work, *A Social History of the American Family* (1917-1919), which was a prominent social service textbook for a number of years. In the third volume, one finds: *"The new view is that the higher and more obligatory relation is to society rather than to the family; the family goes back to the age of savagery while the state belongs to the age of civilization. The modern individual is a world citizen, served by the world, and home interests can no longer be supreme. . . . As soon as the new family, consisting of only the parents and the children, stood forth, society saw how many were unfit for parenthood and began to realize the need of community care."*

As one continues to read Calhoun's third volume, one is amazed at the accuracy of his projections into the future. Writing in 1919, he projected that *". . as familism weakens, society has to assume a larger parenthood. The school begins to assume responsibility for the functions thrust upon it. . . . The juvenile court is developed as a protection to the young, and parents are called to account for disregard of juvenile delinquency. . . . The kindergarten grows downward toward the cradle and there arises talk of neighborhood nurseries. . . . Social centers replace the old time home chimney. . . . The child passes more and more into the custody of community experts. . . . In the new social order, extreme emphasis is sure to be placed upon eugenic procreation. . . . It seems clear that at least in its early stages, socialism will mean an increased amount of social control. . . . There will be an increase of legislation designed to check the mating of the unfit and the procreation of undesirable citizens. . . . We may expect in the socialist commonwealth a system of public educational agencies that will begin with the nursery and follow the individual through life. . . . Those persons that experience alarm at the thought of intrinsic changes in family institutions should remember that in the light of social evolution, nothing is right or valuable in itself."*

• • • • •

In *Labour Monthly* (October 1921), Fabian George Bernard Shaw wrote that *"compulsory labour, with death as the final penalty . . . is the keystone of socialism."* Ten years later, in the May 17, 1931 London *Sunday*

Mail, he would say, *"Never give anything to the poor. They are useless, dangerous, and ought to be abolished."* This type of thinking fit well with elitist eugenicist Margaret Sanger's (founder of Planned Parenthood) views concerning population control. Sanger (1957 Humanist of the Year) was introduced to people of wealth and influence by John D. Rockefeller, and in 1914 she set forth her creed as a woman's right *"to live, to love, to be lazy, to be an unwed mother, to create, to destroy."* During 1914 and 1915, she would have an intimate liaison with the sexual pervert and drug user, Havelock Ellis, who helped found the Fabian Society. In her first newspaper, *The Woman Rebel*, she wrote that *"birth control appeals to the advanced radical because it is calculated to undermine the Christian churches. I look forward to seeing humanity free someday of the tyranny of Christianity."* In *Woman and the New Race* (1920), she said, *"The most merciful thing that the large family does to one of its infant members is to kill it."*

There was also a racist element to Sanger's philosophy. The November 1921 issue of her *Birth Control Review* carried the heading "Birth Control: To Create a Race of Thoroughbreds." In her 1922 book, *The Pivot of Civilization*, she expressed concern that "slum dwellers" (particularly Blacks, Hispanics, and Jewish immigrants) would infect the better *"elements of society with their diseases and inferior genes."* The next year, she editorialized in *Birth Control Review* for restricting immigration on a racial basis, and in 1932 she outlined her "Plan for Peace," which called for coercive sterilization, mandatory segregation, and rehabilitative concentration camps for all "dysgenic stocks" including Blacks, Hispanics,

American Indians, and Catholics. Her "Negro Project" proposal stated, *"The mass of Negroes, particularly in the South, still breed carelessly and disastrously* . . . [and is] *from that portion of the population least intelligent and fit."* In an October 1939 letter to Clarence Gamble, Sanger described how they would use "Colored ministers" to further their plans, because *"we do not want word to go out that we want to exterminate the Negro population, and the minister is the man who can straighten out the idea if it ever occurs to any of their more rebellious members."*

Margaret Sanger also had sympathy for the Nazi's program. In her 1939 *Birth Control Review*, there was an emphasis upon eugenic sterilization, with one article titled "Eugenic Sterilization: An Urgent Need," which was written by Dr. Ernst Rudin, a leader in Hitler's Nazi Third Reich. Similarly, two months after Germany invaded Poland, Sanger's *Birth Control Review* (November 1939) commended the Nazi birth control program, saying that *"the German program has been much more carefully worked out* [than the Italian program]. *The need for quality as well as quantity is recognized."*

President Franklin Delano Roosevelt (a Mason) seemed of a like mind, as British historian Christopher Thorne wrote in his book, *Allies of a Kind* (1978): *"Subjects to do with breeding and race seem, indeed, to have held a certain fascination for the president. . . . Roosevelt felt it in order to talk, jokingly, of dealing with Puerto Rico's excessive birth rate by employing, in his own words, 'the methods which Hitler used effectively.' He said to Charles Taussig and William Hassett, as the former recorded it, 'that it is all very simple and painless — you have people pass through a narrow passage, and then there is a brrrr of an electrical apparatus. They stay there for twenty seconds, and from then on they are sterile.'"*

• • • • •

Pope Benedict XV foresaw the ominous trends toward world government, and its support by what he called on July 25, 1920, *"all the worst and most distorted elements. This state . . . would banish all national loyalties. In it no acknowledgement would be made of the authority of a father over his children, or of God over human society. If these ideas are put into practice, there will inevitably follow a reign of unheard-of terror."*

In the same year, the Supreme Council of the Scottish Rite held a special session at Colorado Springs, Colorado, and drew up a comprehensive education plan for the country. According to Paul Fisher in *Behind the Lodge Door*, the plan called for sending *all* children through *public* schools for a certain number of years, *"and recommended the careful selection of school trustees and teachers, as well as supervisors of school textbooks and libraries in order to exclude 'sectarian propaganda.' The Masonic plan also urged the establishment of 'a national department of public education headed by a secretary appointed as a member of the president's cabinet.'"*

The next year, Fabian socialist George Bernard Shaw wrote *Back to Methuselah*, in which he stated: *"If dwindling sects like the Church of England, the Church of Rome, the Greek Church, and the rest, persist in trying to cramp the human mind within the limits of these grotesque perversions of natural truths and poetic metaphors, then they must be ruthlessly banished from the schools until they either perish in general contempt or discover the soul that is hidden in every dogma. The test of a dogma is its universality."* His meaning of the term "universality" was whether it could be accepted by everyone.

In 1923, Manly P. Hall wrote the Masonically endorsed, *The Lost Keys of Freemasonry*, in which he said that *"Man is a god in the making."* The next year, W.L. Wilmshurst wrote *The Masonic Initiation* (a sequel to his 1922 *The Meaning of Masonry*) in which he refers to the Swiss alchemist Paracelsus (1493-1541, born Theophrastus Bombastus von Hohenheim) as part of a current to which *"one must look for the perpetuation of the secret Masonic science."*

In 1925, Alice Bailey's New Group of World Servers formed to help unite the world. And in the January 1926 edition of *New Age*, W.B. Zimmerman wrote "Let There Be Light," in which he encouraged Masons to be active in Christian churches to help "liberalize and modernize" them. To Christians, the initials "I.N.R.I." inscribed on the crucifix above the head of Jesus mean "Jesus of Nazareth, King of the Jews." However, in Arthur Preuss' *A Study of American Freemasonry* (1908), one finds that in Masonic symbolism, these initials stand for *Igne Natura Renovatur Integra* — "Entire Nature Is Renovated by Fire." In 1927, Nikos Kazantzakis (author of *The Last Temptation of Christ*) wrote that he envisioned a union of individuals *"who might create for earth a brain and heart . . . comrades he might signal 'with a password like conspirators.' "*

Relevant also to conspiracies is the fact that while

many people had (and still have) the impression that all Masons are simply ordinary men engaging in fraternal, charitable, educational, and other works, Manly P. Hall in *Lectures on Ancient Philosophy* (1929) writes: *"Freemasonry is a fraternity within a fraternity — an outer organization concealing an inner brotherhood of the elect. . . . It is necessary to establish the existence of these two separate yet independent orders, the one visible and the other invisible. The **visible society** is a splendid camaraderie of free and accepted men enjoined to devote themselves to ethical, educational, fraternal, patriotic, and humanitarian concerns. The **invisible society** is a secret and most august fraternity whose members are dedicated to the service of the mysterious **arcanum acandrum** (a secret or mystery). In each generation, only a few are accepted into the inner sanctuary of the Work. . . . The great initiate-philosophers of Freemasonry are masters of that secret doctrine which forms the invisible foundations of every great theological and rational institution."*

● ● ● ● ●

It was a time of renovation and revolution toward a New World Order, and in Fabian H.G. Wells' 1928 *The Open Conspiracy: Blueprints for a World Revolution,* he wrote: *"This open and declared intention of establishing a world order. . . . This is my religion . . . a scheme for all human conduct . . . the way of salvation. . . . First comes self-disregard, then service . . . from which the last shred of personality has been stripped. . . . There was no Creation . . . there was no fall. . . . There is the clear hope that directed* [human] *breeding will come within man's scope. . . . The form in which the Open Conspiracy will first appear will certainly not be that of a centralized organization. Its most natural and convenient method of coming into being will be the formation of small groups of friends . . . who will exchange views and find themselves in agreement upon the general idea. Fundamentally important are . . . the entirely provisional nature of all loyalties associated with existing governments, and the supreme importance of population control. . . . The conception of the Open Conspiracy involves a skeptical and destructive criticism of personal immortality religions. . . . The production and distribution of staple necessities is apprehended as one world business. . . . The political work of the Open Conspiracy must weaken, efface, incorporate, or supersede existing governments. . . . The Open Conspiracy is the natural inheritor of socialist and communist enthusiasm; it may be in control of Moscow before it is in control of New York. . . . The character of the Open Conspiracy will now be plainly displayed. . . . It will be a world religion. This large loose assimilatory mass of groups and societies will be definitely and obviously attempting to swallow up the entire population of the world and become the new human community."*

One might call this "new human community's" new "religion" by the name "humanism," as in 1930 Charles Francis Potter's (signer of *Humanist Manifesto*) *Humanism: A New Religion*, in which he stated: "*Education is thus a most powerful ally of humanism, and every American public school is a school of humanism. What can the theistic Sunday schools, meeting for an hour once a week, and teaching only a fraction of the children, do to stem the tide of a five-day program of humanistic teaching?*"

By "humanistic teaching," he not only meant inroads being made in the public schools by evolution after the 1925 Scopes trial, but he was also referring to a shift in emphasis from the academics basics to a socialization process. In John Dewey's (co-author of *Humanist Manifesto*) book, *My Pedagogic Creed* (1897) he stated: "*I believe the true center of correlation on the school subjects is not science, nor literature, nor history, nor geography, but the child's social activities.*" The National Education Association (NEA) made Dewey an honorary president in 1932, which was the same year his disciple, George S. Counts, wrote *Dare the School Build a New Social Order?*

In this book, Counts proclaimed that "*the teachers should deliberately reach for power and then make the most of their conquest*" so that they could "*influence the social attitudes, ideals, and behavior of the coming generation.*" Counts also wrote: "*The growth of science and technology has carried us into a new age where ignorance must be replaced by knowledge, competition by cooperation, trust in Providence by careful planning, and private capitalism by some form of socialized economy.*"

The same year, F.S. Marvin wrote *The New World-Order*, in which one reads that "*nationality must rank below the claims of mankind as a whole*"; and on August 1, Freemason Paul Bezault wrote in the *Bulletin* of the Grand Lodge of France that "*to secularize the constitution of a people is but a small thing, but to secularize the soul of that people is better.*"

All of this, the promotion of a socialist economy, the elimination of trust in God, the secularizing of people's souls, would fit well in the plan outlined by William Z. Foster, the head of the Communist Party in America, in his 1932 book *Toward Soviet America.*

See if what Foster said seems similar to what has been happening recently: *"Class ideologies of the past will give place to scientific materialist philosophy. Among the elementary measures the American Soviet government will adopt to further the cultural revolution are the following: the schools, colleges, and universities will be coordinated and grouped under the National Department of Education and its state and local branches. The studies will be revolutionized, being cleansed of religious, patriotic, and other features of the bourgeoisie ideology. The students will be taught on the basis of Marxism dialectical materialism, internationalism, and the general ethics of the new socialist society. . . . The churches will remain free to continue their services, but their special tax and other privileges will be liquidated. Their buildings will revert to the State. Religious schools will be abolished and organized religious training for minors prohibited. Freedom will be established for anti-religious propaganda. . . . Science will become materialistic. . . . God will be banished from the laboratories as well as from the schools."*

Foster's book title was similar to that of George Count's — *The Soviet Challenge of America* (1931) — in which the latter professed that the Soviet's cultural revolution *"possesses a single mighty integrating principle — the building of a new society . . . in which the mainspring of all industry will be social need rather than private profit . . . in which the curse of Eden will be lifted forever from the soul of woman, in which a condition as essential equality will unite all races and nations into one brotherhood."*

Following Counts' books of 1931 and 1932, fellow educator (and disciple of John Dewey), Harold Rugg published *The Great Technology* in 1933, explaining: *"A new public mind is to be created. How? Only by creating tens of millions of new individual minds and welding them into a new social mind. Old stereotypes must be broken up and new climates of opinion formed in the neighborhoods of America."* Also in 1933, the first *Humanist Manifesto* was published with signers such as Oliver Reiser (who also signed the 1973 *Humanist Manifesto*), who would later write the preface for occultist Alice Bailey's book, *Education in the New Age.* John Dewey was a co-author and signer of the first *Humanist Manifesto*, and he was also a member (along with Edward R. Murrow) of the Institute of International Education (IIE, which today boasts that it *"plays an important role in the Green Revolution"*).

The IIE was established in 1919 at Columbia University (some years after Dewey's arrival there) with a grant from the Carnegie Endowment for International Peace. From 1919 to 1936, the Carnegie Corporation's grants to the institute totalled nearly one million dollars, and substantial additional funds were received from the Laura Spelman Rockefeller Memorial (which was absorbed into the Rockefeller Foundation in 1929) and member universities affiliated with the American Council on Education. In the summers of 1933 and 1934, IIE held Moscow University summer school programs. However, the *Pittsburgh Sun-Telegraph* exposed the programs on February 18, 1935, in an article, "American Professors, Trained by Soviets, Teach in United States Schools," and shortly thereafter the 1935 summer school programs were suddenly cancelled. The Soviet propaganda had already reached thousands, though. Dr. John Almack wrote in a series of articles in the *San Francisco Examiner* (during October 1942) about the programs: *"Many teachers and students returned challenging everything American, breathing fire and defiance to property, the profit system, and the Constitution, and beating the tomtoms for a 'new social order.' . . . They felt they must declare the way* [to revolution], *after insuring their own safety, should things go wrong, by guarantees of 'academic freedom.' "*

Six years later, IIE director Laurence Duggan jumped (or was forced) to his death from his New York office window after Whittaker Chambers linked him to a communist spy network and the FBI interviewed him. This act of suicide (or murder) occurred December 20, 1948, the day before he was to testify (and perhaps name members of the spy network) before a congressional committee.

The same year as the first of these Moscow University summer sessions (1933), the American Historical Association's Commission on Social Studies issued a report funded by the Carnegie Corporation at three hundred forty thousand dollars. According to Robert Henry Goldsborough, this would amount to about six million dollars today, and he indicates that *"the report concluded that the day of the individual in the United States has come to an end, and that that future would be characterized by some form of collectivism and an increase in the authority of the State."*

This movement toward collectivism and an increase in the authority of the state was described in H.G. Wells' futuristic 1933 book, *The Shape of Things to Come*, which was a revision of his 1928 book, *The Open Conspiracy*. In reading this 1933 volume by Wells, it is necessary to constantly remind oneself that the book was written almost sixty years ago rather than today. He states that a Second World War would originate in 1940 over a German-Polish dispute; and after 1945 there would be an increasing lack of public safety in growing criminally infected areas. The plan for the "modern world-state" would succeed on its third attempt (around 1980), and come out of something that happened in Basra, Iraq. At this point, he said, *"Russia is ready to assimilate. Is eager to assimilate."* A world council or "new world administration" would be *"the only sovereign upon this planet,"* which he called "Mother Earth." Although the world government *"had been plainly coming for some years, although it had been endlessly feared and murmured against, it found no opposition prepared anywhere."* The lack of opposition was developed via the "Life Time Plan" which created *"a service mentality in the place of a proprietary mentality."* The Department of General Psychology with its power over both educational and legal controls *"became the thought, as the World Council had become the will, of mankind acting as a whole."*

Not making Hitler's mistake of failing to realize that *"no revolution could be a real and assured revolution until it has completely altered the educational system of the community,"* the new education was *"based on a swiftly expanding science of relationship."* It would be *". . . propaganda passed necessarily into a training for public service and a universal public education . . . to establish a new complete ideology and a new spirit which would induce the individual to devote himself and to shape all his activities to one definite purpose, to the attainment and maintenance of a progressive world-socialism, using an efficient monetary system as its normal medium of relationship."* It would be the *"New Humanity . . . with a common consciousness and a common will."*

The year after *The Shape of Things to Come* was published, Wells published his *Experiment in Autobiography* (1934), in which he stated: *"The organization of this that I call the Open Conspiracy, the evocation of a greater sounder fellow to the first Communist essay, an adequately implemented Liberal Socialism, which will ultimately supply teaching, coercive and directive public services to the whole world, is the immediate task before all rational people. I believe this idea of a planned world-state is one to which all our thought and knowledge is tending. . . . It is appearing partially and experimentally at a thousand points. . . . When accident finally precipitates it, its coming is likely to happen very quickly. . . . Sometimes I feel that generations of propaganda and education may have to precede it. . . . Plans for political synthesis seem to grow bolder and more extensive. . . . The New Plan in America to the New Plan in Russia and how are both related to the ultimate World-State? . . . There must be a common faith and law for mankind. . . . Only after a huge cultural struggle can we hope to see the world-state coming into being. The Open Conspiracy has to achieve itself in many ways, but the main battle before it is an educational battle."*

And what better way to win this educational battle for a "common faith" than for the "father of progressive education," John Dewey, to publish in the same year of 1934 his book, *Common Faith*, in which Dewey describes what he perceives as the need for a syncretization of all religions toward a common faith, saying: *". . . our understanding of our relations to one another and the values contained in these relations. We, who now live, are part of a humanity that extends into the remote past, a humanity that has interacted with nature. . . . Here are all the elements for a religious faith that shall not be confined to sect, class, or race.*" However, we should remember Luke 12:8-9,51-53.

Also in 1934, Willard Givens (who became executive secretary of the National Education Association in 1935, held the position for seventeen years, and then took over the education program of the supreme council thirty-third degree of the Scottish Rite) said: "*A dying laissez-faire must be completely destroyed and all of us, including the 'owners,' must be subjected to a large degree of social control. . . . An equitable distribution of income will be sought. . . . [And] the major function of the school is the social orientation of the individual. It must seek to give him understanding of the transition to a new social order.*"

More recently, former executive director of the Kansas Education Association, John Lloyd, revealed that Saul Alinsky's *Rules for Radicals* (1971) was the NEA's "bible." The socialist Alinsky (1909-1972) has asserted that "*any revolutionary change must be preceded by a passive, affirmative, non-challenging attitude toward change among the masses of our people.*" And during the 1930s, socialists Gunnar and Alva Myrdal often talked of "*creating a new generation, people who would better fit into a new world order.*"

Unfortunately, this "new generation" and "new world order" would demean those choosing to be home-makers, as the Myrdals commented: "*It is still possible to make their way with domestic work, both as housewives and as servants.* " In a letter dated August 12, 1937, Frederick Keppel, president of the Carnegie Corporation, offered Gunnar Myrdal funding for a study published in 1944 as *An American Dilemma,* in which Myrdal claimed the American Constitutional Convention of the late eighteenth century was *"nearly a plot against the common people."* Keppel's foreword to the book was dated December 15, 1942, and refers to the "United Nations" three years before an organization by that name existed. Myrdal, now deceased, had also been a Rockefeller fellow, a Spelman Fund fellow, and among the first endorsers of Planetary Citizens.

In the New World Order's new generation, there would be no room for those not measuring up to the elitist eugenicists' standards, as Nicholas Kristof writing in November 1989 for *The New York Times* said, *"tens of thousands of 'mental defectives' were sterilized across the United States, mostly between the 1920s and the 1950s.'"* Margaret Sanger's 1934 "Baby Code" would have permitted only the "fit" to procreate. In the Supreme Court's *Buck v. Bell* (1927) compulsory sterilization ruling, Justice Oliver Wendell Holmes, Jr., agreed that society should prevent the "unfit" from procreating. The Nazis' compulsory sterilization law of 1933 was taken almost entirely from the Model Eugenical Sterilization Law of Harry Laughlin, affiliated with Sanger's *Birth Control Review.* And a member of her American Birth Control League, Lothrop Stoddard, wrote *Into the Darkness* (1940) applauding the Nazis' sterilization law as *"weeding out the worst strains in the Germanic stock."*

Chapter Seven

Adolf Hitler, World Order and World War II

This mentality of a new generation trained in socialism for a New World Order was picked up by Adolf Hitler, who said, *"Your child belongs to us already. . . . This new Reich will give its youth to no one, but will itself take youth and give to youth its own education and its own upbringing."* In Maria Trapp's book, *The Story of the Trapp Family Singers,* one reads: *"This morning we were told* [by the Nazis] *at the (school) assembly that our parents are nice, old-fashioned people who don't understand the new Party. We should leave them alone and not bother. We are the hope of the nation, the hope of the world. We should never mention at home what we learn at school now."*

The work of implementing the goals of the "new Party" would fall largely to Heinrich Himmler, who transformed the black-clad SS with their skull and bones insignia into a supposedly mystical elite, according to the television documentary *The SS: Blood And Land* (1991). This documentary describes how at the turn of the century, there was a rising tide of materialism in Germany and Austria, with a countervailing reaction that yearned for a more harmonious and spiritual past. Many of Germany's youth became known as "the birds of passage," with vegetarianism, herbal healing, communal living, nudism, and meditation becoming fashionable; and in every major city, cults devoted to spiritualism, astrology, magic, and the occult formed. (Doesn't this sound like today?)

In this regard, the teachings of three individuals were most prominent. First was Madame Blavatsky, whose fifth race in human civilization she termed "Aryan" and which she believed could be reconstituted to return man to the height of spirituality. By 1914 her Aryan doctrine had spread through Germany and Austria. It was a member of the inner circle of the Thule Society, Dietrich Eckart, who first introduced Hitler to the teachings of Madame Blavatsky. Reportedly, Hitler kept a copy of her book, *The Secret Doctrine*, by his bedside, and it was from her writings that he learned the meaning of the Aryan swastika. (The swastika is the symbol of the seventh ray of initiation, and Hitler was a sixth ray initiate.)

The second individual of prominence was Guido von List, who believed in a hidden elect or elite class of priest rulers ("Armenen," with the swastika as their symbol) whose role was to preserve the occult knowledge of Germans' Aryan ancestors. List believed the imposition of Christianity had forced the Teutonic tribes to continue their traditions in secret, but their law had lived on via Freemasons, Rosicrucians, and Knights Templar. A German order was founded on his principles in May 1912 with many military officers joining, and it was ruled by a twelve-man council of initiates.

The third prominent individual was Jörg Lanz, a former Cistercian monk who blended Aryan occultism with eugenics. He believed the original Aryans practiced telepathy, and that it could again be practiced if there were a return to pure Aryan blood. Lanz also believed that Knights Templar were the knights of the Holy Grail, and that the search for the Grail was the search for racial purity. In 1905, he began publication of his journal, *Ostara* (which Hitler had been reading since the age of twenty), and in 1907 Lanz formed the Order of the New Templars, which had as its purpose the harmonization of science, art, and ethics into an occult religion devoted to the purification of an Aryan race which would have psychic powers. This was the origin of the SS, who were the wise priest-kings and leaders of spiritual and secret orders who would rule.

In *The Occult and the Third Reich* (1971), one learns that in the 1930s Hitler said, *"With the nation of races, National Socialism* [Naziism] *will use its own revolution for the establishing of a new world order . . . a new dawning of history."* In occultist Alice Bailey's *The Externalization of the Hierarchy* (1957), one reads that beginning in 1934, there was *"the organizing of the men and women . . . so they can set the note of world goodwill for the new world order. . . . Group work of a new order . . .* [with]*progress defined by service . . . the work of the Brotherhood . . . the Forces of Light . . .* [and] *out of the spoliation of all existing culture and civilization, the new world order must be built."*

The year before, Lucis Trust (formerly Lucifer Publishing Co.) published Bailey's pamphlet, *The Next Three Years (1934-1935-1936),* in which she stated: *"By 1945 we shall have the inner structure of a world faith so clearly defined in the minds of many thousands that its outer structure will inevitably make its appearance before the end of the century. The inner structure of the World*

Federation of Nations will be equally well organized by 1965, and its outer form taking rapid shape by 2025. Do not infer by this that we shall have a perfected world religion and a complete community of nations. Not so rapidly does nature move, but the vision and the idea will be universally recognized, universally desired, and generally worked for. When these conditions exist, nothing can stop the appearance of the ultimate physical form. . . . Approximately four hundred men and women are working consciously with the Plan."

Bailey would also write of the "universal mind" (H.G. Wells published *World-Brain* in 1938), and in 1942 she published *Esoteric Psychology, Vol. II*, in which she wrote: *"Behind the divisions of humanity stand those Enlightened Ones whose right and privilege it is to watch over human evolution and to guide the destinies of men. . . . This they do through the implanting of ideas in the minds of the world thinkers, so that these ideas in due time receive recognition and eventually become controlling factors in human life. They train the members of the New Group of World Servers in the task of changing these ideas into ideals. These in their turn become the desired objectives of the thinkers and are then taught to the powerful middle class and worked up into world forms of government or religion, thus forming the basis of the new world order, into which the masses are patiently incorporated."*

About this same time, the thirty-third degree Freemason Myron Taylor was the United States' special envoy to the Vatican during the Second World War. In 1938, the Jesuit journal, *Civiltá Cattólica*, which was the semi-official voice of the Vatican, no longer included its warnings about Freemasonry, especially in its declared program to create what it termed a "New World Order."

In Hermann Rauschning's 1940 *The Voice of Destruction*, the author recounts his own personal earlier conversations with Hitler: *"Only by accepting the inner law of the new world order, Hitler contended, could the German people become the world people who would give their name to the coming era."* Hitler kept talking of establishing a "new order" which would replace national boundaries, saying: *"Shall we form simply a select company of the really initiated? An Order, the brotherhood of Templars round the holy grail of pure blood? . . . It is not the Christian-Schopenhauerist religion of compassion that is acclaimed, but pure, noble blood, in the protection and glorification of whose purity the brotherhood of the initiated have come together."*

Rauschning then recounts that Hitler described "a new social and economic order," and says, *"Hitler spoke as . . . one of the initiated."* Hitler said: *"We, too, are a Church. . . . Our revolution is . . . in moral ideas and in men's spiritual orientation. . . . National Socialism . . . is more even than a religion: it is the will to create mankind anew. . . . A new age of magic interpretation of the world is coming. . . ."*

Rauschning further states that Hitler spoke of *"the rhythm of life . . . in a spiral,"* and that *"man is God in the making."* (Remember here the words, *"Man is a god in the making,"* in thirty-third degree Mason Manly P. Hall's *The Lost Keys of Freemasonry*.) Rauschning also quotes Hitler as saying, *"We don't want people who keep an eye on the life in the hereafter. We need free men who feel and know that God is in themselves."* Doesn't this sound very much like Masonic leader Albert Pike's statement in *Morals and Dogma* that *"Masonry teaches that the present is our scene of devotion. . . .* [Man] *is sent into this world not to be constantly hankering after, dreaming of, preparing for another. . . . The Unseen cannot hold a higher place in our affections than the Seen and the Familiar. . . . The earth, to the Mason, is both the starting place and goal of immortality."*

Hitler also stated: *"I got illumination . . . from the Freemasons. . . . I learned above all from the Jesuits. So did Lenin, for that matter. . . . There is one dangerous element . . . I have copied from the Freemasons. They form a sort of priestly nobility. They have developed an esoteric doctrine . . . imparted through the medium of symbols and mysterious rites in degrees of initiation . . . by working on the imagination through magic and the symbols of a cult — all this is the dangerous element and the element that I have taken over. Don't you see that our Party must be of this character? . . . An Order, the hierarchical Order of a secular priesthood."*

"Hitler's projected new world order" were also the words used by Ralph Bunche in his article "The Negro in the Political Life of the United States" (*The Journal of Negro Education*, July 1941). Also in this edition were W.E.B. Dubois' "Neuropa: Hitler's New World Order" and Doxey Wilkerson's "Russia's Proposed New World Order of Socialism," which included subparts titled "The Fascist 'New World Order' " and "The Anglo-American 'New World Order.' "

• • • • •

In 1940, Fabian H.G. Wells wrote *The New World*

Order in which he proposed a "collectivist one world state" comprised of "socialist democracies." He advocated "universal conscription for service" and said *"nationalist individualism . . . is the world's disease."* He continued: *"The manifest necessity for some collective world control to eliminate warfare and the less generally admitted necessity for a collective control of the economic and biological life of mankind, are aspects of one and the same process."* He said this would be accomplished through "universal law" and "propaganda (or education)."

Also in 1940, even before the United States had entered the Second World War, the Carnegie Endowment for International Peace published *The New World Order*, which was a select list of references on regional and world federation, together with some special plans for world order after the war. This interesting list of references focused on publications and speeches in 1939 and 1940 and included the following:

1. "The World Federal State" by Lothar von Wurmb in the January 1939 edition of *World Order*.
2. The journal *World Federation* is begun by the Campaign for World Government in April 1939.
3. "Plan for an Unarmed World Federation, Democratic, Non-Military, and All-Inclusive," by the American Campaign for World Government in the May 19, 1939 *Peace News* (London).
4. John Foster Dulles' address on October 28, 1939 proposing that America lead the transition to a new order of less independent, semi-sovereign states bound together by a league or federal union.
5. Pope Pius XII's address on December 24, 1939 outlining

five points considered essential for setting up a new world order.

6. *Building the New World Order* (1939) by E.C. Brunauer (with the aid of the American Association of University Women) is published by the League of Nations Association and advocates building on the foundations of the League of Nations for a union of democracies and peace system in the Western Hemisphere.

7. *World Order (Civitas Dei)* by Lionel Curtis is published in 1939 and considers a working system of human society, concluding that such a system must mean the organization of all human society in one commonwealth. (In Ralph Page's "Designs for a World Order," he calls Curtis' 985-page work the foundation of all thought upon the design of a new order, and he says, *"Curtis' thesis is that to engender in man a desire to serve each other is the end and object of human existence."*)

8. *Federation and World Order* (1939) by Duncan and Elizabeth Wilson examines how federalism has already worked in the British Empire, the United States, and elsewhere, and from this deduces how it might be adopted on a worldwide scale.

9. "The New World Order: A Japanese View" by Iwao Ayusawa was published in the July 1940 edition of *Contemporary Japan.*

10. "Designs for a World Order" by Ralph Page was published in the July 1940 edition of *Annals of the American Academy of Political and Social Science.*

11. In November 1940, the Commission to Study the Organization of Peace issues a preliminary report

setting forth elementary principles essential to a lasting peace, and recommends world federation.

12. "A New World Order" by John G. Alexander was published in the December 12, 1940 *Congressional Record*. (A similar item of his declaring the need for a federation of the world was also in the November 3, 1939 *Congressional Record*.)

In the article by Ralph Page listed above, he quotes John Foster Dulles as saying: *"The fundamental fact is that the nationalist system of wholly independent, fully sovereign states is complete in its cycle of usefulness. . . . Today, more than ever before, are the defects of the sovereignty system magnified, until now it is no longer consonant with either peace or justice. It is imperative that there be a transition to a new order. This has, indeed, become inevitable; for the present system is rapidly encompassing its own destruction. The real problem is not whether there will be a transition, but how can transition be made, and to what."*

Page then goes on to state: *"That the peace of the world depends upon some surrender of national sovereignty has been stated by the leaders, past and present, of most democratic countries in Europe. . . . One purpose, one interest, one loyalty, the brotherhood of man, is the only goal that enlists the life forces of the youth of the world."*

But countering the claim of proponents of world federalism that the U.S. should join a world federation just as the original American states under a confederation joined in the federal republic, Graeme Howard in *America and a New World Order* (1940) argues that this analogy is fallacious. Rather, he stated: *"The American colonies consolidated their power in order to achieve aggregate power in the international community commensurate with other eighteenth century nations. It is one thing for a group of states with low power ratios to consolidate their power and quite another for all states to sacrifice their power."* Instead, Howard argued, *"It is power, morality, and sound economic foundation that must form the framework for support of the new world order. . . . The new international order must provide equality of economic opportunity as a moral factor, for political freedom without social and economic freedom is a mere empty gesture. . . .* [But] *promising both a more ethical and a more realistic solution is the formation of regional economic entities. . . . Cooperative regionalism* [will] *bring about a better world order through internationally balanced economic and political regional blocs."*

Similarly, M.J. Bonn in "The New World Order" (*The Annals of the American Academy of Political and Social Science*, July 1941), wrote: *"National planning means deliberate international anarchy. . . . But we are not yet going to have a world state, and I doubt whether we are on the road to world union. The formation of regional federations by hitherto autonomous groups of countries is much easier. . . . The leveling-up of backward races to full world citizenship cannot be achieved by a few easy steps. . . . I doubt if the world order of tomorrow will be capitalist or socialist. It probably will be both and neither. . . . The genius of History does not march through the ages with the solemn goose-step. . . . But all the time he keeps moving, and with every move a step toward a new world order is taken."*

However, near the beginning of America's involvement in World War II, a group of individuals including Herbert Agar, Lewis Mumford, and Reinhold Niebuhr issued a volume in 1941 entitled *The City of Man: A Declaration on World Democracy*, which declared: *"Universal peace can be founded only on the unity of man under one law and one government. . . . All states, deflated and disciplined, must align themselves under the law of the world-state . . . the new order . . . when the heresy of nationalism is conquered and the absurd architecture of the present world is finally dismantled."* Nelson Rockefeller will refer to this book's phrase, "absurd architecture," in his own promotion of world federalism in his 1962 book, *The Future of Federalism*.

The City of Man continues with other terms, similar to those later used by the Unity-in-Diversity Council (subsequently Unity-and-Diversity World Council) and by President George Bush, when it states: *"Diversity in unity and unity in diversity will be the symbols of federal peace in universal democracy. . . . Society may be likened to a triangular pyramid with its three faces representing the constitutional order, the economic order, the international order. None of them stands alone; each of them leans on the other. All three together converge toward the common apex. . . . A positive plan for world legislation . . . cannot be assigned any longer to pure theoretical thinking . . . even if as august as Mazzini's. . . . And there must be a common creed . . . or ethico-religious purpose."*

Looking toward the future, *The Rosicrucian Digest* for June 1941 printed an article, "The Thought of the Month: Make Your Own Prophecies," which included: *"We predict a mystical-pantheism as the religion of*

*tomorrow. . . . There will not be churches, but a church.
. . . Since the earth is a habitat of humanity, it is also the
common property of all men. . . . The World State will
provide and maintain community hospitals, sanitariums,
and clinics. . . . Physicians will be paid by the state and
their entire professional services will be absorbed by the
state. . . . Every citizen will enjoy these health benefits
and guarantees. . . . Quotas will be placed upon all
professions, in each of the zones of the World-State."*

Two days prior to the Japanese surprise attack on
Pearl Harbor, Fabian Sir Julian Huxley said on December
5, 1941, that he hoped America and Japan would be at
war "next week." The Japanese attack came on Sunday,
December 7, the first day of the week.

The next year, P.E. Corbett's *Post-War Worlds*
(1942) was published under the auspices of the leftist
Institute of Pacific Relations, proclaiming: *"A world
association binding together and coordinating regional
groupings of states may evolve toward one universal
federal government, as in the past loose confederations
have grown into federal unions. Such evolution will bring
with it increasing security and peace and social progress.
World government is the ultimate aim, but there is more
chance of attaining it by gradual development. . . . First
it must be recognized that the law of nations takes
precedence over national law. . . . There is much to be
said for constituting a Supreme World Court. . . .
Nationalism threatens to be a continuing obstacle to
general progress. . . . it may be impossible to 'indict a
whole people,' but quite possible to indict and to coerce,
when necessary, its leaders. . . . Steps will need to be
taken to stop the preaching of the supremacy of the state.*

The process will have to be assisted by the deletion of the nationalistic material employed in educational textbooks and its replacement by material explaining the benefits of wider association. . . . Men engaged in practical affairs, as well as many theorists, are looking to something in the nature of a federal organization with a common police, a supreme court, a legislative and governing body, and common economic agencies for advice and control. . . . An Economic and Financial Organization, embracing Trade, Development, and Migration Commissions, and a Central Bank. The function of these institutions . . . would be to regulate the production and distribution of raw materials and food, control the flow of interregional investment and migration, etc."

During the Second World War, Masonry would do its part in overthrowing the old order, as in 1943 John Stewart Service (a diplomatic advisor to Gen. Joseph Stilwell and Gen. Albert Wedemeyer in China) instituted the Fortitude Lodge at Chungking. And while in China, Service constantly criticized America's ally Chiang Kai-shek in comparison with the Chinese communists. Furthermore, in the Masonic magazine *New Age* itself, one finds in Morris DePass' November 1968 article, "The Hoon Bong or Red Society of China," that years earlier, the Red Society of China, some of whose *"educators were Masons . . . contributed materially to the overthrow of the Manchu Dynasty."*

In 1945, *The New World Order of Islam* by Bashiruddin Ahmad and *The Anatomy of Peace* by Emery Reves were published. Reves called for world goverment as "an immediate necessity," and the *New York Times* proclaimed Reves' book "intelligent, realistic, and eloquent." On August 16 of that year, Stephen King-Hall wrote in his (London) *National News-Letter* that *"world government has now become a hard-boiled, practical, and urgent necessity"* (*Reader's Digest*, November 1945). Two months later, on October 24, Senator Glen Taylor introduced Senate Resolution 183 calling upon the U.S. Senate to go on record as favoring the creation of a world republic, including an international police force. Senator Taylor quoted President Harry Truman in Kansas City, before the atomic bomb was dropped on Hiroshima, as saying, *"It will be just as easy for nations to get along in a republic of the world as it is for us to get along in a republic of the United States."* On this same day (October 24), the U.N. charter went into effect, and American membership was largely achieved due to the involvement of Alger Hiss of the State Department, who was an important advisor to President Roosevelt at Yalta where FDR, Churchill, and Stalin met.

In 1944, Alice Bailey published *Discipleship in the New Age*, vol. 1, in which she talked of "the coming New Age" and its "disciples." Of course, she would be one of these "disciples," and in the book she prints what are supposedly telepathic transmissions from an adept known as "the Tibetan." One of these alleged "communications" was February 1939 in which "the Tibetan" (known as Djwhal Khul) said: *"The world today is in such a distressing condition that the major need in every country is the appearance of 'steadily shining points of light' which can illuminate the way for others."*

Alger Hiss would be selected president of the Carnegie Endowment for International Peace in December 1946, and according to *Lines of Credit: Ropes of Bondage* (1989) by Robert Henry Goldsborough: *"By 1945, Hiss' superiors at the State Department had been completely briefed on his communist activities; but he was chosen to be Secretary General of the United Nations Conference on International Organization at San Francisco, nonetheless. With assistance from two Soviet representatives, Hiss prepared the United Nations Charter. . . . Alger Hiss had finally constituted 'Colonel' House's grand design, and America was at last involved in a one-world socialist government organization."*

Former senior editor of *Time*, Whittaker Chambers, would testify before Congress that CFR member Hiss had been a member of his communist cell, but there were repeated denials that communists were extensively involved in our system of government. However, in Carl Bernstein's *Loyalties: A Son's Memoirs* (1989), his father (who along with Carl's mother had been members of the Communist Party in America) tells Carl: *"You're going to prove McCarthy right, because all he was saying was that the system was loaded with communists. And he was right. You've got to take a big hard look at what you are doing. Because the whole fight against him was that people weren't communists. . . . I'm worried about the kind of book you're going to write and about cleaning up McCarthy. The problem is that everybody said he was a liar; you're saying he was right. . . . I agree that the Party was a force in the country."* And on March 1, 1992, the *Washington Post* admitted that *"a worldwide communist 'conspiracy' really did exist for much of the past seven decades, with the Kremlin secretly funding client Parties (including the Communist Party U.S.A.) from India to El Salvador."*

Chapter Eight

After the Second World War

After the Second World War, Joy Elmer Morgan (editor of the *NEA Journal*, 1921-1955) wrote in "The Teacher and World Government" (*NEA Journal*, January 1946): *"In the struggle to establish an adequate world government, the teacher . . . can do much to prepare the hearts and minds of children for global understanding and cooperation. . . . At the very top of all the agencies which will assure the coming of world government must stand the school, the teacher, and the organized profession."*

In a December 1934 editorial, Morgan had already called for government control of corporations. And in a December 1942 editorial, "The United Peoples of the World," he explained a world organization's or world government's need for an educational branch, a world system of money and credit, a uniform system of weights and measures (note President Bush's July 25, 1991 executive order later in this book), a world police force, and other agencies.

In July 1946, Alger Hiss persuaded the founders of the World Health Organization to include in their constitution the following overly broad definition of "health," so that the social engineers would be provided with a broad latitude under which they could begin to alter society — *"Health is a state of complete physical, mental, and social well-being.*" The head of the World Health Organization, Brock Chisholm (a close friend of Alger Hiss), had written in the February 1946 issue of the journal, *Psychiatry*, that "*a program of re-education or a new kind of education*" needed to be charted whereby "*the science of living should be made available to all people by being taught to all children in primary and secondary schools. . . . Only so, can we help our children to carry out their responsibilities as world citizens as we have not been able to do.*"

And elsewhere at about the same time, Chisholm said: "*To achieve world government, it is necessary to remove from the minds of men their individualism, loyalty to family tradition, national patriotism, and religious dogmas. . . . We have swallowed all manner of poisonous certainties fed us by our parents, our Sunday and day school teachers, our politicians, our priests. . . . The reinterpretation and eventual eradication of the concept of right and wrong which has been the basis of child training, the substitution of intelligent and rational thinking for faith in the certainties of the old people, these are the belated objectives . . . for charting the changes in human behavior*" (*The Utah Independent*, September 1977).

This was not unlike the famous historian Arnold Toynbee's comment regarding world government: "*We are approaching the point at which the only effective scale for operations of any importance will be the global scale. The local states ought to be deprived of their sovereignty and subordinated to the sovereignty of a global world government. I think the world state will still need an armed police [and the] world government will have to command sufficient force to be able to impose peace.*"

Brock Chisholm would later advocate that *"what people everywhere must do is to practice birth control and miscengenation* [racially-mixed marriage] *in order to create one race in one world under one government."* (*U.S.A.* magazine, August 12, 1955). Chisholm would be named the Humanist of the Year in 1959.

• • • • •

In 1947, according to William Still in *New World Order*, Richard Nixon introduced in Congress *"a remarkable piece of legislation which called for the United Nations to be able to enact, interpret, and enforce world law to prevent war."* Likewise in this year, United World Federalists was formed to work for world government, and among its founding organizations was World Federalists of North Carolina, with board member Terry Sanford, now a CFR member and a U.S. senator. And on November 27, 1947, the American Education Fellowship (AEF) issued a statement to the teachers of the nation calling for *"the establishment of a genuine world order, an order in which 'world citizenship' thus assumes at last equal status with national citizenship. . . . The task is to experiment with techniques of learning which look toward intelligent social consensus. . . . The school should become a center of experimentation in attaining communities of uncoerced persuasion.*
The AEF was formerly the Progressive Education Association organized by John Dewey, who in 1941 had become president of the League for Industrial Democracy, which was formerly the Intercollegiate Socialist Society.
In Robert Baron's *Psychology, Understanding*

Behavior (1980), one reads: *"In a book entitled* Walden II *first published in 1948, B.F. Skinner proposed a drastic formula for attaining Utopia — the perfect society. In his new and more perfect order . . . children would be reared by the state rather than by their parents, and they would be trained from birth to demonstrate only desirable characteristics and behavior. Punishment would be outlawed."*

Skinner (1972 Humanist of the Year) followed *Walden II* with *Beyond Freedom and Dignity* (1971), which was paid for by the American taxpayer (via a two hundred eighty-three thousand dollar grant from the National Institute of Mental Health). In this latter book, Skinner argued that man could no longer afford freedom and dignity, and he must therefore be controlled.

About the time *Walden II* was published, realizing the importance of education and social engineering in shaping the "New World Order," Fabian Sir Julian Huxley became the first director general of the newly formed UNESCO (among its founders were Reinhold Niebuhr and Jacques Maritain, and the final editor of its constitution was Archibald MacLeish who was a member of Skull and Bones in 1915). In Huxley's *UNESCO: Its Purpose and Its Philosophy* (1948), he wrote: *"Thus, even though it is quite true that any radical eugenic policy* [controlled human breeding] *will be for many years politically and psychologically impossible, it will be important for UNESCO to see that the eugenic problem is examined with the greatest care, and that the public mind is informed of the issues at stake so that much that now is unthinkable may at least become thinkable."*

In the same year of 1948, the National Education Association with partial funding by the Carnegie Corporation of New York produced the volume *Education for International Understanding in American Schools — Suggestions and Recommendations,* which contained the following statements: *"The idea has become established that the preservation of international peace and order may require that force be used to compel a nation to conduct its affairs within the framework of an established world system. The most modern expression of this doctrine of collective security is in the United Nations Charter. . . . Many persons believe that enduring peace cannot be achieved so long as the nation-state system continues as at present constituted. It is a system of international anarchy — a species of jungle warfare. Enduring peace cannot be attained until the nation-states surrender to a world organization the exercise of jurisdiction over those problems with which they have found themselves unable to deal singly in the past."*

Then, in the May 1949 issue of *Progressive Education,* Kenneth Benne, president of the American Education Fellowship, declared that *"teachers and school administrators* [should] *come to see themselves as social engineers. They must equip themselves as 'change agents.'"* Of course, their proposed changes would not be presented as radical, but rather would be couched in more favorable terms.

This strategy would be similar to that presented in this same year of 1949 when George Orwell's *1984* was published and described a "newspeak" language including "doublethink." These were exemplified in the slogans of "the Party" which were: *"War is peace. Freedom is slavery. Ignorance is strength."* In his book, Orwell explains that *"newspeak had been devised to meet the ideological needs of Ingsoc, or English socialism,"* and that "Big Brother" represents neither the failed German Nazis nor the Russian communists who will also fail, but rather "the Party" which will control men's minds. *"The rule of the Party is forever,"* the character O'Brien tells the character Winston while in the "Ministry of Love," and *"the Party seeks power entirely for its own sake. . . . We are interested solely in power. . . . We are priests of power. . . . We shall crush you down to the point from which there is no coming back. . . . There will be no love, except the love of Big Brother. . . . If you want a picture of the future, imagine a boot stamping on a human face — forever."* Winston replies, *"It is impossible to found a civilization on fear and hatred and cruelty. . . . It would disintegrate. . . ."* But O'Brien retorts that even if hatred were more exhausting than love, *"suppose that we quicken the tempo of human life. . . ."* Keep in mind here the ever-quickening tempo of life since the 1940s and the hyper-reality today of such things as certain types of music and television commercials. On July 26, 1949, eighteen members of the U.S. Senate sponsored Senate Concurrent Resolution 56 calling for the United Nations to be developed into a world federation.

The next year (1950), the syncretistic World Brotherhood was founded at a conference at UNESCO House in Paris. Their official material indicated they *"evolved from the educational program of the National Conference of Christians and Jews, which has been serving the cause of brotherhood in the United States and Canada since 1928."* Its supporters and members would include President Eisenhower, Eleanor Roosevelt, John F. Kennedy, John J. McCloy, and Supreme

Court Chief Justice Earl Warren, among other notables. Warren became chief justice in 1953, and he was a thirty-third degree Mason, an endorser of Planetary Citizens, and head of the Warren Commission that investigated the murder of President Kennedy. The Masonic perspective at this time was likewise one of "coming together," as C. William Smith wrote in the September 1950 issue of *New Age* about *"the unification of all races, religions, and creeds . . . a new religion of 'The Great Light' . . . and the American race will be the sixth Aryan civilization . . . for the dawn of the New Age of the world."*

And what would students be taught in this new civilization? In the January 1949 edition of *New Age*, it was recommended that students be taught the *"balance between good and evil."* And again in a September 1958 *New Age* editorial, a recommendation was made to strengthen *"education for life . . . the knowledge of good and evil."* (It is worth remembering here God's commandment to Adam in Genesis 2 that he should not eat of the tree of knowledge of good and evil, and the serpent's temptation of Eve in Genesis 3 that if she and Adam did eat the fruit, *"you shall be as gods, knowing good and evil."*) The next year, Dr. James D. Carter's "Why Stand Ye Here Idle?" was published in the March 1959 edition of *New Age* and indicated that Masonry is *"the missionary of the new order — a liberal order . . . in which Masons become high priests."* Dr. Carter's article continued that this "Masonic philosophy" which brought about a "new order" became a reality by *"the establishment of the public school system, financed by the State, for the combined purpose of technological and sociological education of the mass of humanity, beginning at an early age in childhood."*

Chapter Nine

Agents of Planned Change

The "sociological education" or "education for life" about which the Masons wrote was the same type of education the Deweyites promoted when they emphasized "social relationships" rather than the three R's. This view was exemplified in A.H. Lauchner's article, "How Can the Junior High School Curriculum Be Improved?" in the March 1951 issue of *The Bulletin* of the National Association of Secondary School Principals, when the author announced, *"The Three R's for All Children, and All Children for the Three R's! We've made some progress in getting rid of that slogan. But every now and then some mother with a Phi Beta Kappa award or some employer who has hired a girl who can't spell stirs up a fuss about the schools . . . and ground is lost. . . . When we come to the realization that not every child has to read, figure, write, and spell . . . that many of them either cannot or will not master these chores . . . then we shall be on the road to improving junior high curriculum. . . . For those thousands who have neither capacity nor desire to work in those areas, the school must provide other types of activities they can and will do. It's high time for us to stop cramming these subject materials down all mouths. . . . Having reached the point at which we are willing to admit that these subjects . . . and I shall now include history, geography. . . . Establish such flexibility in the curriculum as will permit realization of the dream . . . and the improvement will have come about."* This is one example of what the "change agents" wanted to happen in American education, and if they would be able to condition students at ever earlier ages, it would not be too difficult to get them to accept voluntarily the New Age New World Order. Also in 1951, Fabian Bertrand Russell wrote *The Impact of Science Upon Society*, in which he stated that under a scientific dictatorship *"the social psychologist of the future will have a number of classes of school children on whom they will try different methods of producing an unshakable conviction that snow is black. Various results will soon be arrived at: first, that influences of the home are obstructive";* and in order to further condition students, he stated that *"verses set to music and repeatedly intoned are very effective. . . . It is for the future scientist to make these maxims precise and discover exactly how much it costs per head to make children believe that snow is black. When the technique has been perfected, every government that has been in charge of education for more than one generation will be able to control its subjects securely without the need of armies or policemen."* (If this sounds ridiculous, remember the famous study by psychologist Stanley Milgram in the 1960s that showed sixty-five percent of ordinary people, in order to remain "accepted," were willing to inflict severe pain and damage on another person when ordered to do so by "authority.") Bertrand Russell has also been credited with the modern design of the "peace" symbol, which is a broken cross turned upside down, symbolizing Christianity being broken and its influence being reversed.

Children's individuality also had to be broken, so that they could be conformed to the "groupthink," as William Whyte, Jr., referred to it in his book, *Is Anybody Listening?* (1950), where he described the "social engineering movement" as *"a machine for the engineering of mediocrity. . . . It is profoundly authoritarian in its implications, for it subordinates the individual to the group."* This confirmed what Sigmund Freud had said in his *Group Psychology and the Analysis of the Ego* (1922) when he quoted Gustave le Bon as saying: *"As a part of a group, man regresses to a primitive mental state. . . . His critical, intellectual ability and control yield to emotionalism, suggestibility, and inconsistency. . . . As regards intellectual work it remains a fact, indeed, that great decisions in the realm of thought and momentous discoveries and solutions of problems are only possible to an individual working in solitude."*

"The Plan," however, called not for individual initiative, but rather for group control through psychological manipulation. In Alice Bailey's *Problems of Humanity* (1947) and World Goodwill's later accompanying study guides, it was projected that in the future, psychology *"will be the dominating science, and the newer educational systems, based on scientific psychology, will have completely superseded our modern methods. . . . The psychologist will have a sound grounding in mind control. . . . The child will be developed and equipped, trained, and motivated, and then taught his responsibilities to the whole and the value of the contribution which he can and must make to the group. Education, if adequate, is a process whereby unity or a sense of synthesis is cultivated. Young people will be taught to think of themselves in relation to the group."* Then in *Education in the New Age* (1954), Alice Bailey revealed her eugenic mentality when she wrote that *"the emphasis in the future will shift from the urge to produce large families to that of producing quality and intelligence in offspring."* She noted that the *"science of meditation should influence the field of education in the new age"* and it is *"a subsidiary science preparatory to the science of the antahkarana. This is the means of building between the personality and the soul. This is the true science of bridging unconsciousness. It relates the individual mind eventually to the higher mind and later to the universal mind. It will eventually dominate the new educational methods in schools and colleges."*

● ● ● ● ●

But education was not the only way in which people were being scientifically experimented on and affected. John Marks in *The Search for the "Manchurian Candidate": The CIA and Mind Control* (1979) reveals that in 1953, the CIA asked Lilly (Eli Lilly & Co.) executives *"to make up a batch* [of LSD], *which the company subsequently donated to the government. . . . The CIA generally presided over the LSD scene during the 1950s. To be sure, the military services played a part and funded their own research programs. . . . Paul Hoch and James Cattell of the New York Psychiatric Institute . . . forced injections of a mescaline derivative* [which] *led to the 1953 death of New York tennis professional Harold Blauer. (Dr. Cattell later told Army investigators, 'We didn't know whether it was dog piss or what it was we were giving him.')"*

Despite the Nazi horror which had occurred during the Second World War, a contemporary of the period, Jesuit Father Pierre Teilhard de Chardin (who died in 1955, and whose ancestress was a sister of Voltaire), supported totalitarianism and eugenics. This evolutionist-pantheist, who was heavily involved in the 1912 forgery that was called "Piltdown Man," is mentioned in Marilyn Ferguson's 1980 book, *The Aquarian Conspiracy*, as the person leading New Agers listed most often as having *"a profound influence upon their thinking."* He proclaimed the need for a one-world government and *"that the proposed organization must be international and in the end totalitarian. . . . The modern totalitarian regimes, whatever their initial defects, are neither heresies nor biological regressions: They are in line with the essential trend of 'cosmic' movement. . . . The world of tomorrow will be born out of the 'elected' group of those who will decide that there is something big waiting for us ahead, and give their life to reach it. . . . The earth is a closed and limited surface. To what extent should it tolerate, racially or nationally, areas of lesser activity? More generally still, how should we judge the efforts we lavish on all kinds of hospitals on saving what is so often no more than life's rejects? . . . We have only to believe, then little by little, we shall see the universal horror unbend, and then smile upon us, and then take us in its more than human arms"* (from Teilhard's books *Human Energy, The Future of Man, Letters to Two Friends, 1926-1952* and others).

Despite remarks like these, on the centenary (1970) of Teilhard's birth, Cardinal Augustino Casaroli praised him referring to *"the amazing impact of his researches, the brilliance of his personality, the richness of his thought, his powerful poetic insight, his acute perception of the dynamics of creation, his vast vision of the evolution of the world."*

Would Americans really be willing to accept *"little by little the universal horror"* of things which most people in the 1950s found to be morally repugnant? Remember what Mason Alexander Pope (1688-1744) said: *"Vice is a monster of so frightful mien, As to be hated, needs but to be seen; Yet seen too oft, familiar with her face, We first endure, then pity, then embrace."* Americans' later acceptance of those things that were morally objectionable in the 1950s could only be accomplished by a type of subtle brainwashing, and how this might occur was explained in testimony to Congress on March 13, 1958 by Edward Hunter, who had worked for many major American and foreign newspapers. He told a congressional committee: *"These developments include the penetration of our leadership circles by a softening up and creating a defeatist state of mind. This includes penetration of our educational circles by a similar state of mind . . . the liquidation of our attitudes on what we used to recognize as right and wrong, what we used to accept as absolute moral standards . . . by dialectical materialism. . . . The objective of all communist conquest is simply use for power. They seek to conquer the United States in a manner so that it 'voluntarily' falls into the Red orbit. If we have to be conquered by destructive nuclear-age weapons, it will be considered a setback by the Kremlin. Their objective is to make the same use of the American people as they make of the Czechs in the uranium mines of Czechoslovakia, and as they make of the Chinese in the mills of China. We are to become subjects of a 'New World Order' for the benefit of a mad little knot of despots in the Kremlin."*

But what leadership circles would be penetrated, by whom, and how would their attitudes be changed? For the answer to that, one might look at the World Peace Foundation (formerly the International School of Peace) founded in 1910 by educational publisher Edwin Ginn. One of the first books published by the foundation was *The First Book of World Law* (1911) with chapters on "The World Judiciary," "The World Executive," and even one on "The Universal Postal Union" among other chapters. The book also included advertisements for pamphlets available from the foundation, such as "A League of Peace: Rectorial Address Before the University of St. Andrews" by Andrew Carnegie, and "Sir Edward Grey on Union for World Peace: Speech in House of Commons, March 13, 1911."

By 1959, the foundation began preparing a series of seven booklets, titled *Studies in Citizen Participation in International Relations*, which analyzed and described how to change the attitudes of nearly every group in the nation. One of the booklets bemoaned the fact that blacks are *"still predominantly tradition-oriented."* Catholics are identified as a threat to object to Communist China being admitted to the U.N. Both lower- and middle-class Catholic and fundamentalist Protestants are identified as *"constituting the great majority of authoritarian right wingers."* Concerning religious Jews, a booklet indicates *"Jews who go to a synagogue or temple regularly are, on the average, less like our world-affairs criteria than those who go less often."* These remarks are found in the booklet *Americans in World Affairs*, which also states: *"Sons of northeastern old families* [like George Bush who attended Yale University] *are statistically most like our idea for international thought and action."* In syndicated columnist Edith Kermit Roosevelt's article "An American Agitprop" (*News Herald*, Borger, Texas, March 23, 1967), she explains that *"the World Peace Foundation serves as a clearinghouse in the staffing of personnel for various government agencies including the State Department, the CIA, and the Pentagon, and in planning government research programs and recommending goverment and foundation grants to outside scholars. A reading of the foundation's quarterly,* International Organizations, *shows that a primary objective is the meshing of U.S. and Soviet policy in international organizations with the State Department's Bureau for International Organization Affairs coordinating effort."* Among the list of trustees circulated by the foundation in 1966 were Max Millikan (president of the foundation and assistant director of the CIA from 1951 to 1952), Robert Bowie (CFR member and State Department counselor), Joseph E. Johnson (president of the Carnegie Endowment for International Peace, a director of the CFR, and in 1947 with the State Department policy planning staff), and Christian Herter (former secretary of state and CFR member since 1929).

"Penetration of our educational circles" (Edward Hunter's words) would occur in the early 1960s through a type of "brainwashing" known as "sensitivity training." In the National Training Laboratories (founded by the National Education Association in 1946) manual for group leaders, titled "Issues in Training" (1962), they

acknowledge that sensitivity training is "brainwashing." The manual also stated regarding children that *"although they appear to behave appropriately and seem normal by most cultural standards, they may actually be in need of mental health care, in order to help them change, adapt, and conform to the planned society in which there will be no conflict of attitudes or beliefs"* (Lucis Trust/World Goodwill emphasizes "right human relations"). Of course, for children to fit into the coming planned society where there would be no conflict of attitudes or beliefs, they would have to have their existing beliefs destroyed. In Benjamin Bloom's *Taxonomy of Educational Objectives, Handbook II: Affective Domain* (1964), one reads that *"a large part of what we call 'good teaching' is the teacher's ability to attain affective objectives through challenging the students' fixed beliefs."*

In furthering their goal of "no conflict of beliefs," the world planners applauded the removal of state-written or endorsed prayer from the public schools by Supreme Court decisions in 1962 and 1963. And in 1962 Fabian Sir Julian Huxley was named Humanist of the Year. He also acknowledged that humanism's *"keynote, the central concept to which all its details are related, is evolution."* Notice the similarity between Huxley's statement and the statement a few years later by thirty-third degree Mason Leonard Wenz in "Masonry and the Bible" (*New Age,* February 1968): *"The keynote of Masonic religious thinking is naturalism which sees all life and thought as ever developing and evolutionary. . . . The Bible is not today what it once was."* He indicated that current higher criticism *"made obsolete the idea that the Bible is a unique revelation of supernatural truth."* This is why it has been so important for the social engineers and world planners to censor the scientific evidence against evolution out of public school science textbooks, because if students could be programmed to consider man as simply an evolved animal, then society could eventually be conditioned to accept eugenic practices such as abortion, infanticide, and euthanasia. Indeed, the Holy Bible foretold in Matthew 10:21 that this is what would happen: *"And the brother shall deliver up the brother to death* [the Nazi holocaust of yesteryear], *and the father the child* [abortion of today]: *and the children shall rise up against their parents, and cause them to be put to death* [euthanasia tomorrow]*."* Sir Julian Huxley and Aldous Huxley were the grandsons of Thomas Huxley, known as "Darwin's Bulldog" because of his fierce defense of Darwin's theory of evolution. For the scientific evidence against the theory of evolution, one might look at *Evolution: A Theory in Crisis* (1985) by molecular biologist (and agnostic) Dr. Michael Denton, M.D., or one might look at *Darwin's Enigma* (1984) by General Electric Co. aerospace engineer Luther Sunderland. And for evidence of the massive cover-up of the scientific evidence against evolution, one might read *Darwin on Trial* (1991) by University of California law professor Phillip Johnson.

Once society has been programmed and conditioned for this "brave new world," how it would be administered was explained in Roderick Seidenberg's *Anatomy of the Future* (1964), in which he shows how a master race of "administrators" controls the masses of human beings *"by the ever increasing techniques and refined arts of mental coercion"* to the level of mindless guinea pigs. But the secularistic world planners were not satisfied with simply removing state-written or endorsed prayer from public schools, as even voluntary school prayer had to be banned as "religious exercise on public property," thus setting a precedent whereby the ACLU could later even sue a judge for opening court sessions with a brief invocation to God. In 1965, the U.S. Supreme Court allowed to stand a federal appeals court ruling, *Stein v. Oshinsky*, that said the state does not have to permit even student-initiated (voluntary) school prayer. The absurdity and hypocrisy of this decision can be recognized simply by noting that the courts themselves, as well as public school officials and everyone else, use dates on their official records and letters of correspondence that signify "A.D." (*anno Domini*, which means "in the year of the Lord").

● ● ● ● ●

In 1959, Mrs. J. Dickerman Hollister thought of the idea of a Temple of Understanding (the term was suggested by Mrs. Ellsworth Bunker, who was the wife of the American ambassador to India). Mrs. Hollister received encouragement from the Ford Foundation that same year, and the next year the syncretistic temple was founded by Juliet Hollister, with partial financing by the Carnegie Endowment for International Peace. The temple listed its "Founding Friends" as including Pope John XXIII, Thomas Merton, U Thant, the Dalai Lama, and Eleanor Roosevelt. Listed among its advisory council members were Father Thomas Berry, Robert Muller, and Brother David Steindl-Rast.

Relevant to the temple and Alice Bailey's New Group

of World Servers, syndicated columnist Edith Kermit Roosevelt wrote the following in the *New Hampshire Sunday News* (April 1, 1962): *"It is interesting to note that for some time now, a group who call themselves 'the New Group of World Servers' have been holding 'full moon meditation meetings' at the Carnegie Endowment International Centre in New York. On December 21, 1961, this writer attended one of these meetings where pamphlets were distributed describing 'the New World Religion.' One 'World Goodwill' booklet described what some of the backers of the 'Temple of Understanding' may have in mind. 'A new type of mystic is coming to be recognized. . . . He is distinguished by his lack of interest in his own personal development, by his ability to see God imminent in all faiths and not just in his own brand of religious beliefs.' Where the internationalist would-be elite gather to plan and plot world government, I heard a determined group of 'World Servers' led by Foster Bailey chant in unison their eerie Great Invocation (speaking of guiding 'the little wills of men'). Is the real purpose of the world-minded Masters of Unism to guide and control us by pagan rites?"* (As of 1988, the Temple of Understanding was located at the Cathedral of St. John the Divine in New York City, and the dean of the cathedral, James Parks Morton, was the temple's president.)

Also in the early 1960s, *Look* magazine senior editor George Leonard went to California (1962) to report on the beginnings of what would be called the "Aquarian Conspiracy." Aldous Huxley (author of *Brave New World* and pioneer in LSD) had been living in California and promoting a new national constitutional convention, as well as encouraging Michael Murphy (Planetary

Citizens advisory council member) and Richard Price to begin the Esalen Institute in 1961 as a place where "the wisdom of the East and West" could meet in furthering the "human potential" movement through new ideas. Esalen on the West Coast allied or networked with Abraham Maslow on the East Coast, and in 1965 George Leonard joined with Michael Murphy, who in 1948-1949 had gone to Auroville, India, to study collectivism under the aging Marxist revolutionary Sri Aurobindo. The Esalen Institute in September 1989 would sponsor Boris Yeltsin's eight-day trip to the United States where he spoke to the Council on Foreign Relations. While Yeltsin was on his American tour, he reportedly drank heavily, and it is easier to hypnotize someone when he or she is in an inebriated state. The reason this is mentioned is that in "Inhibitions Thrown to the Gentle Winds" (*Life*, July 12, 1968), New York psychiatrist Dr. Milton Kline, a specialist in hypnotherapy, said that Esalen's "guided daydream" sounded to him exactly like hypnosis. The leader of "guided daydreams" at Esalen was Dr. Frederick Perls, the founder of Gestalt therapy. Whether Yeltsin has been hypnotized, I do not know, but it is something to consider.

In 1962, Abraham Maslow, Carl Rogers, Rollo May, Ira Progoff, and others founded the Association for Humanistic Psychology (AHP), which has had as its president New Ager Jean Houston, and out of whose headquarters Planetary Citizens has been working in recent years. Progoff had been a student of Zen master D.T. Suzuki and, earlier, of former Nazi eugenics court member Carl Jung. Professor Michael Waldstein has stated that much of the occult psychologist Jung's work was characterized by *"an ultimate indifference, a dissolution of definiteness in personal relations, and a pervasive aesthetic giddiness."* (Has Jung affected today's youth, often dressed in black and white yin-yang colors, who are indifferent, giddy, and without personal commitment?)

In 1966, Progoff developed his "Intensive Journal" method (workshops now in colleges, the armed forces, and other places, including churches). In Randy England's 1990 book, *The Unicorn in the Sanctuary: The Impact of the New Age on the Catholic Church*, he warns that Progoff's journaling workshops include "imaging" in altered states of consciousness which is "wholly occult," making contact with "spirit guides," and adding the *"common demonic device of dictating written material through a medium."* Progoff's Dialogue House in New York City is listed in the *Directory for a New World*, a "Planetary Guide of Member and Cooperating Organizations for the Unity-in-Diversity Council — A Worldwide Coordinating Body of Groups and Individuals Fostering the Emergence of a New Universal Person and Civilization Based on Unity-in-Diversity Among All Peoples," that is, for *"world integration — a global civilization, a network of planetary citizens, a functional world government."* Previously the International Cooperation Council (ICC), later named Unity-in-Diversity Council (UDC), and presently Unity-and-Diversity World Council (U/D), it began its work during 1965 as the "Pageant for Peace" when the United Nations General Assembly proclaimed International Cooperation Year. However, on May 21, 1972 the Scientific Information and Education Council of Physicians adopted a resolution highly critical of the International Cooperation Council's "Proposal for New

Consciousness Education," submitted March 22, 1972 to the Joint Committee on the Master Plan for Higher Education in California. The physicians' council described the ICC as including occult organizations, as believing America is a "decaying Western civilization," as supporting *"evolution of the United Nations into a world government,"* and as stating in their proposal that *"our narrow tradition-bound values lead to self-destruction"* and we must change *"from reliance largely on one major religion to an absorption from all religions, ancient and modern."* The physicians further noted that the ICC's proposal would bring occultism, yoga, and hypnosis into the schools. Among the organizations affiliated with ICC were the National Training Laboratories (begun by the NEA) and William Glasser's Institute of Reality Therapy, and the physicians' council pointed out that "new consciousness" type programs were already causing serious problems of chaos and dissension in homes, schools, and communities. Therefore, the council stated: *"Taxpayers should not be expected to support programs which would destroy previously held political, moral, and religious convictions, in an attempt to homogenize all individuals into a common human nature and all societies into a one-world government."*

In Caryl Matrisciana's *Gods of the New Age* (1985), one learns that *"the Unity-in-Diversity Council is a powerful New Age promotional network . . . which* [in 1982] *linked arms with the international network of* **'Mind, Body, and Spirit Festivals.'** This formed a vast army dedicated to the merger of all religions into one, under a world leader." Remember here what was said in *The City of Man* in 1941 about a "common creed" and "diversity in unity and unity in diversity." Also remember this when you read President Bush's comments about "unity" and "diversity" in his January 20, 1989 inaugural address.

Just prior to the time this council was beginning its work in the mid-1960s, Pope John XXIII (who died June 3, 1963) initiated the Second Vatican Council in the early 1960s. Pope John XXIII (who sent "Planetary Citizens" and "United World Federalists" co-founder Norman Cousins on numerous diplomatic missions on his behalf) annulled a July 1, 1949 directive of the Holy Office of Pope Pius XII excommunicating communists and all persons cooperating with communists, and initiated the Second Vatican Council which would result in the *Novus Ordo* (New Order) or New Mass, despite the decree *Quo Primum* by Pope Pius V on July 19, 1570: "*We determine and order that **never** shall anything be added to, omitted from, or changed in this Missal. . . . We specifically warn all persons in authority, of whatever dignity or rank . . . **never** to use or permit any ceremonies or Mass prayers other than the ones contained in this Missal ordered by the Sacred Council of Trent. . . . We herewith declare that it is in virtue of our Apostolic Authority that we decree and determine that this our present order and decree is to last **in perpetuity** and can never be legally revoked or amended at a future date. . . . And if anyone would nevertheless ever dare to attempt any action contrary to this order of ours, given for all times, let him know that he has incurred the wrath of Almighty God and of the Blessed Apostles Peter and Paul.*"

On December 7, 1965, Pope John XXIII's successor, Pope Paul VI, issued his "Pastoral Constitution on the

Church in the Modern World," in which he spoke of *"the birth of a new humanism, one in which man is defined first of all by this responsibility to his brothers and to history. "*One would have thought man's first responsibility is to God! In his pastoral letter, the pope went on to talk about such things as "service to the common good," "economic equity," "international order and brotherhood," and "universal authority." Malachi Martin has written that *"the integral humanism of Paul VI permeated the entire policy of his pontificate. What the philosophy has to say is that all men are naturally good, that they will respond to the good and reject the evil if they are shown the difference. The function of the Church is merely to bear witness by service to men in today's world where a new society is being born. "*

"Integral humanism" is similar to Teilhard's theories, but actually was a theory developed by Jacques Maritain. Prior to his becoming pope, Paul VI translated a 1936 Maritain book on the subject, *Humanism Integral*, and wrote an enthusiastic introduction to it. In Cardinal John Heenan's biography of Pope John XXIII, *Crown of Thorns* (1974), the cardinal relates that *"there was no great mystery about Pope John's election. He was chosen because he was a very old man. His chief duty was to make Monsignor Montini, the Archbishop of Milan, a cardinal so that he could be elected (Pope Paul VI) in the next conclave. That was the policy and it was carried out precisely. "*

Just prior to his December 7 pastoral, Pope Paul VI promulgated on October 24, 1965, the "Declaration on the Relation of the Church to Non-Christian Religions." Besides the content of the declaration, what is interesting is the account of events leading to the declaration, as described by senior editor Joseph Roddy in the January 25, 1966 issue of *Look* magazine. Roddy explains that *"both* Time *and the* New York Times *were glad to have an inside tipster"* at the council. He had operated under several pseudonyms, including Michael Serafian, but then *"the cassock had come off the double agent. . . . He was known to be working on a book at a young married couple's flat. The book finally got finished, but so did half of the friendship. He knew it was time for a forced march before his religious superior could inquire too closely into the reasons for that crisis in camaraderie. . . . Apart from his taste for fair ladies . . . he was valuable to the American Jewish Committee and is still thought of by many around Rome as a kind of genuine savior in the diaspora. Without him, the Jewish declaration might well have gone under early."* Of course, the spy Michael Serafian's real name is Malachi Martin, who was laicized in 1965, and who was quoted in *Contemporary Authors* (vol. 81-84) as saying: *"That organization* [the Catholic Church and other high churches] *is going to fade away because it's an organization created by men who were power brokers and still are. They tied it to an economic system and they tied it to political big deals, and now that's all over. It's good that it's happening because dignity, rings, hand kissing, satin slippers, and Latin have nothing to do with the spirit whatever."* Breaking with many years of tradition, Pope Paul VI on April 3, 1969 promulgated the *Novus Ordo Missae* in his apostolic constitution, *"Missale Romanum."*

● ● ● ● ●

Also in the late 1960s, Joy Elmer Morgan (former editor of the *NEA Journal*) wrote in *The American Citizens Handbook* (1968) that *"the coming of the United Nations and the urgent necessity that it evolve into a more comprehensive form of world government places upon the citizens of the United States an increased obligation to make the most of their citizenship which now widens into active world citizenship."* By this time in the United States, there had been a shift in the focus of education from the cognitive domain (academic basics such as reading, writing, and math) to the affective domain (emphasis upon feelings and social relationships). There was also a curriculum shift based on a broader definition of "social studies." In "The 'New' Social Studies" (*NEA Journal*, November 1967), is explained: *"Probably the most obvious change occurring in the social studies curriculum is a breaking away from the traditional dominance of history, geography, and civics. Materials from the behavioral sciences . . . sociology, social psychology . . . are being incorporated into both elementary and secondary school programs."*

Education had come to be referred to by "progressive educators" as a "leveling process," but it became easier for them to level everyone down rather than to level everyone up academically. To some extent, there was a racist element in what the "progressive educators" and world planners were about, because this was a time of increasing school integration, and they believed that minorities could not compete with white students. These people were generally white elitists who simply replaced the white reactionaries in telling blacks what to do. They promoted racial-balance busing to pursue school integration, even though this has meant that the minority population must be bused in inverse proportion to the white population to achieve racial balance (e.g., in a city ninety percent white and ten percent black, ninety percent of the blacks must be bused, but only ten percent of the whites are). Not only has this been a discriminatory burden placed upon blacks, but there are also educational consequences. What they're doing is saying that because these students are black, they are going to deny them an hour or more study time each day that whites are not denied, because they are putting them in the non-studious environment of a school bus for that long every day. If they were really concerned about the civil rights of minorities, blacks would have been given the predominant right of first choice concerning what schools their own children would attend. However, this is not what the white elitist social engineers of the 1960s (or today) wanted. Instead, "social promotions" and "grade inflation" began in the 1960s for students of all races along with the "students' rights" movement that came to mean one student's right to disrupt the learning environment for all other students. SAT and other scores began to fall, and discipline problems, violence, and crime began to rise in the nation's schools.

How did all of this happen? It was the logical outcome of what I would call the world planners' "credentialing process." Not long after the beginning of the twentieth century, they would avoid paying a certain amount of taxes by making donations to tax-exempt foundations. These foundations, in turn, would promote the world view or ideology of their benefactor by providing scholarships or grants to individuals who were "politically correct" in their thinking. Through this funding, these scholars were able to have their works published and thereby establish credentials enabling them to receive appointments to the government or as university departmental chairmen.

From these positions of power, they could determine what college faculty members would be hired, what students would be admitted to programs, and what teachers and administrators would supervise public education. For example, regarding those trained in the "progressive" educational philosophy of John Dewey at Columbia University's Teachers College, one reads in Lawrence Cremin et al's *A History of Teachers College Columbia University* (1954) that *"the single most powerful education force in the world is at 120th Street and Broadway in New York City. Your children's teachers go there for advanced training. . . . With one hundred thousand alumni, TC has managed to seat about one-third of the presidents and deans now* [1953] *in office at accredited U.S. teacher training schools. Its graduates make up about twenty percent of all our public school teachers. Over a fourth of the superintendents of schools in the one hundred sixty-eight U.S. cities with at least fifty thousand population are TC-trained."* By the early 1960s, this trend had progressed to the stage where educational leadership positions across the country were largely in the hands of "credentialed" individuals trained in the "progressive" educational philosophy of John Dewey.

To better understand how the process began and who was involved, it might be helpful to look at several of the alumni of Columbia University and Teachers College after Dewey arrived in 1904. George Betts became a professor of education at Northwestern University; Lotus

Coffman became dean of the College of Education at the University of Minnesota (and later its president); Elwood Cubberly became dean of the School of Education at Stanford University; Edward Elliott became president of Purdue University; Walter Jessup became president of the University of Iowa and president of the Carnegie Foundation for the Advancement of Teaching; William H. Kilpatrick became professor at Teachers College; Bruce Payne became president of the famous educational George Peabody College in Nashville; David Snedden became Commissioner of Education for Massachusetts; and George Strayer became professor at Teachers College and president of the NEA in 1918-1919. These individuals, along with ten others, became known as the "Educational Trust," holding annual meetings known as the Cleveland Conference (because the first meeting was in Cleveland in 1915). Among the other individuals were James Angell, a colleague of Dewey and later a trustee of the Rockefeller Foundation; Leonard Ayers, director of the Russell Sage Foundation; Abraham Flexner, director of the Rockefeller Institute; Paul Hanus, who with the help of the Rockefeller's General Education Board established Harvard University's Graduate School of Education; Frank Spaulding, who received his Ph.D. at Leipzig and became a member of Rockefeller's General Education Board; Paul Monroe, who founded the World Federation of Education Associations; and Dewey colleague Edward Thorndike. The leader of the "Educational Trust" was Dewey colleague Charles Judd, who had received his Ph.D. from Wilhelm Wundt in Leipzig in 1896.

In David Tyack's and Elisabeth Hansot's *Managers of Virtue* (1982), Judd is quoted as urging the Cleveland

Conference to attempt *"the positive and aggressive task of . . . a detailed reorganization of the materials of instruction in schools of all grades. . . ."* Tyack and Hansot also wrote: *"There were 'placement barons,' usually professors of educational administration in universities such as Teachers College, Harvard, University of Chicago, or Stanford who had an inside track in placing their graduates in important positions. One educator commented after spending a weekend with Cubberly in Palo Alto that 'Cubberly had an educational Tammany Hall that made the Strayer-Engelhardt Tammany Hall in New York look very weak. . . . [And] one principal recalled 'Strayer's Law' for dealing with disloyal subordinates was 'Give 'em the ax.' "*

• • • • •

Psychologically, the preparation of the hearts and minds of children for the New World Order would be facilitated by Abraham Maslow's humanistic (Third Force) psychology, emphasizing "self-actualization" at the top of a hierarchy of needs, similar to Erich Fromm's (1966 Humanist of the Year) emphasis upon human needs and "self-realization." Maslow (1967 Humanist of the Year) wrote in *Pace* magazine (December 1969) concerning children's search for values: *"Now religions have cracked up. . . . [Children] have no source of values to go by. So they have to work everything out for themselves. This new humanistic revolution has an alternative source of values."* Even more outspoken, the British Humanist Association published a 1969 discussion document, "Marriage and The Family," which stated that *"some opponents of humanism have accused us of wishing to overthrow the traditional Christian family. They are right. That is exactly what we intend to do."*

Under the guise of promoting "independence" for youth, the "generation gap" was created to separate youth from the values of their parents so that they could be "remolded" (as in the Fabians' slogan) into the "group-think" about which Whyte wrote in his 1950 book mentioned earlier. That is why all the time the rebellious youth of the 1960s were proclaiming their "independence" in hair style, clothing, etc., they all seemed to look like each other (e.g., long hair, faded jeans, etc.)! Instead of truly individualistic motion picture personalities of the past, the new "independent" movie stars all seemed to come out of the same casting studio. In rejecting the standards of the past, the new generation seemed to stand for no standards at all in morality, music, art, and everything else. Morality became "if it feels good, do it"; banging on a guitar became music; and a dot on a blank canvas became art.

The emphasis of the "me" generation of the late 1960s and early 1970s was clearly on "self" (self-gratification, followed in the 1980s by self-esteem). Therefore, the God of the Holy Bible who judged sin became bothersome and was replaced by "man." The Piscean Age had to be replaced by the Aquarian Age (later to be called the New Age). In Caryl Matrisciana's *Gods of the New Age* (1985), Dr. Johannes Aagaard (a world expert on Hinduism) commented: *"New Age really means the Aquarian Age . . . the age of the enlightened man, the age of superman . . . the man with super-consciousness has begun. . . . God is losing all importance, man is the only thing which matters. Man is saving himself by his knowledge, by the development of his mind faculties, by liberating himself from all the powers of this old world and the world of his body."*

In 1967, the musical *Hair* began on Broadway including songs such as "Aquarius," which began with the lyrics, *"When the moon is in the seventh house, And Jupiter aligns with Mars, Then peace will guide the planets, And love will steer the stars. This is the dawning of the Age of Aquarius! Harmony and understanding, sympathy and trust abounding, No more falsehoods or derision, Golden living dreams of visions, mystic crystal revelation, And the mind's true liberation."* A few years later, Foster Bailey (thirty-third degree Mason, director of Lucis Trust, husband of Alice Bailey and later Mary Bailey) wrote *Running God's Plan* (1972) exclaiming: *"Yes, our civilization is dying. Let us move on into the new day and begin now to build a new civilization of the Aquarian Age. . . . The torch of light has been passed to us. The death of our present civilization is inevitable. . . . A world crisis will hasten its passing which is all to the good. The old civilization must give way to the new. . . . The new Aquarian Age has this power. Nothing can stop it."*

Could the "world crisis" Bailey mentioned be the recent crisis in the Middle East? *Running God's Plan* clearly shows that Foster Bailey had a Hitlerian element, as he remarked: *"Another approved hierarchical project is the uniting of the nations of Europe in one cooperating peaceful community. . . . One attempt was to begin by uniting the peoples living in the Rhine River valley using that river as a binding factor. It was an attempt by a disciple, but did not work. Now another attempt is in full swing, namely the six-nation European Common Market.*"

● ● ● ● ●

Morality in the New Age would become "the god within" spirituality; music would become New Age synthesizers and Pan flutes; and art would become the federally-funded "Piss Christ" by Andres Serrano, or whatever was produced by Planet Art Network (PAN, named for a Greek god) founded December 4, 1983 by former art professor José Arguélles as a global association of artists, art groups, and individuals working for New Age transformation. The "youth rebellion" of the late 1960s was something that should have been anticipated, though, as the logical result of a generation of infants reared in the 1950s according to the seemingly "permissive" approach of Dr. Benjamin Spock and others. Dr. Spock (1968 Humanist of the Year) would later say, *"There's this idea in our society that you don't know anything until you take a course in it. Partly I blame professional people like myself who muscled into child care as if they invented it. It's very easy for doctors to be condescending to parents — and, of course, that leaves parents feeling they don't know anything and are sure to make mistakes"* (*People*, May 13, 1985).

With families disintegrating, and "no source of values" for children to go by, according to Maslow, there were obviously no absolutes of right and wrong. As psychiatrist William Glasser said in his 1969 book, *Schools Without Failure*, *"We have to let students know there are no right answers, and we have to let them see that there are many alternatives to certainty and right answers.* "Because American students would no doubt be in need of a great deal of "counseling" due to the trauma of there being "no right answers," the NEA indicated the basic role of the teacher would "change noticeably" over the next decade. In a 1969 *NEA Journal* article, "Forecast for the '70s," authors Harold and June Shane declared that *"ten years hence it should be more accurate to term him* [the teacher] *a 'learning clinician.' This title is intended to convey the idea that schools are becoming 'clinics' whose purpose is to provide individualized psychosocial 'treatment' for the student, thus increasing his value both to himself and to society."* The Shanes also stated that *"educators will assume a formal responsibility for children when they reach the age of two . . .* [with] *mandatory foster homes and 'boarding schools' for children between ages two and three whose home environment was felt to have a malignant influence,"* and children would *"become the objects of* [biochemical] *experimentation."*

At the same time (1969), the Joint Commission on Mental Health of Children presented its report to Congress. It states: *"As the home and the church decline in influence . . . schools must begin to provide adequately for the emotional and moral development of children. . . . The school . . . must assume a direct responsibility for the attitudes and values of child development. The child advocate, psychologist, social technician, and medical technician should all reach aggressively into the community, send workers out to children's homes, recreational facilities, and schools. They should assume full responsibility for all education, including pre-primary education."* At roughly the same time, Dr. Reginald Lourie, former president of the Joint Commission on Mental Health of Children, said: *"There is serious thinking among some of the future-oriented child development people that maybe we can't trust the family alone to prepare young children for this kind of world which is emerging."*

The type of world that had been planned was described in *Report from Iron Mountain On the Possibility and Desirability of Peace* (1967), which explained that in August 1963, high-ranking officials in the Kennedy Administration appointed a secret commission *"to determine the nature of the problems that would confront the United States if and when a condition of 'permanent peace' should arrive, and to draft a program for dealing with this contingency."* Iron Mountain, New York, was "an underground nuclear hideout for hundreds of large American corporations," and the commission concluded that *"lasting peace . . . would almost certainly not be in the best interests of a stable society. . . . War fills certain functions essential to the stability of our society; until other ways of filling them are developed, the war system must be maintained. . . . The following substitute institutions, among others, have been proposed for consideration as replacements for the non-military functions of war — an omnipresent, virtually omnipotent police force . . . new religions or other mythologies . . . and a comprehensive program of applied eugenics."* By the end of the next decade, the National Center for Health Statistics would have a data base including all health statistics (e.g., birth, death, marriage, divorce) for the U.S. and would convert to an international classification of diseases. Hasn't your doctor asked to know your Social Security number?

Chapter Ten

The Population Controllers

The population controllers also had their goals. John D. Rockefeller III was quoted in *Look* magazine, February 9, 1965, as declaring: *"The choice is no longer whether population stabilization is necessary, but only how and when it can be achieved. . . . The population problem is so ramified that only government can attack it on the scale required."* Two years later, Dr. Alan Guttmacher, president of Planned Parenthood-World Population, advocated that an effective contraceptive program could make a "significant contribution" to a New World Order (*Mental Hygiene*, October 30, 1967). And in the June 6, 1969 issue of *Medical World News*, he further explained: *"Each country will have to decide its own form of coercion, and determine when and how it should be employed. At present, the means available are compulsory sterilization and compulsory abortion. Perhaps some day a way of enforcing compulsory birth control will be feasible."* Some years later, in a special supplement to *Family Planning Perspectives* (Planned Parenthood-World Population's journal) entitled, "Examples of Proposed Measures to Reduce U.S. Fertility, by Universality of Selectivity Impact," one finds: *"restructure family, encourage increased homosexuality, educate for family limitation, fertility control agents in the water supply, encourage women to work, compulsory sterilization of all who have two children except for a few who would be allowed three, confine childbearing to a limited number of adults, stock certificate type permits for children, and payment to encourage sterilization, abortion, and contraception"* (this originally appeared in a memorandum to Population Council president Bernard Berelson, found in vice-president of Planned Parenthood-World Population Frederick S. Jaffe's "Activities Relevant to the Study of Population Policy for the U.S." March 11, 1969).

Population controllers also had important allies in the major network media, as well-known ABC news commentator Howard K. Smith wrote in the January/ February 1970 issue of *The Humanist*: *"It is going to cause a wrench in sentiment and attitude, but we are going to have to adjust to limiting population. . . . We may even have to begin penalizing people by tax measures to induce them to do no more than have two children."* In the same year, the U.S. Congress passed Title X of the Public Health Service Act, which established a nationwide system of family planning clinics, and the act was sponsored by the then-Congressman George Bush.

Bush's sponsorship of this act should not be surprising, given that in the July 30, 1968 edition of the *Congressional Record*, George Bush's address titled "Population Control and Family Planning" states: *"I have decided to give my vigorous support to measures for population control in both the United States and the world. Certainly responsible religions have the right to determine their doctrines, but for those of us who feel so strongly on this issue, the recent encyclical was most discouraging. . . . We must seek to provide nations which request them with birth control devices* [with] *such methods as the IUD and contraceptive pill. . . . We must make sure that these are available on a massive scale to the people who need them and want them. . . . For information about what you can do in your own city to advance the cause of family planning, call your local Planned Parenthood center. . . . For years, any public discussion of family planning was most controversial. Things are gradually changing, but they must change faster. In the past, there has been some religious opposition to family planning. I still feel, in spite of the recent encyclical, that there will be a liberalization in this opposition. . . . All of this can change. It must change. It must change soon."*

In 1973, Bush wrote the foreword to Phyllis Piotrow's *World Population Crisis*, a book favorable toward permissive abortion. In the foreword, the future U.S. president said that his father had been narrowly defeated for the U.S. Senate in 1950 when national columnist Drew Pearson "revealed" Prescott Bush's involvement with Planned Parenthood. But George Bush *"was impressed by the sensible approach of Alan Guttmacher who served as president of Planned Parenthood . . . and by the arguments of William H. Draper, Jr., who continues to lead through his tireless work for the U.N. Population Fund. . . . In the federal agencies, there were at first only a few determined individuals like R.T. Ravenholt in AID"* (Agency of International Development). Because Bush mentioned Draper and Ravenholt in his foreword, it is worth remembering that as vice-president, Bush recommended William Draper III to head the U.N. Development Program (which funds abortions in the Third World), and Draper opposed President Reagan's withholding of funds from organizations that include abortion as a method of "family planning." As head of AID, Ravenholt would conduct efforts to set up population programs under the aegis of International Planned Parenthood Federation, and he would also say that *"as many as one hundred million women around the world might be sterilized if U.S. goals are met"* (Paul Wagman's "To Sterilize Millions," *St. Louis Post-Dispatch*, April 22, 1977).

Supposedly in the mid-1980s, Bush had a "conversion" to a pro-life position on issues, but then why did he support Draper's nomination after this? And why did he support pro-abortion-rights Barber Conable for the presidency of the World Bank? And why did he endorse pro-abortion-rights Henry Bellmon over four pro-life opponents in an Oklahoma gubernatorial primary? And why did he endorse the U.S. Senate's number one abortion-rights advocate, Robert Packwood, in a primary against pro-lifer Joe Lutz? And why did he campaign for pro-abortion-rights Lamar Smith in a primary run-off for an *open* congressional seat in Texas against Van Archer, a member of the San Antonio Right-To-Life board?

It was during the general time period of the late 1960s and early 1970s, according to Randy Engel (Human Life International's Tenth World Conference, April 5, 1991, Santa Clara, California), that the March of Dimes began to fund eugenic fetal experimentation. And during the Nixon administration, work was begun by the National Security Council on NSSM, "Implications of Worldwide Population Growth for U.S. Security and Overseas Interests." It was marked "classified" and "confidential" on December 10, 1974, and when one reads what is in it, there is little doubt as to why the U.S. government would not want people to know the role it was playing in the population control movement. The document stated that *"if future numbers are to be kept within reasonable bounds, it is urgent that measures to reduce fertility be started and made effective in the 1970s and 1980s. . . . Intense efforts are required to assure full availability by 1980 of birth control information and means to all. . . . [Financial] assistance will be given to other countries, considering such factors as population growth. . . . Food and agricultural assistance is vital for any population sensitive development strategy. . . . Allocation of scarce resources should take account of what steps a country is taking in population control. . . . There is an alternative view that mandatory programs may be needed. . . . With assistance from the U.S. Agency for International Development, a number of private family planning organizations (e.g., International Planned Parenthood) have significantly expanded their worldwide population programs. . . . AID's population actions would also need to be consistent with the overall U.S. development policy toward each country. . . . No country has reduced its population growth without resorting to abortion. . . . AID sought through research to reduce the health risks and other complexities which arise from the illegal and unsafe forms of abortion. . . . AID funds may continue to be used for research relative to abortion. . . . [There should be] utilization of mass media and satellite communications systems for family planning."*

This was the time of the "sexual revolution," and radical feminism was growing. In 1971, *The Document:*

Declaration of Feminism was published, calling for a "feminist-socialist revolution," and saying: *"We must go back to the matriarchies . . . to ancient female religions* [like witchcraft]. *. . . In order to break the tyranny of class oppression, it is necessary to establish a socialist order. . . . In the final hours of capitalism we will dance on the grave of corporate America. . . . Marriage is the institution that has failed us and we must work to destroy it. . . . The nuclear family must be replaced with a new form of family where individuals live and work together to help meet the needs of all people in the society. . . . With the destruction of the nuclear family must come a new way of looking at children. They must be seen as the responsibility of an **entire society** rather than individual parents."* The women who published *The Document* also published a newspaper called *Gold Flower*, which had on its December 1971/January 1972 cover a picture of a pregnant female as a crucified Christ.

Supporters of radical feminism were not only women, but also New Agers like Fritjof Capra, who likewise advocated a socialist world government, which he said in *The Turning Point* (1982) would *"include, among many other measures, the decentralization of populations and industrial activities, the dismantling of large corporations and other social institutions,* [and] *the redistribution of wealth."* Also applauding sexual liberation and the "humanistic revolution," while disparaging "old-fashioned nationalism," was John D. Rockefeller III (founder of the Population Council in 1952 whose father's cousin, Percy Rockefeller, was a member of the Skull and Bones in 1900) in his book, *The Second American Revolution* (1973).

Chapter Eleven

The 1970s: A Critical Decade

In the year 1970, Lucis Trust president Mary Bailey wrote a letter which announced that *"the decade of the '70s opens to a 'tide in the affairs of men' which can carry us on to the emergence of a new world order. . . . That there is a divine Plan at work behind and within the affairs of men is known and accepted by those who seek to cooperate with the evolutionary tide affecting human consciousness as the era of Aquarius strengthens in potency. Because the changes to be affected are first changes in consciousness, the trained servers and esotericists of the world, the mystics, and meditators, and the spiritually minded men and women of goodwill, have a special function in the years immediately ahead. The spiritual tide is on. In 1975, a vital centennial event, involving in conclave the spiritual Hierarchy of the planet led by the Christ, should result in the formation of specific plans within the Plan."*

And lest anyone think that the timing for the actual beginning of the "New World Order" with the decade of the 1990s was somehow spontaneous or coincidental, Ian Baldwin, Jr. wrote "Thinking About a New World Order for the Decade 1990" in the January 1970 edition of *War/Peace Report*, published by the Center for War/Peace Studies, with board sponsors such as Roger

Baldwin (founder of the ACLU and a communist) and Brock Chisholm. In the article, Baldwin writes that *"the World Law Fund has begun a worldwide research and educational program that will introduce a new, emerging discipline —world order — into educational curricula throughout the world . . . and to concentrate some of its energies on bringing basic world order concepts into the mass media, again on a worldwide level."*

If this New World Order was to begin in 1990, however, something would have to be done about the Judeo-Christian values that parents were instilling in their children. In John Goodlad's 1971 report to the President, "Schooling for the Future," one reads, *"The majority of our youth still hold the values of their parents, and if we do not alter this pattern, if we do not resocialize ourselves to accept change, our society may decay."*

And what kind of "change" did the world planners begin to promote? Society could be most successfully altered by promoting a more permissive lifestyle along with an "exaggerated reality." Such mundane things as a hamburger would be called "fantastic." Television continued to present complicated life problems as solved within thirty-minute programs. Americans came more and more to expect instant solutions and instant gratification of their desires. Therefore, the "present" became all important. Carl Rogers would say at a graduation address at Sonoma State College that *"the man of the future . . . will be living his transient life mostly in temporary relationships. . . . He must be able to establish closeness quickly. He must be able to leave the close relationships behind without excessive conflict or mourning."* Growing numbers of divorces began to occur because many young men and women chose a marital partner on the basis of whether they were presently "sexy" or "fun," rather than whether they were moral, responsible, and held a sense of commitment. Logically, when the spouse was no longer considered "sexy" or "fun," the original reason they were considered attractive was gone, and divorce became a possibility.

This was the "me" generation being promoted, and it would have an effect upon children as well. The world planners indoctrinated young adults with the notion that if a pre-born child was "unwanted," it was better that the child be killed by abortion. The social engineers persuaded many young married adults that if they did have children, these offspring might be placed at an early age in daycare so that the husband and wife could continue to fulfill their own aspirations in their own careers. But what are the results of placing children in daycare? A federally funded National Institute of Child Health and Human Development study concluded that children who attended an academically oriented daycare center which was to improve their IQ were more likely to kick, hit, threaten, push, and argue with others. Joseph Coates' analysis for the Office of Technology Assessment, for Congress, informs that *"children placed together with other children for extended periods of time — as in daycare — may experience slower intellectual growth."* In a special report released in June 1986 by the American Academy of Pediatrics, one reads that *"children who attend daycare are more likely to contract acute infectious illnesses ranging from stomach flu to meningitis than children raised at home."* And according to a study released October 7, 1987, by Dr. Stuart Adler of the Medical

College of Virginia in Richmond, the Associated Press reported, *"Children in daycare centers may be giving their mothers an invisible infection that can cause pregnant women to bear mentally retarded children."*

As children reached the age of adolescence, they would also be affected, as a study in the late 1980s by Prof. Peter Uhlenberg and David Eggebeen of the University of North Carolina, titled "The Declining Well-Being of American Adolescents," found that teens are more prone today than twenty years ago to academic and behavioral problems because their parents are less committed to their children's welfare. The authors noted, *"From the perspective of the child, it appears that parents are becoming available at times convenient to the parents, not at times when the child has the most need for attention."* When some parents did pay attention to their offspring, it was unfortunately the wrong kind of attention for a growing number who had been told by leading sex educator Wardell Pomeroy (his book *Boys and Sex*, which discusses intercourse with animals, is used by many educators): *"It is time to admit that incest need not be a perversion or a symptom of mental illness. Incest between . . . children and adults . . . can sometimes be beneficial"* ("Attacking the Last Taboo," *Time*, April 14, 1980).

A primary focus of societal change would begin in the pre-school years, as *The Futurist*'s introduction to Dr. Chester M. Pierce's (now at Harvard University's Department of Public Health and Department of Human Development) February 1972 article, "The Pre-Schooler and the Future," claims that *"the peaceful world that we hope to have in the twenty-first century may be won in the nursery schools of the 1970s."* In the article, Dr. Pierce indicates that *"Sesame Street has moved American children* [and now children from an increasing number of other lands] *toward becoming planetary citizens."* And in his article "Becoming Planetary Citizens: A Quest For Meaning" (*Childhood Education,* November 1972), he pronounces that *"from infancy on . . . today's children will come to realize that in their own self-interest the only way they can live will be as planetary citizens. . . . A child can enter kindergarten with the same kind of loyalty to the earth as to his homeland."*

According to columnist John Steinbacher, this was about the same time Dr. Pierce told about one thousand teachers at an Association for Childhood Education International seminar in Denver that *"every child in America entering school at the age of five is insane because he comes to school with certain allegiances toward our founding fathers, toward his parents, toward a belief in a supernatural being, toward the sovereignty of this nation as a separate entity. . . . It's up to you teachers to make all of these sick children well by creating the international children of the future."* Steinbacher said this was just after he heard Ashley Montagu (assumed name for Israel Ehrenburg, who frequently appeared on "The Tonight Show") tell about seven thousand school board members in San Diego: *"The reason I didn't salute the flag was that, number one, I do not believe in God and, number two, there is absolutely no justice in this country. And furthermore, every child who enters school at the age of six in the United States is mentally ill because he comes to school with certain values he inherits from the family unit."* Both Dr. Pierce's and Ashley Montagu's statements were similar to Vince Nesbitt's quotation in *Humanistic*

Morals and Values Education (1981) of Paul Brandwein as saying: "Any child who believes in God is mentally ill" (*The Social Sciences*, Teachers edition, levels 3 and 4, 1970). At that time, Brandwein was president of the Center for the Study of Instruction at the University of Pittsburgh, and he would later become director of research for Harcourt, Brace, Jovanovich Publishers, who in 1981 said Brandwein's *"more than thirty books are in daily use in schools today."*

• • • • •

Rather than family values, of course, the world planners wanted children to have internationalist values instilled instead. In 1972, the Organization for Economic Cooperation and Development (OECD) published *Alternative Educational Futures in the United States and in Europe* prepared by the Center for Educational Research and Innovation, which had been created by the OECD in 1968 with the help of grants from the Ford Foundation and the Royal Dutch/Shell group of companies. In the book, Torsten Husen said, *"The school ought to instill receptivity to change. . . . The school must prepare its pupils to live in a society of pluralistic values. Schooling for internationalism and the defeat of present-day educational provincialism is necessary if the world is going to survive."* In the same book, Willis Harman stated: *"The necessity of a shift from a parochial to a 'one world' view of 'Spaceship Earth' hardly needs defense. . . . Emergent change, not homeostasis, is the order of the day. . . . It is apparent that 'new' values* [proposed by humanistic-psychology writers and "forerunner" youth] *are currently challenging the traditional ones* [U.S. middle-class]." Harman then indicated that what Aldous Huxley had called "The Perennial Philosophy" is *present in the Rosicrucian and Freemasonry traditions"* and meant that *"man can under certain conditions attain to a higher awareness, a 'cosmic consciousness,' in which state he has immediate knowledge of a reality underlying the phenomenal world."* He next emphasized Lawrence Frank's remark that *"a social order which tolerates such wide-ranging pluralism of norms must seek unity through diversity."*

To accomplish this, Harman asserted: *"Nothing less than a new guiding philosophy will do. Ferkiss* [1969] *outlines three basic and essential elements for such a new philosophy . . . a 'new naturalism,'. . . 'the new holism,' . . . and 'the new immanentism' (sees that the whole is 'determined not from outside but from within').* . . . *It is not enough to be intellectually aware that at this point in history nationalism is a suicidal course.* . . . *Educational experiences must be contemplated which are akin to psychotherapy . . . that result in a felt realization of the inevitability of one inseparable world, and a felt shift in the most basic values and premises on which one builds one's life. In a sense, this means bringing something like 'person-changing technology' into the educational system (e.g., meditation, hypnosis, sensitivity training, psychodrama, yoga, etc.)."*

At this same time, World Goodwill (Lucis Trust) would also describe its concern for the future of youth in its December 1972 commentary titled, "The Voice of Youth," which set forth: *"At one stage or another, all societies are experiencing the process of evolutionary development toward a new world order. . . . Youth may help guide humanity through the period of transition to the new world order. . . . In their search for new values, many young people are presenting a way of growth to their societies. . . . Through their relentless criticism of the old and affirmation of the new they are unearthing the potent social forces needed to build the new world order."*

World Goodwill would follow this by their October 1973 commentary titled, "Values to Live By," which declared: *"So the principles which should control a new world order for all mankind can emerge with clarity and have great influence on human consciousness, we might define some of these principles and ideals — What is good for all is good for each one. . . . It is the hearts and minds of men and women throughout the world that need to be transformed. . . . Unlike the repressive and puritanical misapplication of spiritual values in the past, these new values can then be recognized as a liberating and fulfilling way of life. The individual whose livingness is expressed daily in terms of right values can be thought of as a point of light. . . . When there are enough men and women of goodwill actively expressing the new value, the world will be aflame with the possibilities of transformation."*

In 1975, Mieczyslaw Kotlarczyk's *Art of the Living Word* was published with a preface by Cardinal Karol Wojtyla (the future Pope John Paul II). Kotlarczyk had founded the Rhapsodic Theater, and he and his wife lived with Karol Wojtyla in Cracow, Poland, during the Second World War. According to George H. Williams in *The Mind of John Paul II* (1981), Kotlarczyk was friend and mentor to Karol Wojtyla, who became a leading member of the Rhapsodic Theater. Commenting on *Art of the Living Word*, Williams states: *"As one takes note of a few of the names and titles dealt with by Kotlarczyk, one will recall that his book wherein they are mentioned has in its subtitle the word 'Magic.' In supplying the dates of the original publications, the present writer intends to suggest that some of these older works would have been discussed with the youthful Wojtyla. Kotlarczyk cited Madame Helena Petrovna Blavatsky, the Russian-born foundress of Theosophy, specifically her* Isis Unveiled *(1877) and* The Secret Doctrine *(1888); Eliphas Levi on the grand arcane (1898) and on the history of magic (1922); Ignacy Matuszewski on mediums (1896) and the mystical and occult in Slowacki (1903); Julian Ochorowicz on mental suggestion (1887) and the secret knowledge in Egypt (1898); and J. Switkowski on occultism and magic against the background of parapsychology (1939). . . . Wojtyla recited in Slowacki's* The King-Spirit . . . *in it is set forth the idea that the whole history of the cosmos was the gradual creation by God of spirits, coming forth from Him in ever more perfect forms, dying only to return. . . . Among the spirits are king-spirits, incarnating themselves in personages and also in nations. . . . The chief figure is the legendary soldier Er, who appears in Plato's* Republic *book X. He reappears in the poem, "The King-Spirit" (1847), as the first Polish king, Popiel,* [and] *is successfully reincarnated in a succession of rulers. . . . It will be recalled that Slowacki is the poet of 'the Slavic pope to come' (1848), who wrote in the same year that the 'exalted mission which is due to us, the oldest among the Slavs,* [is] *. . . the papacy,* [which] *like the Kingdom of God, is not outside us but within.' "*

•••••

Already looking toward the year A.D. 2000, the president of the National Education Association, Catherine Barrett, wrote in the February 10, 1973 issue of *Saturday Review of Education* that *"dramatic changes in the way we will raise our children in the year 2000 are indicated, particularly in terms of schooling. . . . We will need to recognize that the so-called 'basic skills,' which currently represent nearly the total effort in elementary schools, will be taught in one-quarter of the present school day. . . . When this happens — and it's near — the teacher can rise to his true calling. More than a dispenser of information, the teacher will be a conveyor of values, a philosopher. . . . We will be agents of change."*

In the same issue of *Saturday Review of Education*, radical feminist leader Gloria Steinem said, *"By the year 2000 we will, I hope, raise our children to believe in human potential, not God."* Riane Eisler, author of *The Equal Rights* [ERA] *Handbook* (1978), would later say, *"It is absurd to say . . . that one is a humanist but not a feminist. . . . Feminism is the last evolutionary development of humanism. Feminism is humanism on its most advanced level"* (*The Humanist*, November/December 1980).

With the time ripe to promote radical societal change, the second *Humanist Manifesto* was published in 1973 and began with: *"The next century can be and should be the humanistic century. . . . We stand at the dawn of a new age. . . . Only a shared world and global measures will suffice. . . . We affirm a set of common principles that can serve as a basis for united action.*

. . . They are a design for a secular society on a planetary scale. . . . As non-theists, we begin with humans not God, nature not deity . . . a recognition of an individual's right to die with dignity, euthanasia, and the right to suicide. . . . We deplore the division of humankind on nationalistic grounds. . . . The best option is to transcend the limits of national sovereignty and to move toward the building of a world community. . . . Thus, we look to the development of a system of world law and a world order based upon transnational federal government. . . . In closing . . . the true revolution is occuring."

UNESCO would also be involved in the revolution toward a world community. In 1973, UNESCO's Institute for Education, in Hamburg, ran a project referred to as "Getting Children to Learn How They Tick." A news release concerning the project opened with: *"Children at school are invited to repeat to the class, 'the lie you often tell about yourself'* . . . [and] *to write their own obituary notice. . . ."* Furthermore, the UNESCO regional information officer for Latin America at the time described what she witnessed in some of the schools in Colombia during a UNESCO educational experiment there: *"The children spoke of changing traditional patterns, of their parents' attitudes to what they were learning and sometimes to their resistance to progress: 'They need classes too, but we try to teach them.'* " In the same year of 1973, Leonid Brezhnev's *On the Policy of the Soviet Union and the International Situation* was published and included the assertion that *"Soviet society today is the real embodiment of the ideas of proletarian, socialist humanism."*

One area of the United States in which the humanistic revolution was obviously occurring was in schools' sex education programs. The permissive Sex Information and Education Council of the U.S. (SIECUS, which supports pornography) stated in its March/April 1989 report: *"In 1970, the President's Commission on Obscenity and Pornography called for 'a massive sex education effort. . . . It should be aimed at achieving an acceptance of sex as a normal and natural part of life and of oneself as a sexual being. It should not aim at orthodoxy; rather it should be designed to allow for a pluralism of values.' SIECUS' work clearly influenced these statements."* In 1973, one state education department's sex education policy statement announced: *"At one time, sex education was based . . . on innocence, ideals, and moral codes . . . but . . . we are now moving toward a more humanistic approach."* Translated, this meant a movement away from Judeo-Christian moral absolutes toward the moral relativism and situation ethics propagated by Lawrence Kohlberg and Sidney Simon.

What actually happened was all across the nation, teachers bought the secularist propaganda that teachers "should not impose any particular morality" upon students, so that teachers would in effect come to a sex education class and say, "Today we're going to talk about sex, and I'm not going to tell you premarital sex is morally wrong," or they would enter a death education class and say, "Today we're going to talk about suicide, and I'm not going to tell you it's morally wrong." The result of this type of non-directive education was obvious, as Stanford University psychologist Dr. Richard H. Blum's large-scale test in the late 1970s showed that children who went through these non-directive decision-making type programs actually took up with tobacco, marijuana, and alcohol more than did children not in these programs.

• • • • •

The year 1973 was also when the infamous *Roe v. Wade* abortion ruling was handed down by the U.S. Supreme Court. This illogical (and immoral) ruling by the court declared that "personhood" was not constitutionally conferred until birth. The reason this was illogical is that a child born prematurely at six months after conception, for example, would be considered a constitutionally protected "person." However, an older pre-born child seven months after conception, for example, could be legally killed by an abortion simply because he or she still resided in the womb. The population controllers would put forth various arguments for the legalization of abortion, such as the alleged high number of deaths from illegal abortions. But the former medical director for International Planned Parenthood, Malcolm Potts, would acknowledge in his book, *Abortion* (1977), that *"those who want the* [abortion] *law to be liberalized will claim that hundreds or thousands of women die unnecessarily each year, when the actual number is far lower."* Potts also admitted in "Fertility Rights" (*The Guardian*, April 25, 1979) that *"no society has controlled its fertility . . . without recourse to a significant number of abortions. In fact, abortion is often the **starting** place in the control of fertility."* And Potts revealed in the *Cambridge Evening News*, February 7, 1973, that *"as people turn to contraception, there will be a rise, not a fall, in the abortion rate."* He was correct.

• • • • •

Regarding the changing of students' values and the changing content of their textbooks, Ginn Publishers' "New Voices" series included gore-riddled stories like "The City" and blasphemy in "Jack and the Devil's Daughter." Concerning one story, the Ginn's teacher's manual advised, *"Many pupils will feel emotionally drained after reading this story."* Even more widespread has been the Junior Great Books program which includes seven hundred thousand youth in all fifty states. In this program, there are stories like "The Veldt" (for fifth grade) where children tell lions to devour their parents, and "The Lottery" (for ninth grade) where a boy helps stone his mother to death. Then, when students reach high school, they are given a steady dose of depressing works to read, such as the books of Thomas Hardy and Joseph Conrad that are full of symbolism, which is not all that apparent. Rarely are students assigned to read stories like Booth Tarkington's *Seventeen* (1916) that are not depressing or symbolic, and which have a pleasant ending.

The logical consequences of this type of values-changing education have been that teen pregnancies, suicide, violence, crime, etc., have dramatically increased. In a story from the *New York Post*, May 3, 1988, datelined Providence, Rhode Island, a poll was conducted concerning the sexual attitudes of seventeen hundred students. Of the boys in junior high school, twenty-five to forty-one percent said they believed it is all right to rape a girl on the first date if a boy has spent "a lot of money" on her (when asked what "a lot of money" was, the average response was ten to fifteen dollars). In the December 1990 issue of the *Journal of the American Medical Association* is a research article that indicates various suicide prevention programs in schools seem actually to be stimulating students to consider committing suicide.

On the NBC evening news, June 20, 1991, it was stated that one-third of all small businesses fail because of employee theft. It wouldn't surprise me a bit if one day a student accused of date rape or shoplifting, etc., appeared before a judge and said he had been taught in school that no one should impose any particular morality upon him, and therefore there was either no crime, or his teachers should be held accountable. Because the disastrous results of instilling morally relativistic values in students over the past couple of decades is now unfortunately obvious, quite a few of those "cult of change" agents who have been responsible for what has happened are now trying to legitimize their actions by claiming we are all "gods" or have "a god within" and therefore cannot be criticized. Concerning the Masonic view of moral relativism, former high-ranking York Rite Mason, Anokan Reed, described the oath of a master Mason this way: *"It's okay to seduce another man's daughter, or steal his car, as long as he's not a master Mason. . . . In the higher degrees, Masons deny the reality of evil"* (*Minneapolis Star*, May 21, 1980).

Students' religious morality has been undermined in an indirect way as well. At the college level, for example, students in philosophy classes would be asked, "If God is all-good and omnipotent, how can there be evil in the world?" An explanation that God could not be considered "all-good" unless He provided us with freewill, which necessarily means our freedom to choose to do evil, was rarely fully discussed. Relevant to this, Sidney Hook, a signer of the 1973 *Humanist Manifesto*, described in *The Humanist* magazine (January/February 1977) that *"human beings can be influenced to examine critically their religious beliefs only by indirection, [by which] I mean the development of a critical attitude in all our educational institutions that will aim to make students less credulous to claims that transcend their reflective experience."* This technique of using "indirect" means of undermining traditional values was also utilized by New Agers, as in *Occult Preparations for a New Age* (1975) by Dane Rudhyar, one reads: *"In order gradually to convince the old guard of official thinkers in control of most social and educational processes . . . they feel obliged to compromise and tone down their direct . . . realizations by using indirect techniques. . . . References to metaphysical principles unfamiliar to the European tradition are avoided."*

After Rudhyar's 1975 volume and Hook's 1977 *The Humanist* article appeared, a renewed interest in "critical thinking" would enter the nation's schools, building upon research in Dr. Edward Glaser's *An Experiment In the Development of Critical Thinking* (1941). This followed the psychodrama and sociometry work of Rumanian psychiatrist Jacob Moreno in the early part of this century. John Dewey called sociometry "the next stage" after reading Moreno's book, *Who Shall Survive?* (1934); and President Franklin Delano Roosevelt told Moreno one day in Hyde Park after reading Moreno's book, *"When I am back in Washington, I will see where your ideas can be put to use."* Moreno's and Glaser's work was followed by Estonian Hilda Taba's "Thinking Project" in the 1950s and early 1960s. While she received considerable federal funds at San Francisco State College, Taba developed a social studies curriculum that became widely used in the United States.

With "change" a primary goal of education, the U.S. Office of Education (OE) in 1973 awarded a grant to evaluate some of OE's "change agent" programs, and according to the *Congressional Record*, during the spring of 1974 OE gave a grant of $5.9 million for five hundred "change agents" to be trained at twenty-one universities around the country. Naturally, if the advocacy of change was blatant, there would be an outcry on the part of parents. Therefore, in the National Training Laboratories Institute for Applied Behavioral Science newsletter, *Social Change* (1977), a few guidelines were published, such as *"couch the language of change in the language of the status quo"* and *"use the stated objectives of the status quo. They are almost broad enough to encompass innovation."*

About this time, concerning the adolescent literature movement (including themes of homosexuality, rebellion, etc.) in secondary schools, Sheila Schwartz in the January/February 1976 issue of *The Humanist* expressed her thankfulness that *"the crazies* [fundamentalists] *don't do all that much reading. If they did, they'd find that they have already been defeated."* The same year, Harold Shane wrote in *Phi Delta Kappan* (September 1976) that *"as young people mature, we must help them develop . . . a service ethic which is geared toward the real world . . . the global servant concept in which we will educate our young for planetary service and eventually for some form of world citizenship."* And a few years later, James Clavell (author of *Shogun*) published *The*

Children's Story (1981) depicting how in just a short period of time, young school children's thinking could be so manipulated that they would consider cutting into pieces the American flag a wonderful thing.

• • • • •

Some individuals did try to speak out against what was happening in American society and in our schools, as Martin Gross did in *The Psychological Society* (1978). In 1963, Gross had published *The Brain Watchers*, which actually led to congressional hearings with Gross as the leading witness. In his new book (1978), he stated: *"Our schools are taking on the aura of a psychiatric clinic, without taxpayer consent. . . . The school child is immersed in a psychological environment in which he is cajoled, invited, seduced, even bludgeoned into seeking counseling. . . . Almost all the* [school psychology] *personnel are actually laymen. The entire practice of school psychology may be seen as an intrusion of bureaucracy into the family structure. Further school counseling may not be legal. In most states, school personnel may not practice psychotherapy on children. By labeling it as 'counseling' instead of 'psychotherapy,' they may have invented a semantic subterfuge to circumvent the law. . . . There is no real evidence that the anxieties, neuroses, or eventual psychosis rate of children is in any way reduced by school intervention. There is the equal possibililty that the effort is actually a **neurotic stimulus**. With our taxes, we are helping poorly trained specialists to tamper with the psyches of an already overpsychologized generation."*

Chapter Twelve

Psychological Preparation
for the New World Order

By the early 1980s, the humanist revolution was in full tilt. The director of the American Humanist Association from 1975 to 1980, Morris Storer, declared in his 1980 book, *Humanist Ethics*, that *"a large majority of the educators of American colleges and universities are predominantly humanists, and a majority of the teachers who go out from their studies in colleges to responsibilities in primary and secondary schools are basically humanist, no matter that many maintain a nominal attachment to church or synagogue for good personal, social, or practical reasons."* The next year, H.J. Blackham (a founder of the International Humanist and Ethical Union, which has four million members) wrote in the September/October issue of the American Humanist Association's *The Humanist* that if schools teach dependence on one's self, *"they are more revolutionary than any conspiracy to overthrow the government."* Then in the January/February 1983 issue of *The Humanist*, John Dunphy's prize-winning essay proclaims that *"the battle for humankind's future must be waged and won in the public school classroom . . . between the rotting corpse of Christianity . . . and the new faith of humanism . . .* [and]

humanism will emerge triumphant."

It's indeed proper to refer to humanism as a religion, for in the *Encyclopedia of Associations*, one reads that the American Humanist Association *"certifies humanist counselors, who enjoy the legal status of ordained pastors, priests, and rabbis."* When secular humanism in the schools was challenged in a federal court case originating in Alabama in the mid-1980s, even liberal *Washington Post* columnist Colman McCarthy wrote in his April 5, 1987 column: *"U.S. District Court Judge W. Brevard Hand is reasonable to conclude that 'this highly relativistic and individualistic approach constitutes the promotion of a fundamental faith claim opposed to other religious faiths.'"*

Obviously with this humanistic attack upon Judeo-Christian values, there would be a counter movement, led by the "religious right." Anticipating this counterattack, certain secularists may have initiated activities designed to discredit some religious leaders who were becoming politically involved in 1980. In the February 25, 1988 *Washington Post*, Rev. Jimmy Swaggart is said to have had a problem with pornography "for years." The minister who exposed Rev. Swaggart, the Rev. Martin Gorman, the article said, had admitted to a sexual dalliance "seven or eight years ago." The *Post* article indicated this was about the same time PTL's Rev. Jim Bakker had his sexual escapade. What is notable here is the time frame of "seven or eight years ago." This would have been about the time when fundamentalists and evangelicals were first becoming a potent political force in the United States, and it may be that these religious leaders were "set up" by individuals concerned about the threat these leaders posed in terms of political power and influence.

What is also interesting is that it was seven years after Jim Bakker's escapade with Jessica Hahn in Florida in 1980 that the scandal became public. This was almost at the beginning of the 1988 presidential campiagn, at about the same time the Swaggart scandal just happened to break in the news. No long after Jessica Hahn broke her story to the press and media, she posed topless in *Playboy* magazine. Was this all just coincidental?

This theory is not so farfetched when one remembers that in the 1980s, New Age networker Deena Metzger wrote the peculiar book, *The Woman Who Slept with Men to Take the War Out of Them*, regarding a fictional account of a woman's use of sex to gain political ends (like the German spy Mata Hari allured men to divulge their governments' secrets early this century, and like the 1987 arrest of American Marines who had sex with female Soviet spies and let them enter security areas of the U.S. embassy in Moscow). In the *Utne Reader* (August/ September 1985), Ms. Metzger also wrote, "Re-Vamping the World: On the Return of the Holy Prostitute," in which she advocated that all women become "holy prostitutes" as a means of regaining spiritual power lost with the beginning of patriarchal religion. Relevant here is Rev. Paul Trinchard's *Apostasy Within* (1989, with a foreword by Malachi Martin) in which he presents his interpretation of a hypothetical radical feminist plan as follows: *"Since 1960, diabolically feminine seduction has been one method of de-evangelization within the Catholic churches in America. We have had great success in turning shepherds into wolves. . . . Like Eve, you are to* *become their **helpmate**, or, better yet, their **playmate**, in order to make them your hellmate. . . . So shall you rule priests and bishops!"* (The principle involved here was described by prominent Hungarian sociologist Elmer Hankiss in the January 6, 1988 *New York Times as "if you corrupt, you can dominate."*)

More recently, one will recall the events surrounding Vicki Long and several members of the clergy in Atlanta. Ms. Long said she had been interested in becoming a nun, but then developed an intimate relationship with Rev. Donal Keohane of Columbus, Georgia, and unsuccessfully sued the priest in 1987 for allegedly fathering her daughter. Incredibly, the year after this paternity suit occurred, Archbishop Eugene Marino of Atlanta began a relationship with Mr. Long within two to four months after his arrival, and he resigned in July 1990. When Father John F. O'Connor notified the Vatican that homosexuality was rampant in the Dominican Order, he was dismissed from the Dominicans with Vatican approval, and was denied — after forty-two years with them — all Social Security benefits, Medicare, and pensions. A prominent American canon lawyer accredited to the Vatican told Father O'Connor his appeal would go nowhere *"because there are too many homosexuals in the Vatican Curia."*

In the secular arena of sexual activity, the *Milwaukee Sentinel* (February 3, 1990) reported Debra Chapple in Wisconsin confessing to be a prostitute at conventions nationwide attended by businessmen, mayors, and aldermen. She told the judge that uniformed police officers provided security for the events in Shreveport, Houston, and Birmingham, and in Chicago she *"was driven from one location to another by a sheriff's deputy."*

At about the same time, a "madame" was arrested in Tampa and related that for quite some time she had a number of prostitutes working for her, specializing in sexual activities with "politicians." It is interesting that the press for some reason has not vigorously pursued the names of these politicians.

• • • • •

Likewise laying the groundwork to counter the religious reaction against the increasing secularization of society, one state's 1980 State Health Plan listed "religion" as a socioeconomic precursor of "mental retardation" (a concept supported by Brock Chisholm). The plan was endorsed by the then-governor of the state, James B. Hunt, Jr., not long after his notorious "Child Health Plan for Raising a New Generation," which was part of a national strategy suggested by what was then HEW to regionalize child health care. "Barriers to service" listed in the Child Health Plan included "modesty and confidentiality" and "parental and community attitudes." If asked, Hunt would probably say he doesn't support all aspects of either plan, yet he endorsed both plans without demanding the withdrawal of their objectionable parts prior to his endorsement. Hunt is now chairman of the National Board for Professional Teaching Standards, which he described as *"the linchpin of a larger strategy to affect the transformation of our nation's schools."* The board wants to nationally certify teachers, and this would be not simply on the basis of academic competence, but also on such things as how they would teach students with different religious backgrounds.

Even the American Bar Association would participate in the attack upon religious values that was occurring in the United States. A brochure announcing an ABA seminar in San Francisco on May 4 and 5, 1989, said the seminar was for *"attorneys who want to be on the leading edge of an explosive new area of law."* The seminar's opening area was "Expanding Use of Tort Law Against Religions," and the first speaker's topic was "Tort Law as Ideological Weapon." He was followed by another lawyer speaking on "Tort Law as Essential Restraint On Religious Abuses."

These would all reflect the increasingly changing values of the 1980s, and public schools were not exempt from changing values and innovations either. In 1982, the "Wizards" simulation game was introduced to help students in spelling, and the "eight levels of spelling power" exercise had third-graders advance in power from being just "humans" (level 1) up to "wizards" (level 8). Ironic is the fact that at the front of the game is a message signed by "The Wizard" which ends with *"May you have a save journey."* (Note that "safe" was misspelled.) In addition, there's a Merrill Publishing Co. teacher's manual *Health: A Wellness Approach* that tells teachers how to instruct students in meditation; a Prentice-Hall *Creative Drama Resource Book for Grades K-3* which contains picture captions such as, *"You're looking in a crystal ball"* and *"Be a mean witch mixing a brew in your cauldron";* and a Holt, Reinhart, and Winston series *Impressions* (marketed by Harcourt Brace Jovanovich) for elementary students that has themes of occultism and witchcraft.

The response of many parents to these trends in public education was to remove their children from these schools and send them to private schools or homeschool them. While this was a logical reaction, a large number of these parents were no longer interested in what was happening in the public schools which their tax dollars were still supporting, and those schools became even more secularized. Unfortunately, graduates of those schools will probably go on to become public school teachers, lawyers, and legislators, all of whom may work together to regulate private and homeschools in the future.

For those members of the public who still send their children to public schools, if they do not accept the secularists' desired changes or innovations in schools, then "crises" can be manufactured to create a climate receptive to change. How such techniques are used by educators is described in "The Uses of Crisis: Guidelines for School Leaders" (*The Education Digest*, October 1984). This reference to using crises (like the recent one in the Persian Gulf) is reminiscent of what Alice Bailey said in *Esoteric Psychology*, vol. 2 (1942): *"Builders of the new civilazation . . . make their presence felt immediately after a crisis has occurred. . . . The general method employed is one of inspiration and of the presentation of moments of crisis. These moments offer opportunity for the activity of some disciple."* Perhaps one such "disciple" is New Ager and former democratic vice-presidential candidate Barbara Marx Hubbard (author of *The Evolutionary Journey* and president of Futures Network, Inc.), who spoke at the 1984 Heart to Heart Festival, sponsored by the New Age "Network of Light, " calling upon humanity *"to pull itself back from the brink of destruction."*

● ● ● ● ●

During the 1980s, there was a continued push for early childhood education, as Mortimer Adler (author of *The Paideia Proposal*) advocated perhaps three years of preschool tutelage, saying *"the sooner a democratic society intervenes to remedy the cultural inequality of homes and environments, the sooner it will succeed in fulfilling the democratic mandate of equal educational opportunity for all."* Among the many sessions at the World Future Society Fourth General Assembly in Washington, D.C. (welcomed by Sen. Albert Gore as a host and moderator for a session including New Agers Barbara Marx Hubbard of Futures Network and Willis Harman of the Institute of Noetic Sciences) on July 20, 1982 was "Early Childhood Education" with the following description: *"Education begins at infancy. Attitudes, values, skills, and capacities are formed under the age of five. A major problem today is how to teach children of the world about ways of achieving and maintaining peace and preserving the environment. Individuals with worldwide experience are taking part in a revolution which is changing society by their influence on children. This is a global education approach that can result in a better and more peaceful world for our children's children."*

Not only in preschool activities were children to be prepared for the New World Order, but for school-age children there were activities outside of school as well. For the Girl Scouts, there was the "My World in My Community" badge, which closely resembles the occultic yin-yang symbol, including the Luciferic dark and light points or dots. In children's literature, there is the Prentice-Hall series of "Little Witch" books by Linda Glovach, with titles such as *The Little Witch's Black*

Magic Cookbook and *The Little Witch's Book of Yoga.*
In cartoons, there are the Smurfs from Bavarian occultic
origins, as Papa Smurf sometimes calls upon "Azazel" for
help. "Azazel" is a biblical term for Satan, or in Milton's
Paradise Lost it refers to one of the angels who with Satan
rebelled against God. In toys as well as on television there
were The Transformers, who were human beings who
could transform themselves into machines and back
again. (Not only is the rainbow a favorite New Age
symbol, but so too is the butterfly because its meta-
morphosis symbolizes radical "transformation.") Similarly, there was the individual who looked like part
human and part cat in *Beauty and the Beast.* "Cuteness"
was the selling point in the movie *The Littlest Mermaid*
with the half human and half fish mermaid. In music and
the movies were the Teenage Mutant Ninja Turtles,
combining human and animal characteristics.

In a 1962 nationally syndicated column, Edith
Kermit Roosevelt quoted Madame Blavatsky as having
said, *"What is one to do, when in order to rule men, it is
necessary to deceive them? . . . For almost invariably the
more simple, the more silly, and the more gross the
phenomenon, the more likely it is to succeed."* Could it be
that such things as the Beast (in the *Beauty and the Beast*)
and the Teenage Mutant Ninja Turtles are to prepare or
condition youth to accept the New Age New World Order
occultic, mythical part-humans part-animals such as the
sphinx or the centaur of Sagittarius. Mary Bailey, thirty-
third degree Mason Foster Bailey's wife after Alice
Bailey, said in 1983 that *"Sagittarius rules Washington,
D.C., the nation's capitol."* Earlier, she had written an
editorial, "The World of Tomorrow," in the September/

October 1977 issue of *The Beacon* (Lucis Trust), in which she posed the questions: *"What are the goals of the Aquarian Age? How should our own personal attitudes and activities be directed, as a contribution to the building of a new world order?"* Mary Bailey had succeeded Foster Bailey as director of Lucis Trust, which distributed Lola Davis' *Toward a World Religion for the New Age* (1983), in which the author relates that Foster Bailey *"agrees that the Ancient Wisdom's teachings are found in the symbolism, numbers, and rituals of Masonry. He states that the first degrees of Masonry are similar to the plan of spiritual development taught in the Ancient Wisdom. For example, in the first degree, the disciple moves from 'darkness into light' or to awareness of the spiritual self or soul; in the second degree, the member gains wisdom; and in the third, he is 'raised from the dead' or from the personal self which is subject to physical death, to the soul-self which is immortal."*

• • • • •

Returning to the movies, George Lucas directed *Star Wars*, which he described as based upon Eastern and Indian (of the Americas) mysticism, and in which a primary saying was, *"May the Force be with you."* In *The Aquarian Gospel of Jesus Christ* (subtitle: "The Philosophic and Practical Basis of the Religion of the Aquarian Age of the World of the Church Universal Transcribed from the Book of God's Remembrances Known as the Akashic Record") by Levi H. Dowling (pseudonym) in 1911, one reads that *"one may enter fully into the spirit of the God of Force. . . . "* However, remember here that in

Daniel 11:36-38 regarding the fall of man, it states that
" . . . *he shall exalt himself. . . . Neither shall he regard*
the God of his fathers. . . . But in his estate shall he
honour the God of forces. . . ." Lucas also produced
Captain EO for Disney with a New Age space adventure
plot and with a small monkey-like creature with wings
(reminiscent of the monkey-like creatures with wings in
Oz). "EO" is also pronounced in some languages as the
word for "I," which could symbolize the "third (or 'all-
seeing') eye." Perhaps not coincidental is the recent
commercial for an "Eos" (meaning "dawn" in Greek)
camera which zooms in close on only one of the sports
figure's eyes. There are also recent television ads (e.g., by
Glidden Paint) that focus on one eye (the left eye) for a
long time. In Egyptian mythology, there are many legends
that relate to the left eye (which symbolizes the moon,
while the right eye symbolizes the sun). One of these
legends concerns the myth of the Eye of Horus, which is
said to be the seat of the soul and all-powerful.

Perhaps the best way to compare motion pictures of
years past that upheld biblical values, and the motion
pictures of today is to look at the old and new "Westerns."
For example, in the classic movie *Shane*, starring Alan
Ladd, he was probably in love with the heroine, but
because she was married, he did not pursue an illicit
affair. Instead, he went so far as to fight her husband for
the heroic honor of facing death against the villains so
that the heroine and her husband and son could remain
together. Today, however, "Westerns" starring Clint
Eastwood or Charles Bronson usually depict the villains
as committing acts so heinous that no matter how violent
or immoral the star acts, the viewer is supposed to

sympathize and/or empathize with him — a sort of situation-ethics approach to values and life that is characteristic of secular humanism. The same could be said about the popular "James Bond" movies, as millions of so-called "Christians" flocked to these motion pictures year after year to see "007" defeat the villains, ignoring the fact that in every film, Bond engaged in fornication and was what one university psychology instructor described as a "sociopath."

A variation on this is also used today in a political sense by the world planners. For example, if they had openly attacked the biblical values of families and children, there would have been an immediate strong resistance. However, by branding certain leading individual conservatives as "far right" and their concerns as "extremist," the media and press could be counted on to portray them unfavorably. Thus, when the general population began to become concerned about these same issues (e.g., legalization of abortion, impact of communism, etc.), their views had already been labeled and propagandized as "far right extremism," thereby undercutting the forcefulness of their objections.

Regarding one specific activity of the media, repetitive showing of certain television commercials can condition youth to accept New Age humanistic values of moral relativism and situation ethics, as a Pontiac truck ad ends with the words *"New Age — New Values,"* and a Burger King ad ends with the words, *"Sometimes you gotta break the rules."* For older teens and young adults, there is also an ad for the U.S. Marines that could be a Knight Templar entering the castle for his initiation ceremony. His horse's armor includes a pointed frontispiece like a unicorn. Lightning appears from above and runs through a sword into the knight's hand, but doesn't harm him.

The same type of conditioning occurs via repetitive showing of certain themes on television programs. Despite the bemoaning of network news announcers and reporters regarding an increase in violence and the consequences of illicit sex in society, these same networks in their primetime programming and "soaps" hypocritically bombard viewers daily with shows that glorify this very behavior. Characters such as Luke on "General Hospital," Ross on "All My Children," and John on "As The World Turns," rape women and later become heroes on these "soaps." In one of the first episodes of the primetime series "Hardball," the two leading characters, police officers, don't flip a coin to see who rides the bike, but they toss rocks at a streetlight instead, causing one of them to say, *"Now we're lawbreakers."* And what kind of medium message is sent when those youths trying to resist the temptation to take drugs see Dan Rather receiving plaudits and financial rewards as a top network news anchor, even though he has revealed: *"As a reporter . . . I've tried everything. . . . I had someone at the Houston police station shoot me with heroin so I could do a story about it"* (*Ladies Home Journal*, July 1980).

The October 5, 1990 Juvenile Law Study Commission report, presented by Dr. Linnea Smith, M.D., listed scientific study after study demonstrating that television and other media violence can contribute to aggressive behavior. For example, at a recent annual meeting of the American Psychiatric Association, Dr. Brandon Centerwall showed that homicides by people of white European descent had increased dramatically in the United States,

Canada, and South Africa after the introduction of television and TV violence, even though the television was introduced at very different times in those nations. Within the U.S., there were also increases in murder and property crime rates in those areas that received television earlier. Psychiatrist Paul Kettl of Pennsylvania State University showed that the rates of teenage depression and suicide increased sharply since the introduction of television. There has also been an anti-Christian bias on television. Howard Rosenburg, TV critic for the *Los Angeles Times*, on May 21, 1991, said: *"A recent rerun of* [Norman] *Lear's old series 'The Jeffersons,' for example, was brutal and mean-spirited in its ridiculing of a 'born-again' preacher. . . . In the main, primetime has done to religion what dogs do to fire plugs, pouring on the ridicule."*

What one must remember, though, is that some television messages are not obvious. At the World Future Society's Fourth General Assembly in Washington, D.C., on July 19, 1982, a session titled "Media Communication As An Agent For Change" (co-moderated by New Age networkers Carol Rosin, of Educators for World Peace and a special envoy to the U.N., and Barbara Marx Hubbard) was described as follows: *"The mass media create our social nervous system. The signals that go forth affect the body politic, creating a shared sense of reality. As we see ourselves, so we act; as we act, so we become. Therefore, the media create our sense of reality and consequently shape reality itself. We must become conscious of the effect of the media and design programming to enhance the potential for a positive future."*

Shortly after this (around 1985), many of the people who had produced music videos became involved in commercial advertising. A concept was developed that no longer appealed to the reasons viewers should buy a particular product, but rather through quickly changing images showed a lifestyle with which a target audience associates. In what amounts to a form of psychological terrorism, these are often shown by "cult-of-change" agents in a hyper-reality style of quickly changing images, music, and flashing lights (one knowledgeable individual said they sometimes simulate a drug experience), like Aldous Huxley's description in *The Devils of Loudon* (1952) of how the masses could be conditioned. He said: *"If exposed long enough to the tomtoms and the singing, every one of our philosophers would end by capering and howling with the savages. . . . Assemble a mob of men and women previously conditioned by a daily reading of newspapers; treat them to amplified band music, bright lights . . . and in next to no time you can reduce them to a state of almost mindless subhumanity. Never before have so few been in a position to make fools, maniacs, or criminals of so many."* This technique can also be applied to individuals, such as the American government's musical bombardment of Manuel Noriega in the Vatican Embassy in Panama. William Sargent in *Battle for the Mind: A Physiology of Conversion and Brainwashing* (1957) states: *"If these underlying physiological principles are once understood, it should be possible to get at the person, converting and maintaining him in his new belief by a whole variety of imposed stresses that end by altering his brain function."*

Relevant here are the findings of *Snapping: America's Epidemic of Sudden Personality Change* (1978) by Flo Conway and Jim Siegelman. "Snapping," according to the authors, *"depicts the way in which intense experience may affect fundamental information-processing capacities of the brain. . . . The experience itself may . . . render the individual extremely vulnerable to suggestion. It may lead the changes that alter lifelong habits, values, and beliefs. . . . At the Esalen Institute . . . techniques for creating intense sensory . . . experiences were experimented with."* Pertaining to television's effects, the authors note that *"TV stills the mind through repetition . . . in the . . . assault of momentary images upon vision. . . . Television also may be a potent neutralizing force of human thought and feeling. Its incessant transmissions of information physically trains an individual to hear and observe without stopping to think. . . . Advertisers have long known that this rapid-fire kaleidoscope of consumption may make television viewers more vulnerable to their suggestions."* And in their conclusion, Conway and Siegelman warn that *"our culture seems to be embarking on a destructive new course of manipulation and escapism, of human abdication."*

Planetary Citizen's board member and New Ager, Prof. Willis Harman (a consultant to the National Goals Research Staff of the White House) of Stanford University's Engineering Economic Systems Department, believes that a person's behavior is governed far more extensively than one might realize by the unconscious or subconscious mind. Research has already shown that quick flashes of subliminal messages have been successfully used as conditioning or programming tools. Furthermore, research around 1985 by Benjamin Libet, professor of neurophysiology at the University of California, San Francisco, in the scientific journal *The Brain and*

Behavioral Sciences, indicates that *"the conscious mind doesn't initiate voluntary actions."* Monitors revealed that about a half-second before a muscle flexes, for example, an unconscious part of the brain sends signals seemingly to prepare the conscious part of the brain for action. Libet says the conscious part of the brain can veto the unconscious signal, but my question is, "What if the person's 'will' has been conditioned not to veto the signal?" What if the person has seen the Nike slogan *"Just Do It"* so many times that he or she "just does it" — whatever "it" is? Dr. Robert Assagioli, founder of psychosynthesis, believes it is actually possible to train the "will." He was a lifelong friend of Alice Bailey and one of the "disciples" referred to in her book, *Discipleship in the New Age.* In Constance Cumbey's 1983 book, *The Hidden Dangers of the Rainbow*, she describes the New Age movement as *"a movement that includes many thousands of organizations networking throughout every corner of our globe with the intent of bringing about a New World Order — an order that writes God out of the picture and deifies Lucifer. . . . The Age of Aquarius was at last arriving and it meant nothing pretty as far as the Judeo-Christian world was concerned. And that world well needed to be concerned. For sadly, apathy was the order of the day — an apathy that if not soon shaken would result in the New Agers' long-awaited 'New World Order.' "* This apathy was not something that happened accidentally, either, as drugs and various scandals over the past thirty years caused people to "tune out" or "turn off" or become disillusioned, thereby engendering a kind of "what can I do?" helplessness mind-set resulting in apathy. In this mental state, people could be more easily manipulated, and in Karen Cook's article, "Scenario for a New Age," in the business world section of the *New York Times* magazine (September 25, 1988), she describes the movement of New Age consultants into programs for some of the nation's largest corporations, with Pacific Bell employees, for example, complaining *"that they were being subjected to mind control and coercion."* In February 1988, the federal Equal Employment Opportunity Commission issued notice number N-915.022, which was its policy statement on "new age" training programs which conflict with employees' religious beliefs, indicating that employees could not be forced to participate in such programs.

• • • • •

At about this same time, New Age psychological techniques were being used in the area of music as well. Plato in his *Republic* stated that *"the introduction of a new kind of music can alter the character of a nation."* Not only can music alter the character of a nation, but Henry David Thoreau (1817-1862) said, *"Even music may be intoxicating. Such apparently slight causes destroyed Greece and Rome, and will destroy England and America."* In recent years, even traditional singers with religious backgrounds, such as Perry Como, have sung songs that contain lyrics like *"I would sell my very soul."* Debbie Boone sang "You Light Up My Life" which says, *"It can't be wrong when it feels so right."* Moreover, in several large school systems in the United States not long ago, elementary students were being taught the theme song from "M*A*S*H," which is actually titled "Suicide Is

Painless," and informs students that *"cheating is the only way to win, the game of life is lost anyway, and suicide is painless."*

The new rock music was also bringing about a revolution for older youth. Paul Cantor of the Jefferson Airplane was reported as saying, *"The new rock music is intended to broaden the generation gap, alienate parents from their children, and prepare young people for revolution."* David Crosby (of Crosby, Stills, & Nash) similarly stated in *Rolling Stone*, vol. 1: *"I figured the only thing to do was to steal their kids. I still think it's the only thing to do. By saying that, I'm not talking about kidnapping. I'm just talking about changing young people's value systems which removes them from their parents' world effectively."* Frank Zappa, leader of the rock group Mothers of Invention, said, *"The loud sounds and the bright lights of today are tremendous indoctrination tools."* (Aldous Huxley had said something similar to this in *The Devils of Loudon*.) A member of The Who boldly proclaimed, *"What we dish out is the musical equivalent of war — war upon quiet, war upon dullness, war upon certainty and stability."* Noted composer and conductor Dimitri Tiomkin has been quoted as saying: *"The big beat is deliberately aimed at exciting the listener. There is actually very little melody, only rhythm. . . . We seem to be reverting to savagery. . . . Youngsters who listen constantly to this sort of sound are thrust into turmoil. They are no longer relaxed, normal kids."* Rock music has harmonic dissonance and melodic discord which violate man's natural body rhythms, according to Dr. David Noebel, who reported on experiments at Temple Bell College in Denver that indicated rock music could even kill plants within a month. Similarly, Dr. John Diamond, a New York City psychiatrist, studied beats of over twenty thousand recordings and concluded *"that a specific beat ('stopped anapestic rhythm,'which is contrary to our natural body beats and rhythms) found in over half of the top hits of any given week can actually weaken you. . . . It interferes with brain wave patterns, causing mental stress. . . . Tests conducted in schools showed that students performed fifteen percent better without rock music."* According to an Associated Press story, the first week in July 1991 in Maryland Heights, Missouri, about three thousand of over fifteen thousand fans "went wild" at a Guns N' Roses concert after lead singer Axl Rose jumped off the stage, then stopped the concert. At least sixty-four fans and fifteen police officers were injured. This is not surprising given that a September 1990 report by the American Medical Association described the link between rock music (especially heavy metal rock) and drug use, premarital sex, satanic cult involvement, and emotional and psychological disturbances. And lest one think that surely vocal sounds cannot affect anyone physically in any significant way, Dr. Venkat Ramani reported July 11, 1991, in the prestigious *New England Journal of Medicine* that a woman had epileptic seizures when hearing the voice of Mary Hart, co-host of the television program "Entertainment Tonight."

• • • • •

The "war on stability" would also be evident in the new architecture (Secretary of State Baker would also use the term "new architecture" in his December 12, 1989, speech in Berlin) beginning to go up in the form of buildings at about this time. Pyramids, domes, arches, and other forms and shapes have recently begun to be emphasized as part of what New Agers would call "sacred geometry" based upon Hermetic philosophy (e.g., New Ager Buckminster Fuller's geodesic domes were early examples of this). If one looks at the Nazi architectural designs of the mid-1920s, there is an emphasis upon domes and arches, and the pitched roof design was part of Hitler's architectural credo, according to John Toland. In Toland's *Hitler: The Pictorial Documentary of His Life* (1978), he quotes Hitler as writing in 1924 that *"the house with the flat roof is Oriental — Oriental is Jewish — Jewish is bolshevistic."* Through most of American history, buildings have had either spired or flat, functional tops, but over the past decades there has been an increasing number of buildings with pitched, triangular, or pyramid-shaped roofs in addition to those with domed or arched tops or designs on the buildings' facades. These are not only unlike traditional American architecture, but they are also unlike the unique and radically different earlier designs by Frank Lloyd Wright, who became involved in Theosophy which had come from Russian intellectuals. Wright's books show his concern with spiritual issues, such as when he said, *"Humanity is the light of the world,"* as represented by his Unity Temple built with many stained glass windows near Chicago early this century.

Another leading architect, Louis Sullivan ("will to power" concept), was also concerned about spiritual issues, according to John Lobell's November 20, 1984 speech, "The Importance of Art and Culture in World Transformation," presented at the World Service Forum and distributed by Lucis Trust. Lobell's wife, Mimi, an architect, designed a "Goddess Temple" with a labyrinth and ring of fire (upper level) symbolic of the conscious, and a lower level symbolic of the unconscious. In his speech, Lobell said, *"Most important modern architects have had spiritual issues as their primary concern, and there's sort of been a secularization of art history and of our culture that has kept that fact from us, almost as a conspiracy."* He quoted Ludwig Mies van der Rohe as saying, *"Architecture is the will of the age conceived in spiritual terms,"* and *"architecture is the battleground of the spirit."* Lobell explained that *"the Renaissance was a period of humanism. Humanism meaning the human being is the essentially important thing . . . unlike the Medieval period where God was essentially important. . . . Perspective is totally generated by the point of view of the viewer. . . . I am the measure . . . as in Palladio's Villa Rotunda. . . . Van Gogh could sit in a room and actually feel the forces, actually feel the table interacting with the floor . . . and that's the direction our consciousness is moving."*

Noted architect Louis Kahn talked about "order," and bringing buildings from the realm of potential into the realm of realization, from silence (in the mind) into light, philosophically like Lao-tzu's Taoism. Kahn's Salk Center near La Jolla, California, is designed with concentric circles, like Tibetan mandalas and the seven chakras. It's like a cathedral without a ceiling, which has its outer circle (with stairs, etc.) serving the body, the next inner circle (lab operations) serving the mind, the next inner circle (walkways) serving society, the next inner circle (the "studies") serving cultural activities, and the last inner circle (open space) serving the spirit. Kahn believed that people actually "experience" a building's "realization" when they enter it, and he said, *"In the end, the spirit of the building takes over . . . a work is made . . . and when the dust settles, the pyramid, echoing silence, gives the sun its shadow"* (symbolic language). One should pay close attention to these modern architectural philosophies when examining buildings today.

For example, a tall building has just been completed in a capitol city. The ominous-looking building has one large window at the top of each side, and the top of each window is in the shape of George Washington's "Rising Sun" chair, as is the front entrance of the building, as is the background for the final scene of Mozart's *The Magic Flute*. On the east side of the building where the large window faces the rising sun, there is a spiral staircase leading to the top floor which looks down on the floor below. Viewed from above, both the top of the building and the water fountain on the ground have a cross in the middle. From the front of the building, on the right side is an unnecessary structure that is in the shape of a Masonic master's station with four pillars. This same type of structure (but with an arch at the top) has just been added to the front right side of the state university library in the same capitol city.

●　●　●　●　●

In the mid-1980s, the World Policy Institute was preparing a 750-page curriculum guide endorsed by the

NEA, titled *Peace and World Order Studies*, for our schools. Not long afterward, the University of Denver's Center for Teaching International Relations (CTIR) developed *World Citizen Curriculum*, which *"recommends out-of-body experience as a way of visualizing the world without national boundaries,"* according to the *New York Times* magazine. CTIR also published a "death education" book, *Death: A Part of Life*, which contains "kamikaze" letters. Planetary Citizens proclaimed that it sought to "redesign education," and has as its pledge: "As a member of the planetary family of humanity, the good of the world community is my first concern." In an effort to further "the good of the world community," New Ager Jacques Cousteau was reported in the June 13, 1985 *Los Angeles Times* (about two weeks after President Reagan awarded him the Medal of Freedom) as having decided to devote the rest of his life to *"the compulsory exchange of children, at a relatively low age, seven to eight, or eight to nine,"* as the only way to avert nuclear annihilation.

If you're thinking Cousteau's suggestion would contribute to the breakup of the family, you might also remember that in *Many Missions* (1991), C.X. Larrabee wrote that the Research Triangle Institute of North Carolina and the Carolina Population Center *"took the position that effective population control relies on aspects of national development that offer greater incentives to have fewer children, incentives such as . . . a bigger role for women in the workplace. It's no accident that 'Integrated Population and Development Planning' was the name of a decade-long RTI/USAID project that provided technical assistance on policy analysis and planning to 50 countries in all regions of the developing world."*

Chapter Thirteen

Carnegie and
the Anita Hoge Story

Heavily involved in promoting "world order" and in reshaping education in 1985 as well as earlier was the Carnegie Corporation. For example, in 1914 Andrew Carnegie founded the Church Peace Union, which believes that the major religions hold in common certain religious and ethical principles and *"it works for the promotion through religion of international cooperation and the establishment of world order."* At the end of the First World War, James Shotwell became a founding member of Col. Edward House's "Inquiry" group planning the League of Nations. Shotwell became the Carnegie Endowment for International Peace's director of the Division of Economics and History. From that position, he was a leading planner of the U.N. Earlier he inspired the founding of the International Labor organization, and he developed the "abolition of war" concept of the Kellogg-Briand Pact.

But if "world order" were to be achieved through a type of "common thinking," it would be necessary to develop the "correct" mentality in youth. Therefore, in a book, *Human Relations in the Classroom, Course I,* published in 1947 by the Delaware State Society for

Mental Hygiene (with acknowledgments to the Supreme Council, Scottish Rite Masons, Northern Jurisdiction), one finds in the preface the following: *"In 1932, the president of the Carnegie Foundation for the Advancement of Teaching said to Dr. C.M. Hincks, distinguished psychiatrist, 'You, in the mental hygiene field are making little real progress with educators. . . . They need simple mental hygiene manuals.' "* The preface went on to say there was a need to preach *"positive mental hygiene principles to normal children in public schools."* One must wonder, if these children were already "normal," what were these "positive" mental hygiene principles they needed to be taught? Could they be the principles taught in "Project Read"?

In the late 1960s, the Carnegie Corporation funded "Project Read" used particularly by millions of children in "culturally deprived areas," and one of the books depicts step-by-step a man torching the porch of a shack, while one depicts a boy stealing a girl's purse. Commenting on this, Ellen Morphonios, prosecutor for Florida in its attorney-general's office and a chief of its criminal court division at the time, said that it is an insult to blacks to think the only way to communicate with their children is to show a robber or violence. She continued, *"It's like subliminal advertising. If this isn't subversive and deliberately done as part of a master plan . . . only a sick mind could have produced it."* Other pictures in the Carnegie-funded texts compare a flag with a rag, show people kneeling in a church praying beside a picture of a horse being taught to kneel, and show a boy throwing darts at a companion. Could it be that the man shooting darts at women in New York City in 1990 read these books and saw these pictures when he was a boy?

On May 16-17, 1970, all meetings (including medita-tions) of the Arcane School Conference were held in the Carnegie Endowment International Centre in New York. The Arcane School is with Lucis Trust (formerly Lucifer Press or Lucifer Publishing Co.).

In 1985, the Carnegie Corporation negotiated the Soviet-American Exchange Agreement (signed by CFR member Secretary of State George Shultz on November 21, 1985) that agreed to let the Soviets work with the United States in the development of curricula and teaching materials for elementary and secondary school children. That agreement, along with one succeeding it in 1988, also allowed the Soviets to *"put up statues of well-known Soviet cultural figures in American parks,"* and it allowed the exchange of police officers (see April 30, 1991 *Los Angeles Times* regarding exchange of Los Angeles and Leningrad police officers, and the June 14, 1991 *New York Times* regarding the exchange of New York and Moscow police officers). The first coordinator of the U.S.-Soviet Exchange Initiative was CFR member Stephen Rhinesmith, who has also been with the Aspen Institute for Humanistic Studies and the World Bank. Facilitating the new spirit of cooperation with the U.S.S.R. was the February 1-5, 1988, "Soviet-American Citizens' Summit" (Barbara Marx Hubbard was an organizer) held in Alexandria, Virginia, with a delegation of approxi-mately one hundred Soviets coordinated by the Soviet Peace Committee (SPC). According to a 1985 State Department report on Soviet "Active Measures," the SPC is linked to the Soviet Central Committee's International Department, which was created by Stalin to carry out subversion within other countries. Interesting is the fact that the education task force at the summit recommended that the National Education Association (NEA) guide a global computer program. Just think of it — the NEA in charge of a global computer program with the approval of Soviets coordinated by the subversive SPC!

Not only had Carnegie been instrumental in the Soviet-American Exchange Agreement, but they had also persuaded the National Governors' Association (when Lamar Alexander was chairman in 1986) to endorse the principle of state takeovers of local schools (removing locally elected school boards and administrators) which did not meet certain state educational standards. In a report titled, "Teaching as a Profession — Teachers for the Twenty-first Century," Carnegie called for the establishment of the National Board for Professional Teaching Standards, which would nationally certify teachers, and in the 1988 annual report from the Carnegie Corporation of New York, it lists grants of nine hundred thousand dollars to the generally liberal Brookings Institution; six hundred fifty thousand dollars to the Aspen Institute for Humanistic Studies; three hundred three thousand dollars to the Alan Guttmacher Institute (affiliated with Planned Parenthood) to look at sex education and the impact of AIDS on this education in the U.S.; two hundred thousand dollars to the Center for Population Options for a "Support Center for School-Based Clinics"; two hundred thousand dollars to the American Civil Liberties Union; two hundred thousand dollars to Parliamentarians Global Action for Disarmament, Development, and World Reform; and one hundred thousand dollars to

People for the American Way (these are examples of the use of philanthropy as social change agentry).

Also in 1988, the February issue of *Education Reporter* reported that Ernest Boyer (CFR member), president of the Carnegie Foundation for the Advancement of Teaching, said the following startling things the month before in Washington, D.C. He said that schools should no longer be seen as academic centers but should be turned into "social service centers," that school-based health clinics should be combined with daycare facilities, and that schools should assume the responsibility for feeding students all three meals since they would be in the school building from seven a.m. to six-thirty p.m.

Probably oblivious to the fact that something cannot be "voluntary" if it is "required," Boyer earlier had said in his book, *High School* (1983), that *"we* [Carnegie Foundation for the Advancement of Teaching] *recommend that every high school student complete a service requirement — a new 'Carnegie Unit' — involving volunteer work in the community or at school. . . . The goal of service in the schools is to teach values — to help all students understand that to be fully human one must serve."* Malachi Martin in *The Keys of This Blood* also identifies Boyer as one of the "transnationalists," and he stated that *"their formula for education was summed up by Boyer, who said schools must possess an 'understanding of a new global agenda' and must reform their curricula so as to communicate that agenda to their students."*

It was obvious Carnegie organizations wanted to direct the future of American education and society as well. Marc Tucker had been an associate director of the National Institute of Education (part of the federal government) in

Washington, D.C., and then went to the Carnegie Forum (later, National Center) on Education and the Economy. Tucker then returned for a meeting at the National Institute of Education where I was in attendance, and he was quite critical of the speaker, Henry Levin of Stanford University, for the speaker's lack of perspective that we should be shaping our own future rather than simply meeting the educational and other needs of society as they naturally occur.

At this point, it might be useful to give several examples of what is, in effect, a kind of "revolving door" between Carnegie and the U.S. Department of Education. Tucker, mentioned above, had come to the National Institute of Education (NIE, part of the U.S. Department of Education) from the Northwest Regional Laboratory, which was funded by NIE. He became an associate director of NIE before leaving to become executive director of the Carnegie Forum on Education and the Economy. Another individual, Gary Sykes, who worked across the hall from me at NIE, went to Stanford University, which was then given eight hundred fifteen thousand dollars by the Carnegie Corporation of New York to develop a means of assessing teachers for national certification. Down the hall from me at NIE was Michael Cohen, who left and directed a project on "Restructuring the Education System: Agenda for the '90s" for the National Governors' Association Center for Policy Research. The project was given six hundred ninety-one thousand dollars by Carnegie in 1988, and in part helped implement the recommendations of the Carnegie Forum's report, "A Nation Prepared: Teachers for the Twenty-first Century." After leaving office, the

U.S. secretary of education, Terrel Bell, accepted a position on the board of the Carnegie Corporation. And former CFR member and U.S. Commissioner of Education Francis Keppel, along with former NIE Deputy Director Michael Timpane (now president of Columbia University Teachers College) were two of the three individuals leading conferences at Teachers College for reassessing the federal role in education, which was given seventy-five thousand dollars by Carnegie in 1988. (Francis Keppel's father, Frederick, had been dean of Columbia College earlier, and later became president of the Carnegie Corporation.) The 1988 annual report of the Carnegie Corporation in New York also showed that another seventy-five thousand dollars was given to the Institute for Educational Leadership for a project under the direction of Harold Hodgkinson, who had previously been director of NIE.

• • • • •

Perhaps the most important connections, though, between the Carnegie Foundation for the Advancement of Teaching (CFAT) and the U.S. Department of Education (including a supercomputer) is found in a new book, *Educating for the "New World Order"* (1991), by B.K. Eakman. In this new book, Eakman suspensefully details incidents and information leading to a supercomputer, Elementary and Secondary Integrated Data Systems (the ESIDS), brought on-line by the U.S. Department of Education in 1988. The author, who used to be a liaison to the U.S. Department of Education, knows whereof she speaks and describes the ominous threat that this computer system poses to every American's right to privacy.

The story begins simply enough with a complaint filed by Anita Hoge against the Pennsylvania state education agency for administering a test, the Educational Quality Assessment, to her son without parental permission. After seeing that the test asked questions such as under what circumstances would her son throw rocks at windows, Mrs. Hoge found that the purpose of the EQA curriculum her son was taking was *"to discourage transmittal of certain attitudes held by parents."* Pressing further, she found that the teacher's edition of the curriculum alluded to ten quality goals of eduction "that reflect NAEP objectives." But what was NAEP? she wondered.

This is where in the book one begins to learn of the fascinating connection between the federal Department of Education and the Carnegie Foundation for the Advancement of Teaching. Through her investigation, Mrs. Hoge found out that the creators of NAEP (National Assessment of Educational Progress) were among the same people who created the EQA. Digging further, she learned that because the Carnegie Foundation had quite a few of its leaders on the board of the Educational Testing Service, it "virtually owned" the college boards (SATs), the National Teachers' Exam, and NAEP, all of which were administered by ETS. After the ten quality goals had been in effect for a while, since the 1960s, ETS began to work in 1975 with Terrel Bell *"to get the whole business moving according to a specific timetable."*

Ralph Tyler, who had been president of the Carnegie Foundation and defined education as *"a process of changing behavior patterns,"* undertook the major part of designing NAEP (created by Francis Keppel). In George Henderson's *Introduction to American Education* (1978), one reads that, *"there are those who charge that the people chosen by the Carnegie Corporation to develop the objectives of national assessment were no more qualified for that task than were numerous others, of perhaps different perspectives. One critic has charged that the program has been characterized by elements of secrecy on the part of those responsible for its formation, casting a shadow of doubt upon it from its conception."*

Tyler was also a principle designer of the EQA, and his mentor was the Estonian "change agent" psychologist Hilda Taba. Her work has been followed by such programs as "Tactics for Thinking" by Robert Marzano, director of research at one of the U.S. Department of Education-funded laboratories (McRel). According to Eakman's book, McRel is also the lab from whence came the Robert Muller School's World Core Curriculum, which is based upon the teachings of occultist Alice Bailey. Perhaps most of the psycho-behavioral programs in our schools were researched and developed at the U.S. Department of Education's labs and centers thanks to Title IV of the Elementary and Secondary Education Act of 1965, and ESEA was largely crafted by men like Ralph Tyler, John Gardner, and Francis Keppel, all former Carnegie Foundation (CFAT) presidents. Eakman writes that *"CFAT and their proxies in federal and state governments co-control three computer banks of test result data — including personal, non-academic information, opinions, and attitudes — which in 1988-89 were integrated into one large, supercomputer: the Elementary and Secondary Integrated Data System (the ESIDS)."* Anita Hoge noted that the ESIDS would be linked to individuals' social security numbers, and alarm bells went off because this should not be allowed under Section 7 of the Public Law 93-579, the Privacy Acts of 1974.

Former U.S. Senator Sam Ervin (D-NC) and Attorney-General Elliot Richardson in 1974 became very concerned over the potential abuse of the social security number in federal data banks. Senator Ervin had become outraged at many of the behavioral-attitudinal learning programs being disseminated by the National Diffusion Network of HEW, calling it *"the biggest scandal in the history of the United States."* He co-sponsored Amendment 1289 to Senate Bill 1539 which, he said, *"would prevent schools from making guinea pigs out of children and delving into their personal attitudes and privileged information about their families, as has been done in schools throughout the United States."* After he was named to the Watergate Committee, though, his legislative assistant, Anne Sullivan, started to complain that some of the documentation he'd been collecting started "disappearing" from his office and was never found.

Success did occur, though, in 1978 when Senator Orrin Hatch (R-UT) was successful in passing the Protection of Pupil Rights Amendment (PPRA), using such examples as *"an ESEA—sponsored program which actually had the students of an elementary school class collectively put their parents on trial — following which the mother and father were always found guilty."* The PPRA was used by Anita Hoge as the basis for her complaint, and she finally heard April 18, 1990 from U.S. Senator Arlen Specter's office that she had won, with the Education Department and Justice Department acknowledging that the EQA was a psychological test, that federal funding had been involved, and that areas protected by the PPRA had been violated. Then, Eakman writes, *"all those other letters forwarded earlier on by Arlen Specter's office would prove conclusively that officials at the highest levels of government had been lying for three years when they denied the charges earlier."* However, in December 1990, a U.S. Department of Education official notified Anita Hoge that the statute of limitations had run out on her complaint, and the investigation was therefore closed.

Thus, the threat to Americans' privacy still looms. Eakman describes how a National Institute of Education (part of the federal government) 1981 working paper, "Measuring the Quality of Education," makes absolutely clear the connections between CFAT, ETS, and NAEP, *"along with the work toward a centralized computer bank and the funding arrangement to make it all happen."* The document states that *"achievement data are not the primary focus of the studies, which also collect data on educational attainment, student characteristics and attitudes, parent attitudes, and school programs."* The data base for the supercomputer will include pupil files containing personal information about "home environment and family characteristics," which will be linked to personnel files on teachers, etc., and everyone can be tracked from kindergarten into the job force. Eakman states that *"NAEP is not about mere academic testing, but, rather, is a first step toward a permanent, interlinkable dossier and data bank on the nation's citizens — and a way of imposing a national curriculum."*

The Washington Post had reported on May 11, 1986, that *"while the federal government could not require a state to computerize its records, it could craft its regulation in such a way as to make it prohibitively expensive or impossible for states to meet federal requirements unless they did so."* This fulfilled what Walcott Beatty in 1969 had written in *Improving Educational Assessment and an Inventory of Measures of Affective Behavior* that *"federal funding for schools would hinge on data collection at the local level and that the use of NAEP objectives in obtaining this data was important."* Why didn't someone in the U.S. Department of Education blow the whistle on all this? The author of this insightful book asserts that *"such whistle-blowing is the exception in government rather than the rule. One can easily jeopardize a career — and maybe even one's life — by too much prying or outspokenness in the wrong place at the wrong time."*

Concerning what NAEP is doing with the data it has collected, Eakman refers to a highly placed source within NAEP itself as revealing that data is being sold to just about any domestic or international group billing itself as a research organization. The implications are ominous, according to the author — *"personal and attitudinal information (which, again, tends to reflect the parents' views), gathered over many years of the child's school life, may soon determine, if it hasn't already, whether an otherwise qualified student is accepted or rejected by the college of his/her choice, whether the student is turned down for employment, whether a person is later passed over for a promotion."*

What type of mentality is behind this? Eakman contends that it is a controlling elite of education futurists who favor such things as global education and who see to it that people with the "right attitude" are selected for leadership positions. A key to their control over education personnel was the Behavioral Science Teacher Educational Project (B-STEP) published in 1967 by the U.S. Office of Education, which stated as one of its goals *"the development of a new kind of elementary school teacher who . . . engages in teaching as a clinical practice . . . and functions as a responsible agent of social change."* The whole of page 253 of the document B-STEP is devoted to an intended manipulation of the media.

Toward the end of Eakman's book, she notes that in 1978 the GAO published a report, "Questions Persist about Federal Support for Development of Curriculum Materials and Behavior Modification Techniques Used in Local Schools," but Ernest Boyer (current CFAT president) was the U.S. commissioner of education. Why didn't anyone ask if this was a conflict of interest? The author concludes her very readable and worthwhile book by noting that angry parents and activists are calling on the Administration, Congress, or the states to, among other things, revoke CFAT's charter and shut down the Department of Education's labs and centers.

In Laura Rogers' article, "In Loco Parentis" (*Chronicles*, February 1991), she also describes a program where children are given a computer code number so that they can be tracked the rest of their lives. The program is the federally-funded "Parents as Teachers," now in about forty states, where a "parent educator" is assigned to the home and bonds with the family. A battery of tests are administered, free services are offered, and the "parent educator" must legally report any "suspected" child abuse, such as if the parents "refuse to take recommended services." The program also receives state tax dollars and funding from the Ford, Carnegie, New World, Rockefeller, and other foundations. The program should be fully implemented by about 1995 and cost seventy-five to one hundred billion dollars. The Education Commission of the States has also announced eight spinoff programs with different names but similar goals.

• • • • •

Elsewhere desiring to direct education and nations on a global scale, on October 13-14, 1989, at a conference co-sponsored by the Wichita State University "War and Peace Group" and "Global Learning Center," Gerald and Patricia Mische (founders of Global Education Associates in 1973 and authors of *Toward a Human World Order*) spoke on topics such as "Global Transformation and World Order," "Economic Dimensions of World Order," and "Religions and World Order."

Regarding higher education, the Council on Learning conducted a "Global Awareness" survey among college students, which Victoria Sackett and Jeffrey Salmon described in "Shaping Undergraduates' World View: Global Disinformation" (*Public Opinion*, February/March 1982) as *"merely a small part of a larger effort to restructure the whole of undergraduate curricula so that it will reflect the Council on Learning's view of the world,"* which the authors characterized as *"the United States should reject sovereignty in favor of an interdependent relationship with the world."* The problem with this type of attitude on the part of the planners for the New World Order is that the United States is not simply a national entity, but it stands for Judeo-Christian moral absolute principles, and certain cherished ideals such as freedom, which many other countries do not have. Our moral absolutes have been undermined for years, however, as Allan Bloom describes in *The Closing of the American Mind* (1987): *"There is now an entirely new language of good and evil, originating in an attempt to get 'beyond good and evil' and preventing us from talking with any conviction about good and evil anymore. . . . The new language is that of value relativism, and it constitutes a change in our view of things moral and political as great as the one that took place when Christianity replaced Greek and Roman paganism."*

Students no longer had the biblical moral standards taught them by their parents constantly reinforced in the American public schools, and the 1985 edition of the popular "Family Life" textbook *Contemporary Living* stated that *"if you follow the guidance of your parents, you might risk the criticism of your peers. The best approach is to try to combine family and peer influence."* Instead, students were being instructed in humanistic world values so that they could become "world citizens," and in the January 1990 edition of *Education News* in the state of Washington, one reads that *"an increasing number of teachers in our public schools are taking the opportunity to teach students to expand the vision of their role as citizens of the world."* And where did these teachers in the state of Washington come up with this "vision"? One possibility is that at Western Washington University, Prof. Philip Vander Velde taught a course called "Foundations of Education" to prospective teachers using a textbook he co-authored titled *Global Mandate: Pedagogy for Peace* (1985). Teachers graduating from this university are sought by schools across the nation, and in this textbook they have been told: *"Men may cling to much of the language and symbolism of old creeds — secular and religious — but unless a new faith . . . overcomes the old ideologies and creates planetary synthesis, world government is doomed. . . . Citizenship education, found in every respectable nation claiming to be civilized, is replete with curricula through which it teaches its citizens chauvinism, patriotism, and nationalism: the by-products of a world view which pits man against his fellow human beings. . . . Nation-states have outlived their usefulness, and a new world order is necessary if we are to live in harmony with each other. . . . The task of re-ordering our traditional values and institutions should be one of the major educational objectives of our schools. . . . A new political order of control over human relationships will come into being. This clearly implies that a national sovereignty, which is the basis of the current nation-state system . . . can be whittled away."* The same year as this textbook was published, there appeared a memo dated April 19, 1985, on Seattle public schools stationery from "Jim Grob, Rockefeller Project," which cautioned that *"the term 'global education' is an extreme, political hot potato at this time"* with "right-wing Christian groups" opposing its use, and that instead of using the term "global education," district personnel should note that a *"temporarily safe term is — multicultural/international curriculum development."* (This was the year after the superintendant of education for the state of Washington issued a technical assistance handbook titled *School District Implementation of Multicultural Education*, which included the notorious, "Man: a Course of Study," or MACOS, that contained cannibalism.) New Agers use the same tactic to hide what they are doing in schools. Jack Canfield and Paula Klimek in "Education in the New Age" (*New Age*, February 1978) wrote that *"centering can also be extended into work with meditation in the classroom. (Advice: If you're teaching in a public school, don't call it meditation, call it 'centering.' Every school wants children to be relaxed, attentive, and creative, and that's what they will get.)"*

On the September 29, 1988 edition of "Nightline," host Ted Koppel (who has been a CFR member) referred to nationalism as a "virus." Soviet Foreign Affairs Minister Boris Pankin did likewise at the U.N. on September 24, 1991. Remember here that *The City of Man* in 1941 referred to "the heresy of nationalism," and Nelson Rockefeller referred to "the fever of nationalism" in his 1962 book, *The Future of Federalism*.

Concluding this chapter on Carnegie and psychological testing, I will relate my own personal experience. Carnegie provided half the funds for the 1963 Governor's School (NC), the first of its kind in the nation. I and 399 others there as exceptional high school students were given an extensive battery of tests, including the Minnesota Multiphasic Personality Inventory. A place for our names was on this test of 771 True-False items, such as "I believe in the worth of humanity, but not of God," "One of the most important things children should learn is when to disobey authority," and "In illegitimate pregnancies, abortion is in many cases the most reasonable alternative." I was a guinea pig! The Carnegie Corporation and Ford Foundation also financed ECAPE (Exploratory Committee on Assessing the Progress of Education), the forerunner of NAEP, beginning in 1966.

Chapter Fourteen

The Council on Foreign Relations, the Atlantic Union, and the Trilateral Commission

Concerning the CFR view of the world, syndicated columnist Edith Kermit Roosevelt (granddaughter of President Theodore Roosevelt) wrote in the *Indianapolis News* (December 23, 1961) that they think *"the best way to fight communism is by a one world socialist state governed by 'experts' like themselves. The result has been policies which favor . . . gradual surrender of United States sovereignty to the United Nations."*

Prior to America's entrance into the Second World War, the Council on Foreign Relations' journal, *Foreign Affairs*, ran advertisements for Clarence Streit's *Union Now: A Proposal for a Federal Union of the Leading Democracies* (1939). In 1939, Streit, the former Fabian Rhodes Scholar and *New York Times* correspondent at the League of Nations, founded the Association to Unite the Democracies (incorporated in 1940 as Federal Union). And by the 1980s, the organization would boast such directors as Speaker of the House James Wright, Jr., and a former director Barbara Marx Hubbard (New Ager).

At the end of the Second World War, in the CFR's *Foreign Affairs* (July 1948), Sir Harold Butler wrote "A

New World Takes Shape," in which he stated: *"How far can the life of nations, which for centuries have thought of themselves as distinct and unique, be merged with the life of other nations? How far are they prepared to sacrifice a part of their sovereignty without which there can be no effective economic or political union? . . . Out of the prevailing confusion a new world is taking shape . . . which may point the way toward the new order. . . . The breath of a new spirit is beginning to reanimate it. . . . It will abjure war except in defense of freedom itself. That will be the beginning of a real United Nations, no longer crippled by a split personality, but held together by a common faith."*

Other renowned non-CFR members believed that ideas such as Butler's did not go far enough, and in the same year as Butler's article (1948), the University of Chicago Press published *Preliminary Draft of a World Constitution*, produced by Robert Hutchins, Mortimer Adler, Rexford Tugwell, and others. It advocated regional federation on the way toward world federation or government, with England incorporated into a European federation. Believing that the U.N. Security Council was paralyzed, the world constitution provided for a more efficient "World Council," along with a "Chamber of Guardians" to enforce world law. One commentator said the draft *"does not contain a single paragraph that would run counter to socialism."* The constitution's preamble contained the words, *"the governments of the nations have decided to order their separate sovereignties in one government of justice, to which they surrender their arms; and to establish, as they do establish, this constitution as the covenant and fundamental law of the Federal Republic of the World.*" The constitution itself also provided the world government with sweeping powers such as *"the appropriation, under the right of eminent domain, of such private or public property as may be necessary for federal use."*

On February 17, 1950, a prominent member of the CFR and a co-founder of the United World Federalists (now known as the World Federalist Association, perhaps the foremost organization today working for world federal government), James P. Warburg (son of former Federal Reserve banker Paul Warburg), told a U.S. Senate Foreign Relations Subcommittee: *"We shall have world government, whether or not we like it . . . by consent or by conquest."*

Just a few days earlier, on February 9, Senate Concurrent Resolution 66 was introduced into the Foreign Relations Subcommittee of the Senate, and it begins, *"Whereas, in order to achieve universal peace and justice, the present Charter of the United Nations should be changed to provide a true world government constitution."* The document was prepared by the same Robert Hutchins, Mortimer Adler, Rexford Tugwell, and others, and the resolution was introduced into the full Senate on September 13, 1949 by Senator Glen Taylor of Idaho. Senator Alexander Wiley of Wisconsin called it *"a consummation devoutly to be wished for,"* and said, *"I understand your proposition is either change the United Nations, or change or create, by a separate convention, a world order."* Senator Taylor later said, *"We would have to sacrifice considerable sovereignty to the world organization to enable them to levy taxes in their own right to support themselves."*

At about the same time as these hearings were taking place, CFR member Dean Acheson as U.S. secretary of state was directing the drafting of the infamous National Security Council Document Number 68. This was formally known as "The Report of the Secretaries of State and Defense on 'United States Objectives and Programs for National Security,' April 7, 1950." Acheson had been a member of Yale University's secret Scroll and Key society, and even before the U.S.S.R. was recognized by the United States, he was representing Bolshevik interests in this country. He addressed the Soviet-American Friendship Society, and assisted Alger Hiss in obtaining a high government position. He was so bad that on December 15, 1950, the Republicans of the U.S. House of Representatives voted unanimously that he should be removed from office. However, on April 12 of that year (two months before the start of the Korean War), President Truman wrote a letter to the National Security Council requesting *"further information on the implications of the conclusions"* of NSC-68 which was stamped "top secret." Truman would later order: *"It is my desire that no publicity be given to this report or its contents without my approval."* The basic details of the document were that the United States and its allies would simply try to deter Soviet aggression and engage in counteractions only to contain them. NSC-68 stated: *". . . We must with our allies . . . seek to create a world society based on the principle of consent. . . . In 'containment' it is desirable to exert pressure in a fashion which will avoid, so far as possible, directly challenging Soviet prestige, to keep open the possibility for the U.S.S.R. to retreat before pressure with a minimum loss of face."*

It was probably from this type of thinking that both the Korean and Vietnam Wars, in which tens of thousands of American soldiers lost their lives, were "no-win" wars by design from the outset! In May 1951, the acclaimed publisher of *U.S.A.* magazine, Alice Widener, had an exclusive private interview with General Douglas MacArthur, in which the general revealed: *"Always in war when I visited my wounded in the hospital, I could look them in the eye, no matter what their condition or how tragic their wounds, knowing that our country had backed them to the hilt. But when I went to see my Korean wounded, I just couldn't look them in the eye, knowing that they had been forced to fight with one hand tied behind their backs. . . . I am convinced I was restrained in Korea by some secret Administration policy directive or strategy about which I was not informed."*

On November 6, 1953, U.S. Attorney-General Herbert Brownell indicated that CFR member Harry Dexter White's spying activities for the Soviets had been revealed to the White House by the FBI as early as 1945, yet President Truman after that nominated White to be executive director for the U.S. International Monetary Fund, of which White and John Maynard Keynes were the primary architects.

Also in 1953, John J. McCloy became chairman of the CFR and of Chase Manhattan Bank. He has been an intimate advisor to presidents from Ronald Reagan back to Franklin Roosevelt, and under FDR he was assistant to Secretary of War Henry L. Stimson, who was a founder of the CFR. Stimson was also a member of Skull and Bones in 1888, and when George Bush was tapped to be a member in the spring of 1947, he found *"none other than Colonel Stimson, there to initiate a new class into the society's mysteries and rituals"* (*Newsweek*, August 20, 1990). While Stimson was FDR's secretary of war, he questioned *"whether anyone in the Administration ever acted without having a word with McCloy."*

McCloy was the force behind the lend-lease program that gave fifteen billion dollars to Soviet dictator Josef Stalin. McCloy was also a primary figure behind the firings of General George Patton and, later, General Douglas MacArthur. McCloy became president of the World Bank in 1947, and U.S. commissioner in Germany in 1949 where he had almost dictatorial powers and influenced the establishment of what would become the Common Market (later the European Economic Community). He was the architect of the European postwar reconstruction "Marshall Plan" (General George C. Marshall was a Mason), and later became head of the Ford Foundation in the United States.

In Malachi Martin's *The Keys of This Blood* (1990), the author states that *"no one was a greater champion than McCloy with the fervent faith that the nations can be unerringly guided to a new world order — provided that talented and visionary globalists themselves design, install, and maintain a controlled balance among the nations that deal in raw power. . . . He originated many of the 'New World Order' projects as chairman of the Ford Foundation. "*(The reader should remember here Norman Dodd's quotation of H. Rowan Gaither, when Mr. Dodd was director of research for the Reece Committee in the U.S. House of Representatives, and Mr. Gaither was president of the Ford Foundation in 1953. Mr. Gaither told Mr. Dodd that most of the foundation's personnel had worked for the OSS, the State Department, or the European Economic Administration, and that during those times they operated *"under directives from the White House to so alter life in America as to make possible a comfortable merger with the Soviet Union."*)

Malachi Martin, in his book, continued to describe how the New World Order would come about: *"The father of the new world order is to be the interdependence of nations. Its mother is to be that peculiarly modern process called international development. It is to be midwifed by the entrepreneur, the banker, the technocrat, the scientist, and, ultimately, the lawyer. It is to be born between the printed sheets of compacts and agreements; joint ventures and mergers; contracts and covenants and international treaties signed and countersigned by the political bureaucrat, and sealed with the stamp of united nations."*

In 1936, McCloy sat in Hitler's Olympics box, and in 1956 he invited a young Henry Kissinger to join a task force on U.S.-Soviet relations. It was McCloy who was largely responsible for the U.S. government's agreement not to overthrow Fidel Castro after the 1962 Cuban Missile Crisis. The essence of the agreement was that in exchange for Soviet withdrawal of offensive missiles from Cuba, the U.S. would agree not to attempt another overthrow of Castro. But I would suggest that this is what the Soviets expected all along! With nuclear missiles on submarines off the American coast, offensive missiles in Cuba were not critical to the Soviets. What they expected all along was the guarantee (provided by McCloy, et al) that the U.S. would not overthrow Castro, and therefore Cuba could be used as a base for training revolutionaries in

Latin America, Africa, etc. What evidence is there for this conclusion? According to CFR member Graham Allison of Harvard University in his book, *Essence of Decision* (1971), *"Missile deployment and evidence of Soviet actions toward detente poses an apparent contradiction"*; the Soviets knew of American U-2 flights over Cuba, yet the missiles were left uncamouflaged; the Soviets didn't coordinate installation of the medium-range ballistic missiles with the completion of the surface-to-air missile covers; the Soviets had never before placed missiles in any nation beyond its borders, not even in its satellites in East Europe. Cuba could have expelled the Soviets as Egypt had done, and the U.S. had already attempted one invasion and would certainly succeed with a second one if it were well-planned. In late January 1989, Sergei Khrushchev (son of Nikita) admitted, *"Even in event of an American invasion or air strike, Soviet officials in Cuba had no orders to use the missiles."* The Soviets' secretive method of transporting the missiles to Cuba was to avoid an American quarantine or surgical air strike, but once there, the deal could be made that the Soviets planned for all along.

In Walter Isaacson's and Evan Thomas' *The Wise Men* (1986), there is a photo of CFR chairman McCloy swimming with Soviet dictator Nikita Khrushchev at the Black Sea in late July 1961. Both are smiling, and Khrushchev has his arm around McCloy, who is wearing swim trunks loaned to him by Khrushchev. McCloy was also a member of the Warren Commission that investigated the assassination of President Kennedy, and he was a senior partner in a Wall Street law firm whose clients included the Rockefeller family and all of Big Oil's "Seven

Sisters." He was behind the creation of OPEC, and was chairman of the CFR through 1970 (succeeded by David Rockefeller). Finally, he was an honorary trustee of the Aspen Institute for Humanistic Studies, and a longtime friend of Jean Monnet (banker who was the architect of the Common Market).

In 1958, the "Rockefeller Panel Reports" on page 34, included the statement that *"the U.N. stands, finally, as a symbol of the world order that will one day be built."* The next year, CFR member James Warburg's *The West in Crisis* was published, proclaiming that *"a world order without world law is an anachronism . . . a world which fails to establish the rule of law over the nation-states cannot long continue to exist. We are living in a perilous period of transition from the era of the fully sovereign nation-state to the era of world government . . . [and] a deliberate search for methods and means by which American children may best be educated into . . . responsible citizens not merely of the United States but of the world."* On November 25 of the same year (1959), the CFR published "Study No. 7" which advocated: *"Build a new international order [which] must be responsive to world aspirations for peace, [and] for social and economic change . . . an international order . . . including states [nations] labeling themselves as 'socialist' [communist]."*

In 1960, a study titled "The Technical Problems of Arms Control" was conducted for the Institute for International Order, and among those conducting the study were Jerome Weisner (CFR member who would become President Kennedy's top aide on science), Brock Chisholm (former head of the World Health Organization), and Arthur Larsen (director of the World Rule of

Law Center and law professor at Duke University). Weisner recommended that to insure compliance with official disarmament arrangements, an "international intelligence network" be developed which could "recruit and train competent secret agents" to find any resistance. In addition, those conducting the study recommended that in order for an arms control inspection system to be developed into "a system of enforced world law," there should be research on developing informants and how to extort information from "key people" using drugs, hypnosis, and polygraphs.

Then in the early years of the Kennedy administration, the State Department (led by CFR member Dean Rusk) in 1961 published Document No. 7277 titled, "Freedom from War: The U.S. Program for General and Complete Disarmament in a Peaceful World," which described how the nations of the world could be disarmed in three phases, and the U.N. could be armed, with the last phase, *"where no state would have the military power to challenge the progressively strengthened U.N. Peace Force."* This same year, the *New York Times* on August 16 editorialized that *"we must seek to discourage anti-communist revolts in order to avert bloodshed and war. We must, under our own principles, live with evil even if by doing so we help to stabilize tottering communist regimes, as in East Germany, and perhaps even expose citadels of freedom, like West Berlin, to slow death by strangulation."* The chairman of the board of the *New York Times* at that time was CFR member Arthur Hays Sulzberger, and the president and publisher was CFR member Orvil Dryfoos (the newspaper was later passed on to CFR member Arthur Ochs Sulzberger). Alfred

Ochs had purchased the newspaper in 1896 with the backing of J.P. Morgan, Rothschild agent August Belmont, and Jacob Schiff of Kuhn, Loeb & Co.

In the January 16, 1962 issue of *Look* magazine, the late Israeli Prime Minister David Ben-Gurion said, *"In Jerusalem, the United Nations, a truly United Nations, will build a Shrine of the Prophets to serve the federated union of all continents. . . ."* This was the same year that the State Department and Defense Department (led by CFR member Robert McNamara) financed a study by CFR member Lincoln Bloomfield, titled "A World Effectively Controlled by the United Nations," which included: *". . . if the communist dynamic was greatly abated, the West might lose whatever incentive it has for world government."*

The world planners could not allow that to happen, and in the same year of 1962, Harvard University Press published CFR member Nelson Rockefeller's *The Future of Federalism*, in which the future presidential candidate would exclaim that current events compellingly demanded "a new world order," as the old order was already crumbling, and there was *"a new and free order struggling to be born."* Note here that in President Bush's September 11, 1990, address to Congress, the president will say *"a new world order can emerge . . . that new world is struggling to be born."* These and other remarks by President Bush seem strikingly similar to the statements and concepts in Nelson Rockefeller's *The Future of Federalism*, which proclaims that there is a *"fever of nationalism . . . [but] the nation-state is becoming less and less competent to perform its international political tasks. . . . These are some of the reasons pressing us to lead vigorously toward the true building of a new world order . . .* [with] *voluntary service . . . and our dedicated faith in the brotherhood of all mankind. . . . Sooner perhaps than we may realize . . . there will evolve the basis for a federal structure of the free world. "*Remember here that in Col. House's *Philip Dru: Administrator* (1912), he wrote: *"Thus Dru had formulated and put in motion an international policy, which, if adhered to in good faith, would bring about the comity of nations, a lasting and beneficent peace, and the acceptance of the principle of the brotherhood of man."* Supreme Court Justice William O. Douglas described Rockefeller's volume as a *"plea for a 'new world order' with the United States taking the lead in fashioning a new federalism at the world level."* Americans for Democratic Action international director David Williams had written in the February 1959 issue of *The Progressive* that if Nelson Rockefeller *"escaped the limitations of his own party"* and *"tapped fresh resources of power,"* he might make an acceptable president of left liberal standards. In *The Intelligent Socialist's Guide to America*, Williams had said that ADA *"operates very much as the early Fabian Society did, seeking to permeate existing parties."*

It had always been a favorite tactic of the Fabians to "educate" the offspring of prominent families, and in Rose Martin's *Fabian Freeway*, one reads: *"Nelson Rockefeller seems to have been exposed to such psychological seduction since childhood. As a boy he attended the experimental Lincoln School, together with three of his brothers, Winthrop, Laurance, and David. The Lincoln School was operated by Columbia University's School of Education, then dominated by the ideas of*

John Dewey, father of so-called progressive education and a president of the Fabian Socialist League for Industrial Democracy"(formerly called the Intercollegiate Socialist Society). In addition, one finds in Jules Abel's *The Rockefeller Billions* (1967) just how disastrous the "progressive education" of the Lincoln School was, as he related: *"Laurance gives startling confirmation as to 'Why Johnnie Can't Read.' He says that the Lincoln School did not teach him to read and write as he wishes he now could. Nelson, today, admits that reading for him is a 'slow and torturous process' that he does not enjoy doing but compels himself to do. This is significant evidence in the debate that has raged about modern educational techniques."*

When founding member of the CFR John Foster Dulles died in 1959, President Dwight Eisenhower (CFR member) replaced him as U.S. secretary of state with CFR member Christian Herter (thirty-third degree Mason). Eisenhower had said, *"If we got effective political union of the Atlantic, we could cut our defense costs by half,"* and Herter, like many other CFR members, had promoted during the 1950s and then into the 1960s a bilateral federation of America and Europe called "The Atlantic Union." In 1963, Herter wrote *Toward an Atlantic Community* regarding this proposed federation, which he further explained in "Atlantica," in the January 1963 issue of the CFR journal, *Foreign Affairs*. Through lobbying efforts by the Atlantic Union Committee and its successor, the Atlantic Council, several bills were actually introduced in Congress to bring about this federation of Europe and America, probably as a stepping stone toward an eventual world federation, which unlike the confederation would demand that its member nations relinquish much of their sovereignty to the world government.

● ● ● ● ●

At this time, it is probably worthwhile to look more closely at the effort to bring about a federal union of the NATO countries under an Atlantic union. This is not only because quite a few CFR members were involved, including current President George Bush, but also because the communists had a similar plan which they specified in their 1936 Communist International. Their three-stage plan for world goverment was:

1. Socialize the economies of all nations
2. Bring about federal unions of various groupings of these socialized nations
3. Amalgamate the regional unions into a world union of socialist states

One should remember here that Mikhail Gorbachev recently suggested that NATO should become more of a political than military entity.

Ever since about 1940, Clarence Streit has been promoting the idea of a federal union basically for the countries that make up NATO today. Streit indicated that he had the private support of President Roosevelt for this idea, and in 1949 Senator Estes Kefauver introduced a resolution on behalf of Streit's Atlantic Union Committee that proposed a convention be called to discuss plans for world government beginning with the

NATO countries. The resolution failed, and about this time Atlantic Union Committee president Owen J. Roberts (former Supreme Court Justice) testified that *"in joining the Atlantic Union, the U.S. government would have to surrender its rights and powers to coin money, to levy taxes and tariffs, to regulate immigration, to enact citizenship laws, to declare war, and to maintain standing armies"* (see testimony of Myra Hacker in July 1971 to the House Committee on Foreign Affairs regarding House Concurrent Resolutions 163 and 164, "Atlantic Union Delegation").

In 1951, Clarence Streit was in the intelligence service and had a talk off the record with General Dwight Eisenhower, who expressed his support for a "political union in the Atlantic." In 1956, Senator Kefauver again presented a resolution (SJR 12) regarding an Atlantic Union. Then in 1960, with over half of the members of the Altantic Union Committee also members of the CFR and promoting the concept of a federal Atlantic Union, Senate Joint Resolution 170 passed and was signed by CFR member President Eisenhower on September 9, 1960. Atlantic Union Committee treasurer Elmo Roper delivered an address titled "The Goal Is Government of All the World," in which he said: *"For it becomes clear that the first step toward world government cannot be completed until we have advanced on the four fronts: the economic, the military, the political, and the social. By chance, the economic came first, and this was a very positive step. The military has now come next, and that is a necessary defensive step. The political must come next, and the social will follow the political organization."*

In 1961, when President Kennedy came into office,

he made CFR member George Ball the under-secretary of state. Ball had been the American lawyer for Jean Monnet, who designed the plan for the European Common Market. The Atlantic Union Committee was dissolved about this time, but was simply replaced by the Atlantic Institute, headed by CFR member Henry Cabot Lodge and comprised primarily of CFR members. From their meeting in Paris in 1962 came a declaration, largely directed by CFR member Christian Herter, which included a recommendation that the government of the Atlantic Community countries accept compulsory jurisdiction of the International Court of Justice (World Court).

In 1964, CFR member Richard Gardner (deputy assistant secretary of state, 1961-1965) wrote *In Pursuit of World Order*. In 1966, Senate Resolution 128 was introduced concerning an Atlantic Union. On March 2, Governor Nelson Rockefeller gave his support to the resolution, and on September 1, Richard Nixon wrote the following: *"It is fitting that the United States, the world's first truly federal government, should be a main force behind the effort to find a basis for a broad federation of free Atlantic nations. Although the accomplishment of the ultimate goal of the resolution may well be impossible to attain for many years, recent events of history and numerous scientific and technological advances of the past twenty years point the way in this direction. . . . I have been deeply disturbed of late by the trend of events in Europe. The renewed nationalism of France has for the moment halted the pace at which the nations of Western Europe were moving toward becoming a unified and federated community. By adopting a measure such as the Atlantic Union resolution, we could give new impetus to the spirit of federalism in Western Europe. To be sure, the concept of an 'Atlantica' is at present only a dream, but in the age of the rocket, dreams become reality with a speed which is difficult to imagine."* Nixon had been a sponsor of resolutions regarding an Atlantic Union when he was earlier in the U.S. House of Representatives and U.S. Senate.

In the October 1967 issue of the CFR's *Foreign Affairs*, Richard Nixon wrote of nations' disposition *"to evolve regional approaches to development needs and to the evolution of a new world order."* CFR member Nixon's Republican opponent for the presidential nomination in 1968 was CFR member Nelson Rockefeller, who was reported by the Associated Press on July 26 of that year as saying that *"as president he would work toward international creation of 'a new world order.'"* In October of this same year, the U.S. Disarmament Agency issued a document titled "Arms Control and National Security," which stated: *"Since 1959, the agreed ultimate goal of the negotiations has been general and complete disarmament, i.e., the total elimination of all armed forces and armaments except those needed to maintain internal order within states and to furnish the United Nations with peace forces. . . . While reductions were taking place, a U.N. peace force would be established and developed, and, by the time the plan was completed, it would be so strong that no nation could challenge it."* Remember here that the U.S. Disarmament Agency wasn't established until September 1961, but in 1959 (date mentioned in the quote above) the CFR "Study No. 7" was published.

The year after the U.S. Disarmament Agency's "Arms Control and National Security" document was issued, Congressman George Bush on December 2, 1969, introduced House Concurrent Resolution 460, which in part stated, *"Whereas a joining together for such purposes of the democratic nations of the Atlantic community to create an Atlantic Union within the framework of the United Nations would reduce the cost of the common defense, provide a stable currency . . . a declaration that the goal of their peoples is to transform their present alliance into a federal union."* The same wording was used in House Concurrent Resolution 164 in 1971 sponsored by Rep. Paul Findley of Illinois, who said, *"If new difficulties should arise in the Middle East . . . not only military but economic and spiritual* [resources] *as well would be brought together in a single course of action."* Findley, along with CFR member and Mason Gerald Ford, supported a similar resolution in 1973, and Findley argued that *"some joint exercise of sovereignty is needed"* among the Atlantic nations. This was necessary, he said, because the U.N. *"is not a government; it does not have the authority to raise revenue* [levy taxes and collect them]; *it does not have legislative authority; it does not have any kind of a real police force or military establishment. So it is not a government."*

In the congressional hearings, the resolution was challenged in a moving statement by Mrs. Lillian Williams, who declared: *"If we cannot cooperate in an alliance* [NATO], *how can we do so in a federal union, short of police-state controls? . . . How would you explain to the mothers and fathers that their sons and daughters may be called upon to fight and die on some distant shore, not in defense of their homeland, but as policemen for a regional or world government? Once committed to a federal union, we are forever trapped, betraying the sacrifices made by all our honored war dead, who gave to the last bitter drop that we might live free and independent. We must never betray them; they must not have died in vain."* Did Rep. Findley's remark regarding the Middle East and Mrs. Williams' comments in 1973 sound an ominous warning concerning the war in the Persian Gulf in 1991 and its contribution toward the formal launching of the New World Order by President Bush?

• • • • •

In 1970, the CFR's Zbigniew Brzezinski (who became the first director of the Trilateral Commission, established in 1973, and later President Carter's national security advisor) had published *Between Two Ages*, in which he explained his view that *"Marxism is simultaneously a victory of the external, active man over the inner, passive man and a victory of reason over belief . . .* [and] *the fiction of* [national] *sovereignty . . . is clearly no longer compatible with reality . . .* [but] *a* [world community] *cannot be achieved by fusing existing states into one larger entity. . . . It makes much more sense to attempt to associate existing states through a variety of indirect ties and already developing limitations on national sovereignty."* Formalizing the supposed "fiction" of national sovereignty, the Fabian-certified historian Arnold Toynbee in *Surviving the Future* (1971) declared that to secure a true and lasting peace, *"The people of each local sovereign state will have to renounce their state's sovereignty and subordinate it to the paramount sovereignty of a literally worldwide world government. . . . I want to see a world government established."*

In the same year, CFR member James Reston wrote "Cautious Nixon Strategy" in the May 21, 1971 *New York Times*, saying, *"Mr. Nixon would obviously like to preside over the creation of a new world order, and believes he sees an opportunity to do so in the last twenty months of his term."* One year later, the former CFR member Richard Nixon was opening the door to Communist China, and in his 1972 visit there, he toasted Chou En-lai and mentioned *"the hope that each of us has to build a new world order."* On May 18, 1972, Roy M. Ash of the Office of Management and Budget in the Nixon Administration projected regarding the coming of world government that *"within two decades the institutional framework for a World Economic Community will be in place . . . [and] aspects of individual sovereignty will be given over to supernational authority."*

Facilitating this, the Club of Rome (founded 1968) published *The Limits to Growth* (1972) by CFR member Dennis L. Meadows, et al, calling for a global economic and ecological (population control) management, because their MIT computer models showed that the earth *"probably cannot support present rates of economic and population growth much beyond the year 2100, if that long, even with advanced technology."*

Even though the preparers of this report would later indicate some of their calculations were in error, the Club of Rome proceeded with its global agenda and four years later (1976) published another report, *RIO: Reshaping the International Order* (with an emergent Tao on the cover) calling for a new international order, including an economic redistribution of wealth, saying that *"a new* *world order must of necessity be based upon the recognition of the interdependence between both rich and poor nations. . . . The process of initiating . . . and guiding change in preferred directions . . . can and should be organized. . . . A **new value system** more appropriate to future needs may well emerge kicking and screaming in the decade ahead."* The next year (1977) Ervin Laszlo, et al, made their report to the Club of Rome entitled *Goals for Mankind*. The Club has indicated that *"only a global revolution, the substitution of a New World Economic Order, can save us."* And it was founded by Bilderberger member Aurelio Peccei, who exclaimed that a *"charismatic leader . . . would be the world's only salvation from the social and economic upheaval that threatens to destroy civilization."*

In the April 1974 issue of *Foreign Affairs*, CFR and Trilateral Commission member Richard Gardner (later President Carter's ambassador to Italy) wrote in "The Hard Road to World Order" that *"the 'house of world order' will have to be built from the bottom up rather than from the top down. It will look like a great 'booming, buzzing confusion,' to use William James' famous description of reality, but an end run around national sovereignty, eroding it piece by piece, will accomplish much more than the old-fashioned frontal assault."* And in the same year, Rexford Tugwell (of FDR's "brain trust") published *The Emerging Constitution* containing a "Constitution for the Newstates of America," which would replace our fifty states with ten to twenty regional "newstates," but which are described in William Still's *New World Order* as *"not states at all, but rather subservient departments of the national government. The government would be em-*

powered to abridge freedom of expression, communication, movement, and assembly in a 'declared emergency.'" If such an emergency were declared today, the Federal Emergency Management Administration (FEMA) would have almost dictatorial powers, and our constitutional rights would be thrown out the window.

Bayless Manning was president of the CFR in New York in 1974, and he was also a "faculty member" of the Bohemian Grove, about which G. William Domhoff wrote that year. In Harper & Row's publicity for this 1974 volume, *The Bohemian Grove*, it stated: *"Domhoff does valiant battle against hothouse sociologists who appear to believe the corporate overlords are all strangers to each other, unconnected. But it turns out that they are all really lodge brothers. When it comes time to meet for semi-public arm's-length decision making about corporate and political schemes, the decisions, as it happens, are made by long-familiar playmates, clubmates from the Bohemian Grove of California, the Rancheros, and the Roundup Riders."*

CFR member George Bush had been a guest at the Grove, as had President Reagan, and CFR member Richard Nixon had been a member of the Grove since 1953. The Bohemian Club was founded in 1872, with early members like Ambrose Bierce (author of *The Devil's Dictionary*), and the Grove encampment began in 1878. The "Mandalay Camp" at the Grove is *"an all-star team of national corporate elite,"* according to Domhoff, including Stephen Bechtel (chairman of Bechtel Corporation, trustee of Ford Foundation, and director of Morgan Guarantee Trust and Stanford Research Institute, where New Ager Willis Harman has been). Another camp has a "pornographic collection." CFR members Nelson Rockefeller and Henry Kissinger have been speakers at the Grove, where men with pointed red hoods and flowing red robes cremate the "body of Care," and where the "high priest" at the Owl Shrine says, *"Let all within the Grove be reverent before him"* and *"Weaving spiders, come not here"* (from Shakespeare). Domhoff also mentioned *"ladies of the evening who are available in certain inns and motels near the Grove."*

There were CFR members who became disenchanted with that organization's activities, as in William Still's *New World Order*, one finds that *"Admiral Chester Ward, former judge advocate general of the U.S. Navy, and former CFR member, wrote in 1975 that the goal of the CFR was the 'submergence of U.S. sovereignty and national independence into an all-powerful one-world government.' "* (This is similar to what Senator Barry Goldwater said in his book, *With No Apologies*.) Admiral Ward continued regarding how the CFR works: *"Once the ruling members of the CFR have decided that the U.S. government should adopt a particular policy, the very substantial research facilities of the CFR are put to work to develop arguments, intellectual and emotional, to support the new policy, and to confound and discredit, intellectually and politically, any opposition."*

Also in 1975, the first issue of *Alternatives: A Journal of World Policy* was edited by CFR member Saul Mendlovitz, who has been chairman of the Planetary Citizens' Advisory Council and is a director of the World Order Models Project, which was supported by the Carnegie Endowment for International Peace and the Rockefeller Foundation, and had as one of its sponsoring institutions the Novosti Press Agency of Moscow (a propaganda agency staffed by the Soviet secret police). Mendlovitz said there *"is no longer a question of whether or not there will be world government by the year 2000. The questions are how it will come into being (cataclysm, drift, more or less rational design), and whether it will be totalitarian, benign, or participatory (the possibilities being in that order.)"* Alternatives: A Journal of World Order is published by the Institute for World Order (now named World Policy Institute), which has had as its honorary chairman CFR director C. Douglas Dillon (secretary of the treasury under President Kennedy), who stated, *"it will take a while before people in this country as a whole will be ready for any substantial giving-up of sovereignty to handle global problems. . . . Global authorities will develop, possibly through the United Nations or parallel organizations."*

Mendlovitz edited *On the Creation of a Just World Order* (1975), in which CFR member Richard Falk projected that the 1970s were to be the decade of "consciousness raising," the 1980s would be the period of "mobilization," and the 1990s would be the decade of "transformation." Falk in the same year wrote *A Study of Future Worlds*, in which he advised that *"to achieve this* [better world order], *central institutions would have to be equipped with police capabilities while national institutions would be substantially deprived of military capabilities. . . . The first and central priority of the movement for a preferred world is to make progress toward **diminishing the role of the war system in international life and toward dismantling the national security apparatus in the major states of the world."***

Likewise in 1975, CFR member James Reston wrote in an August article in the *New York Times* that President Ford and Soviet leader Leonid Brezhnev should *"forget the past and work together for a new world order."* On September 22, 1975, however, an attempt was made on the life of President Ford, a former CFR member and Bilderberger, by Sara Jane Moore (only seventeen days after Lynette "Squeaky" Fromme had pointed a gun at the president). In the *Arizona Daily Star* article, "Assailants Stalked Eight Other Presidents" (March 31, 1981), Moore remarked: *"Ford is a nebbish. . . . Killing Ford would have shaked a lot of people up. More importantly, it would have elevated Nelson Rockefeller to the presidency, and then people would see who the actual leaders of the country are."* In June 1976, Moore had already told a national publication regarding her attempt upon President Ford's life: *"I had done something very valuable for them* [the FBI] *in the fall of 1974. . . . That was the point at which the seed of what finally happened on September 22, 1975, was planted. That was the one time when my political beliefs, what I wanted to have happen, coincided with something that the Bureau and the Secret Service wanted."* Of course, there has been a great deal of skepticism regarding Ms. Moore's comments concerning the FBI and the Secret Service.

Almost exactly one month after the second attempt upon President Ford's life was made, CFR member Henry Steele Commager on October 24, 1975 wrote *The Declaration of Interdependence* (signed by one hundred thirty-one members of the U.S. Congress in Washington, D.C., including Alan Cranston, George McGovern, Robert Packwood, Claiborne Pell, Christopher Dodd,

Paul Simon, Les Aspin, Pat Schroeder, Ron Dellums, and Paul Tsongas) for the World Affairs Council of Philadelphia. This includes the words: *"Two centuries ago our forefathers brought forth a new nation; now we must join with others to bring forth a new world order. . . . Narrow notions of national sovereignty must not be permitted to curtail that obligation. . . . We affirm that a world without law is a world without order, and we call upon all nations to strengthen and to sustain the United Nations and its specialized agencies, and other institutions of world order, and to broaden the jurisdiction of the World Court, that these may preside over a reign of law that will not only end wars but end as well that mindless violence which terrorizes our society even in times of peace."*

Congresswoman Marjorie Holt refused to sign the *Declaration*, saying: *"It calls for the surrender of our national sovereignty to international organizations. It declares that our economy should be regulated by international authorities. It proposes that we enter a 'new world order' that would redistribute the wealth created by the American people"* (*Don Bell Reports*, January 30, 1976). Congressman John Ashbrook would also relate that the World Affairs Council *"has even joined with the Philadelphia school system to develop model fifth- and sixth-grade school programs promoting the declaration of interdependence. Children are even asked to pledge themselves to the declaration's concepts, thus repudiating their own patriotic heritage, and to lobby for signatures from their friends and relatives for the declaration of interdependence. . . . Unlike the Declaration of Independence, whose great hallmarks are guarantees of individual personal freedom and dignity for all Americans and an American nation under God, the declaration abandons those principles in favor of cultural relativism, international citizenship, and supremacy over all nations by a world government. The declaration of interdependence is an attack on loyalty to American freedom and institutions,* which the document calls 'chauvinistic nationalism,' 'national prejudice,' and 'narrow notions of national sovereignty.' "

The movement toward global interdependence was growing, however. In the Rockefeller Foundation's annual report at the end of 1975, president John Knowles stated: *"The web of interdependence is tightening. We are one world and there will be one future — for better or for worse — for us all. Central to a new ethic of making less more is controlled economic growth which conserves scarce resources, provides equitable distribution of income and wealth. . . . It is also necessary to control fertility rates at the replacement level and to achieve zero population growth as rapidly as possible."*

The next year, 1976, Trilateralist Jimmy Carter campaigned for the presidency, and in March he told the Chicago Council on Foreign Relations that the United States should "coordinate" its policies with the Trilateral nations. Then in May, he told the American Chamber of Commerce in Tokyo that the U.S. needed a "commitment" to Trilateralism, and the next month he told the Foreign Policy Association that *"the time has come for us to seek a partnership between North America, Western Europe, and Japan."*

One year later in 1977, Laurence Shoup's and William Minter's *Imperial Brain Trust* about the Council on Foreign Relations was published with chapter titles, "Shaping a New World Order: The Council's Blueprint for Global Hegemony, 1939-1944" and "Toward the 1980s: The Council's Plans for a New World Order." In that same year, CFR member Harlan Cleveland's (with the Aspen Institute for Humanistic Studies) volume, *The Third Try at World Order*, was published in which he talks of "changing Americans' attitudes and institutions," of "complete disarmament (except for international soldiers)," of "fairer distribution of worldly goods through a New International Economic Order," and of "international standards for individual entitlement to food, health, education. . . ."

At the beginning of the year 1977, Jimmy Carter had become president of the United States. And on the day of his inauguration (January 20), he delivered a speech, "Statement to the World," in which he declared, *"I want to assure you that the relations of the United States with the other countries and peoples of the world will be guided during our administration by our desire to shape a world order that is more responsive to human aspirations. The United States will meet its obligations to help create a stable, just and peaceful world order. . . ."*

On February 5, 1977, former *Washington Post* columnist Jeremiah Novak wrote in *America: "According to sources in the State Department, the trilateral papers have directly influenced the summoning of the Rambouillet and Puerto Rican conferences, the sale of IMF gold, the Law of the Sea conferences, the formation of the International Energy Agency, and steps to establish a new international currency, which replaces the U.S. dollar and gold. . . . New structures are recommended to meet the needs of oil users and producers to 'bridge the economic systems' of communist and non-communist states. These interest-group institutions are seen as subordinate to a superstructure of planetary institutions. . . . The Trilateral Commission's most immediate concern is the creation of a new world monetary system to replace gold and the dollar as the international exchange units with a new currency called special drawing rights (SDR's). In fact, as a move in this direction, the commission was instrumental in the IMF's sale of its gold and in the creation of a system of denoting all currencies in terms of SDR's as a first step in the push for a new world system."* Later in this same year, Novak would write in "The Trilateral Connection" (*Atlantic Monthly,* July 1977): *"For the third time in this century, a group of American scholars, businessmen, and government officials is planning to fashion a New World Order. Discouraged by U.N. inadequacies, disheartened by chaos in the Bretton Woods institutions* [the Establishment's International Monetary Fund and their World Bank], *and worried about the United States' waning strength, these men are looking to a 'community of developed nations' to coordinate international political and economic affairs. . . . The Trilateralists' emphasis on international economics is not entirely disinterested, for the oil crisis forced many developing nations, with doubtful repayment abilities, to borrow excessively. All told, private multinational banks, particularly Rockefeller's Chase Manhattan, have loaned nearly fifty-two billion dollars to developing countries. An overhauled IMF would provide another source of credit for these nations, and would take the big private banks off the hook. This proposal is a cornerstone of the*

Trilateral plan. . . ." At this point, it might be worth remembering the slogan "get a sovereign (or nation) in debt" to control him or it.

The objectives of the Trilateralists were further described in Barry Goldwater's book, *With No Apologies* (1979): *"In my view the Trilateral Commission represents a skillful, coordinated effort to seize control and consolidate the four centers of power — political, monetary, intellectual, and ecclesiastical. All this is to be done in the interest of creating a more peaceful, more productive world community. What the Trilateralists truly intend is the creation of a worldwide economic power superior to the political governments of the nation-states involved. They believe the abundant materialism they propose to create will overwhelm existing differences. As managers and creators of the system they will rule the future."*

In the same year that Barry Goldwater's book was published, Secretary of State (and CFR member) Cyrus Vance indicated on March 30 that the United States would increase economic aid to developing nations to further *"progress toward a more equitable and healthy new international economic order."* The next year, and toward the end of the Carter Administration, on September 15, 1980, a special session of the U.N. General Assembly ended that had attempted to lay the groundwork for a New International Economic Order. It was clear from the U.N.'s report that it is being influenced by the occult, as it quoted from occultist Alice Bailey. The U.N. report, "The New International Economic Order: A Spiritual Imperative," stated: *"Over the centuries humanity has drawn a line of demarcation between what was considered human and what was considered spiritual.*

*But today a new understanding of spirituality is emerging which recognizes that all efforts to uplift humanity are spiritual in nature. Alice Bailey said, 'That is spiritual which lies beyond the point of present achievement; it is that which embodies the vision and which urges man on toward a goal higher than the one attained.' In another context she said, 'The word **spiritual** relates to attitudes, to relationships, to the moving forward from one level of consciousness (no matter how low or gross, from the point of view of a higher level of contact) to the next; it is related to the power to see the vision, even if that vision is materialistic as seen from the angle of a higher registration of possibility. . . .' Given this new understanding of spirituality, the work of the United Nations can be viewed not only within a political and social sphere, but can be seen within the **entire evolutionary unfoldment** of humanity. The work of the U.N. is indeed spiritual and holds profound import for the future of civilization."* The same month (September 1980), "The New International Economic Order" (World Goodwill Commentary Number 14) was published emphasizing Alice Bailey's explanation that *"in the destruction of the old world order and in the chaos of these modern times, the work of the new creation is going forward; the task of reconstruction, leading to a complete reorganization of human living."* Recall the Masonic phrase, "order out of chaos."

This chapter began with information about the Association to Unite to Democracies (AUD), and it will end with a quotation from Thomas Ehrenzeller, who has been active with both the World Federalist Association and AUD. In 1985, Ehrenzeller wrote *Solar Man*, and then became a staff member of AUD. Sounding very much like Alice Bailey's reference to "solar," he exclaimed: *"As the sun rises on the coming age, we see a great task before us. . . . A great human civilization is to be built. . . . World unity alone can create permanent world peace. . . . The era in which the people of the world finally cast off the bonds of nationalistic self-deception, freeing themselves to join together in one free community, will be a true Solar Age. As solar citizens, we will be part of one mighty race. . . . We can build a mighty Solar Nation, a nation of nations. . . . World government will have the power to do that which only world government can do: secure every nation from aggression. . . . We could build a world society . . . and so we will. . . . There is no force that can stop such a movement. . . . Human society must finally become one single society, united in its diversity. . . . The New Era is coming, whether the guardians of the old are ready or not. . . . There can be a New World Order. . . . We will save the world by making of it a bright New Age. . . . We will do this by creating regional groups of nations. The different nations can become more compatible. Then, we can form our nations into regional groupings, and we can align those groupings into one unit which can ultimately encompass the entire world. . . . The dawn of the Solar Age will herald the coming of a new Solar Race which will last for centuries, millennia even."*

Chapter Fifteen
Thinking Globally

If there was going to be a "New World Order" under the U.N., "managers" would have to be prepared in various areas, including transnational corporations. Ervin Laszlo, director of the Program on Regional Cooperation for the United Nations Institute for Training and Research (and member of the board of directors of Planetary Citizens, and speaker to the Association for Humanistic Psychology), has edited the journal *World Futures*, which contained a 1981 (vol. 17, No. 3/4) article, "Developing Managers for a New World Order" by Bohdan Hawrylshyn, director of the Centre for Education in International Management in Geneva. The article indicated that in the New World Order, *"Company training centers will be increasingly internationally staffed . . . [with] 'partnerships in learning,' . . . and institutions supporting each others' determination to internationalize executives. . . . The world order, or disorder, will likely be based on multiple sources of power, with power shared through and moderated by agreements, numerous international conferences, special agencies, official, semiofficial, and private networks, in what has been aptly labelled 'the planetary bargaining process.'"* Laszlo also wrote *The Objectives of the New International Economic Order* (1979).

The year after the *World Futures* article appeared, Camilo Dagum wrote "Elements for a New World Order" in the Summer 1982 issue of *International Social Science Review*. After describing philosophical types of rulers from Plato's "philosopher-king" to St. Augustine's and St. Thomas Aquinas' "philosopher-saint," to Immanuel Kant's "philosopher-scientist" (described in his *Critique of Pure Reason* and *Critique of Practical Reason*), Dagum reaches the concept of the "philosopher-technologist" developed by Ludwig Wittgenstein. Dagum writes that *"a highly relevant contemporary triad for the design of a NWO* [New World Order] *includes science, technology, and industry, which is known by the name of Research and Development* [R&D]. *. . . The purpose of this human endeavor is to achieve a more efficient composition and utilization of human and natural resources. And the utilization of science and technology is done by industry, completing the side of development in the social quest for R&D. . . . Any national project of R&D has an impact on the rest of the world . . . and the tragic war between Iraq and Iran constitutes an example of the vulnerability and interdependence of all nations, including the superpowers of the world. This is also a forceful appeal for the construction of a NWO that has to take into consideration the human species as a whole. We have to become citizens of the world even if we are only concerned with the welfare of our own motherland. . . . For the first time in history, the statement advanced by Thomas Paine, an Englishman by birth, a French citizen, an American by adoption, acquires compelling power. Paine said: 'I am a citizen of the world and my religion is to do good.' And there is today a need for us to become* *citizens of the world if we want a future for it. Of course, such citizenship is opposed to a well-defined national citizenship."*

And "there was the rub" for the planners of the New World Order. As James McGregor Burns in *The Power to Lead* (1984) stated: *"Let us face reality. The framers of the U.S. Constitution have simply been too shrewd for us. They have outwitted us. They designed separate institutions that cannot be unified by mechanical linkages, frail bridges, tinkering. If we are to 'turn the Founders upside down' — we must directly confront the constitutional structure they erected."* Then in 1985, the national weekly newspaper, *Human Events*, in its August 10 edition reported CFR member Norman Cousins as having said, *"World government is coming. In fact, it is inevitable. No arguments for or against it can change that fact."* These were almost the exact words James Warburg had used in his congressional testimony in 1950.

Not only was the goal to change the Constitution and have a world government, but to change culture as well, using environmental issues as a primary vehicle. In October 1987, the World Commission on Environment and Development (the U.S. Commission member was CFR member William Ruckelshaus) presented its report, "Our Common Future," to the U.N., which had established the commission as an independent body in 1983. The report is actually a map or program for the world's future covering nearly all areas of life, and calling for *"new norms of behavior at all levels . . . changes in attitudes, in social values"* and population control. Paul Ehrlich had written his doomsday book, *The Population Bomb* (1968), in which he suggested that because the Third

World was hopeless, the death rate there could be increased by withholding food and technology from them, and their birthrate could be reduced by mandatory birth control and sterilization. Much of the message of this 1968 volume was reiterated in Paul and Anne Ehrlich's 1990 *The Population Explosion*, despite the fact that the conclusions from *The Population Bomb* had been proven almost totally fallacious. For example, after Ehrlich's 1968 book, the prestigious National Academies of Sciences and Engineering published its own frightening report on population growth and economic development in 1971, but by 1986 this organization almost completely reversed itself saying, *"The scarcity of exhaustible resources is at most a minor constraint on economic growth."* It had discovered that more people caused economic growth (see "Population Panic" by Julian Simon in the May 21, 1990 issue of *Fortune* magazine). Still, the population controllers had allies at some of the highest levels of government, as the executive assistant to the administrator of the Health Services Administration at HEW under President Carter advocated licensing parents before they could have children. In a speech to the Mental Health Association's annual Child Abuse Conference for Dallas and Tarrant counties in Texas in the late 1970s, Executive Assistant Eddie Bernice Johnson justified her advocacy of licensing parents before they are permitted to have children by saying, *"We require almost every endeavor or profession to be licensed — why not the most single important responsibility which a parent can ever have?"*

Similar advocacy of governmental licensure of parents came from outside government as well, as David Brower of Friends of the Earth advocated that *"childbearing* [should be] *a punishable crime against society, unless the parents hold a government license. . . . All potential parents* [should be] *required to use contraceptive chemicals, the government issuing antidotes to citizens chosen for childbearing."* Also, a First Endorser of Planetary Citizens, Kenneth Boulding (originator of the "Spaceship Earth" concept), supported government regulation of childbearing, stating: *"The right to have children should be a marketable commodity, bought and traded by individuals but absolutely limited by the state."*

• • • • •

There was also an element of racism in the population control movement. At the beginning of the 1980s, Rev. Peter Proeku Dery of Tamale, Ghana, revealed: *"The World Bank denied loans to Ghana until my country agreed to institute a nationwide contraception and family-planning policy. There was also pressure to legalize abortion. . . . The people have so far been able to prevent this,* [but] *for how long, I don't know."* A few years later, there was even mention of "birth quotas" in the World Bank's "World Development Report 1984." In the United States, even Black liberals like Dick Gregory denounced funding abortion-on-demand as amounting to genocide against Blacks, and respected Black Pittsburgh physician Dr. Charles Greenlee found that many poor Blacks had been intimidated into having abortions, and the *"intimidation takes the form of implicit and explicit threats that welfare payments will be cut off if the recipient has more children."* The president of Planned

Parenthood, Faye Wattleton (1986 Humanist of the Year) even acknowledged, *"We have received contributions from people who want to support us because they want all welfare mothers and all Black women to stop having children."* She also declared in the October 17, 1987 *Los Angeles Times* that *"we are not going to be an organization promoting celibacy or chastity."*

Another organization about which the public should know more concerning its activities is the March of Dimes. Randy Engel in "The A-Z of Eugenic Killing" (*All About Issues*, Spring 1991), reveals, *"As the battle over the use of fetal tissues and organs of aborted babies heats up in the U.S. and abroad, we should recall that the March of Dimes (MOD) has funded such practices for more than two decades. . . . The MOD has been funding NOAPP (National Organization on Adolescent Pregnancy and Parenting) — a pro-abortion, pro-school-based clinic agency — since 1983. . . . On March 25-27, 1985, the MOD co-sponsored and co-funded (with NOAPP) an adolescent pregnancy seminar titled 'Inventing the Future.' . . . Included in the 'New Futures' summary report were numerous anti-life references and scenarios promoting school-based clinics, compulsory population control, homosexuality, birth control ads, and divorce."* And in the "Pregnancy Prevention" section of the report was a recommendation that boys be sterilized at age thirteen after depositing their sperm! More specifically, it was suggested that by the year 2008, the federal government should mandate "conception immunization" for all preteen boys and girls (via a reversible sterilization procedure performed at school-based clinics), who could apply after reaching adulthood to get a certificate-type permit to have children.

The eugenics of today and tomorrow not only involve children and young adults, but older adults as well. Not only is it becoming increasingly difficult to be admitted to medical school if a prospective medical student is pro-life regarding abortion, but those graduating from medical school increasingly have a eugenic attitude toward older adults. For example, my aunt was recently told by her cardiologist that she needed a hip operation as soon as possible, but he told her point-blank that other doctors were delaying her operation and similar operations for older adults because they hoped these people would simply die and be gone. This is not good news, given Initiative 119 that was on the ballot in the state of Washington in November 1991. The first and second provisions of the initiative redefined the word "terminal," allowing nutrition and hydration to be removed from someone in a coma or persistent vegetative state. The third provision exempted from prosecution under Washington State's homicide statute any physician who administers a lethal injection "voluntarily" requested by a terminally ill patient. One can just imagine a doctor saying to a patient in pain, "If you would like something that will cause you to feel no more pain, just voluntarily sign this form." If the doctor then gave the patient a lethal injection, the physician would not be prosecuted.

● ● ● ● ●

In Peter LaLonde's *Blueprint for Building the New World Order* (1991), he describes the political technique of "management by crisis" where *"those who desire a change in a specific direction and those who have sufficient resources, create, invent, or find an existing crisis; then they widely publicize that crisis; and when there is sufficient alarm among the people they always, citing renowned academics, propose their solution to the crisis."* Using the example of the current "environmental crisis," he then refers to former Congressman Bob Edgar (chairman of the Congressional Clearinghouse on the Future and member of Members of Congress for Peace through [World] Law) arguing that the environmental problem lies in national sovereignty and that only a world government can now "save" the environment. Similarly, LaLonde says: *"Ervin Laszlo of the United Nations Institute for Training and Research in speaking of how all the various crises — environmental, overpopulation, economic, and political — combined with the new image of man could bring about a moment of critical instability and thus a transformation to a New World Order. . . ."* Along this same line, Donald S. McAlvany in his *Toward a New World Order* (1990) states: *"The environmental crisis is the vehicle upon which the New Age movement, the New World Order . . . plan . . . to move the world to global government before the close of the 1990s."* In March 1988, twenty-four nations met at the World Court (the Hague, Netherlands) and proposed a *"supranational agency within the framework of the U.N. that could impose sanctions against any country negatively impacting the environment."*

Perhaps the first major event of this scenario for achieving world government via environmental issues was the 1970 Earth Day, organized in part by New Ager José Arguelles. Then in 1972, CFR member Lester Brown, president of Worldwatch Institute, which promotes world government, wrote *World Without Borders* which stated: *"Effective supernational institutions . . . invariably require that countries sacrifice a measure of sovereignty. . . . Arresting the deterioration of the environment does not seem possible within the existing framework of independent nation-states. . . . The list of national problems which can be solved only at the global level is lengthening. These range from drug addiction and the energy crisis in the United States to poverty and rising unemployment in the poor countries. The existing international system based on competition and conflict and superpower dominance will not work over the longer term. It must be replaced by a new world order, one based on cooperation and a sense of community."*

More recently, Brown has been on the board of Ted Turner's Better World Society, which supports population control. And even more recently for José Arguelles, he was chief coordinator of the August 16-17, 1987, Harmonic Convergence and wrote that there was a *"call for another way of life, another way of doing things . . . a redistribution of global wealth . . . in short, a New World Order."* He also stated that by August 18, 1987, *"a new paradigm, a New World Order, will be established, characterized by an end to the arms race, demilitarization, a redistribution of global wealth, an end to pollution, environmental harmony, and deindustrialization."*

On March 18, 1991, a U.N. conference gave out information about the "Mandate for Life on Earth" project founded by Paul Clark and which was launched at the 1991 Earth Day celebrations. The mandate aims to raise a minimum of one hundred million signatures/ thumbprints worldwide to present to the June 1992

United Nations Conference on the Environment ("Earth Summit") due to take place in Brazil. The mandate calls for the establishment of a set of international environmental standards and an International Court of Justice with the power to fine individuals, organizations, and governments that breach the newly instituted regulations. This far-reaching initiative already has the support of the Ecological Centre of Moscow, the Club of Rome, the Center for Our Common Future, and the Worldwide Fund for Nature (headed by Prince Philip, which will be mailing to thirty-two thousand schools).

A question I'd like to ask is why, if environmentalists are so concerned about ending pollution, do so many of them drive old vans or VWs with "Save the Earth" and other stickers on them, but which are so poorly maintained that they belch exhaust fumes and smoke each time they start? The large vehicles that city governments send up and down neighborhood streets to pick up material to recycle in order to help the environment also often emit a large amount of dirty exhaust, polluting the air.

In the 1980s, Donald Keys convened "The Planetary Initiative for the World We Choose" with endorsers like Steve Allen, Father Robert Drinan, and the Dalai Lama, and with the theme, "Think Globally, Act Locally." The initiative (a project of Planetary Citizens) would lead to a planetary congress meeting with a "world council of wise persons" present. ("Council of Wise Men" is the name often given to the members of the Council on Foreign Relations, and CFR member Joseph E. Slater [who has been president of the Aspen Institute for Humanistic Studies, where Henry Kissinger has been a trustee and Special Fellow] proposed in the early 1970s *"that there be a council of wise persons. . . . They could work on the question of genetic engineering or DNA."*) Donald Keys has been a speechwriter for foreign ministers and ambassadors, on the board of directors for the Baconian Foundation, representative of World Federalists U.S.A. officially accredited to the headquarters of the U.N. in New York, and co-founder of Planetary Citizens in 1974. He is currently president of Planetary Citizens, which has consultative status in the U.N. In July 1984, Keys delivered an address, "Integral People for a Whole Planet," at the Arcane School Conference in London (published in *The Beacon*, May/June 1985, Lucis Publishing Co., United Nations Plaza, New York City), in which one reads: *"From now on, civilization will be global. . . . We will in fact become a creative hierarchy. . . . We have the bare beginnings of a notion of world order in the embryonic United Nations. . . . Humanity is not suddenly going to become a race of adepts. . . . We are at the point of interpretation. . . . We can be a point of reference, a point of strength, and a point of responsible action. . . . In the lives of some of us . . . the devic world has opened as a reality. . . . We can exemplify a sensitive relationship to the spirit of earth at a higher turn of the spiral . . . in the hue and cry and in the storm of crashing old institutions and disruption of old values, we have been trained to see clearly. . . . It's a wonderful thing to be crucified here . . . to be as members of the new group of world servers. . . . So be your cellular part of this initiation of the earth."*

Then at a symposium, "Toward a Global Society," held in Asheville, North Carolina on November 11, 1984, Keys delivered an address, "Transformation of Self and

Society," in which he said, *"We're at the stage now of pulling it all together. It's a new religion called 'networking.'. . . When it comes to running a world or taking people into a New Age. . . . Don't anyone think for a moment that you can run a planet without a head. . . . This planet has to be managed. . . . We have meditations at the United Nations a couple of times a week. The meditation leader is Sri Chinmoy, and this is what he said about this situation:'. . . The United Nations is the chosen instrument of God; to be a chosen instrument means to be a divine messenger carrying the banner of God's inner vision and outer manifestation. One day, the world will . . . treasure and cherish the soul of the United Nations as its very own with enormous pride, for this soul is all-loving, all-nourishing, and all-fulfilling.'"*

Endorsers of Planetary Citizens have been Chief Justice of the U.S. Supreme Court Earl Warren, Judy Collins, Robert Hutchins, Coretta Scott King, Linus Pauling, and Aurelio Peccei (founder of the Club of Rome), and on its advisory council have been Isaac Asimov, René Dubos, Robert Muller, David Spangler, Brother David Steindl-Rast (a Benedictine monk who has written for the Theosophical quarterly, *Quest*), and Father Theodore Hesburgh. Father Hesburgh has been president of the University of Notre Dame, an advisory board member of the World Federalist Association, a CFR director, and chairman of the Rockefeller Foundation. On April 15, 1991, at a convocation at Notre Dame, he said virtually the same thing World Federalist Association Vice-President John Logue said on December 4, 1985 to the Human Rights and International Organizations Subcommittee of the U.S. House Foreign Affairs

Committee. Logue said: *"Peace people — and all people — must see that if we really want to stop the arms race we must have effective world political institutions. . . . Yes, people must stop patronizing the people of the world. It is time to tell the world's people not what they want to hear, but what they ought to hear. What they ought to hear is that if we really want to have peace and promote justice, we must reform, restructure and strengthen the United Nations and give it the power and authority and funds to keep the peace and promote justice. The Security Council veto must go. One-nation, one-vote must go. The United Nations must have taxing power or some other dependable source of revenue. It must have a large peacekeeping force. It must be able to supervise the dismantling and destruction of nuclear and other major weapons systems. In appropriate areas, particularly in the area of peace and security, it must be able to make and enforce law on the individual."*

Regarding "Global Oneness" and the environment, a new book has just been published. Berit Kjos, who authored *Your Child and the New Age* (1990), has just written *Under the Spell of Mother Earth* (1992). It describes how concern for the environment has joined with mysticism to spark a return to ancient forms of nature worship, and the author relates how Christians can responsibly care for the earth but still resist the pervasive pagan beliefs that are entering our lives through media, schools, and the church.

Chapter Sixteen

"Back to the Garden," a New Age, and the Third Attempt at World Order

---

P. Shannon Cuddy, in "The New Age and Population Control, Part 2" (*The National Pro-Life Journal*, Summer 1985), wrote that New Agers *"worship the creation rather than the Creator, God."* Indeed, as was stated earlier, the New Age is actually taking us back to Satan's lies in the Garden of Eden that we can all be "gods" and never die.

Two of the most prominent individuals promoting the New Age are Robert Muller and David Spangler. Muller is a "karma-nized" Catholic whose "master" was a Buddhist monk, U Thant, who was secretary-general of the United Nations. Muller was a friend of Norman Cousins and has been in close contact with a number of popes in his former capacity of assistant secretary-general of the United Nations. Pope John Paul II even presented Muller with a large cross which he wears around his neck. In his own book, *New Genesis: Shaping a Global Spirituality*, Muller talks about *"our brethren the animals, our sisters the flowers"* and how we must *"create common world religious institutions."* He further states, *"I often visualize in my mind another even more accurate painting:*

that of the United Nations which would be the body of Christ" and that we should *"display the U.N. flag in all houses of worship"* and *"happiness can be achieved by elevating oneself to God."* In *Blueprint: For Building the New World Order*, Peter LaLonde quotes Muller as saying: *"I have come to believe firmly today that our future, peace, justice, and fulfillment, happiness and harmony on this planet will not depend on world government but on divine or cosmic government . . . my great personal dream is to get a tremendous alliance between all major religions and the U.N."*

In a description of the Robert Muller School located in Texas, one reads that the underlying philosophy of its World Core Curriculum (which is endorsed by the Association for Supervision and Curriculum Development) *"is based on the teachings set forth in the books of Alice A. Bailey by the Tibetan teacher Djwhal Khul* [Lucis Pub. Co.] *and the teachings of M. Morya."* Khul and Morya are allegedly adepts (with Khul supposedly being a reincarnation of Confucius) who telepathically transmitted their thoughts to the occultist Bailey. The Center for World Servers, Asheville, N.C., also promotes this World Core Curriculum, along with a set of materials and instructions for a program, "Balanced Beginnings," which was developed by the Robert Muller School and in which, according to Dr. Dorothy Maver, an astrological chart is done *"from the moment of conception and then also at the moment of birth."*

David Spangler has been co-director of the New Age Findhorn Community in Scotland, which was founded by Eileen Caddy and her husband Peter Caddy, along with Dorothy MacLean. Peter Caddy emphasizes *"learning to trust inner guidance and creating a world of synthesis."* MacLean worked with the British Secret Intelligence Service in the Second World War in North and South America, and now is president of the Canadian Lorian Association (an offshoot of Findhorn). At the "Toward a Global Society" symposium held November 9-11, 1984 in Asheville, North Carolina, MacLean mentioned "the higher self, the god within, the intuitional level," and said that *"everything in nature has intelligence."* She explained that she had gotten in touch with the intelligence behind the garden pea (her favorite vegetable), which told her that humans "weren't using our potential." Then this former member of the British Secret Intelligence Service said, *"As we take this Earth initiation . . . we are immediately linked with that level in nature and everything else. . . . Trees are for transformation of energy from the earth below to the cosmos above. . . . The gift of mental stability is given to us from large trees. . . . The Garden of Eden . . . to me was a forward, not a fall. . . ."* She later explained some experiences in communicating with the angels or devas of minerals, trees, plants, and other things in nature, and indicated regarding Gaia that she *"has contacted the oversoul of the planet* [and] *it was a very wonderful experience."*

David Spangler was co-director of the Findhorn Community from 1970 to 1973, at which time he returned to the United States and founded the Lorian Association. Spangler has said that laser beam projectors have been placed on St. John the Divine Cathedral in New York City to create holographic images in the sky. He, along with Benjamin Creme, Alice Bailey, and Madame Blavatsky, have said the "Luciferic initiation" will be the heart and core of the "New World Religion" in the New Age. Malachi Martin in *The Keys of This Blood* quotes Spangler as writing: *"Lucifer is the angel of man's inner light. . . . Lucifer, like Christ, stands at the door of man's consciousness and knocks. . . . If man says, 'Come in,' Lucifer becomes . . . the being who carries . . . the light of wisdom. . . . Lucifer is literally the angel of experience. . . . He is an agent of God's love . . . and we move into a* **new age** *. . . each of us in some way is brought to that point which I term the Luciferic initiation. . . . We must say, 'Thank you, Beloved, for all these experiences. . . . They have brought me to you.' . . . At some point each of us faces the presence of Lucifer. . . . Lucifer comes to give us the final gift of wholeness. If we accept it, then he is free and we are free. That is the Luciferic initiation. It is one that many people now, and in the days ahead, will be facing, for* **it is an initiation into the New Age.**"

In Spangler's *Revelation: The Birth of a New Age* (1976), one reads: *"Thus, the Cosmic Christ united with the consciousness of the Earth Logos in which were sunk the foundations of Earth and its past development and future potentials. Through that union, a seed-atom of Christ-power began to radiate within the inner spheres of Earth, summoning forth the beginnings of a new consciousness. . . ."* This is similar to occultist Alice Bailey's writing in *Glamour: A World Problem* (1950), where she indicates that a *"new world religion is now on its way to externalizing . . . the inauguration of the New Age . . .* [and] *the only ritual which is still regarded as of value to the human family as a whole — particularly to the advanced person — is the Masonic ritual."* She stresses the role of the "solar Angel" (Lucifer), and urges New

Agers to make the effort *"to see in the light which the Angel radiates, the point of light behind all phenomenal appearances. . . . The esotericist knows that in every atom of his body is to be found a point of light. . . . Then he shines forth as a Light Bearer"* ("Lucifer" comes from *lucis,* meaning light, and *ferre,* meaning bearer; concerning the "solar Angel," remember that Isaiah 14:12 states: *"How art thou fallen from heaven, O Lucifer, son of the morning!"*).

Bailey continues: *"Once the disciple has taken the necessary steps, the response of the Angel is sure, automatic, and all-enveloping. Complete obliteration of the personal self in three successive stages is the immediate and normal result. . . . This occult waxing and waning is portrayed for us . . . in the sign of Gemini. When this 'occult obliteration' has taken place, what then is the destiny of the disciple? It is complete control by the soul (solar Angel) and this, in practice, connotes . . . group service and eventually group initiation."*

According to J. Gordon Melton, et al's 1991 *New Age Almanac, "As early as 1920, Alice Bailey introduced the idea of 'points of light' and 'light groups' which channel the higher spiritual forces necessary to build the New Age."* Masonry also uses the term "point of light" and emphasizes group service and initiation, and perhaps coincidentally, President Bush (a Gemini, born June 12) in his August 18, 1988 nomination acceptance speech, emphasized "service," pursuing "the better angels," "a thousand points of light," and said that the election was *"about philosophy. And I have one. At the bright center is the individual. And radiating out from him or her . . . I hope to stand for a new harmony, a greater tolerance. We've come far, but I think we need a new harmony."*

(Remember that "New Harmony" was the name of Robert Dale Owen's commune of the early nineteenth century, located in Indiana.) Prior to Mr. Bush's nomination acceptance speech, President Reagan (an honorary Mason) delivered the convention's keynote speech, saying: *"With George Bush . . . we'll have . . . a nation confidently willing to take its leadership into the uncharted reaches of a new age"* (*New York Times*, August 16, 1988).

● ● ● ● ●

Regarding the possibly coincidental use of terms such as "new age," "points of light," "service," and "new world order" by Masons, occultist Alice Bailey, and Presidents Bush or Reagan, it would be worth looking at President Bush's Points of Light Initiative Foundation. In early January 1990, the foundation's advisory committee issued a report recommending community and national service. Although service was supposed to be "voluntary," some of the recommendations seemed to be of a more "mandatory-voluntary" nature. For example, the report stated that *"every significant sector of American society will form and lead 'peer-to-peer pressure groups,' "* and the Points of Light Foundation *"will determine what each kind of 'institution' (e.g., family, place of worship, etc.) can distinctively contribute to the community service movement and then persuade each such 'institution' to make that contribution."* Regarding "places of worship," most of which have the worship of God as central to their members, the report said: *"Every place of worship will be asked to make community service central to the life of their congregation."* Even five-year-old children are challenged to *"make community service part of their daily pattern of living, "* and the report disturbingly stated that *"at the heart of problems like . . . crack-cocaine, gangs . . . are essentially good people."* Other examples of the report's mandatory "volunteerism" are that the foundation asks *"every employer to include community service among the criteria to determine hiring, compensation, and promotion decisions,"* and *"every college and university is urged . . . to weigh an applicant's community service record in admissions decisions."*

The only way this type of service could be considered "voluntary" is if an individual did not want to go to college or have a job! In early April 1991, the Points of Light Foundation (a private organization started by President Bush's Points of Light Initiative; he serves as the foundation's honorary chairman) sent a letter to every church across the nation promoting and praying for unity and "the new world order." On September 17, 1991, I saw a television ad sponsored by the Points of Light Foundation, which proclaimed concerning service, *"the light to do it is within us all."* This was not long after President Bush took another action that would cause Americans to "voluntarily" choose the New World Order. Despite Americans' rejection several years ago of attempts to impose the metric system upon our lives, Mr. Bush seems determined to ram it down our throats, whether we want it or not. On July 25, 1991, he issued an executive order which stated: *"The head of each executive department and agency shall . . . use, to the extent economically feasible by September 30, 1992 . . . the metric system of measurement in federal government procurements, grants, and other business-related activities. Other business-*

related activities include all use of measurement units in agency programs and functions related to trade, industry, and commerce. . . ."Such a sweeping use of the metric system by the government is not only necessary if the U.S. is to be forced to become like the rest of the world, which already uses the metric system, but it will also force American businesses and individuals to accept and use the metric system, which is a necessary step in forcing the New World Order upon us. Napoleon also imposed the metric system.

Additionally concerning whether President Bush's selection of certain words and phrases that sound New Age is purely coincidental, New Age networker Dorothy Maver of the Seven Ray Institute in New Jersey delivered an address titled "Global Education: The Esoteric Connection" to a group of educators in October 1990, in which she pointed out, *"President Bush has implemented a 'Points of Light' initiative. You may be familiar with this. He suggested it will lead to fuller service, better communications, group work, recognition, and acceptance of our roles as responsible citizens. Again, we can identify and recognize the esoteric connection."*

Constance Cumbey addressed the Human Life International Tenth World Conference at Santa Clara on April 4, 1991, and said that New Ager Donald Keys (a former administrator of Lucis Trust) indicated that he had started many a trend at the U.N., where President Bush used to be an ambassador.

Furthermore, according to *Mind Wars* (1984) by Ron McRae (former associate of columnist Jack Anderson): *"1976 was the first time that parapsychology research got direct and enthusiastic support from the CIA director, then George Bush. Bush was approached by*

[New Age former astronaut] *Edgar Mitchell, a personal friend for many years. Mitchell's Institute of Noetic Sciences in San Francisco, which he founded to promote psychic research, had worked closely with Stanford Research Institute* [where New Ager Willis Harman, now president of the Institute of Noetic Sciences, was located]. *Bush gave Mitchell permission to organize high-level seminars at the CIA to discuss possible intelligence applications of parapsychology."*

This book also contains an entire chapter on the "New Age warrior monks" (the Knights Templar of several centuries ago have also been called "warrior monks") of the First Earth Battalion formed by U.S. Army Lt. Col. Jim Channon. The FEB's charter initiation was conducted at the second quarterly meeting of Task Force Delta, an army think-tank of officers, futurists, and psychologists. New Ager *"Barbara Marx Hubbard, a Delta psychologist, suggested that the First Earth Battalion could 'bombard the Soviets with psychic love rather than hate and suspicion.' Task Force Delta bought the idea, and the First Earth Battalion was born."* The creed of the FEB "guerilla gurus" or "warriors of the spirit" includes: *"I take personal responsibility for generating evolutionary conspiracies as a part of my work. I will select and create conspiratorial mechanisms . . . that will create and perform evolutionary break-through actions on behalf of people and planet. One people, one planet."*

How this might transpire is described by Willis Harman in a World Goodwill (Lucis Trust) Occasional Paper, "For a New Society, a New Economics," published in the April, May, and June 1987 issues of *Development*

Forum, by the United Nations Division for Economic and Social Information and the United Nations University. In this paper, Harman borrows from Abraham Maslow's "self-actualization" theories and his Eupsychean Network to say *"a respiritualization of society is taking place, but one more experiential and non-institutionalized, less fundamentalist and sacerdotal, than most of the historically familiar forms of religion. With this change comes a long-term shift in value emphasis. . . . There may indeed be a conflict between dogmatic esoteric religion and positivistic science. However, there is **not** an inevitable conflict between the esoteric 'perennial wisdom' of the world's spiritual traditions and a science based on certain metaphysical assumptions."* He further states that during the transition period between now and this future time, we *"will see some sort of partial breakdown of the world economic system. This could be triggered by . . . the oppressive debt structure."*

Only a few months after Harman made these remarks, the Dow Jones Industrial Average plunged five hundred eight points on October 19, 1987. In the *Wall Street Journal*'s front page article, "Will Foreigners Shape Bush Policies?" (December 5, 1988), one finds that *"as a result in the rapid rise of overseas debt since 1981, the United States has ceded considerable control over its economy to foreign investors. They now hold the power to help keep the U.S. economy growing or to help plunge it in recession. . . . Secretary of the Treasury Nicholas Brady concluded after his study of last October's* [1987] *market crash that Japanese investors triggered the debacle."*

The Economist in its January 9, 1988 issue wrote that in part to avoid the collapse of the dollar in the future,

"Pencil in the phoenix for around 2018, and welcome it when it comes." The "phoenix" will be the name for the new international monetary unit (or coin). *The Economist* continued: *"National economic boundaries are slowly dissolving. As the trend continues, the appeal of a currency union across at least the main industrial countries will seem irresistible. . . . There would be no such thing . . . as a national monetary policy. The world phoenix supply would be fixed by a new central bank, descended perhaps from the IMF. The world inflation rate — and hence, within narrow margins, each national inflation rate — would be in its charge. . . . This means a big loss of economic sovereignty."* According to radical feminist Barbara Walker's *The Women's Encyclopedia of Myths and Secrets* (1983), the Egyptians closely associated the phoenix bird with the Horus hawk (Horus is associated with the "all-seeing eye" in the top of the pyramid on the reverse side of an American dollar bill). The Egyptians and Phoenicians believed the phoenix to be the representation of a god who *"rose to heaven in the form of a morning star, like Lucifer, after his fire-immolation of death and rebirth,"* as quoted from Walker's book.

Don McAlvany recently warned that the economic planners of the New World Order are moving us toward a cashless society. This is so that through "smart cards," which are like computerized credit cards, it will be possible not only to monitor all of our financial transactions, but also our physical locations and movements, too.

● ● ● ● ●

But what about those who don't go along with the

new values of the New Age and those who don't accept the unity of all people under a one-world government? Their cruel fate might have been revealed by Task Force Delta psychologist Barbara Marx Hubbard, who has been praised by such notable New Agers as Norman Cousins and Buckminster Fuller (the latter of whom received our nation's highest civilian honor, the Presidential Medal of Freedom, from President Reagan on February 23, 1983). In the 1980s, Hubbard published a three-part book, *The Book of Co-Creation*, the first part of which was called "Jesus the Christ — Our Potential Self." In this book, she admonishes: *"Out of the full spectrum of human personality, one-fourth is electing to transcend. . . . One-fourth is destructive* [and] *they are defective seeds. In the past they were permitted to die a 'natural death.' . . . Now as we approach the quantum shift from creature-human to co-creative human — the human who is an inheritor of god-like powers — the destructive one-fourth must be eliminated from the social body. . . . Fortunately, you are not responsible for this act. We are. We are in charge of God's selection process for planet Earth. He selects, we destroy. We are the riders of the pale horse, Death. "*Here, she is alluding to Revelation 6:7-8, but the "God" to which she refers is not the God of the Holy Bible. Rather it is the New Age "god of forces" or "god within."

A few years before Hubbard's book, M. Scott Peck professed in his best-seller *The Road Less Traveled* (1978) that *"the ultimate goal of spiritual growth is for the individual to become as one with God. It is to know with God. Since the unconscious is God all along, we may further define the goal of spiritual growth to be the attainment of godhood by the conscious self. It is for the individual to become totally, wholly God."* And a few years earlier, British socialist Vera Stanley Alder wrote *When Humanity Comes of Age* (1974) describing an existing "Plan" for a "world organization," a "world economy," and a "world religion" where there would be a "Council for Economics" and a "World Food Authority" which operates in manners that seem to fulfill Revelation 13:17, *"And that no man might buy or sell, save he that had the mark, or the name of the beast, or the number of his name."*

At about the same time as Hubbard's book was published, Peter Russell in 1983 wrote *The Global Brain: Speculations on the Evolutionary Leap to Planetary Consciousness* (reminiscent of Alice Bailey's "universal mind" concept and H.G. Wells' *World Brain* published in 1938). Heralded as the next Buckminster Fuller, Russell has written *Encyclopaedia Britannica's Relaxation Programme*, has translated *The Upanishads* (late Vedic metaphysical treatise concerning man's relation to the universe), has been on the advisory board of the Networking Institute (along with Robert Muller and John Naisbitt), and has conducted seminars for major corporations such as IBM and Shell. At a November 9-11, 1984 symposium "Toward a Global Society," he spoke on "The Global Brain: Our Next Evolutionary Step," in which he remarked: *"Evolution is now occurring in our own mind — consciousness. We are God's way of beginning to look back and enjoy what He, She, It has done. God's way of evolution — it's got to the stage with us where She can, through our eyes and through our senses, begin to explore Her own creation. . . . We're beginning to link together to form one world — minds and souls . . . [in] understanding, compassion . . . let go of our own beliefs ('crap stuff'). . . . We stand now at the threshold of the first true spiritualization of humanity. That is probably what the Second Coming is really about. It's nothing to do with an individual coming. It's with the Christ in all of us. . . . The Christ didn't come to say there was only one Son of God."* This is the same lie of Satan in the Garden of Eden, that we can all be "gods."

● ● ● ● ●

According to *New York Times* News Service writer Bill Keller, *Pravda* and *Izvestia* on September 17, 1987, reported that Mikhail Gorbachev *"called for giving the United Nations expanded authority to regulate military conflicts, economic relations, environmental protection and . . . also called for enhancing the power of the afflicted International Court of Justice to decide international disputes."* In this same year (1987), Gorbachev's *Perestroika* was published, in which he revealed that *"the essence of* perestroika *lies in the fact that* **it unites socialism with democracy** *and revives the Leninist concept of socialist construction both in theory and in practice. . . . We want more socialism."*

Barbara Hanna and Janet Hoover in *World Government on the Horizon* (1988) note that the message in Gorbachev's book is similar to that of M. Scott Peck in his 1987 book, *The Different Drum*, in which he suggests world government as a solution to our problems. Hanna and Hoover conclude: *"Both wish to turn more power over to the United Nations. They feel a revolution is necessary. Disarmament is touted as essential to world peace. In the end, we must adopt a new order. Ingredients which may lead us to the desired destination are: interdependence, inclusivity, integrity, peace, and new thinking."* Gorbachev's proposals reported September 17, 1987 in *Pravda* and *Izvestia* also are similar to proposals put forth by Grenville Clark and Louis Sohn in *World Peace Through World Law.*

Less than four months after these newspapers' accounts of Gorbachev's proposals, President Reagan (a former member of the World Federalist Association) on January 11, 1988, addressed the City Club of Cleveland, Ohio, and made the following remarks: *"Even more than in the past, this new world economy is a one-world economy. . . . In this new world economy, national boundaries are increasingly becoming obsolete. . . . These new economic realities dictate a world economy."*

Thirteen days later, on January 24, 1988, the *New York Times* published an interview with former Under-Secretary of State George Ball, who was a key figure in the Vietnam conflict, as well as a member of the CFR and Trilateral Commission. He was also a member of the Bilderbergers (as were David Rockefeller, Henry Kissinger, Baron Edmond de Rothschild, and Father Theodore Hesburgh of Notre Dame University). He said in the *Times* interview: *"The Cold War should no longer be the kind of obsessive concern that it is. Neither side is going to attack the other deliberately. . . . If we could internationalize by using the United Nations in conjunction with the Soviet Union, because we now no longer have to fear, in most cases, a Soviet veto, then we could begin to transform the shape of the world and might get the U.N. back to doing something useful. . . . Sooner or later we are going to have to face restructuring our institutions so that they are not confined merely to the nation states. Start first on a regional, and ultimately you could move to a world, basis."*

Soon after the Republican Convention in 1988, Mikhail Gorbachev (who takes "radon baths") addressed the U.N. on December 7 and praised the *"tremendous impetus to mankind's progress"* that came from the French and Russian revolutions, and he called for a new role for the U.N., saying: *"World progress is only possible through a search for universal human consensus as we move forward to a new world order. . . . What we are talking about . . . is unity in diversity."* (The *Newsweek* article regarding this on December 19, 1988, was titled, "Brave New World.")

Between the time of Gorbachev's statement of December 7, 1988, and the beginning of 1990, a tremendous series of events occurred in Eastern Europe as the world planners' strategy for promoting "democratic socialism" there as the synthesis of Western capitalism (thesis) and Eastern communism (antithesis) was rapidly succeeding. Even though the United States is actually a constitutional republic because our founders rejected democracy as "mobocracy," political leaders increasingly began to refer to the U.S. as a "democracy" and to say that "democracy" should be promoted around the world. (Remember the enthusiasm when the Chinese students in Tiananmen Square erected a statue called "The Goddess of Democracy"?) James Madison said in *Federalist Papers* (No. 10), that *"democracies have ever been spectacles of turbulence and contention; have ever been found incompatible with personal security or the rights of property;*

and have in general been as short in their lives as they have been violent in their deaths." Perhaps that is one reason both Marx and Lenin referred to "democracy" as the necessary stage through which a nation would pass on the road to the communist state.

It should be remembered at this time of Gorbachev's "peace" overtures, that another temporary "one step backward" component of communism's "one step backward, two steps forward" strategy may be occurring, because Lenin said, *"Peace can be a weapon,"* and one should recall what Dimitri Manuilski told students at the Lenin School of Political Warfare in Moscow in 1930. One of the students, Zack Kornfeld, said that Manuilski, who would later serve as Soviet delegate to the U.N., told them in 1930 that to defeat the capitalists beginning several decades from then, *"we shall need the element of surprise. The bourgeoisie will have to be put to sleep. So we shall begin by launching the most spectacular peace movement on record. There will be electrifying overtures and unheard of concessions. The capitalist countries, stupid and decadent, will rejoice to cooperate in their own destruction. They will leap at another chance to be friends. As soon as their guard is down, we will smash them with our clenched fist"* (*Congressional Record*, May 31, 1955). Regarding the supposedly transformed peaceful Russian "bear" today, one might recall the words of Mason Rudyard Kipling in 1898: *"When he shows at seeking quarter, with paws like hands in prayer, that is the time of peril — the time of the Truce of the Bear."*

One year after Gorbachev's December 7, 1988 statement, the December 28, 1989 newsletter of the Association to Unite the Democracies (AUD) applauded Secretary of

State James Baker's call on December 12, 1989, in Berlin for *"the architecture of a New Europe and a New Atlanticism"* and an emphasis upon the Conference on Security and Cooperation in Europe (CSCE) process. AUD highlighted the fact that Gorbachev had called recently for a more "political" NATO and that Baker supported the CSCE process, which AUD included in its "Four Concentric Spheres of Unification" heading toward an Atlantic Community and Atlantic Union.

Who would be at the head of this final federal union? In Malachi Martin's April 6, 1991 speech to Human Life International's Tenth World Conference held at Santa Clara, California, he said: *"It is a matter of public record, and in the words of President George Herbert Walker Bush, Mikhail S. Gorbachev, Francois Mitterand of France, Chancellor Kohl of Germany, and Toshiki Kaifu of Japan, that their aim is to create a new structure for the world. . . . The new Economic Union will be set up. In the meanwhile, the organs already set up — the International Monetary Fund, the World Bank, the GATT (General Agreement on Trades and Tariffs), which will create an omni-nation closed system of export-import which we must join or die! . . . The CSCE is assuming the governing functions of this new . . . concentric structure, and the chosen president of the CSCE is going to be Mikhail S. Gorbachev. This is a matter of public record."*

The faster the world planners could incorporate the nations of Eastern Europe into this process, the faster they might achieve their objective of world government. In that regard, their recent success at promoting socialist democracies in Eastern Europe was succeeding so rapidly by early 1990 that an article titled "New World Order

Galloping Into Position," by Don Oberdorfer (CFR member) in the February 25, 1990 *Washington Post* stated that *"a new world order is taking shape so fast that governments as well as private citizens find it difficult just to absorb 'the gallop of events,' in the apt phrase of Soviet journalist Stanislav Kondrashev."*

Several months later, Gorbachev came to North America, and David Ellis reported in "Gorby, The New Age Guru?" (*Time*, May 18, 1990): *"Fans of Harmonic Convergences and the like have been noting Mikhail Gorbachev's frequent use of phrases associated with the New Age movement, that mystical universal philosophy that preaches — as the Soviet president does — of the need for 'a New World Order.' As Gorbachev said in California, 'All mankind is entering a New Age, and world trends are beginning to obey new laws and logic.' More strikingly, he* [Gorbachev] *held a private meeting in Canada earlier in the week with one of the leading gurus of the New Age movement, Sri Chinmoy, who read him a 'spiritual song' and gave him a volume of admiring letters."*

The next month, Gorbachev would follow up on his earlier theme about "a New World Order" with a speech at Stanford University on June 4, 1990, where he iterated: *"All of us have felt how much we need the United Nations if we really are to move toward a new world, a new kind of relationship in the world in the interest of all countries. . . . The Soviet Union and the United States have more than enough reasons to be partners in building it, in shaping new security structures in Europe and in the Asian Pacific region. And also in the making of a truly global economy, indeed, and the creation of a new civilization. . . . .*"This speech was made about two months **before** Iraq's invasion of Kuwait; about two weeks **prior** to the invasion, Soviet General Makashov (specialist in tank warfare and swift territory seizure) arrived in Baghdad! Secretary of State Baker's spokesperson, Margaret Tutweiler, would also say that *"the U.S. was not obligated to come to Kuwait's aid if the emirate was attacked."*

Picking up on Gorbachev's statements, and almost repeating him, President Bush (former member of the CFR and Trilateral Commission) delivered a speech on September 11, 1990 to Congress in which he said *"the crisis in the Persian Gulf offers a rare opportunity to move toward an historic period of cooperation. Out of these troubled times . . . a new world order can emerge, in which the nations of the world, east and west, north and south, can prosper and live in harmony. . . . Today, that new world is struggling to be born."* Remember here CFR member Nelson Rockefeller's statement in his 1962 book, *The Future of Federalism*, about *"a new world order . . . a new and free order struggling to be born."* And also remember that in the January 30, 1989 *Time*, article, "A New Breeze Is Blowing," President Bush's national security advisor, Brent Scowcroft (a former CFR director), referred to the president as a "Rockefeller Republican."

Interestingly, it was this former vice-chairman of Kissinger Associates, Scowcroft, who seventeen days *before* President Bush's September 11 "New World Order" speech to Congress told Cable News Network on August 25 that the Gulf crisis was reflecting "the emergence of a new world order," with the United Nations functioning as originally intended *"to mobilize the civilized world against aggression and against aggressors."* This was reported in the *New York Times* on August 26, as was also the fact that Henry Kissinger (CFR member) and Alexander Haig (CFR member) were warning the president *"about the dangers of wearing out popular support by waiting too long to act in his effort to control the expanionist ambitions of Saddam Hussein."* This advice was likewise interesting, given that the murderous Saddam Hussein had not invaded Saudi Arabia when he could have easily done so before the arrival of American forces, which would have made the landing of Allied ground troops and the establishment of Allied military bases for combat soldiers and aircraft far more difficult.

Concerning Gorbachev's December 7, 1988, "unity-in-diversity" statement, as well as his June 4, 1990 "new civilization" statement, and President Bush's September 11, 1990 "east and west, north and south" statement, it should be remembered that the Unity-in-Diversity Council's framework for "Implementing the New Civilization" has for years included *"building bridges between . . . east, west, north, south . . . to promote world harmony and cooperation. . . . Creating a new global civilization* [including the emergence of a New Universal Person] *based on unity-in-diversity, a network of planetary citizens, a functional world government."*

Two weeks after President Bush's September 11, 1990 address to Congress, Soviet Foreign Minister Eduard Shevardnadze on September 25 told the United Nations concerning Iraq's invasion of Kuwait that *"an act of terrorism has been perpetrated against the emerging New World Order."* One week later, on October 1, President Bush addressed the United Nations General Assembly and asked the nations of the world *"to press forward to cap a historic movement toward a new world order."* He concluded his speech by proclaiming: *"And so let it be said of the final decade of the twentieth century, this was a time when humankind came into its own . . . to bring about a revolution of the spirit and the mind and began a journey into a new day, a new age, and a new partnership of nations. The U.N. is now fulfilling its promise as the world's parliament of peace. . . ."* Humankind came into its own? A revolution of the spirit and mind? A journey into a new age?

Eleven days later, on October 12, *Newsweek* conducted a survey which showed the president's approval rating had dropped to fifty-four percent from sixty-five percent in July, and in the November 5 issue of *Newsweek* just before the elections, it was reported that President Bush's rating had slipped even further to forty-eight percent. Almost immediately after the elections, the president announced a shift in his policy concerning the American military presence in the Gulf. Instead of being there primarily to protect Saudi Arabia from invasion by Iraq, he announced that American troop levels would be almost doubled there to provide an "offensive capability" against Iraq, thereby almost guaranteeing an American attack in the near future (five hundred thousand troops could not sit there indefinitely, and to withdraw them would be perceived as a humiliating defeat which would seriously undermine the effort to achieve a "New World Order").

About two weeks later, Prime Minister Margaret Thatcher's resignation on November 23, 1990, was forced in part due to her opposition to Great Britain's economic union with Europe officially in 1992, because she believed that would adversely impact upon British sovereignty.

The question of whether Americans have complete "sovereignty" was also cast into doubt in a December 28, 1990 article by Geraldine Brooks and Tony Horowitz in the *Wall Street Journal*, where they related the following comment by a high-ranking official from one of the Arab Gulf states: *"You think I want to send my teenaged son to die for Kuwait? We have our white slaves from America to do that."* What was occurring was not in doubt as far as the World Federalist Association was concerned, as deputy director (until December 31, 1991) Eric Cox had written in their Summer/Fall 1990 newsletter: *"It's sad but true that the slow-witted American press has not grasped the significance of most of these developments. But most federalists know what is happening. . . . And they are not frightened by the old bug-a-boo of sovereignty."*

In the December 1990 issue of *World Press Review*, Yevgeny Primakov (member of the Presidential Council and director of the Soviet Institute of World Economics and International Relations) explained what the Persian Gulf crisis was really all about when he said that the development *"of a new world order that, after the Cold War, can insure stability, security, justice, and the creation of conditions for progress for all people"* is the goal, and that the crisis in the Persian Gulf *"is the kind of laboratory, where our efforts to create a new world order after the Cold War are being tested. These efforts must include the impossibility of imposing one's will on other countries and the right of any people to be free to choose its path of development and system of government. Unquestionably, the mechanisms of the U.N. should play a special and growing role in this process."* And on

December 31, 1990, Mikhail Gorbachev would say that *"the New World Order would be ushered in by the Gulf crisis."* Perhaps this is one reason why President Bush one month later, on January 29, 1991 in his "State of the Union" message, declared: *"What is at stake is more than one small country, it is a big idea — a new world order. . . to achieve the universal aspirations of mankind . . . based on shared principles and the rule of law. . . . The illumination of a thousand points of light. . . . The winds of change are with us now."* Remember here that many years ago, Gustave le Bon said: *"In politics, things are less important than their names. To disguise even the most absurd ideas with well-chosen words is enough to gain their acceptance."*

In the World Association for World Federation's (which has a U.N. office) "Action Priorities Post Gulf War Period 1991," one reads that the WAWF *"proposed that all nations allocate **standing forces** to the U.N. in advance of conflict. . . . An important new initiative for WAWF is to organize for the creation of a United Nations Parliamentary Assembly. This is part of our answer to the question of 'how can world federation be achieved?' . . . We believe a U.N. Parliamentary Assembly could provide the missing political leadership on behalf of world unity and U.N. charter reform. If we can succeed in seeing such an assembly created, citizens will gain a permanent ally in the U.N. system to help get governments to move on larger U.N. charter reforms. Change can then come more quickly."*

Only about one week after the president's "State of the Union" message, he told the Economic Club of New York on February 6, *"My vision of a new world order foresees a United Nations with a revitalized peacekeeping function."* He explained that as a member of the Security Council, China could veto peacekeeping operations, and he admitted that is why he thinks *"it is vital to this new world order that that veto* [his veto of congressional legislation denying "most favored nation" status to China after the Tiananmen Square massacre] *hold."*

This contention regarding the role of China as a permanent member of the Security Council was supported in the Spring 1991 issue of the CFR's *Foreign Affairs* in an article, "The U.N. in a New World Order," by Bruce Russett and James Sutterlin (the latter being a former director of the Executive Office of the U.N. Secretary General). The authors commented that *"the Gulf action became possible because the permanent members of the Security Council cooperated. . . . Representatives of the United States and the Soviet Union have repeatedly suggested that such action is an important element in a new world order. . . . The new world order envisioned by Presidents Bush and Gorbachev would be founded on the rule of law and on the principle of collective security. That principle necessarily entails the possibility of military enforcement measures by the United Nations. . . . But to be acceptable to the majority of U.N. members, such a force must retain an indisputable U.N. identity and must not be dominated by one member state. . . . The manner in which the gulf military action was executed by the United States and its coalition partners will likely limit the willingness of council members to follow a similar procedure in the future — a procedure that leaves council members little control over the course of military operations and over the conclusion of hostilities. . . . The*

Security Council should be able to mobilize a force to serve under U.N. command for enforcement purposes. That capacity may be virtually indispensable in an emergent world order."

Just two days after President Bush's February 6 address in New York, however, Senator Jesse Helms on February 8 at the Conservative Political Action Conference (CPAC) in Washington, D.C., said he believed and hoped that it would be a *"long time before a 'new world order' emerged and that there never could be one based on atheistic materialism."*

When Howard Phillips addressed several hundred conservative leaders in Washington, D.C., on April 13, 1991, he told them that *"the New World Order constitutes no proper part of the heritage of American liberty. . . . Today, America's autonomy and independence are profoundly challenged — not by the armies of foreign tyrants or even the intrigues of domestic enemies, but by the immense power of forces which seek openly to diminish or abolish our distinctiveness as a free nation. Their perverted idealism is based on a secular humanist vision of 'one world' — a Utopian world unified by the abolition of borders, conflicts, and the enforced disregard of distinctions in character, heritage, and faith. . . . Submitting to a New World Order requires that America eventually surrender its independence, its unique political institutions and laws, and even the control of its own foreign policy to institutions and individuals beyond accountability, in which governing bodies bear no direct relation to the people from whose consent their legitimacy is properly derived. . . . The New World Order is not a new idea. It has long been a dream of Utopian humanists and of commercial activitists who seek to break down political entities which are inconvenient to their pursuit of profits."*

Howard Phillips' concerns regarding the threat to American sovereignty posed by the current U.N. actions against Iraq were not unwarranted, because on CNN's "Crossfire" in late July 1991, former CIA director Stansfield Turner (CFR member), when asked about Iraq, answered: *"We have a much bigger objective. We've got to look to the long run here. This is an example — the situation between the United Nations and Iraq — where the United Nations is deliberately intruding into the sovereignty of a sovereign nation. . . . Now this is a marvelous precedent* [to be used in] *all countries of the world."*

Turner's comments came shortly after *The Economist* editorialized in "The World Order Changeth" (June 22, 1991) that *"America itself needs to remember that a willingness to involve others is not enough to make a collective world order work. There must also be readiness to submit to it. If America really wants such an order, it will have to be ready to . . . submit itself to the International Court . . .* [and] *make a habit of consulting the U.N. Is it ready to do so?"*

This was just four days after Secretary of State James Baker delivered an address on June 18 in Berlin to the Aspen Institute for Humanistic Studies, saying, *"Our objective is both a Europe whole and free and a Euro-Atlantic community that extends east from Vancouver to Vladivostok. . . . To me, the Trans-Atlantic relationship stands for certain Enlightenment ideals of universal applicability. . . . Our structures need to promote Euro-Atlantic political and economic values, the ideals of the*

Enlightenment," and he emphasized the Conference on Security and Cooperation in Europe (CSCE) as becoming "a true community of values."

The New World Order is supposed to be a socialist synthesis of Western capitalism and Eastern communism, but there is a fundamental flaw in the thinking that socialism will benefit man better than capitalism. When capitalist economic activities are used to promote biblical principles through charitable acts, capitalism is better than socialism, as illustrated in the following example. A capitalist and a socialist each had $5,000 which they invested and doubled. The socialist gave all of his profit to the poor, but the capitalist kept $1,000 of his profit, giving only $4,000 to the poor. At first glance, it appears that socialism is more helpful to the poor than is capitalism. However, if the above process were repeated four more times, one would see that the socialist would have given $25,000 to the poor, but the capitalist would have given $30,000 while having $10,000 for himself (the second time, the capitalist would have invested his $6,000, doubled that, given $5,000 to the poor, and kept $7,000, etc.) The comparative results obviously favor capitalism.

The Swedish model of socialism has been used as an example to be followed by other countries, but Sweden has the highest inflation and lowest economic growth rates in Western Europe. Swedish-born Prof. Eric Brodin, director of the Foundation for International Studies, was quoted in *Reader's Digest* (September 1991) as saying: *"Socialism, whether of the Marxist, democratic, or nationalist kind, is bound to fail. . . . If the Swedish experiment in cradle-to-grave welfarism serves as an eye-opener to those who would imitate it, then it will have served an important purpose."*

Chapter Seventeen

The Houses of
Orange and Rothschild

Throughout the centuries, revolutionary change has often come in times of crisis. In a November 12-13, 1977, interview with Michael L. Chadwick, Norman Dodd predicted that the United States and the Soviet Union would be brought together by some emergency or crisis (foreshadowing the war with Iraq?). Largely controlling the events over the past four hundred years, he said, was the House of Orange (established as a corporation at the turn of the eighteenth century). What is interesting about this is that just as President Bush today promotes a "New World Order," the *Encyclopaedia Britannica* informs us that King William III of England (William of Orange from Holland) had *"an ideal which he had pursued doggedly for thirty years, an international order in which no single power was able to tyrannize the rest."* Both President Bush and William of Orange had a common ancestor in King Henry III of England in the thirteenth century, and President Bush also has ancestors from Holland through Francis Cooke fifteen generations ago. Interesting also is the quotation, *"Despite the birth of the disctinctive Masonry of William of Orange in 1694,"* that one finds in *Freemasonry and the Vatican* (1968) by

Vicomte Léon de Poncins.

Here it should be remembered that the powerful Habsburg family became connected with the House of Orange when Queen Mary died suddenly in 1482 and Holland passed to her son Philip, who was under the guardianship of his father, the Austrian Archduke Maximilian. Philip was succeeded by his son Charles (the Holy Roman emperor), who was succeeded by Philip III of Holland, who in 1559 appointed William I of Orange as stadholder. William was assassinated in 1584, and in 1585 Robert Dudley (Earl of Leicester who after his wife had suddenly and mysteriously died, began to court Queen Elizabeth I of England by whom he allegedly had Francis Bacon, who possibly wrote the works of Shakespeare) arrived and exercised sovereignty over northern Holland for two years.

Around three hundred years later at the beginning of the twentieth century, Juliana was born to Queen Wilhelmina of the House of Orange. Juliana became Queen of the Netherlands in 1948 and in the 1970s was among the "First Endorsers" of Planetary Citizens. At about that time, it was estimated that she owned five percent of the stock of Royal Dutch/Shell (worth around four hundred twenty-five million dollars in 1978). Her husband, Prince Bernhard, had founded the Bilderbergers in 1954 and has also been an international director of the World Wildlife Fund with Prince Charles of England (who has experimented with shamanism, and whose mentor, Lord Mountbatten, was into Theosophy and such Madame Blavatsky writings as *The Secret Doctrine*).

Currently very active is the Worldwide Fund for Nature, with Prince Philip of England as its president. In

Trashing the Planet by Dixy Lee Ray with Lou Guzzo (1990), Prince Philip is quoted as saying in 1989 that *"were he to be reincarnated, he would wish to return as a 'killer virus to lower human population levels.' "* And according to Hamish Fraser's *Approaches* 1970 study document "Sex Education: Its Role in the Anti-Life Conspiracy," Prince Philip suggests population control *"by additives to the food or water supply."* (It is noteworthy here that President Jimmy Carter's chief advisor on health and drug abuse and an advocate of abortion-on-demand, Peter Bourne, went to the United Nations as a consultant on the world's water needs after Bourne was forced out of the White House by a drug scandal before he could implement a strategy involving the establishment of *"a massive network of government family planning clinics."*) After a meeting of Prince Philip (a Mason) and Pope John Paul II on April 11, 1990, the Vatican accepted the Worldwide Fund for Nature as a consultant on nature conservation.

In a related activity, banking magnate Baron Edmund de Rothschild (of the House of Rothschild) attended the September 11-18, 1987 "Fourth World Wilderness Congress" held in Colorado, and was there creating the International World Conservation Bank (called "a New Magna Carta") that would collateralize thirty percent of the earth's land surface ("debt for nature" swap). The congress was opened with the reading of a personal message and greeting from President Ronald Reagan, and speakers at the congress included current Secretary of State James Baker and David Rockefeller. The congress was a project of the International Wilderness Leadership Foundation, with trustee Edmund de Rothschild and advisory board members including Jay Hair (now president of the National Wildlife Federation, U.S.A.) and William Reilly (then president of the World Wildlife Fund, and currently head of the federal Environmental Protection Agency). The official hosts of the congress were the New Age "Findhorn Group" (an ashram in Loveland, Colorado) calling themselves the "Emissaries of Divine Light." George Hunt, who attended the congress, said it *"set in motion a one-world economic system with the United Nations becoming the legislative congress."* Hunt compiled a packet of material on the congress which he distributed along with a videotape in June 1988, and in the packet is an item titled, "Sri Swami Aurobindo's 'Fourth World Wilderness' of Auroville (India) and Baca (Colorado)," in which Hunt writes: *"Aurobindo's 'truth consciousness' philosophies describe the beginnings of a 'consensus reality,' to be employed by the elite rulers in the New Era, for the new world order of society. Individuality and personal rights are stifled and a group mentality will take its place. Perhaps this is what the head of 'Live Earth' was referring to in the videotape and the technique to be used to 'harness love' as Edmund de Rothschild proposes."*

• • • • •

Regarding the House of Orange (Holland) and the House of Rothschild, the Bank of Amsterdam was established in Holland in 1609 and made possible the establishment of the Bank of England (almost synonymous with Rothschild) in the following manner. The Bank of Amsterdam had financed Oliver Cromwell's rise to power in England, and the same bankers also financed William of Orange's becoming king of England with his wife Mary as queen in 1689. He then had the British treasury borrow one and a quarter million pounds from these bankers and issued them a royal charter for the bank of England to be established. By 1698, the British treasury owed the Bank of England sixteen million pounds, and with interest the debt rose to eight hundred eighty-five million pounds by 1815. Norman Dodd has indicated that it was through the mechanism of getting sovereigns in debt that the House of Orange has been able to wield so much power in the world (and remember that the U.S. currently has a staggering international debt). Now, enter the Rothschilds.

Mayer Amschel Rothschild was born February 23, 1744, and his original last name was Bauer (he adopted the name Rothschild, meaning "red shield"). In *Twenty-Eight Years in Wall Street* (1888), Henry Clews (who twice declined the position of U.S. secretary of the treasury), writes that Rothschild's intention was to make his five sons *"dominate Europe by the power of their wealth, so that the ordinary kings would become their subjects."* Clews goes on to reveal that *"it is not generally known that Rothschild's first great start in financial life was given to him by the use of the twenty million dollars which was paid to the Landgrave of Hesse, Frederic II* [a Mason], *by George III of England, for seventeen thousand Hessians to retain the American colonies. This blood money was the original basis of the vast fortune of the Rothschilds."* King George IV (the Prince of Wales) was the grand master of the Grand Lodge of England from 1791 to 1812.

Nathan, Mayer's son, made six million pounds in

one day by personally witnessing the Battle of Waterloo in 1815, and quickly returning to London to mislead members of the stock exchange into thinking Napoleon had won so that they would sell their stock cheaply. Nathan's agents secretly bought them, making a huge profit when news of Napoleon's defeat finally arrived. As Richard Lewinsohn described it in *The Profits of War* (1937), *"it was the Rothschilds, Napoleon's most implacable of enemies, who came off best. Under Metternich, after long hesitation finally agreed to accept financial direction from the House of Rothschild. The least important of the five brothers, who was at Naples, established a veritable financial dictatorship."* In Frederic Morton's *The Rothschilds* (1961), one reads that *"someone once said that the wealth of Rothschild consists of the bankruptcy of nations."* (Remember the above statement concerning the House of Orange "getting sovereigns in debt.")

In 1844, eight years after the death of Nathan Rothschild, Benjamin Disraeli wrote the novel *Coningsby; or the New Generation,* in which he stated, *"So you see, my dear Coningsby, that the world is governed by very different personages from what is imagined by those who are not behind the scenes."* In the book, Disraeli modeled the character, Sidonia, after Nathan Rothschild, writing that *"Sidonia had become one of the most considerable personages in Europe. He had established a brother, or a near relative, in whom he could confide, in most of the principal capitals. He was lord and master of the money-markets of the world, and of course virtually lord and master of everything else. . . . But in the height of his vast prosperity he suddenly died."* Nathan Rothschild had believed his enemies were trying to kill him, and according to Henry Clews in *Twenty-Eight Years in Wall Street*, Nathan's last words were, *"He is trying to kill me. Quick, quick, give me the gold."*

Mayer Amschel Rothschild supposedly once said, *"Let me issue and control a nation's money, and I care not who writes its laws."* In the United States, this would be relevant to the Bank of the United States. In Gustavus Myer's *History of the Great American Fortunes* (1936), one finds that *"under the surface, the Rothschilds long had a powerful influence in dictating American financial laws. The law records show that they were the power in the old Bank of the United States."* This bank, which existed from 1816 to 1836, was abolished by President Andrew Jackson, who warned: *"The bold effort the present bank had made to control the government, the distress it had wantonly produced . . . are but premonitions of the fate that awaits the American people should they be deluded into a perpetuation of this institution or the establishment of another like it."* Col. Edward Mandell House's father, Thomas, had come to America from England to fight for Sam Houston (who along with Davy Crockett and Jim Bowie were members of the same Strict Observance lodge), and according to Rose L. Martin's 1968 book, *Fabian Freeway* (acclaimed by the *Los Angeles Times*), *"Thomas William House acted as an American agent for London banking interests, said by some to be the House of Rothschild, which had invested in Texas rice, cotton, and indigo from 1825."* And according to Arthur D. Howden Smith in *Mr. House of Texas*, Thomas House *"was one of the few residents of a Confederate state to emerge from the Civil War with a handsome personal fortune in cotton, land, and private banking."*

At the beginning of the twentieth century, an associate of the Rothschilds, a German banker named Paul Warburg, immigrated to the United States in 1902. Warburg became associated specifically with the banking firm of Kuhn, Loeb, & Co.; and the Rothschilds were also behind American bankers like J.P. Morgan and Brown Brothers Harriman (as in Averell Harriman's family; President Bush's father, Prescott Bush, was a senior partner in this latter firm and was the financial organizer of Columbia Broadcasting System). J.P. Morgan specifically fronted for Nathan Meyer Rothschild of London, and by 1905 all the Rothschilds had about sixty million dollars in American securities. In "Masters of Capital in America: The Seven Men" (*McClure's* magazine, August 1911), John Moody and George Kibbe Turner expose how *"seven men in Wall Street now control a great share of the fundamental industries and resources of the United States."* These men included J.P. Morgan, John D. Rockefeller, and Jacob Schiff of Kuhn, Loeb, & Co., which was associated with Citibank. An editorial in the same issue of *McClure's* warned that *"all fundamental resources, and all industries capable of forming a unit, are being drawn together toward monopoly control . . . a central monopoly in the great security and money market of New York. . . . And if corporate centralization of power continues unchecked, what is the next great popular agitation to be in this country? For state socialism?"*

The Rothschilds' ownership and influence was spreading far and wide. Kent Cooper of the Associated Press wrote in *Barriers Down* (1942) that at the beginning of the twentieth century, the Rothschilds heading a group of international bankers either bought or had tremendous influence over Reuters International News Agency, Wolff News Agency (Germany), and Havas News Agency (France). Speaking primarily about international banking interests, President Woodrow Wilson in his book, *The New Freedom* (appearing serially in *World's Works* from January to July, 1913), wrote: *"Since I entered politics, I have chiefly had men's views confided to me privately. Some of the biggest men in the United States, in the field of commerce and manufacture, are afraid of somebody, are afraid of something. They know that there is a power somewhere so organized, so subtle, so watchful, so interlocked, so complete, so pervasive, that they had better not speak above their breath when they speak in condemnation of it."* Wilson knew whereof he spoke, because it was largely through these banking interests that he became president in 1913. His "alter ego," Col. House had, like his father, Thomas House, become a front man for these banking interests, like Paul Warburg who helped craft and obtain Wilson's approval of the Federal Reserve, which became law in December 1913, and Warburg served on its original board. Almost twenty years later, President Roosevelt, in his first year in office, wrote a letter to Col. House on November 21, 1933, stating: *"The real truth of the matter is, as you and I know, that a financial element in the larger centers has owned government ever since the days of Andrew Jackson — and I am not wholly excepting the Administration of W.W."*

Concerning the origin of the Federal Reserve legislation, the president of the Rockefeller National City Bank of New York, Frank Vanderlip, wrote in "From Farm Boy to Financier" (*The Saturday Evening Post*, February

9, 1935) that *"there was an occasion, near the close of 1910, when I was as secretive — indeed, as furtive — as any conspirator. . . . I do not feel it is any exaggeration to speak of our secret expedition to Jekyl Island as the occasion of the actual conception of what eventually became the Federal Reserve System. . . . Since it would be fatal to Senator Nelson Aldrich's* [father-in-law of John D. Rockefeller, Jr.] *plan to have it known that he was calling on anybody from Wall Street to help him in preparing his report and bill. . . . We were told to leave our last names behind us. . . ."* To later assure that Woodrow Wilson was "in line" with what the planners were doing, Col. House's papers reveal that he wrote on December 19, 1912: *"I talked with Paul Warburg over the telephone regarding currency reform. I told of my Washington trip and what I had done there to get it in working order; that the senators and congressmen seemed anxious to do what Governor Wilson desired and that I knew the president-elect thought straight concerning the issue."*

During the First World War, George Mandel (real name Jereboam Rothschild, according to John Gunther's *Inside Europe*, written in 1938) actually ran the government of France in 1917 and 1918 while Clemenceau was preoccupied with the war. (The actual rulers of the Banque de France were its regents, and a Rothschild had become a regent in 1855.) At about the same time, Col. House, according to Rose Martin in *Fabian Freeway,* *"formed a lasting friendship with journalist George Landsbury, a lifelong pillar of the Fabian Society . . .* [who] *once persuaded the American soap millionaire, Joseph Fels* [a member of the London Fabian Society, thanks to the prodding of his wife Mary Fels, née Rothschild], *to lend five hundred pounds sterling to underground Russian social democrats including Lenin and Trotsky, when they were stranded in England."*

Contributing about twenty million dollars to the Russian Revolution was Jacob Schiff (of Kuhn, Loeb, & Co.) whose ancestors had been connected with the Rothschilds for almost one hundred years. Also contributing to Aleksandr F. Kerensky and the Russian Revolution was Federal Reserve Bank of New York director William Boyce Thompson. According to Hermann Hagedorn in *The Magnate: William Boyce Thompson and His Time (1869-1930),* published in 1935, Thompson in September 1917 contacted the Morgans to give one million dollars of Thompson's own money to Kerensky et al.

Earlier, via his J.P. Morgan partners, Thompson had been secretly acting for the British government in marketing high-grade American securities. When Kerensky finally fell, Thompson argued that the U.S. could work with the Bolsheviks (Lenin and Trotsky), and after he returned to the U.S., he authorized an interview in the *New York World* (January 13, 1918), in which he said: *"Russia is pointing the way to great and sweeping world changes. It is not in Russia alone that the old order is passing. There is a lot of the old order in America, and that is going too. We may just as well open our eyes to it — all of us. The time has come everywhere when affairs must be handled for the benefit of the many — never again for the comparatively few, and what I call legislation by proxy must cease. I'm glad it is so. When I sat and watched those democratic conclaves in Russia, I felt that I would welcome a similar scene in the United States."*

In Albert Fox's interview with Thompson published in the February 3, 1918 *Washington Post*, Thompson advocated that the United States recognize the Bolshevik government. He also became a founding member of the CFR, which in 1923 made Averell Harriman (Skull and Bones, 1913) a member. Harriman's father had made a fortune in railroads with the support of Jacob Schiff of Kuhn, Loeb, & Co., and in 1920 Harriman & Co. gave a loan to Lenin. Averell Harriman also formed a joint shipping firm with the Russian communists, and all of this was prior to their recognition by the United States government as the legal government of Russia. At this time, one might be perplexed as to why capitalists would be conducting business with the leaders of the U.S.S.R. who had vowed to overthrow the capitalist nations of the world. Here however, one must remember that the U.S.S.R. stands for the Union of Soviet Socialist Republics (emphasis on *socialist*), and there is a difference between capitalists and monopoly capitalists. Socialism imposes more government regulations or controls than capitalism, and monopoly capitalists can believe that through financial contributions they can persuade politicians to impose government regulations or controls favorable to the monopoly capitalists against potential competitors.

Seeing what was happening in Russia, Winston Churchill wrote in the February 8, 1920 *Illustrated Sunday Herald* (London): *"From the days of Weishaupt to those of Karl Marx, to those of Trotsky, Bela Kuhn, Rosa Luxembourg, and Emma Goldman, this worldwide conspiracy has been steadily growing. This conspiracy has played a definitely recognizable role in the tragedy of the French Revolution. It has been the mainspring of every subversive movement during the nineteenth century; and now at last, this band of extraordinary personalities from the underworld of the great cities of Europe and America have gripped the Russian people by the hair of their heads, and have become practically the undisputed masters of that enormous empire."* Similarly in his essay on Leon Trotsky in *Great Contemporaries*, Churchill wrote: *"The citadel will be stormed under the banners of liberty and democracy; and once the apparatus of power is in the hands of the brotherhood, all opposition, all contrary opinions, must be extinguished by death."*

Returning to the Rothschilds, they have been quite active in recent years, too. Victor Rothschild (1910-1990) was a British intelligence agent, and Carola Warburg Rothschild (died in 1987 at ninety-one years of age) was vice-president of the Girl Scouts of America (and chairman of its camp committee), a board member of Planned Parenthood, and helped organize Lord Louis Mount-batten's United World Colleges project. And for many years, the price of gold has been fixed each day in an upstairs room at N.M. Rothschild in London.

Perhaps relevant at this point concerning the New World Order are the thoughts of leading New Ager William Irwin Thompson as expressed in the Spring 1991 edition of *Quest*. In the magazine, he says that America *"created a process of planetization of the economy . . . [and] has energized and set up our previous enemies, Germany and Japan, and created the system that enabled them to very rapidly become wealthy and dynamic. . . . It's sort of a return to the Middle Ages in the sense that nationalism is not as important as it used to be. Money and economic class now dictate who reigns over the earth.*

*Society is beginning to take on very medieval charac-
teristics."* Does this sound like the Knights Templar?
Thompson continued: *"There is a ruling class at the top
that communicates through oral means, face-to-face
. . . and at the bottom there is an underclass. So it's
almost like a return of the Vedic* [Hindu] *caste system.
. . . The ruling oral class has the right accent, and has
wealth. . . . The rich get richer and the poor poorer, and
the smaller ruling class just rules the masses through
pageantry and **illusion**. . . . We have now a new spirituality, what has been called the New Age movement. The
planetization of the esoteric has been going on for some
time. . . . This is now beginning to influence concepts of
politics and community in ecology. . . . This is the Gaia*
[Mother Earth] *politique . . . planetary culture. . . .
Japan got Detroit's automotive industry and the United
States got* [Buddhist] *Zen monasteries in California.
. . . The esoteric tradition of the New Age has been going
on for a long time."* He also stated that *"the independent
sovereign state, with the sovereign individual in his
private property are over, just as the Christian fundamentalist days are about to be over. We are fast becoming
a planetary culture."*

It was in this planetary culture that the BCCI
banking scandal occurred. The bank operated around the
world, employing pimps and prostitutes, and engaging in
political payoffs, too. When the first hints occurred that
something unsavory might be going on, the chief investi-
gator was dismissed as believing in conspiracies. He has
now been proven correct, and one should remember this
when considering the information presented in this book.

Chapter Eighteen

Big Business

In addition to banking interests, political influence and power today is also exercised via multinational corporations like Royal Dutch/Shell (headquartered in the Netherlands), in which the Rothschilds have been heavy stockholders. For example, the Shell Oil representative in North Carolina has been Bert Bennett, who was referred to by Vice-President Hubert Humphrey as the "Lord God Almighty of Politics," and who is responsible for the political rise of individuals such as former Governor James Hunt (now chairman of Carnegie's National Board for Professional Teaching Standards) and U.S. Senator Terry Sanford (on the board of directors of World Federalists of North Carolina in 1947 when that organization called a uniting conference from which emerged the United World Federalists, today known as World Federalist Association, an affiliate of World Association for World Federation, headquartered in Amsterdam, the Netherlands). Interestingly, in the recent conflict in the Middle East, Royal Dutch/Shell has significant interests in Egypt, Syria, the United Arab Republics (Saudi Arabia), the United Arab Emirates, Turkey, Cyprus, Oman, and Libya, but *not* in Iraq or Kuwait! It will take five to seven years to restore Kuwait's oil production to pre-war levels and about one hundred million dollars a day was burning up in smoke there. The tremendously profitable job of rebuilding Kuwait (and Iraq) will go largely to Bechtel Corporation, from which came former Secretary of State George Shultz, former Secretary of Defense Caspar Weinberger, and former CIA director Richard Helms — all of whom have been CFR members. The only current American oil concern in Kuwait has been Aramco, of which Exxon owns twenty-eight and one-third percent, and Exxon is one of the corporations that came from Standard Oil. Because of the embargo in the Gulf, also affected have been Exxon affiliates Kuwait Oil Tanker Co. in Mina al-Ahmadi, Kuwait, and the Iraqi Maritime Transport Co. in the devastated city of Basra, Iraq. The oil industry in Kuwait was originally developed by Gulf Oil, which is now BP, which bought Standard Oil. Did the war in the Middle East just happen?

And did the *Exxon Valdez* just happen to run aground? It probably did, but on March 13, 1991, the Exxon Corp. agreed to pay one hundred million dollars in criminal liability and nine hundred million dollars in civil damages because of what happened (Exxon would later withdraw from the agreement when the state of Alaska indicated it would not be paid enough). And what happened, according to Art Davidson's *In the Wake of the Exxon Valdez* (1990), is revealed in the following curious statements: *"Captain Hazelwood said, 'I am going to . . . reduce speed to about twelve knots to wind my way through the ice.' However, despite Hazelwood's assurance to the Coast Guard, the ship's speed was not reduced. . . . Hazelwood did not notify the Coast Guard when he left the traffic separation zone . . .* [as they] *enter the gap between the ice and the reef. The ship was still accelerating. . . . Hazelwood gave the helmsman two last orders: to accelerate to sea speed and to put the ship on automatic pilot. Both commands were highly unusual. Speed was normally reduced when ice was encountered. . . . The automatic pilot — almost never used in the Sound. . . . Hazelwood neither gave the third mate an exact course to follow nor plotted a line on the chart. . . . The vessel was increasing speed. . . . Impact. . . . The tanker ground to a halt. . . . For fifteen minutes, Hazelwood held the throttle forward on sea speed. . . . The ship groaned as rock ground metal. . . . The stench of crude oil filled the air. . . . Twenty-three minutes after grounding, Hazelwood finally radioed the Coast Guard traffic control."*

● ● ● ● ●

For years, there's been a mighty economic (and political) struggle between the Rothschilds (Royal Dutch/Shell) and the Rockefellers (Standard Oil). In Frederic Morton's *The Rothschilds* (1961), one finds that Edmond Rothschild in the early twentieth century *"engaged in the customary activities on the Family program (his specialty was dividing the world's oil with Shell and Standard Oil)."* And in "Frenzied Finance" by Thomas Lawson (one of the famous "muckraker" journalists) in *Everybody's Magazine* (August 1904), one reads: *". . . There gather each day, between the hours of eleven and twelve o'clock, all the active men whose efforts make 'Standard Oil' what 'Standard Oil' is. . . . Reports are presented . . . republics and empires made and unmade. . . . The success of 'Standard Oil' is largely due to two things — the loyalty of its members to each other and to 'Standard Oil,' and the punishment of its enemies. Each member before initiation knows its religion to be reward for friends and extermination of enemies. Once a man is within the magic circle . . . punishment for disloyalty is sure and terrible, and in no corner of the earth can he escape it, nor can any power on earth protect him from it. . . . Every twist and turn in the pedigree and records of Republicans and Democrats are as familiar to* [the head of Standard Oil] *as the 'dope sheets' are to the gambler, for is he not at the receiving end of the greatest information bureau in the world? A 'Standard Oil' agent is in every hamlet in the country."*

According to Norman Dodd, the House of Orange is known today as the Société Générale de Belgique (founded in 1822) and owns hundreds of corporations around the world, having gained and wielded power by following the principle that "if you get a sovereign in debt, you have control of him." Remember here Willis Harman's statement quoted earlier that *"the oppressive debt structure"* could induce a *"partial breakdown of the world economic system,"* which would provide the crisis needed to issue in the managed New World Order he desired.

Perhaps this matter of "debt" also helps explain the tremendous changes that have occurred over the past two dozen years in such institutions as the American family and the Catholic Church, as both parents in American families entered the work force in increasing numbers to pay for items purchased on credit, and as the Vatican faced a crisis of debt. It is fairly well established that the "P-2" Freemasons' lodge was heavily involved in the

Vatican banking scandal, and there has been speculation that Pope John Paul I was murdered just after he discovered and was about to act upon this matter (remember the speculation regarding the possible poisoning of Pope Leo XIII in 1903). In Rupert Cornwell's *God's Banker* (1983), one reads, *"Then there was the puzzle of the two transfers in spring 1981, of ninety-five million dollars and forty-eight million dollars from Bellatrix . . . to those peculiar Zirka and Recioto accounts held at Rothschild Bank, Zurich."* Were the Rothschilds involved? There is no proof of this, and no accusation is made. It is a fact, though, that the Rothschilds have been doing business with the Vatican since the early nineteenth century, and have lent millions of dollars to the Holy See. For example, Pope Pius XII's grandfather's brother, Ernesto Pacelli, was a member of the Rothschild banking firm who came to Rome in the early 1840s and facilitated a large loan to the papal states and set up the first offices of Banco di Roma. Interesting also is the fact that a unicorn is on the Rothschilds' coat-of-arms. Curious, though, is the question of how, if the Vatican is hard-pressed for funds, it could jointly sponsor with the Smithsonian Institution and the University of Arizona a two hundred million dollar observatory in Arizona in 1990? And the Smithsonian a few years ago with the Institute of Noetic Sciences (New Ager Willis Harman is president) planned a symposium that included topics on altered states of consciousness and "Death and Dying: A Buddhist Perspective." Remember here that the Smithsonian was originated by Robert Dale Owen, who desired revolutionary change in America.

Chapter Nineteen

The Grand Design
and the Future

Revolutionary change brought about by crisis is also one of the principles upon which Alice Bailey and her followers have relied to bring forth the New Age one-world government and one-world religion. The World Conference of Religion for Peace at Louvain, Belgium (August 28-September 3, 1974), was characterized in a *Toronto Star* article (August 17, 1974) by Dr. Ernest Howse as *"possibly . . . one small step on the pathway to one world,"* and one of Douglas Roche's reports at the conference was titled, "We *Can* Achieve a New World Order." In William Irwin Thompson's *Evil and World Order* (1976), he speaks of lending "a little New Age lustre" to a particular candidate's political campaign, and predicts that systems scientists will extend their systems to include areas of culture that are likely to be a feature of the creation of a "new world order based on general systems theory." Thompson is a trustee of the Aspen Institute for Humanistic Studies, on the advisory council of Planetary Citizens, and founder of Lindisfarne, which is supported by the Rockefeller Fund and has its official headquarters at the Cathedral of St. John the Divine (begun in 1892 with funding from J.P. Morgan). The

Encyclopedia of Occultism and Parapsychology indicates that Thompson developed his concept of a new "planetary culture" involving a synthesis of science, art, and spiritual awareness, and founded Lindisfarne in 1973 after visiting Findhorn community in Scotland. According to the encyclopedia, he *"regarded Lindisfarne as typifying a historic clash between esoteric Christianity and ecclesiastical Christianity, between religious experience and religious authority. . . . All this has much in common with contemporary outlooks loosely labelled **New Age**."*

David Spangler is on the faculty of Lindisfarne, and the financial officer is Canadian Maurice Strong, who is with the U.N. and seems to be connected with the Rothschilds. He is custodian of a politically conscious group of New Age ashrams called "the Baca" at Crestone, Colorado, which has been visited by David Rockefeller, Henry Kissinger, and members of the British royal family. The Lindisfarne Temple has been built with "sacred architecture" principles from Babylonian and Egyptian systems supposedly for the "communion of the mystical body of Christ" which is supposed to be the union of the "God of the Heavens" (sky god) with "Gaia of the Earth" (earth mother) in the "holy grail," surrounded by a Rosicrucian rose-shaped seating arrangement, to usher in the "Aquarian Christ" who will head the new world religion. There is also a Carmelite Hermitage at "the Baca" where fourteen male and female "monks" live, including Abbot William McNamara who received his "mandate" for an ecumenical eremitic community from Pope John XXIII, and who says the "Our Father" backward (which is satanic and part of the "Black Mass"). Likewise at the hermitage is Abbess Tessa Bielecki, who has stated that *"the affective energy which the mystic consumes in the love of God is the same as that which others make use of in erotic love."* She speaks of man's *"feminine principle — the woman within, the eternal woman . . . every man must make his soul feel like a woman."* Father Dave Denny is also at the hermitage, and in "Christ the Wolf," he exercises his wild imagination and describes Christ as a wolf. If you've wondered where these people get all the money it takes to do the many things they do, it seems that many of the individuals and organizations behind the New World Order are also the ones who are funding the New Age movement.

In "The Wizard of Baca Grande" (*West*, May 1990), Daniel Wood recounts that as he rode from the Baca with Maurice Strong one day, Strong told him of a novel he was planning about a group of world leaders who decide the only way to save the planet is if the industrialized civilizations collapse, so they form a secret society and engineer a worldwide financial panic while simultaneously preventing stock markets from closing. Wood writes: *"This is not **any** storyteller talking. This is Maurice Strong. He knows these world leaders. He is, in fact, co-chairman of the Council of the World Economics Forum. He sits at the fulcrum of power. He is in a position to **do it**."*

In 1980, Benjamin Creme of the Tara Center (and spokesman for "the Christ" or "Lord Maitreya") wrote *The Reappearance of the Christ and the Masters of Wisdom.* Creme claims to have descended to Earth from Venus about eighteen million years ago, and therefore is reminiscent of Oscar Zoroaster Diggs (the Wizard of Oz) who descended in his balloon and spoke as "the Great Oz."

which he projected as a large head. In his book, Creme states, *"According to Djwhal Khul* [supposedly the same adept who spoke to occultist Alice Bailey] *the Master Jesus will take over the throne of St. Peter in Rome, and the true apostolic succession will begin. This event is now imminent, following the declaration of the Christ. . . . It is more than likely that the present pope, John Paul II, will be the last. . . . The new religion will be manifest, for instance, through organizations like Masonry. In Freemasonry is embedded the core or the secret heart of the occult mysteries."* Creme believed in the fulfillment of Alice Bailey's 1934 statement that *"eventually there will appear the Church Universal, and its definite outlines will appear toward the close of this century. . . . The three main channels through which the preparation for the New Age is going on might be regarded as the church, the Masonic fraternity, and the educational field. . . . The* **Masonic movement** *. . . will meet the needs of those who can, and should, wield power. It is the custodian of the law; it is the home of the mysteries and the seat of initiation. It holds in its symbolism the ritual of Deity, and the way of salvation."*

The Theosophists are also involved, especially through infiltration of Christian churches. Speaking at the Human Life International's Tenth World Conference at Santa Clara, California, on April 6, 1991, attorney and author Constance Cumbey related that she had been able to attend a board of directors meeting of the Theosophical Society, and *"found to our dismay and amazement that most of the board members of the Theosophical Society, the organization that started out with their magazine being named* Lucifer, *were Sunday school teachers in conventional churches."* Similarly concerning the New Age movement, the *Houston Chronicle* reported on June 9, 1990 that the "Texas Poll" conducted by Texas A&M University indicated the New Age religion was the fastest-growing religion in Texas, even though one-fifth of the individuals who identified themselves as New Agers still attend mainline churches. This is very much like what Morris Storer said earlier concerning humanists, and it would therefore be a mistake to think the only New Agers are those who are on the fringe, like Shirley MacLaine.

What should be understood is that Shirley MacLaine is an example of what I would call the "progressive extremism strategy" of the world planners. Regarding the New Age, the Shirley MacLaine-types cause other New Agers to be perceived as not "extremists," and therefore less threatening or more tolerable. Pertaining to environmental issues, when one environmental group becomes identified as extremist, then another even more extreme group is formed to make the first organization appear as not so extreme after all. This same type of tactic is used in foreign relations as well. For example, in the Cuban Missile Crisis of the early 1960s, the Soviets took the "extreme" action of placing offensive missiles in Cuba. However, they then appeared less extreme, or more reasonable, when they backed off and accepted a compromise that their missiles would be withdrawn if the U.S. promised not to overthrow Castro. This "more reasonable" position, though, is probably what they expected to achieve all along, so that Cuba could be used as a revolutionary training base. Those opposing the New Age New World Order should watch out for the use of this strategy against them.

• • • • •

Regarding religion and the subject of world governance, the pastoral letter of the National Conference of Catholic Bishops, titled "The Challenge of Peace," included the words, *"Just as the nation-state was a step in the evolution of the government . . . we are now entering an era of new global interdependence requiring global systems of governance to manage the resulting conflicts. . . . These growing tensions cannot be remedied by a single nation-state approach. They shall require the concerted effort of the whole world community."* Even more specific is Malachi Martin's 1990 *The Keys of This Blood*, in which this former Jesuit advises that Pope John Paul II and Mikhail Gorbachev *"intend to infuse the present inchoate globalism with the values it lacks, give it flesh-and-blood reality, and transmute it into a veritable new world order . . . a geopolitical world to come — the new world order, the world of the Grand Design of the nations. . . .* [Concerning] *the design Mikhail Gorbachev has formed for the new world order . . . at the geopolitical level, the Gorbachevist design for a new world order envisages a condition in which all national governments as we now know them will cease to exist."*

In *Jean Monnet, A Grand Design for Europe* (1988), author Pascal Fontaine states, *"Monnet was aware of the role that a united Europe could play in creating a new world order. . . . The concluding words of Monnet's memoirs — 'And the Community itself is only a stage on the way to the organized world of tomorrow.' "*

And where will President Bush be when the "world of tomorrow" arrives? In a March 16, 1989 radio address,

President Bush asked, *"What are we doing to prepare ourselves for the new world coming just eleven short years from now?"* For the president, the answer was found in a January 3, 1989 Associated Press story which stated: *"President-elect Bush . . . in ten years he may be in Egypt. Organizers of the Millennium Society say he's already committed to ushering in the next century at the Great Pyramid of Cheops in Giza."* The article then quoted from a telegram President Bush sent the society: *"Barbara* [Mr. Bush's wife] *and I wish you the best of luck in the next year, and we're looking forward to your celebration in Egypt in 1999."*

Seventeen days later, President Bush delivered his inaugural address on January 20, 1989, which included his statement, *"I take as my guide the hope of a saint. In crucial things, unity; in important things, diversity."* (Remember here the statement of the 1941 *The City of Man* which said, *"Diversity in unity and unity in diversity will be the symbols of federal peace in universal democracy. . . . A positive plan for world legislation. . . ."*) Later in 1990, concerning the controversial alleged apparitions at Medjugorje, a believer in the apparitions and former parish priest there, Jozo Zovko, said that he met with President Bush on November 15, 1990, but would not say what they discussed. He would only say that another meeting with President Bush had also been scheduled. There is also speculation that former President Reagan and the Dalai Lama may be visiting Medjugorje.

● ● ● ● ●

Relevant to all three subjects of President Bush, the

Middle East, and religion is that in the final chapter of *The Keys of This Blood*, Malachi Martin writes the curious alarm, *"Red-alert code: 'The dove is loose! the dove is loose!' "* What Martin means by this is not clear, but there are a number of possibilities. First, because he is Irish, it may refer to the first line of an ancient Celtic poem, *The Holy Man*, which is *"He is a bird round which a trap is closed. "* In this sense, "the holy man" could be the pope who has escaped the manipulative forces within the Vatican bureaucracy.

A second possibility is that in Greek and Roman mythology, the dove is associated with the "goddess of love." In this sense, the book *The Dove in the Stone: Finding the Sacred in the Commonplace* by Alice Howell may be relevant. Its advertisement by the Theosophical Publishing House indicates that it *"is an exploration of some aspects of Hagia Sophia . . .* [whose] *reemergence was heralded by Jung, and her disguises in other cultures and religions now are being recognized. . . . Alice Howell's photo-illustrated book is set on the sacred isle of Iona, 'transformed by her loving eye into the* **unus mundus** *of the timeless realm — heaven and earth,' according to Christopher Bamford, co-author with William Parker of* Celtic Christianity: Ecology and Holiness [published by Lindisfarne Press in 1982]. *'It teaches in the gentlest possible way the profoundest truth of all: "The dove can only be released from the stone through love." ' "*

And a third possibility is that "the dove" refers to Saddam Hussein, who sees himself as a modern-day Nebuchadnezzar (the ancient king who conquered Jerusalem, destroyed the temple, and deported many Jews into Babylonia), who was called "the dove." In Malachi

Martin's article, "The Rule of Man, the Rule of God, and the Gulf War," in *The Remnant*, February 15, 1991, he states: *"More than once, on special evenings, huge laser beams throw two portraits into the deep black of the desert sky: Nebuchadnezzar's and Saddam's side by side, the leader's features modelled to closely resemble Nebuchadnezzar's."* Both dramatic and revealing! One should remember at this point that lasers at the Cathedral of St. John the Divine in New York City can project holographic images into the sky, and in *The Keys of This Blood*, Malachi Martin said Pope John Paul II is waiting for a vision in the skies. Is it possible that the Antichrist will attempt to fake the second coming of Jesus in order to establish himself as world ruler? In *The Rays and the Initiation* (1960), Alice Bailey refers to "the Coming One" as "Sanat," which is obviously the word "Satan" with rearranged letters.

• • • • •

The U.S. Congress voted in favor of President Bush's action against Iraq, but even if they hadn't done so, Section 6 of the "United Nations Participation Act of 1945" states: *"The president shall not be deemed to require the authorization of Congress to make available to the Security Council on its call in order to take action"* (unless prohibited by special agreement), and on April 12, 1952 John Foster Dulles (later to become secretary of state) said that *"treaty law can override the Constitution."* To celebrate United Nations Day, on October 24, 1990, the U.N. flag was raised over the City Hall in Asheville, North Carolina, as well as probably over other cities around the United States. The Center for World Servers is located in Asheville (remember Alice Bailey's New Group of World Servers and World Goodwill, which is with Lucis Trust, formerly the Lucifer Publishing Co., which printed Bailey's works). In Randy England's *Unicorn in the Sanctuary*, the goals of the Lucis Trust are described as including *"the establishment of a new world order, a new world religion, and a new world leader."* On November 17, 1990, World Goodwill held a symposium titled "The Psychology of Nations: Revealing the Plan," with addresses such as "The Role of the Media in Illuminating the Significance of Global Change." An announcement for the symposium was mailed by Lucis Trust and mentioned the "forces of light." And, incidentally, when Saddam Hussein gave the order for Iraqi troops to withdraw, he said, *"They have been engaged in an epic, valiant battle which will be recorded by history in letters of light"* (*The Washington Post*, February 26, 1991).

A book titled *New World Order Through Cooperative Democracy* was scheduled for publication in 1991 and was largely a republication of some of the earlier works of James Warbasse (1955 Humanist of the Year). The "New World Order" which President Bush is proposing seems to be where the collective will of the world's nations, exercised through the United Nations, will be used against those who violate international law. Unfortunately, a majority of the countries that make up the "New World Order" do not have governments like ours, but rather are basically socialist in nature and voted with the Soviet Union and against us the vast majority of the time in the U.N. (The 1985 U.N. voting record, for example, shows that sixty-one percent of the time, the U.N. as a whole votes against American interests.) What then if the countries that comprise the NWO now decide that a Palestinian state should be carved out of Israel regardless of what the Israelis think? *The Economist* in "The World Order Changeth" (June 22, 1991) wrote that the New World Order about which President Bush was talking is *"an epic made possible by Mikhail Gorbachev, realized by Saddam Hussein, starring the United States and shortly to be showing in a conflict near you."* So, what if the NWO says the U.S. should be attacked because it sees no real difference between our invasion of Panama due to Noriega's violation of American law, and Saddam's invasion of Kuwait due to Kuwait's violation of Iraqi law when it stole Iraq's oil from the field bordering both nations? Of course, the U.S. could respond that Noriega wasn't democratically elected in Panama, and that Saddam Hussein was posing a threat to Saudi Arabia. But what if the NWO said that the rulers of Kuwait weren't democratically elected either, and that after our invasion of Panama, Secretary of Defense Dick Cheney (CFR member) on national television offered the implied threat that Nicaragua's Daniel Ortega should learn a lesson from our invasion of Panama?

In addition, an article in *Newsday* by Sydney Schanberg after the war with Iraq (which we had supplied with arms to use against Iran) asks whether we will now take our troops to Cambodia. Schanberg explains: *"I speak of the Khmer Rouge, like Iraq a foul regime to which the United States has given aid and comfort. And think of the certain moral high ground to be gained, for Pol Pot's genocidal atrocities (perhaps two million Cambodians killed between 1975 and 1979) make Saddam*

Hussein look like a wimp. It was only a thought. I know Mr. Bush isn't going after the Khmer Rouge. That's because they're the creatures of our good friends, the dictators of China — and Mr. Bush wants to keep the dictators of China happy, no matter how many students they slaughter." President Bush even went so far as to extend "most favored nation" status to China after the Tiananmen Square massacre in Peking, and the administration's callousness concerning this mass murder can be seen from the fact that although perhaps tens of thousands of Chinese were slaughtered by their dictators in June 1989 and only three soldiers were killed, Secretary of State James Baker remarked, *"It would appear that there may be some violence being used here on both sides,"* seeming to somehow justify that government's brutalization of its own people. And just prior to the July 3, 1991 expiration date for "most favored nation" status for China, President Bush hypocritically stated in his commencement address at Yale University on May 27, that *"the most compelling reason to renew MFN trading status and remain engaged in China is not economic, not strategic, but moral."* The Chinese communists have continued to engage in massive human rights violations since the Tienanmen Square massacre, even though President Bush argued then that we needed to maintain their MFN status so that we could persuade them to change their ways. Regarding the president's Yale commencement address as it pertained to MFN status for China, U.S. Senate Democratic leader George Mitchell of Maine retorted, *"What is especially offensive about the president's statement is that he seeks to clothe what is an immoral policy in moral terms."*

Earlier, when President Bush sent National Security Advisor Brent Scowcroft and Deputy Secretary of State Lawrence Eagleburger (the respective former vice-chairman and former president of Kissinger Associates in the late 1980s) secretly to meet Chinese leaders about a month after the massacre, even though June 20, 1989 the president said he'd suspended high-level exchanges between the two nations, Secretary Baker covered up the meeting and later said, *"I only misled them* [the American people] *for seven days."* Baker himself had met with a Chinese foreign ministry official, Qian Qichen, in Paris shortly after the Tiananmen Square massacre, and President Bush's brother, Prescott Bush, visited China in September 1989 representing a company looking for potential investment possibilities, including a satellite-linked computer network. The secret Scowcroft-Eagleburger meeting with the Chinese was also at the exact moment the communist leaders there were arresting dozens of Roman Catholic bishops and priests, causing "Free the Fathers" (an independent human rights group supportive of the Catholic Church in China) to say, *"This is probably the worst crackdown on religion since the Cultural Revolution in the 1960s"* (*Human Events*, February 10, 1990). It seemed that President Bush wanted to maintain friendly relations with the Chinese communist leaders regardless of what atrocities they might commit, just as he would later want to maintain friendly relations with and be protective of Gorbachev even after Soviet troops killed independence-minded Lithuanians. The one billion Chinese consumer market simply could not be lost as far as President Bush's multinational corporate friends were concerned, and the same is true for the Soviet Union.

What is of growing concern regarding the Chinese is their connection with Iran. From the Washington, D.C., office of the *St. Petersburg Times* on November 1, 1991, Jack Payton wrote: *"Iran is working on nuclear weapons and with crucial help from President Bush's 'most favored nation,' China. . . . The Bush Administration has known what the Chinese have been up to for some time and hasn't done anything about it. In fact, it's looking more and more like the Bush Administration deliberately misled Congress about what China was doing so that it could stay on friendly terms with the communist leaders in Beijing."*

Concerning the U.S.S.R, early in June 1991, President Bush tapped Robert Strauss (known as "Mr. Democrat") to be the new American ambassador to the Soviet Union. What is revealing about this nomination is that Strauss is a director of Archer-Daniels-Midland, whose head, Dwayne Andreas, was described by the *Wall Street Journal* as "Moscow's favorite businessman." In this regard, he's considered Armand Hammer's (friend of Lenin and Stalin) successor. He said, *"Gorbachev and I go hand in hand"* (he helped bankroll the presidential campaigns of Hubert Humphrey, Richard Nixon, Jimmy Carter, and Robert Dole). At about the time of the Strauss nomination, Gorbachev delivered what amounted to an extortionist's statement, saying he was "entitled to" financial aid from the West or there could be chaos in the Soviet Union and a resumption of the Cold War.

In "What's Wrong with Chaos? And Who Says Soviet Order Will be Better?" (*Defense Media Review*, December 1990), Stephen Aubin observed the *"false semantic opposition created between the terrible state of 'chaos' and the wonderful state of 'order'* [repression] *in the Soviet Union."* However, what Aubin, Schanberg, and others apparently do not realize is that the CFR-Fabian-Masonic world planners want a "managed order" in the Soviet Union and elsewhere. Many feel they also want to manage the chaos (which many believe they create) out of which their "New World Order" will emerge via economic enticements or pressures (remember the motto of the thirty-third degree Mason is *"Ordo ab Chaos,"* meaning "Order out of Chaos").

This thinking is described in Max Lerner's unfortunately approving article, "Toward a Federative Principle" (*Washington Times*, April 1, 1991), in which he writes: *"Mr. Bush has wisely pointed America's resulting world leadership toward the objective of a 'world order.' In doing so, he has gone beyond the rhetoric of 'national interest' that still narrowly dominates conventional thinking. . . . One could argue with the Bush camp that the world had to break up its old patterns of order and grow disorderly before it could be ready for new patterns of order. True enough. . . . Since the disorders of the world flow from divisiveness of every sort they must be met by a tissue of connectedness. Let's call it, broadly, the federative principles. . . . The Middle East will be the hardest case, but not insuperable, if the moderate Arab states and Israel can forge ties of economic common interest. . . . Finally, on issues of a sustainable world ecology and of collective security, only a federative principle will work. Can we hope for a world motto that declares, 'Federate or bust'? "*

The problem with Lerner's thinking, besides the

obvious, is that deep ideological differences separate many nations and cultures. The world planners have regrettably had a great deal of success in shifting America's ideological principles from Judeo-Christian ones to those which are humanistic, but they will have a far harder time persuading Israel, for example, to forsake their principles. One should remember here that the *Washington Times* was financed by Rev. Moon, who sees himself as the world's savior, and Max Lerner wrote the foreword to the 1980 edition (John Naisbitt the 1987 foreword) of New Ager Marilyn Ferguson's *The Aquarian Conspiracy*, in which Lerner uses key words such as "radiating," "whirlwind," "gaia," "the initiates," "open conspiracy," and "this is a book drenched in sunlight."

• • • • •

Just as the world planners determined that the American people could be manipulated into participating in the New World Order if it were initiated by a crusade against a tyrant like Saddam Hussein, a strategy had to be developed also to cause the Soviet people to join the New World Order. Since a foreign military action was out of the question after Afghanistan, that only left an alleged coup against Mikhail Gorbachev, which occurred August 19, 1991. The chairman of the U.S. Senate Intelligence Committee, David Boren (member of Skull and Bones), said he was carefully watching the situation. But the authenticity of the coup was suspect right from the start as its leaders isolated Gorbachev, cutting off his telephones in the Crimea, but they supposedly forgot even to flip a switch cutting off Boris Yeltsin's phone and other means of communication with the press and foreign leaders. Also, satellites revealed no major troop movements during the alleged coup. Thus, we are supposed to believe that the head of the mighty Soviet armies and navies and the ruthless head of the KGB could only muster a handful of armored vehicles to bump into a few barricades in Moscow, never even firing one round of cannon shot to penetrate the barricades! Even former Soviet Foreign Minister Eduard Shevardnadze on August 21 told ABC's Diane Sawyer that the whole thing looked suspicious, and remember that Shevardnadze used to head the Interior Ministry, which controls the secret police.

One cannot help but think at this point about what high-level KGB defector Anatoliy Golitsyn wrote in his 1984 book, *New Lies for Old*, regarding information he had conveyed to the CIA as early as the 1970s. He related there were to be Soviet strategies such as *"the introduction of false liberalization in Eastern Europe and, probably, in the Soviet Union and the exhibition of spurious independence on the part of the regimes in Romania, Czechoslovakia, and Poland. . . . The KGB would be 'reformed.' . . . Demolition of the Berlin Wall might even be contemplated. . . . Dissolution of the Warsaw Pact would have little effect on the coordination of the communist bloc. . . . The pressure on the United States for concessions on disarmament and accommodation with the Soviets will increase. During this period, there might be an extensive display of the fictional struggle for power in the Soviet leadership."*

The result of the failed coup was that Gorbachev returned after only seventy-two hours, like the "phoenix" from the ashes, claiming the traitors had been defeated by the Soviet people who supported his reforms. Thus, the "comfortable merger" between the U.S. and the U.S.S.R., that Ford Foundation president H. Rowan Gaither in the early 1950s said had been directed from the White House, would continue under the New World Order now accepted by the American and Soviet people. On August 21, both CFR members Dan Rather of CBS and Ted Koppel of ABC noted that some people had said that if the United States and other industrialized nations had only given Gorbachev the money he asked for, the coup may not have occurred. And U.S. Senator William Cohen on the same day claimed that Boris Yeltsin, who had "manned the ramparts" during the coup, would be "the real moral leader" of the U.S.S.R.

But what kind of "morality" would this be that would lead the Soviet Union? Commenting in September 1989 on a U.S.-Soviet "partnership," columnist Gary Potter wrote: *"The convergence is more than economic and political. It also has its spiritual dimension; and, interestingly enough, that dimension corresponds to the esoteric side of the New Age movement, which is centered on the vision of all lands and peoples coming together as One World to make a New Order. Reference is here being made to the spiritual dimension of the convergence and its correspondence to New Age teaching because of the fact that the principle sponsor of Yeltsin's trip* [to the U.S.] *is the California-based Esalen Institute,"* which engages in "hot tub diplomacy" for diplomats. Yeltsin's trip was also partly underwritten by the Rockefeller Brothers Fund, and David Rockefeller himself introduced Yeltsin to a luncheon of three hundred members of the

CFR. Pertaining to the alleged coup against Gorbachev, it should also be remembered that British and French intelligence analysts believe Yeltsin has strong support within the Soviet military, having been present at the founding of "Shield," a pressure-group of reform-minded military officers.

Regarding this most suspicious coup, the question comes to mind, "What if like the Cuban Missile Crisis, the final outcome was what was planned all along?" What if the world planners wanted Yeltsin to rise in stature as a possible successor to Gorbachev because he could be manipulated? Wouldn't the only way for that to happen be an unsuccessful coup that would eliminate the hardliners and lower the stature of Gorbachev because he had put the hardliners in positions of prominence? How else does one explain the ineptitude of those involved in the coup who didn't even bother to take Yeltsin into custody the moment the coup began? In fact, the troops used at key points in Moscow during the initial hours of the coup were conscripted troops led by commandos loyal to Yeltsin rather than the coup leaders! For additional curious aspects of the coup, see Peter Schweizer's (American Foreign Policy Council) op-ed article in the August 22, 1991 *New York Times*. Regarding Yeltsin as a possible successor to Gorbachev, remember that Secretary of Defense Richard Cheney predicted some time ago that Gorbachev would not last, and on August 25 on national television, Cheney told members of the press that he'd rather deal with Yeltsin than Gorbachev.

It is also important to remember at this point when members of the press and media are joyfully proclaiming the death of communism, that books like *Brave New*

World and *1984* never said there would be some type of
nuclear war with communism winning. Rather, they
indicated that "Big Brother" and the totalitarian state
would be some form of socialism in which a centralized
government would be dictator over our lives. One should
recall that in H.G. Wells' *The Open Conspiracy: Blueprints
for a World Revolution* (1928), he emphasized that his
new world order, which would succeed communism,
*"may be in control of Moscow before it is in control of
New York."* And one should also note that according to
the *New York Times*, August 23, 1991, when Gorbachev
returned to Moscow after the coup failed, he was asked,
*"Is it possible that Mikhail Sergeyevich would cease
being the leader of the Communist Party?"* And he
responded, *"I am one of those people who's never
concealed his position. I am convinced that socialism is
correct. I'm an adherent of socialism. . . . Unless we get
rid of Stalinism, we will never achieve the implementation
of socialism. . . . Some sentence of Lenin's in which he
said that socialism is the vital creativity of the masses, this
is the model that we have to implement, this is something
that Lenin said, that we have to develop the process of
democratization in all areas — political, economic, and
in the sphere of reconstructing our federation. We have to
move ahead democratically in all areas and this movement
toward great justice and greater liberty, that is the same
thing as the movement to socialism and to the implementation of the socialist idea."*

If the objective of the New World Order is to
synthesize Western capitalism and Eastern communism
into an "Order" of world socialist control, then as far as
the world planners are concerned, events like the attack

upon Iraq, the failed Soviet coup, and the short-term denial of complete independence for the Baltic states (though independence would come later), were necessary not only in a governmental sense, but in a religious sense as well. "Order" is being established in the Middle East after the "chaos" (crisis) of the war against Iraq. "Order" was re-established in the U.S.S.R. after the "chaos" (crisis) of the alleged coup attempt. And after Gorbachev's position appeared less threatened, independence for the Baltic states was granted. In fact, on August 29, 1991, President Bush notified Gorbachev and the Soviet government that they should recognize the independence of the Baltics because *"they should not stand against the will of the inevitable."* One might interpret Bush's use of the term "the inevitable" rather than "the people" to mean the "New World Order" is "inevitable."

John Steinbruner, director of foreign policy studies at the Brookings Institution, had months earlier said that Gorbachev's staying in power far outweighed, as far as Washington was concerned, any aspect of independence for the Baltic states. Steinbruner was referred to by the *New York Times* (January 13, 1990) as claiming that Gorbachev's continued presence was crucial in negotiating "a new world security order." And supporting a new world security order, Gorbachev said on October 30, 1991, at the Middle East Talks in Madrid: *"We are beginning to see practical support. And this is a very significant sign of the movement toward a new era, a new age. . . . We see both in our country and elsewhere . . . ghosts of the old thinking. . . . When we rid ourselves of their presence, we will be better able to move toward a new world order . . . relying on the relevant mechanisms of the United Nations. "*

• • • • •

Pertaining to governments in general, Paul Mazur wrote *Unfinished Business* in 1979, in which he foretold that *"the large number of governmental bureaus that will have their orbits in the atmosphere of our planet cannot be allowed the freedom to compete and collide with one another. So, in order to control the diverse bureaucracies required, a politburo will develop, and over this group organization there is likely to arise the final and single arbiter — the master of the order, the total dictator."*

And to the extent that the New World Order will have a religious component when it is fully in place, it will be the New Age New World Order. Regarding religion, remember that a slogan of Masonry (which is a religion) is "Order out of Chaos." In Malachi Martin's *The Keys of This Blood*, he indicates that Pope John Paul II believes the vision which everyone will see in the skies, and which will affirm him as the world's spiritual leader, will come out of chaos. Martin writes: *"The competition* [between the pope, the Soviet leader, and the Western capitalist leaders] *was not a tug of war to decide whether in fact there would be a global society. Every major player in the competition understood that John Paul's competitors were even then well along in their work of reorganizing and reassembling the economic, political, and cultural resources of the world. Everyone who was a major player understood that structures were already being built that would soon enough include the world's every nation and race, its every culture and subgroup. John Paul knew that neither he nor anyone else could reverse that momentum. . . . The real competition had to be far more profound than would ever be apparent in the merely visible rush of change and innovation. It had to be nothing less than a fight to capture the minds — to direct the very impetus of will — of men and women everywhere, at the unique moment when all the structures of civilization, including those of John Paul's church, were being transformed into the framework that would not only house the new global society, but shape everything about it."*

Concerning the "deterioration" of the Catholic Church today, Martin comments: *"Ever since he* [Karol Wojtyla] *became pope* [John Paul II], *all statistics still continue to pursue the downward plunge. Apart from now and again repeating traditional doctrine, he did nothing and is doing nothing to halt the deterioration. Isolated words not followed by concrete application have done nothing effective to correct it. John Paul has, in sum, not even attempted to reform the very obvious deformations afflicting and finally liquidating his churchly institutions."*

In a list of questions and answers that the publisher of *The Keys of This Blood*, Simon and Schuster, sent out as part of a press kit, Malachi Martin relates: *"Willing or not, ready or not, Pope John Paul II says that by the end of this decade, we will all live under the first one-world government that has ever existed in the society of nations . . . a government with absolute authority to decide the basic issues of human survival and human prosperity . . . our food supply . . . war, population control. . . ."* And when the questioner asks, *"Suppose Gorbachev or John Paul or some of the really powerful*

Western leaders leave the scene one way or another? Would the pope's prediction of a one-world government still stand?" Martin replies: *"John Paul says that the forces that have propelled these people to the top — himself included — are exactly the forces that are propelling us toward a one-world government. And he says that those forces won't change, just because our leaders come and go. One-world government is inevitable in his view."* This sounds exactly like the words of Norman Cousins, who had been sent on diplomatic missions by a previous pope.

Just as Baha' U'llah many years ago called for a world religion, world government, world police force, world language, and world currency, in 1948 the Marxist millionaire publisher Victor Gollancz proclaimed: *"The ultimate aim should be that Judaism, Christianity, and all other religions should vanish and give place to one great ethical world religion, the brotherhood of man,"* which would provide mankind with harmony of mind and heart. Gollancz concluded by indicating that the political systems of the world would follow the syncretization of religions and be fused into a one-world government.

Unfortunately, many Catholic, Protestant, and Jewish leaders at the highest levels are increasingly talking about searching for their "common ground." They fail to realize that it is not what they have in common which is important, but rather what Christianity has that is different which is most important. And that difference is that Jesus Christ died for our sins, rose from the dead, and our salvation is in Him alone.

• • • • •

President Bush recently remarked, *"I commend the United Nations Association of the United States for working to keep Americans informed of the United Nations' efforts in fields ranging from environmental protection to drug-interdiction and counterterrorism."* This was quoted in a recent mailing from UNA-USA (cover letter signed by CFR members Cyrus Vance and Elliot Richardson) that noted the U.N. was also involved in "population control," and urged: *"Become a Citizen of the World"* and subscribe to UNA-USA's *The Interdependent* — "an insiders guide to what's happening in the United Nations along with news and analyses of global issues shaping international politics." President Bush's national security advisor, Brent Scowcroft, was a vice-chairman of UNA-USA, and on their Council of Organizations are Planned Parenthood Federation of America, the National Organization for Women, and the National Education Association, among others. Another organization, the Southeastern World Affairs Institute, held a program July 26-28, 1991, including topics such as "The United Nations: From Its Conception to a New World Order" and "Legal Structures for the New World Order," with participants such as a former director of the U.N.'s general legal division and a former secretary-general of International Planned Parenthood.

But what exactly is happening today at the U.N. which President Bush wishes to invest with greater authority under the New World Order? In the October 24, 1991 *Wall Street Journal*, deputy features editor Amity Shlaes comments on the editorial page that the U.N. Secretariat headquartered in New York City is still under the domination of old-line communists and Third World ideologues. She indicates that rather than becoming *"the cornerstone in President Bush's oft-mentioned 'new world order,' many of those working within the Secretariat, or at its missions in its vicinity, argue that communism left a legacy.... 'It works like a scorpion's stinger,' says one U.N. professional. 'The scorpion — East bloc socialism — dies. But the stinger remains poisonous, and strikes new victims.' "* Shlaes reports that *"Westerners who worked at the U.N. ... found themselves surrounded by what many have called a communist mafia,"* among whom is Vasily Safronchuk, who heads the U.N.'s influential Department of Political and Security Council Affairs, and who before coming to the U.N. helped supervise in 1978-1979 the Soviet occupation of Afghanistan.

If President Bush believes that in the New World Order, the United Nations should play not only a greater peacekeeping role, but also a greater role in the area of human rights, he might unfortunately sign the United Nations Convention on the Rights of the Child. At UNICEF's "World Summit" for children on September 29-30, 1990, ratification of this convention was described as "critical." In article after article of the convention, the state determines how children should be reared, and no country (including the U.S.) will be permitted to have reservations concerning this, including Article 13, which states: *"The child shall have the right to freedom of expression; this right shall include freedom to seek, receive, and impart information and ideas of all kinds, regardless of frontiers, either orally, in writing, or in print, in the form of art, or through any other media of the child's choice"*; and including Article 21 which declares that parents are to be counseled to agree to adoption if the child cannot be cared for in a manner deemed suitable by the state. This treaty uses vague terms such as "appropriate" and "adequate" and "highest attainable standard," but who will define those terms in areas ranging from freedom of expression to health care in the treaty? The answer is "ten experts" will sit in judgment as an international committee on the rights of the child, and according to nationally syndicated columnist James J. Kilpatrick, *"States that failed to adjust their civil and criminal laws according to the experts' judgment would find themselves pilloried before the world."*

To see what plans there are specifically for American children and families, one need simply look at "Beyond Rhetoric: A New American Agenda for Children and Families," a federally-funded report of the National Commission on Children, with Chairman John D. Rockefeller IV (a U.S. senator, CFR member, and possible 1996 presidential candidate), which was approved May 1, 1991, as *"the bold blueprint of a national policy for America's children and families."* While there are positive aspects of the report, such as the recognition that *"subliminal media messages that promote sexuality as the key to social acceptance and personal happiness can be harmful to young people,"* there are some serious problems with this report which the commission says "shares a similar vision" with the Carnegie Council on Children's 1977 report, "All Our Children: The American Family Under Pressure." A majority of the National Commission called for regulation of the entire health care system *"from setting provider payment rates to defining the basic set of benefits all insurers, both private and public, must provide."*

Regarding schools, the National Commission's report refers approvingly to "the Mental Health Team," including a social worker and school psychologist, who *"provide direct counseling to students and consult with teachers, staff, and parents."* Note that they do not say they must obtain the approval of the parents before anything is done, or that the parents are the ultimate authority in any decisions made. Similarly, the National Commission states that *"health professionals and educators, employers, leaders from business and labor, voluntary and religious institutions, and the media must help children form attitudes."* Note that they do not say these individuals and organizations should "reinforce" the attitudes taught by parents. The National Commission also proposes values education programs built upon "common values," but this necessarily precludes specifically biblical values which would be vetoed by secularists as "not common" to them. Troubling, too, are the National Commission's misleading statements, such as *"studies indicate that while music may reinforce listeners' dangerous or antisocial behavior, it does not appear to cause it."* This plays down the fact that it is that which reinforces or promotes immoral or violent behavior which is a large part of the problem today in American society.

When the social engineers do advocate reducing "violence" in society, they often are referring to corporal punishment in the schools. What is curious about this is the fact that there was far less violence in American society years ago when spanking was more prevalent. A growing number of states have banned corporal punishment in public schools. Obviously, this form of discipline shouldn't be administered by the government, represented by school officials, without parental permission. However, a total ban on corporal punishment in schools is actually government telling parents what type of discipline cannot be administered regarding their children even if parents want that type of discipline used. This sets a dangerous precedent for government to ban spanking in the home and to forcibly intervene in other private family matters.

To persuade Americans to accept more government intervention into and regulation of their lives, of course "crises" will have to occur and be publicized. For example, there is a great deal of publicity today concerning private daycare scandals. The result has been a call for greater government regulated or operated daycare. And in the area of banking, the recent BCCI scandal caused *The Honolulu Advertiser* to editorialize on July 31, 1991 that *"the BCCI scandal rudely shows up both the absence and need for a system of strict, impartial, global financial regulation."* The use of "crises" has always been a favorite device used by the world planners to accomplish their objectives, because "crises" cause the people themselves to request drastic action.

Chapter Twenty

Education in the
New World Order

What type of education will there be in the New World Order? Past presidents of the powerful National Education Association Catherine Barrett, George Fischer, Helen Wise, and John Ryor respectively commented: *"We are determined to control the direction of education";* *"To determine who will enter, who will stay, and who will leave the profession"; "We must defeat those who oppose our goals";* and *"We will become the foremost political power in the nation."* There is already a move for national teacher certification (which the NEA hopes to control) and state takeovers of local schools (removing locally elected school board members) that don't meet state standards (perhaps eventually federal takeover of state schools that don't meet federal standards). The sorry state of education today is in part revealed by the contradictory mindset of most NEA and other educational leaders, who will tell you in practically the same breath that there are not serious academic problems today because they are doing a wonderful job teaching, yet more money is the solution to the problem of declining test scores. This is similar to the double contradiction found in Robert K. Mueller's *Corporate Networking* (1986), which states,

"Our world's greatest problems are the boundless constraints of our expanding limitations." This is reminiscent of former Secretary of Education Terrel Bell's position that he opposed forced busing, but advocated that if it couldn't be ended, it should be expanded metropolitan-wide! When the NEA does admit education is in serious trouble in this country, it is not comforting, yet quite revealing, to hear that they have no answers to our problems. In national columnist David Broder's interview with NEA executive director Terry Herndon (*Washington Post*, July 9, 1980) at the NEA's annual convention, Broder asked about parents' and voters' concern over the poor quality of public schools, and Herndon replied that the convention speakers and delegates *"don't know what the answer is. . . . We don't have the answers. Our executive board spent more time talking about the crisis in urban education than any other topic this year, but we have no answer."*

Instead of genuinely trying to improve students' academic performance, the NEA seems to be more interested in other things (in addition to gaining and exercising political power). Mary Faber of the NEA's Human and Civil Rights Division wrote in the October 1990 issue of *NEA Today* that *"both right-wing and religious extremists have . . . secured bans on textbooks containing stories about violence and sorcery."* And Ms. Faber recommends that teachers *"report 'anti-satanist' activity immediately to your local [NEA] association. It's your best defense against what's usually the real aim of such activity — an attack on public education."* There are even materials showing teachers how to counter parents' objections regarding what is occurring in the schools.

The NEA also supports more comprehensive sex education, despite the evidence that sex ed has not reduced teen sexual activity or reduced venereal diseases to even 1960s levels. In 1969, when venereal diseases were a relatively minor problem in the U.S., only a little over one percent of American students were taking sex ed classes. But in 1981 when venereal diseases were (and still are) at almost epidemic proportions, almost seventeen percent of American students were enrolled in sex ed courses.

These facts aren't surprising, given that one reads in sex ed proponents Lester Kirkendall's (1983 Humanist of the Year who advised teachers regarding sex ed to "sneak it in" the classroom) and Ruth Osborne's *Teacher's Question and Answer Book on Sex Education: "To make the elimination of premarital pregnancy, venereal disease, or divorce the main purpose of sex education is to make certain its failure."* Perhaps this is why nationally syndicated columnist Thomas Sowell wrote concerning the real purpose of comprehensive sex education in the *Detroit News*, October 1, 1990: *"Breaking down inhibitions is the first order of business. . . . That is why so-called 'sex education' courses go on for years in some schools. It doesn't take that long to convey the facts of life. But it does take that long to relentlessly undermine what children have been taught at home. . . . Movies showing close-ups of childbirth have been shown in elementary school (even though one child fainted in class)."*

In Planned Parenthood's own journal, *Family Planning Perspectives* (September/October 1980), one finds: *"More teenagers are using contraceptives and using them more consistently than ever before. Yet the number and rate of premarital pregnancies continue to rise."* And a 1986 Planned Parenthood-Lou Harris poll showed that children taught contraception were fifty percent more likely to be sexually active. But why should this be surprising? Dr. Robert Kistner of Harvard Medical School, who developed the oral contraceptive, has indicated that its increased availability has led to increased promiscuity, venereal disease, and cervical cancer among adolescents.

Relevant to this is the statement by Rabbi Yosef Friedman, executive secretary of Jews for Morality, concerning the free condom distribution that was to begin in New York City high schools in September 1991: *"The idea that handing out condoms will reduce the spread of AIDS is overly simplistic and indeed insidiously misleading. . . . The increase in promiscuity outweighs the prevention effects of the condoms. Since the net result is clearly more pregnancies, there will certainly be an increase in the spread of AIDS which is more transmissible than pregnancy . . . [and] the debauchery of our children."* Some time ago, Jack E. Robinson, president of the National Association of Black Americans (and former president of the Boston NAACP), assailed the dispensing of contraceptives in public schools, saying if implemented there, he would seek an injunction in federal court.

And has sex ed helped? Research by William Marsiglio and Frank Mott in *Family Planning Perspectives* (July/August 1986) showed an association between taking sex education and starting intercourse at ages fifteen and sixteen. What parents should have been asking over the past quarter century is, if school prayer was banned because it was government promotion of religion, why isn't non-morally-based sex education banned as government promotion of immoral sexual activity? Instead, the U.S. Department of Health and Human Services has given Planned Parenthood over two billion dollars in Title X funds over the past twenty years, supposedly to reduce teen sexual activity, among other things, but what has been the result? According to government figures, in 1971, almost thirty-two percent of teenagers were sexually active, compared to over fifty-two percent in 1988. And in 1970, twenty-nine and a half percent of teen pregnancies were out of wedlock, compared to over sixty-five percent in 1988. Despite the obvious failures of sex education, SIECUS in 1991 called for the development of national guidelines for sex ed, including the use of explicit terminology and classroom discussions of controversial topics related to sex. Not long afterward in the same year, the National Guidelines Task Force coalition, underwritten by the Carnegie Corporation, proposed such guidelines K-12 on October 16, 1991.

In addition to sex education, now a number of schools have even established school-based clinics (SBCs), some of which dispense contraceptives and give abortion-referrals. This is despite the fact that a 1986 study by Prof. Jacqueline Kasun of Humboldt State University in California found that providing government-funded contraceptives and abortions to teenagers is leading to an increase in teen pregnancies. Why the push for SBCs? In "Adolescent Pregnancy Prevention Services in High School Clinics" by Laura Edwards et al (*Family Planning Perspectives*, January/February 1980), it is admitted that SBCs were invented in Minneapolis in 1973 only for family planning and sexual services. Only a few students came though, so services were expanded to provide *"a measure of anonymity for the sexually active student."*

• • • • •

There is not only an attempt now under way to nationalize education via a national exam which would facilitate a national curriculum, but there is also an attempt to internationalize or globalize education as well. In *World Order: Its Intellectual and Cultural Foundations* (1945), a series of 1944 addresses, edited by F. Ernest Johnson (professor of education at Teachers College, Columbia University), one reads that as far back as 1914, the secretary of the New England Education League, Walter Scott, succeeded in having a bill introduced in Congress (H.R. 12247) *"to create an international board of education and a fund for international or world education."* More recently, the NEA in 1972 established a Bicentennial Committee whose initial work culminated in the *NEA Bicentennial Ideabook*, which contained the idea of developing a definitive volume to *"contain a reframing of the cardinal principles of education and recommendations for a global curriculum"* (*Today's Education*, September/October 1976).

Several years later, John Goodlad reasoned that if global education were to be accepted, parents and the general public would have to be reached. In 1979, Goodlad was dean of UCLA's Graduate School of Education and wrote the foreword to James Becker's edited volume, *Schooling for a Global Age* (1979), in which Goodlad remarked: *"Parents and the general public must be reached also. Otherwise, children and youth enrolled in globally oriented programs may find themselves in conflict with values assumed in the homes. And then the educational institution frequently comes under scrutiny and must pull back."*

Ann Herzer, who ran for the office of superintendant of education for the state of Arizona, relates that she was in France in 1984 when a million people marched in the streets of Paris because the national government was about to take over the schools of France, and the people forced the resignation of the entire executive branch except the president because of this. She then quotes a woman there who had a Ph.D. from Columbia University and who had taught in the U.S. for fourteen years as saying: *"You Americans are fools. Don't you know there is a worldwide movement to control all education? No government should ever control education, because education must remain in the hands of the people to remain free. Parents have to say how they want their children to be educated. We did not march* [in Paris] *for religious purposes; we marched for freedom. You Americans had better wake up or you are going to lose your freedom."*

That "global education" would be truly "global" in the sense that it would be promoted in countries besides the U.S., and that it would have a socialist inclination was revealed in a 1984 Victorian (Australia) Fabian Society pamphlet in which Joan Kirner (former minister of education, and now premier of Victoria) explained: *"If we are egalitarians in our intention, we have to reshape the education so that it is: part of the socialist struggle for equality, participation and social change, rather than an instrument in the capitalist system; a vital weapon in the transition to more equal outcomes for disadvantaged groups and classes, rather than a ladder to equal educational opportunity for individuals; a catalyst for system change, rather than the legitimization of system maintenance."*

As "global education" became more accepted in the 1980s, it added a New Age element, and in the February 1991 *Concerned Women* newsletter, one reads that Iowa's Department of Education plans to introduce "global education" with recommended reading references to "Gaia" (New Age religion "Earth Mother"). Writing in the *Minneapolis Star-Tribune* on March 30, 1991, Mary Jane Rachner explained that *"today in the Minneapolis schools, the liberal elite stands guard. When I served as a substitute teacher in a third grade room and announced to the children that we would begin the day with the pledge to the flag, a teacher who apparently had been listening outside the door stepped in and told me that saying the pledge was not customary in the Putnam School. She said the custom was to pledge allegiance to the Earth, and she pointed to where the Earth-worshippers' pledge was posted on the wall. . . . One of the children asked the teacher, 'Can't we do the pledge to the flag if we want to?' A stern look was the reply."*

A number of progressive educators and government leaders are seeking a transformation of American society to fit into the "New World Order" by using "nuclear education." For example, a group called "Peace Links" has entered a number of schools, and when asked in an *Arkansas Gazette* article whether she thought the U.S. Constitution might eventually be set aside, Arkansas state coordinator for Peace Links, Olivia Guggenheim, responded, *"Yes, it would be a natural progression of events.* "In the same article, Betty Bumpers, who founded Peace Links and is the wife of U.S. Senator Dale Bumpers, is quoted as saying: *"At some time . . . we all would be in a progression toward a one-world government. It's the logical progression of events. We are all one people. "* From October 30 through November 1, 1991, the United States Coalition for Education for All held a conference on "Learning for All: Bridging Domestic and International Education," with First Lady Barbara Bush as the "honorary chair." The coalition is part of a one hundred fifty-six nation network working to "reform" education worldwide. One of the conference programs was "Education for a New World Order" with keynote speaker Elena Lenskaya, deputy to the minister of education of Russia.

Also relevant to the type of education there will be in the "New World Order" is the Committee for Economic Development's *The Unfinished Agenda: A New Vision for Child Development and Education* (1991), which emphasizes preschool and early childhood education, using schools as bases for delivering social services, and removing the barriers to change. (This sounds like former Governor James B. Hunt, Jr.'s "Child Health Plan" mentioned earlier.) Not only does *The Unfinished Agenda* refer favorably to the notorious Parents as Teachers program described elsewhere in this book, but it also refers favorably to a "New Futures School" in Albuquerque, New Mexico. The school is supported by New Futures, Inc., and the proposal to New Futures from Pittsburgh was based upon the premise that no one institution (including the "home") can solve all of the problems of "at-risk" youth (defined as students who "might" become unproductive adults). This, too, sounds very much like the "Child Health Plan" mentioned above. Under the Pittsburgh proposal's "intensive home-based counseling" and "advocacy services to all family members," there is the obvious danger that a governmental agency may intervene on behalf of one family member against another. In addition, the sharing of "confidential client service information" poses a threat to individuals' right to privacy.

Increasingly, the schools are taking over more and more of the responsibilities of parents. In "Get Ready for the Post-Modern Family: Changing Parental Values Leave Greater Role for Educators" (*The School Administrator*, June 1990), Tufts University Professor David Elkind declares, *"The values and thrust of this new* [post-modern] *era often directly conflict with the values and drives of the modern period, leaving both families and schools to adjust to a new social order. . . .* [Now] *children are no longer an economic asset . . . children are an economic liability. . . . Childrearing . . . ranks low on post-modern parents' priority lists. That may be one reason why post-modern parents also are more willing than parents in previous times to share their childrearing functions with others. . . .* [In] *the modern period, when teachers and schools are treated as partners with parents, schools in the post-modern era are expected, at the behest of parents, to take a leadership role in childrearing* **and** *education. . . . As parents give up more of their childrearing functions to the schools, they will have to accept educational leadership in domains heretofore unaccepted. . . . In addition, parents will have to accept the school's leadership role in dealing with emotional and family as well as educational problems. . . . For administrators, perhaps the most general message* *in the post-modern era is they must be prepared to take on more responsibility for childrearing and nurturing. This is already happening in some school systems which provide full-day kindergartens, programs for 3- and 4-year-olds, before- and after-school programs, and comprehensive school health clinics."*

Then there is the "brand-new American school" proposed by Lamar Alexander, who was confirmed by the U.S. Senate on March 14, 1991, as U.S. secretary of education, and who now sends his youngest son to private (rather than public) school. In a November 1, 1989 speech at the Governor's Conference on Education in Wichita, Kansas (the state from which Dorothy supposedly traveled to Oz), Alexander said that while each community's school would be different to meet their differing needs, he envisioned that America would go through "its own *perestroika*" and form a "brand-new American school" that would be open year round from six a.m. to six p.m. He also said: *"I would go down to the maternity ward of the local hospital . . . and find out how many babies are born out of wedlock"* (his wife had been a volunteer worker for Planned Parenthood). And he added, *"These schools will serve children from age three months to age eighteen. That may be a shocking thought to you, but if you were to do an inventory of every baby in your community, and think about what the needs of those babies were for the next four or five years, you might see that those needs might not be served any other way."*

That is a shocking statement, because it sounds like education in the New World Order would not be different from what one would find in Aldous Huxley's *Brave New World*! It also sounds like the statement by Orestes

Brownson (a confidant of Frances Wright of the New Harmony, Indiana experiment in communism) in the early nineteenth century, when he said, *"Our complete plan was to take the children from their parents at the age of twelve or eighteen months, and to have them nursed, fed, clothed, and trained in these* [national] *schools at public expense; but at any rate, we were to have godless schools for all the children of the country."*

Lamar Alexander said in his books *Steps Along the Way* (1986) and *Six Months Off* (1988) that the volume that changed his thinking the most during the past ten years, and which he's tried to read once a year since the early 1970s, is René Dubos' *A God Within* (1972). The title in Greek is *Entheos*, from which is derived "enthusiasm," which according to Dubos implies "divine madness" in the original Greek sense. Dubos says this is Socrates' "mania," and he quotes Plato as saying: *"In reality the greatest blessings come to us through madness, when it is sent as a gift of the gods. . . . Madness, which comes from god, is superior to sanity, which is of human origin."* (Perhaps this is why most gurus have a goofy look, like *Mad* magazine's Alfred E. Newman.) Dubos explains that *"apparently, certain drugs can help in generating this inspired state."* The "god" of this book is not the Judeo-Christian God of the Holy Bible, but rather a pantheistic "god" where the rocks and plants are supposedly our brothers and sisters. Reincarnation is also introduced through Dubos' quote of Mirandola: *"Thou shalt have the power to degenerate into the lower forms of life, which are brutish. Thou shalt have the power . . . to be reborn into higher forms, which are divine."*

The basic elements of New Age philosophy found in

Dubos' *A God Within* can be found earlier in the writings of Carl Jung, who believed *"God dwells in the depth of our consciousness. The archtype of Self is the same thing as God. Who I really am in my deepest, truest self is God. God is at the core of me and you and everyone else."* These same elements would be found later in John Randolph Price's *The Planetary Commission* (1984). Price founded the Planetary Commission and was the mastermind behind the December 31, 1988, "World Healing Day."

• • • • •

Recently, there has been an attempt to reintroduce religion in the public schools. After school prayer was banned in the early 1960s, secularists even went so far as to delete religious references (e.g., Pilgrims giving thanks to God) from history texts. Now, however, not only are historical religious facts being presented, but there are courses on "comparative religions" as well. In 1950, at Oxford University in England, a "Union for the Study of Great Religions" was founded, with chairs in many of the world's universities. Then some years later, the World Religions Curriculum Development Center in the U.S. developed a high school course titled, "Religion in Human Culture," to develop attitudes of respect for and the legitimacy of others' beliefs and practices, *"safeguarding against dogmatic 'right answerism.' "* Then, toward the end of the 1980s, the Williamsburg Charter Foundation (editorial review board chairman and CFR member Ernest Boyer) introduced a curriculum to foster religious liberty and respect for others' beliefs in "our pluralistic society." The problem with this approach, however, is that while no one should be persecuted for her or his religious beliefs, the "equal treatment" of all religions (and witchcraft is a religion) places biblical principles on an equal basis with Hindu, Buddhist, and other religious beliefs. Commenting on these events, Princeton University sociologist Robert Wuthnow said the movement to reintroduce religion into the public schools did help to "bring values back" into discussions of social policy. However, he noted, *"when everyone — right and left — is talking about values, the distinctive claims of the Religious Right tend to be muted. Its potential strength may, therefore, be diminished by having a less distinct identity."* Regarding Christians' concerns, Charles Haynes, who is the executive director of the First Liberty Institute (formerly the Williamsburg Charter Foundation), said, *"I understand their frustrations — they feel they're losing their institutions. However, public education will not go backward. We are a pluralistic society."* I believe students should not be taught to respect false religions.

Increasingly in public schools, yoga is being taught. There are several types of yoga, such as Hatha yoga, where *Ha* means "sun" and *tha* means "moon." Then there is the Tantric (esoteric) form of yoga, which teaches that at the base of the spine lies coiled, like a snake, a latent power called *kundalini* ("the earringed one," a name of the "goddess" Kali, or sometimes "*kundalini* within" is called "God within").

The author of *A God Within*, René Dubos, is listed by New Ager Marilyn Ferguson in her book, *The Aquarian Conspiracy*, as one of the *"many authors whose thinking was influential in the Aquarian Conspiracy."*

Ferguson has a section in her book titled, "God Within: The Oldest Heresy," and she also recounts that six years after Dubos' *A God Within* was published in 1972, the Berkeley Christian Coalition (sponsor of the Spiritual Counterfeits Project) devoted its August 1978 journal to the threat to the Judeo-Christian tradition. *"The idea of a God within was particularly disturbing,"* wrote Ferguson concerning the SCP, which said about this concept that *"it is fundamentally hostile to biblical Christianity."* Ferguson commented, *"Now the heretics are gaining ground, doctrine is losing its authority, and knowing is superseding belief."*

In her book, one reads: *"There are legions of conspirators. . . . Whatever their station or sophistication, the conspirators are linked, made kindred by their inner discoveries and earthquakes. . . . Their **lives** have become revolutions. . . . They have coalesced into small groups in every town and institution. . . . They are at once antennae and transmitters, both listening and communicating. They amplify the activities of the conpiracy by networking and pamphleteering, articulating the new options through books, lectures, even congressional hearings and the national media, and through school curricula. . . . Of the Aquarian conspirators surveyed, more were involved in education than any other single category of work. . . . [There is] the need for innovation . . . experiments. . . . Educators are belatedly examining a holistic Greek concept, the* 'paidea' *. . . in which the community and all its disciplines generated learning resources for the individual, whose ultimate goal was to reach the divine center in the self. . . . Educators engaged in transpersonal and humanistic methods have begun* *linking in national networks and centers. . . . The new school community is very close, more a family than a school. . . . Virtually no subject is too difficult, controversial, or offbeat to think about. . . . Altered states of consciousness are taken seriously: centering exercises, meditation, and fantasy are used. . . . Eduation is a lifelong journey. . . . Part of the transformative process is becoming a learner again, whatever your age . . . openness to lifelong learning. . . . A major ambition of the curriculum is autonomy. This is based on the belief that if our children are to be free, they must be free even from us — from our limiting beliefs. . . . A top-level government policymaker for education speculates that we may eventually have the equivalent of the GI Education Bill in lieu of compulsory curricula — an allotment to be spent by the individual for whatever learning, specialized or general, he seeks: 'funding the student and not the institution.' "*

• • • • •

Perhaps coincidentally, in President Bush's and Lamar Alexander's "America 2000" education plan, released April 18, 1991, there was an emphasis on innovation and experimentation, on community-wide strategies for achieving goals, on transformation of schools, on lifelong learning, and on the GI Education Bill as a rationale for educational choice where the dollars follow individual students. Regarding improving American education, President Bush said, *"There will be no renaissance without revolution"* (*Los Angeles Times*, April 18, 1991), and his new education plan called for creating "new American schools." It would be a "revolution," all right, in the sense that elements of the plan smacked of Walter Mondale's (S. 626) and John Brademas' (H.R. 2966) "Child and Family Services Act," which was described in *Human Events* (January 10, 1976) as *"simply a new version of the radical child development legislation vetoed by President Nixon in 1971 that was described by columnist James J. Kilpatrick as 'the boldest and most far-reaching scheme ever advanced for the Sovietization of American youth.'"*

In developing "America 2000," Lamar Alexander consulted with a number of so-called educational "experts," including Theodore Sizer. Sizer is the chairman of the education department at Brown University, and he is director of the Coalition of Essential Schools, which Alexander has cited as an example of an effort to design "new American schools." But Sizer has said concerning his Coalition of Essential Schools that it is a concept intended for the whole world (not just the U.S.). He said, *"We want to move away from nationalism toward the concept of world family."* Sizer has also been developing a program called "Re: Learning" that involves developing "thinking skills" rather than knowledge, per se, and in which parents have no role of any great consequence. An editorial in Denver, Colorado's *Rocky Mountain News*, June 23, 1991, described it as reminiscent of the 1970s educational fads falderal. In one Albuquerque, New Mexico elementary school, three-fourths of the teachers have requested a transfer rather than continue another year with the program. And if a student completes the program in high school, he or she will receive a "diploma of exhibition" (e.g., showing that a student has exhibited that he or she can build a boat, or do some other things), which almost no university currently recognizes as fulfilling their admission requirement.

The Carnegie Corporation chipped in one million dollars to the program, and a small group of anonymous donors gave it ten million dollars through the New York-based Atlantic Philanthropic Services. Another three million dollars came from Citibank, and one should remember here Citibank's close association early in this century with **Kuhn, Loeb, & Co.**, for whom Paul Warburg (Federal Reserve member) worked, and his son James Warburg (prominent member of the CFR and co-founder of United World Federalists) said, *"We shall have world government, whether or not we like it . . . by consent or by conquest."* To promote "Re: Learning," Sizer has formed a partnership with the Education Commission of the States, whose president, Frank Newman, said about Chicago's move toward more local control of schools: *"Will it work in Chicago? Will it eliminate corruption in Chicago — when you've had a hundred years of using the schools as a primary focal point for patronage, because you've changed the focus of power from a central board to a local board? No, of course not. . . . New teachers entering the profession must come in from higher education and teacher education as change agents."* Prior to becoming the president of ECS in 1985, Newman was a presidential fellow at the Carnegie Foundation for the Advancement of Teaching from 1983 to 1985.

Like Sizer, another group that wants to *"move away from nationalism toward the concept of world family,"* are the teachers of Impact II. Early in 1991, Impact II:

The Teachers Network published *The Teachers' Vision of the Future of Education: A Challenge to the Nation*, prepared with the support of Metropolitan Life Foundation. Praised by advisors Ernest Boyer of the Carnegie Foundation, Keith Geiger of the NEA, Albert Shanker of the AFT, and others, this report advocated that teachers be in charge of everything (curriculum, funds, personnel decisions, etc.) and it recommended that *"rather than narrow nationalism, in our future, we must emphasize that we are members of the world community. Therefore, our vision of teacher empowerment extends beyond the United States and includes the idea of the United League of Teachers, based at the United Nations."*

The Bush Administration's new education plan calls for the establishment of a national test (that would inevitably lead to nationalization of American education via a national curriculum designed to "teach to" the national test) which would be "voluntary," but the Administration urged employers to consider the test results in their hiring decisions, and colleges to consider the test results in their admissions decisions. Thus, just like the president's community and national "voluntary" service proposals, taking the national test would be "voluntary" only if someone did not want to go to college or have a job!

The "choice" aspect of the Administration's new education plan is also suspect. First, Lamar Alexander has stated that those schools participating, including private and religious schools, would come under federal regulations. Secondly, the plan indicates that these "brand-new American schools" will have to obtain state recognition or accreditation, which raises the question of just how much "choice" there will actually be. For example, if the states still control textbook decisions, this brings to mind the case of the fundamentalists in Tennessee who requested that their children in public schools not be required to read a series of stories containing thirty-five examples of children lying or rebelling against their parents with no negative consequences. The state of Tennessee refused their appeal, and the governor of Tennessee, Lamar Alexander, refused to support the fundamentalist parents who simply requested that their children be allowed to read another series of state-adopted textbooks. They had not requested that any books be "banned," but on February 28, 1987, George Bush at the forty-fourth annual convention of National Religious Broadcasters chided fundamentalist parents in Tennessee for trying to "ban" books from schools when they were deemed offensive to Christians. Bush unfairly criticized, *"There are those who would seek to impose their will and dictate their interpretation of morality on the rest of society. There are those who would forget the need for tolerance."*

Perhaps the person most influential on Lamar Alexander in his construction of the president's new education plan is Chester Finn, a former head of the U.S. Department of Education's Office of Educational Research and Improvement. After reading a copy of Finn's recent book, *We Must Take Charge: Our Schools and Our Future*, Alexander told him, *"You saved me six months"* in organizing the president's education initiative. In the book, not only does Finn advocate a national curriculum, but he also writes: *"The school is the vital delivery system, the state is the policy setter (and chief paymaster), and nothing in between is very important. This formulation turns on its head the traditional American assumption that every city, town, and county bears the chief responsibility for organizing and operating its own schools as a municipal function. That is what we once meant by 'local control,' but it has become an anachronism no longer justified by research, consistent with sound fiscal policy or organizational theory, suited to our mobility patterns, or important to the public."*

Every student must meet a core learning standard or be penalized, according to Finn, who says, *"Perhaps the best way to enforce this standard is to confer valuable benefits and privileges on people who meet it, and to withhold them from those who do not. Work permits, good jobs, and college admission are the most obvious, but there is ample scope here for imagination in devising carrots and sticks. Drivers' licenses could be deferred. So could eligibility for professional athletic teams. The minimum wage paid to those who earn their certificates might be a dollar an hour higher."* The use of the term "carrot and stick" was reminiscent of a July 1987 U.S. Department of Education "White Paper on Accountability: Tying Assessment to Action" (probably prepared largely by Finn), with a cover letter saying, *"Assessment can be used as both a carrot and stick — to recognize and reward school systems that are doing exemplary jobs in raising student performances, and in extreme cases, to intervene in districts and institutions that are not making the grade."*

Under the White Paper's section, "Intervening in Academic Bankruptcy," it indicates that some school districts may be unwilling to meet their educational responsibilities, and in those cases, state intervention may mean *"replacing district superintendents and local school boards with state-appointed officials."* This is the same "state takeover" of local schools not meeting certain state standards that Carnegie persuaded the National Governors Association to recommend when Lamar Alexander was its chairman in 1986. Leading conservatives around the country were warned about the Alexander/Finn educational philosophy, but most refused to oppose the nomination of Lamar Alexander as U.S. secretary of education.

Americans must vigorously defend local control of schools. Bills being pushed through legislatures across the land providing for "state takeover" of schools not meeting certain standards set a dangerous precedent for a state (and eventually the federal) government to take over a local school system for any reason. "State takeover" of schools is the critical link in the effort to nationalize American public education, because once authority is centralized at the state level, it will be much easier for a national authority to control fifty state authorities than have to contend with thousands of local school systems.

Besides, we know that to the extent there has already been some centralization of public education into the hands of state and federal bureaucrats, education has suffered. As nationally syndicated columnist Warren Brookes noted in the April 1990 issue of *Imprimis*: *"American public education suddenly went into . . . a tailspin in the middle 1960s. That tailspin coincided with the rapid centralization of public education away from parental control and local accountability, and into the hands of state and federal bureaucrats."* Brookes showed that in 1963, when SAT scores were highest (983), local funding composed fifty-nine and a half percent of educational appropriations, but in 1987, when scores had dropped to 904, local funding was only forty-four percent according to U.S. Department of Education figures.

• • • • •

"America 2000's" emphasis on innovation and experimentation may have come from Dee Dickinson and Linda MacRae-Campbell on the White House Task Force on Innovative Learning. MacRae-Campbell has spoken on "Educators as Change Agents," and Dickinson is in the project network of the New Age publication, *In Context.* Both individuals are with New Horizons for Learning (Dickinson as president and MacRae-Campbell as director), with board members such as leading New Ager Jean Houston. In the early 1980s, Dickinson visited the largest maternity hospital in Venezuela (remember Alexander's statement about visiting maternity wards) when she was vice-president of the International Association of Accelerated Learning, and Luis Machado was Venezuela's minister for the development of human intelligence and responsible for "The Family Project" which Dickinson visited (Machado worked with Edward DeBono, a noted teacher of "lateral thinking").

Board member for New Horizons for Learning, Jean Houston, founded the Possible Society with *Megatrends* author John Naisbitt and with Elsa Porter (former President Jimmy Carter's assistant secretary of commerce). This society sponsored a seminar in Denver in 1985 in which the attendees re-created the myth of *The Wonderful*

Wizard of Oz. According to the National Research Institute's *Trumpet* (March 1989), this was accomplished by Houston's employing *"hypnosis, enchanting spells, trances, dances, and a series of exercises supposedly designed to release the latent God within each. 'You are simply God in hiding. You must achieve your potential Godhood,' Houston commanded. By the second night, she had worked the crowd into a frenzied emotional peak then slowly to a regressed stage where they became hideous monsters or animals, slithering and groaning about on the darkened hall floor."* Houston would later be a keynote speaker at the Association for Supervision and Curriculum Development's forty-fourth annual conference (1989). She and her sexologist husband, Robert Masters, have both experimented with clinically controlled hallucinogenic drugs like LSD, and they developed the Altered States of Consciousness Induction Device, better known as "the Witches' Cradle" (like when witches were suspended from a tree branch in a swinging bag).

Jean Houston has been bridging and networking in other countries as well. The latest (as of the writing of this book) was in Australia, 1990, when Sister Marian McClelland, a Catholic nun for twenty-one years, was part of the team which brought Houston to Australia. Sister McClelland *"spent several months with Dr. Houston in U.S.A., Canada, Venezuela, and India, learning more of the work,"* according to a flier announcing workshops scheduled for 1991 in Australia, where the nun would be a "facilitator." Houston, a former Catholic, wrote a letter of authorization on January 7 of that year, stating: *"Sister Marian knows the range and extent of this work to a degree that few others do. . . . I give her full authority to teach my work."*

Those parents thinking they have removed the New Age threat to their youth by removing them from public schools and placing them in parochial schools should be very careful. New Age elements are also creeping into Catholic schools, and New Agers Robert Muller and Jean Houston both have been featured speakers at annual National Catholic Education Association (NCEA) conventions. Houston has also been a featured speaker at NEA and ASCD (Association for Supervision and Curriculum Development) conventions, as well as at the Temple of Understanding.

●●●●●

In 1985, Robert Marzano of the Mid-continent Regional Educational Laboratory (McRel) published a paper in June of that year, and it became the basis for his "Tactics for Thinking" program. McRel is also where the radical education change agent Shirley McCune works now, after she was director for the Education Commission of the States and worked for the (John) Naisbitt Group of Washington, D.C. She recently said at an ASCD conference in Aurora, Colorado: *"Radical change is necessary now; you cannot escape it. . . . Strategies and behaviors must be changed because the dawning of this new age is far more significant than the transformation of the national and world economics taking place."*

Marzano's "Tactics for Thinking" program references individuals such as the Russian psychologist A.R. Luria. Luria was influenced by Karl Marx, Wilhelm Wundt, I.P. Pavlov, and William James. He was famous for his brainwashing techniques, and may be a descendant of the sixteenth century Kabbalist (Jewish esoteric mysticism) Isaac Luria. Marzano's "Tactics for Thinking" was published by the ASCD, which recommends Robert Muller's (former assistant secretary-general of the U.N.) "World Core Curriculum" based upon the teachings of occultist Alice Bailey.

"Thinking" skills were also emphasized in *Super-learning* by Lynn Schroeder (and two others) who traveled extensively in the Soviet bloc countries and began researching learning systems there. In 1970, she introduced "Suggestology" (developed by Bulgarian Georgi Lozanov) to the West in her co-authored international best-seller, *Psychic Discoveries Behind the Iron Curtain* (perhaps relevant are the supposed psychic readings of New Ager Edgar Cayce). Schroeder developed New Age/holistic learning materials for individuals, businesses, and educators, and her book *Superlearning* is listed as a reference in the chapter of Ferguson's *The Aquarian Conspiracy* from which the above quotes were taken for this chapter of my book. Ferguson's volume is classified as occult literature in libraries and bookstores.

The concept of "the god within" (Dubos' book title) is Benjamin Creme's New Age pantheistic occultism. Remember also regarding pantheism that Dostoyevsky said, *"Anything is permissible if everything is God. There is no way of making any distinction between good and evil."* Now doesn't that sound like Masonic philosophy? Since thirty-third degree Mason Manly P. Hall wrote, *"Man is a god in the making,"* it is appropriate here to mention the relevancy of the Tower of Babel for today. Because ancient architects did not have the steel with which to make vertical "towers" as we know them, the Tower of Babel was a ziggurat or giant pyramid in Babylon, built theoretically to reach to heaven so that men would be as "gods." Thus, it was not simply the structure to which God objected and reacted, but also the concept of man becoming a "god," or in today's New Age parlance, man having "a god within."

Since the world planners are moving us toward a New Age New World Order, the movement has to be spread beyond the United States. In that regard, Dorothy Maver is a founder of the Seven Ray Institute, an adjunct faculty member of Kean College in New Jersey, and currently serving on the design team of the U.N.'s Global Education Program for Peace and Universal Responsibility, sponsored by Robert Muller's University for Peace. In October 1990, she presented a workshop in Sydney, Australia, titled "Creative Esoteric Education," in which she spoke of *"bridging esoteric principles into mainstream education. . . . There's a paradigm shift happening in education . . . linking heart and mind. . . . It is the process and not the content that is most important."*

To the extent that this pantheistic, New Age concept spreads across the country and the world now, man runs the risk of God's reaction once again, as the first of God's Ten Commandments is that He shall have no other "gods" before Him. Commenting upon the future, the nationally prominent Rev. Charles Stanley recently said, *"There will be consummated one person, an Antichrist, who will come upon the scene, and again, you know what his message is — New World Order."*

Many of the New Age principles are entering American schools via psychological "counseling" today, but some of the problems with this approach have been effectively characterized in Ronald Kohl's editorial in *Machine Design* (April 25, 1991) when he writes: *"When World War II broke out, children were told that family members in the service might never come home, and we were put through repeated air drills. . . . We took this all without 'counseling' or noticeable psychological trauma. . . . However, when war erupted recently in the Persian Gulf, school administrators were whipped into a frenzy of emotional support aimed at making sure that youngsters didn't have their psyches injured. Even worse, the tidal wave of psychological counseling swept over adults, sometimes reaching farcical proportions. A force of eight thousand psychologists announced that they were ready to shore up the fragile emotional foundations of our nation. This sets bad patterns for both kids and adults. Courage and stability are largely learned attributes picked up from role models. If psychological volatility is viewed as socially acceptable, we simply will get more of it. . . . The impact is being felt in the workplace. Children don't grow up to be productive employees when they are raised with the wrong models with regard to emotional stability. The situation has deteriorated to the point where the prerogative to flip out is now an employee fringe benefit. . . . When we encounter emotional problems, we should try harder to tough them out before pouring dollars into the pockets of psychologists."* This is good advice, especially when one considers the type of psychological counsel being given today. On NBC's "Today Show," January 22, 1990, Dr. Michael Lewis of the New Jersey Robert Wood Johnson Medical School said, *"Lying is an important part of social life, and children who are unable to do it are children who may have developmental problems."*

• • • • •

The real shame here is that even though our schools are in bad shape academically (Motorola must test ten job applicants to find one who can meet seventh grade reading and fifth grade math), we really do know how to solve our educational problems, but just are not doing it. For example, statistics show that students who do more homework and watch less television have better academic performance, but about fifty-three percent of our nation's high schools have no policy requiring homework. In addition, there is abundant research that shows intensive phonics is the best method of reading instruction, yet only about fifteen percent of our schools teach reading this way. One school that does use phonics is in Houston, Texas, whose principal is Thaddeus Lott. Nearly all of the students are poor Black youth, but on ABC television's "Prime Time Live," June 6, 1991, it was reported that the students were scoring two grade levels above average. They were also using the Saxon method of teaching math, using drills and repetition. The principal and teachers said the school system's bureaucrats were short-changing them and harassing them because of their traditional educational philosophy and the bureaucrats' racist attitude that poor Black youth should not be scoring as well as affluent white students.

Ironically, this "Prime Time Live" program aired the same day as the National Assessment of Educational Progress math results were released showing how badly

American students are doing in that subject. For example, thirty-four percent of the eighth graders and twenty-three percent of the twelfth graders tested could not add the prices of soup, hamburger with fries, and cola, which were given in the test. However, many of them watched several hours of television daily. Similarly, seven thousand eight hundred and twelve eleventh graders recently took a test in history, and one-third thought Columbus discovered the New World after 1750, while forty-three percent could not correctly name the half-century in which the First World War occurred. This lack of historical knowledge is not surprising, though, as one fifth grade history text had only one paragraph on George Washington, but seven pages on Marilyn Monroe because she was more "relevant." Another text had three and a half chapters on immigration, but no mention of Lincoln's Gettysburg Address. Thus, many Americans are likely to accept the New Age New World Order revolution taking place today, because they are subject to George Santayana's statement in volume I ("Reason in Common Sense") of *The Life of Reason* (1905-1906): *"Those who cannot remember the past are condemned to repeat it."*

To give some idea of just how much American education has deteriorated, one might simply reflect upon the test Avis Carlson passed in 1907 in a one-room schoolhouse in Kansas when she was only eleven years and eight months old. In her book, *Small World, Long Gone: A Family Record of an Era* (1977), she recalls, *"The orthography quiz asked us to spell twenty words, including elucidation and animosity. . . . An arithmetic question asked us to find the interest on an eight percent note for nine hundred dollars running two years, two*

*months, six days. . . . In reading, we were required to tell
what we knew of the writings of Thomas Jefferson . . . and
give the meanings of words such as panegyric and eyrie.
. . . Among geography's ten questions was, 'Name two
countries producing large quantities of wheat, two of
cotton, two of coal.' . . . In history, we were to 'name the
principle political questions which have been advocated
since the Civil War and the party which advocated each.' "*

There is simply no comparison between this test and
the relatively easy multiple choice nationally standarized
tests American students take today, yet today's students
still score disappointingly low. Many "progressive
educators" criticize tests based upon facts as not reflecting
students' ability to "think." However, they miss the point
concerning such tests and what they reveal. Just as one
must know the "fact" that two plus two equals four before
one can do the "thinking" required of a civil engineer,
factual tests do reveal some very important things. For
example, if a student has a good understanding of South
American geography, one could ask him or her to analyze
the economic variables affecting Argentine agriculture —
a "thinking" question. Or one could ask the student the
simple "factual" question, "What is the capital of
Argentina?" Chances are, if the student doesn't even
know that Buenos Aires is Argentina's capital, the student
isn't going to know how to analyze the economic variables
which affect that nation's agriculture. Thus, students'
ignorance regarding simple factual information reveals a
great deal about their ignorance concerning many subjects.

One should also be wary of the educational establishment's attempt to dress its failed approaches in a slightly
different manner and resell them to the public as something

new. In J'Aime Adams' "The 'New Math' Rides Again" (*Human Events*, September 7, 1991), she explains how many of the failed principles behind the disastrous "new math" of the 1960s are resurfacing today in the promotion of calculators and computers, at the expense of basic math skills. For example, she notes that the National Council of Teachers of Mathematics (NCTM) in 1989 produced "Curriculum and Evaluation Standards for School Mathematics," which bemoaned the fact that *"students might like mathematics yet believe that problem solving is always finding one correct answer using the right way."* Similarly, *Newsweek*, in its June 17, 1991 issue decried that *"most math classes are still mired in the Victorian Age, eschewing the use of calculators and computers. . . . Children are wasting time practicing adding, subtracting, multiplying, and dividing when they could be moving on to more interesting and challenging math."* Both the NCTM and *Newsweek* seem oblivious to the fact that the Japanese spend a great deal of time on practicing math fundamentals and score far above American students on math tests.

When American schools did emphasize computers, what happened? The May 20, 1991 issue of *Time* features the Belridge school district in McKittrick, California, which began to use computers in all subjects. But when the standardized test scores showed a *decline* for Belridge students, *Time* commented: *"There is a growing sense among educators and parents that as an educational cure-all, the computer has failed."* The same is true for calculators, as Dr. Richard Berg, University of Maryland professor of physics and author of *Physics of Sound*, stated: *"A lot of kids are coming into the colleges now who use the calculator for everything, and they make crazy mistakes — mistakes in the times tables — mistakes that a person well grounded in computation with a pencil and paper could never make. In my opinion, the calculator very quickly becomes a substitute for thinking.*

What should be done regarding the dismal state of American education? Congress should immediately begin an investigation into why our schools have not been doing that which has been proven to improve our students' academic performance. Unfortunately, up to this point, all we have gotten from government is an endless line of commissions appointed to study the problem, and these commissions are often comprised of the same people who have been in leadership positions while American education has been deteriorating. These should be the last people we rely upon to solve our problems. On May 22, 1991, the *MacNeil/Lehrer Newshour* showed President Bush going to what they called one of his "New World Order schools" in St. Paul, Minnesota. At this Saturn School of Tomorrow, where the president said he wanted *"to build revolutionary schools,"* students decide what they study and move at their own pace with the help of computers, into which one of the students typed: *"Will you go to collage some day, and if so witch one"*(Washington Post, May 23, 1991). Note the two misspelled words.

One of the more ominous aspects of what the New World Order holds in store for us is described in the recently published *Educating for the "New World Order"* (1991), in which author B.K. Eakman states: *"Whatever faction winds up in control of American politics in the year 2000 will inherit the new supercomputer, the Elementary and Secondary Integrated Data System, brought on line in 1988. With easy access to cross-referenceable personal information, including value judgments and political viewpoints, this faction will become powerful beyond imagination."*

● ● ● ● ●

Not only are there problems in elementary and secondary education, but colleges and universities are also under siege from a "new (politically correct, 'PC') thinking." In Dinesh D'Souza's "Illiberal Education" in *The Atlantic* (March 1991), he states that at American colleges and universities today, *"a new world view is being consolidated. . . . It is no exaggeration to call it a revolution . . . [that] seeks a fundamental restructuring of American society."* He refers to the American Council of Learned Societies' recent document, *Speaking for the Humanities*, as maintaining *"that democracy cannot be justified as a system of government inherently superior to totalitarianism; it is simply an 'ideological commitment' that the West has chosen to make."* He then identifies Duke University as one of the leaders in this "new thinking," and quotes Prof. Henry Louis Gates, Jr., there as one of its supporters who *"identified what he called 'a rainbow coalition of Blacks, leftists, feminists, deconstructionists, and Marxists' who have now infiltrated academia and are 'ready to take control.' It will not be much longer, he predicted. 'As the old guard retires, we will be in charge. Then, of course, the universities will become more liberal politically.'"* D'Souza also quotes Marxist theorist, Frederic Jameson, at Duke University as seeing the new scholarship as consistent with Jameson's mission: *"To create a Marxist culture in this country, to make Marxism an unavoidable presence in*

American social, cultural, and intellectual life. In short, to form a Marxist intelligentsia for the struggle of the future." This, they hope, will be the New World Order.

What one should recognize here is the hypocrisy of the PC advocates. Most of these people have for years been screaming that neither teachers nor society in general should impose any particular morality on anyone, yet they are now trying to impose their "politically correct" views on everyone. But there is also a bit of irony here, because for years it was the now challenged liberal "old guard" professors who themselves used "politically correct" thinking to see that the vast majority of faculty appointments went to their ideological comrades rather than to conservatives. History professor Alan Kors of the University of Pennsylvania recounted, *"I have had members of history departments elsewhere say to me point-blank, 'My department would never hire a conservative.' And these were not conservatives complaining. These were people on the left boasting."* Now these people on the left are being challenged by those seeking power who are even more radical than themselves, and they don't like it.

● ● ● ● ●

In conclusion regarding education, we recently heard Saddam Hussein refer to "the mother of all battles," but what we urgently need in the U.S., according to Mary Jo Heiland (founder of the Educational Research Institute), is "the battle of all mothers (and fathers)" against the social engineering educrats for the control and improvement of our children's education before it is too late.

Chapter Twenty-One

New Age Spirituality
and the New World Order

Linking the New World Order with the New Age, "PC" with "the god within" spirituality, is the radical philosopher Mary Daly, who teaches feminist ethics in Boston College's theology department. She describes the next stage of feminism as "cronehood," where they will see *"that our sister the Earth is in mortal danger . . . and seize the decade of the 1990s."* She continued, *"I see the voyage happening over a sea of subliminal knowledge that every woman has: background, unconscious knowledge of our history. . . . Now is the time for us to take care of our own craft. . . . We are breaking through, so what is necessary is to continue courageous voyaging in a spiraling form so that we keep regathering our energies and the memories . . . [in] our own spiral image. . . . I have absolute faith that we have it in us to save ourselves. . . . But very, very important is courage. The courage to be, the courage to see, the courage to sin in the boldest way imaginable, which is to Be . . . recalling the courage to sail on being a radical feminist pirate in the 1990s. . . . I see us and other radical feminists plundering back what really belongs to us and smuggling it back to women. . . . I took the concept of the second coming of*

Christ and said the real concept would be the second coming of women with the . . . celebration of goddess" (*Charlotte Observer*, April 7, 1991).

Also mentioning the "worship of the goddess" is radical feminist Riane Eisler in her 1987 book *The Chalice and the Blade*, wherein she states that "the Eye" and the serpent are the symbols of "the goddess." Then, quoting from Marija Gimbutas' *The Goddesses and Gods of Old Europe, 7000-3500 B.C.*, published in 1982, one reads, *"The snake and its abstract derivative, the spiral, are the dominant motifs of the art of Old Europe."*

Closer to our own time in history, the Apprentice Pillar at Rosslyn Chapel in Scotland, built in the fifteenth century, has a spiral effect. This was a Templar chapel, and the Templar churches were circular in design, just as many of the more "modern" Catholic churches being built today (some have said they are like "theater-in-the-round" design). In the south chapel of the Templar church at Garway, Herefordshire, one can see engraved a winged pyramid, solar emblem, and snake. *Encyclopaedia Britannica* notes that the Barberini family of Italy commissioned the famous sculptor Gian Lorenzo Bernini *"to build a symbolic structure over the tomb of St. Peter"* in St. Peter's Church in the Vatican. The resulting bronze baldachin (built between 1624 and 1633) has four spiraling columns, *"and the entire monument is studded with bees, suns, and laural tendrils, emblems of the Barberini family."* Bees and suns had also been associated with the Pharaohs of ancient Egypt.

Returning to Eisler's *The Chalice and the Blade*, she proclaimed: *"Ours was to be the modern era, the Age of Reason. Enlightenment was to replace superstition;*

humanism was to replace barbarism; empirical knowledge was to take the place of cant and dogma. . . . The gradual erosion of the absolute authority of the father and husband was a critical prerequisite for the entire modern movement toward a more equalitarian and just society. As the sociologist Ronald Fletcher, one of few to focus on this critical point, writes in The Family and Its Future, *'The fact is that the modern family has been created as a necessary part of this larger process of approximating to the central ideals of social justice in the entire reconstitution of society.' . . . Not just biological parents, but many other adults will take various responsibilities for that most precious of all social products: the human child. Rational nutrition as well as physical and mental exercises, such as more advanced forms of yoga and meditation, will be seen as elementary prerequisites . . . where the minds of children — both boys and girls — will no longer be fettered. It will be a world where limitation and fear will no longer be systematically taught us through myths about how inevitably evil and perverse we humans are. . . . Children will be taught new myths, epics, and stories in which human beings are good."*

Lest one think this type of values education would surely be prevented in our public schools by "separation of church and state," it should be remembered that this concept seems only to apply to those with biblical beliefs, as secular humanists have no trouble incorporating their tenets in the curricula of the government schools. In leading secular humanist John Dewey's *Education Today* (1940), he wrote (originally in the July 1907 *The Hibbert Journal*): *"Our schools . . . are performing an infinitely significant religious work. They are promoting the social unity out of which in the end genuine religious unity must grow.”*

Just two years later, the Masonic philosopher (and dean of Harvard Law School) Roscoe Pound in 1942 wrote *Social Control Through Law.* One might recall here that prior to the Second World War, many Masons were not opposed to the Fascists or Nazis, as in the April 1934 edition of the Masonic *New Age,* one reads that *“Masons adhered to Fascism at the beginning and even contributed toward the march on Rome.”*

One year earlier, on April 24, 1933, the *New York Times* reported that German Masonry had been *“pleading for the admission of its members to the Nazi Party.”* Hitler (greatly influenced by the writing of Mason Henry Ford, who contributed to the Nazis, according to James and Suzanne Pool’s *Who Financed Hitler: The Secret Funding of Hitler’s Rise to Power 1919-1933*) was concerned about secret societies, however, just as Benjamin Disraeli (Lord Beaconsfield) had been when the latter said on September 20, 1876, in a speech at Aylesbury: *“In the attempt to conduct the government of this world, there are new elements to be considered which our predecessors had not to deal with . . . the secret societies — an element which at the last moment may baffle all our arrangements, which have their agents everywhere, which have reckless agents which countenance assassination, and which, if necessary, could produce a massacre.”*

More recently regarding the New Age, radical feminist Madonna Kolbenschlag is quoted in Donna Steichan’s excellent exposé of Catholic feminism, *Ungodly Rage* (1991), as describing in *Lost in the Land of Oz: The Search for Identity and Community in American Life*

(1988) the way *"women's spirituality . . . is building a kind of chrysalis of the future"* out of which the "New World Order" will emerge. It is not surprising that Kolbenschlag would refer to the "Land of Oz," because symbolism is very important in New Age spirituality. In the motion picture, *The Wonderful Wizard of Oz* (shown by CBS each year to the present), before Dorothy dreams she is in Oz, she crosses a pyramid-shaped bridge and meets Prof. Marvel (who closely resembles the Wizard of Oz appearing later), who consults a crystal ball which he claims belonged to the priests of Isis and Osiris. The yellow-brick road begins in Munchkin City (which has a Lollipop Guild) as a "tao," which means "way," or "road" in Taosim. When the witch corners Dorothy and her companions, the witch says, *"Ring around the rosie, a pocket full of spears,"* (remember the symbolism of a rose and a spear). Dorothy had said she and her companions will receive their desires *"if the Wizard is a wizard who will serve,"* and Dorothy accomplishes her goals by "serving" her companions. There are Masonic overtones to this.

There is also the question of colors and gestures as symbols. In Malachi Martin's *The Keys of This Blood*, he writes concerning Pope John Paul II: *"He was, himself, the head of the most extensive and deeply experienced of the three global powers that would, within a short time, set about ending the nation system of world politics that has defined human society for over a thousand years."* Martin refers to the pope's thinking and working in terms of the Roman Catholic Church as the "Black *Internationale*." This is strange, because traditionally the Church has been symbolized as the Bride of Christ arrayed in white. Another internationally known Catholic priest a year earlier had said that the beast (leopard, perhaps of the black variety) of the book of Revelation in the Holy Bible is "international Freemasonry."

Regarding gestures, Martin writes supposedly about a future pope that the cardinals *"had learned to expect things from him: a deluge of well-chosen words and a panoply of gestures heavily laden with symbolism."* Some Christians have wondered why the current pope seemed to use a hand gesture when photographed with Gorbachev in December 1989, that was similar to the "real grip" of the master Mason (a grip shown in Malcolm Duncan's *Masonic Ritual and Monitor*, third edition, 1976) and *Star Trek* Spock's "Vulcan salute."

● ● ● ● ●

And how is New Age spirituality being manifested in the United States today? At the very time there is a vigorous attempt by the ACLU and others to remove not only any representation of Jesus (e.g., Nativity scenes at Christmas), but also any audible mention of Jesus (e.g., a prayer or invocation) from public life, there are increasing numbers of giant pagan statues (e.g., Athena in Nashville, Zeus at the U.N., Demeter in Annapolis, Vulcan in Birmingham, etc.) across America. And concerning children, the July 1991 *Reader's Digest* describes Turner Broadcasting System's New Age cartoon series "Captain Planet and the Planeteers" as *"the slickest political propaganda piece ever aimed at America's young people . . . promoting a leftist agenda."*

Also promoting the "New World Order" New Age spirituality is the Omega Institute for Holistic Studies, which on August 3-10, 1991, held its first annual international conference at Prague, stating in its announcement: *"We find ourselves at the edge of a 'new world order.' . . . For those interested in global unity . . . the main emphasis of the conference is on building community as an active contribution to global consciousness. . . . Among the faculty are Peter Goldman* [former director of White Lodge, a society for transpersonal psychotherapy] *and Erik van Praag* [working to establish the International School for Global Leadership]. *"*

In the July 1991 *New Age Journal*, it was announced that from August 30 to September 1, a "Transformational Politics Group Annual Meeting" would be held in Washington, D.C., with panel topics including, "The '90s as a Green Decade" and "Humanistic Psychology in Politics." Also for August 30 to September 1, "Choices for the Future," with speakers such as Matthew Fox, was hosted by New Ager John Denver's Windstar Foundation. One doesn't truly appreciate John Denver's famous line, "Far out," until one learns that, according to author Randall Baer, Denver believes he originated from a place near the Lyra nebula. In his "Choices for the Future" announcement letter, Denver wrote: *"We hear current discussion about a 'New World Order' . . . and in an effort to take personal responsibility for this proposed new order . . . we can make sure the 'New World Order' includes an environmentally sustainable and peaceful future for all."* (Windstar Foundation, founded in 1976, presents each year a Windstar Award to *"a global citizen who is contributing to the creation of a healthy, peaceful future, whose personal and professional life exemplifies commitment to a global perspective."*)

Other celebrities promoting world government are actor Ed Asner and film producer Oliver Stone who, along with Philadelphia mayor Wilson Goode, Linus Pauling, and others, were honorary sponsors of the World Constitution and Parliament Association's (WCPA) World Constituent Assembly (WCA) and the Provisional World Parliament (PWP). The WCPA was founded in 1959, with its most prominent member being World Union, which was founded in 1958. Speakers at the PWP (formerly called the Peoples World Parliament) discussion series during the 1980s included Jesse Jackson and Ramsey Clark. Among the organizations collaborating in the preparatory committee for the WCA (formerly called the World Committee for a World Constitutional Convention) held in Lisbon, Portugal on April 29-May 9, 1991, were the Millennium Project U.S.A. and the Rainbow Coalition of California.

Most of this information is included in *En Route to Global Occupation* (1991) by Gary Kah, who feels that the WCPA apparently *"has been destined to replace the U.N. "* In his book, Kah publishes documents showing the WCPA's Diagram for World Government under the Constitution for the Federation of Earth (including the "World Police"). He also includes interesting quotations by notable Americans and others, such as Frederick Gates (appointed by John D. Rockefeller as chairman of the General Education Board, founded in 1902), who wrote in the board's "Occasional Letter, No. 1" (1913), *"In our dream, we have limitless resources, and the people yield themselves with perfect docility to our molding hand. The present educational conventions fade from our minds; and, unhampered by tradition, we work our own good will upon a grateful and responsive rural folk. "* He also quotes Woodrow Wilson after signing the Federal Reserve Act, as saying, *"I have unwittingly ruined my country."* Giovanni Agnelli, head of Fiat and a leading Bilderberger, is referred to as asserting, *"European integration is our goal and where the politicians have failed, we industrialists hope to succeed."*

The Bilderberger organization has been funded by the Rockefeller and Ford Foundations among others, and its founder, Prince Bernhard of the Netherlands (whose family is principal owner of Royal Dutch/Shell Oil Co.), is quoted as stating: *"It is difficult to re-educate the people who have been brought up on nationalism to the idea of relinquishing part of their sovereignty to a supernational body. . . . This is the tragedy."* Kah also refers to organizations such as the Arcane Schools, Triangles, and World Goodwill, all established by the Lucis Trust in the 1920s and 1930s.

In *Triangles* (June 1991, Bulletin 96) is written: *"Through visualization and imagery we are able to experience realms of beauty, truth, and knowing that we would not be able to experience any other way. We know this in our regular Triangles work, where the creative imagination enables us to **see** and **experience** the inner light that radiates through the network and to **know** ourselves as points of light in a pulsating web of triangles."* This is typical New Age spirituality, and those who believe and follow the teachings of the Holy Bible should remember that Colossians 2:8 warns: *"Beware lest any man spoil you through philosophy and vain deceit, after the tradition of men, after the rudiments of the world, and not after Christ."*

Chapter Twenty-Two

Conclusion

Thus, it seems that many groups are promoting the concept of a New World Order, but national columnist Pat Buchanan wrote: *"The Trilateralist-CFR, Wall Street-Big Business elite, the neo-Conservative intellectuals who dominate the think tanks and op-ed pages, the Old Left, with its one-world, collective security, U.N. 'uber alles' dream: All have come together behind the New World Order. Everyone is on board, or so it seems. But out there, trying to break through, is the old authentic voice of American patriotism, of nationalism, of America first!"*

I hope that Mr. Buchanan is right, but I would also offer three cautionary notes. First, never underestimate the willing ignorance and lethargic indifference of the general public. This even applies to many conservative fundamentalist Christians who have been told by their pastors that because they are "saved," they do not have to be concerned about anything. At the "Capitol Fourth" celebration on Capitol Hill in Washington, D.C., on July 4, 1991, over three hundred thousand people cheered wildly at the conclusion of Cab Calloway's rendition of Ira and George Gershwin's song, "It Ain't Necessarily So," which contains the anti-biblical lyrics, *"De t'ings dat you' li'ble, To read in de Bible, It ain't necessarily so. . . . Dey tell all you chillun, De debble's a villun, But 'taint necessarily so. . . ."* Similarly at a recent Boston Pops concert on Public Television (supported by our tax dollars), the audience applauded wildly at the end of a song by Bobby McFerrin's singers, which contained the words to Psalm 23 except that everywhere God is referred to as "He" or "His," they said "she" or "her" and concluded with *"In the name of the mother, and the daughter, and the holy of holies, Amen."* Do those listening to and applauding such music understand what these songs are saying? Abraham Lincoln said, *"To sin by silence when they should protest makes cowards out of men."* Regarding the instances above, those who did not protest were moral cowards or have "lost their salt."

Secondly, never underestimate the ability of so-called conservative national leaders to sit by while the country is being undermined or even destroyed. Just as conservative leaders did not oppose the nomination of Lamar Alexander to become U.S. Secretary of Education, how many conservative leaders have you heard speak out about the possible permanent placement of foreign military troops on American soil? According to a report in the *Dallas Morning News* and other newspapers around the nation on May 11, 1991, *"German lawmakers said U.S. officials reacted favorably to the idea of a permanent German military presence"* in the United States. Think about it! At a time when American military bases are being closed, why would German soldiers be permanently stationed here, especially when they refused to send any forces to the Persian Gulf War? Perhaps the answer lies in a map adopted in 1952 by the World Association of Parliamentarians for World Government which showed how foreign troops would occupy and police the six regions into which the United States and Canada would be divided as part of a world government plan.

In a speech from the White House on the evening of September 27, 1991, President Bush announced drastic unilateral reductions in our nuclear arsenal which had served as a very successful deterrent against aggression. Brent Scowcroft was the architect of the reduction, just as he had planned President Nixon's 1972 trip to Moscow and President Ford's plan to reduce our offensive nuclear arsenal; Scowcroft was also the architect of our shift in nuclear strategy from one of first-strike capability to one based merely upon deterrence. President Bush on September 27, assured the American people that there was no need to be concerned about this, but then one must remember that he has lost a great deal of credibility having promised ("read my lips") the public there would be no new taxes, and then he broke his word. In Mr. Bush's speech, he declared: *"Twenty years ago, when I had the opportunity to serve this country as ambassador to the United Nations, I once talked about the vision that was in the minds of the U.S.'s founders — how they dreamed of a new age when the great powers of the world would cooperate in peace. . . . The Soviet people and their leaders can join us in these dramatic moves toward a new world of peace and security. Tonight, as I see the drama of democracy unfolding around the globe, perhaps we are closer to that new world than ever before."*

This was similar to President Bush's reference to a "New World Order" and the *"vision of* [the U.N.] *founders"* in his March 6, 1991, address to Congress at the end of the Gulf War. And because of his reference (in his

September 27 address) to a "new age" and "new world" based upon "the vision" of the United Nations' founders, it is interesting to note that Soviet agent Alger Hiss was the secretary-general of the U.N. founding conference in San Francisco in 1945 and helped draft the U.N. Charter. Furthermore, over forty of the American delegates to the founding conference were members of the CFR.

The states of the former Soviet Union today are very unstable, and no one knows for sure who will be in control there next year or next month. Also, remember that decades ago Dimitri Manuilsky revealed a Soviet plan whereby they would use a great peace initiative to lull the West into a vulnerable position. Therefore, rather than greatly reduce our military strength, we might remember what Winston Churchill told his countrymen in 1938 concerning the impending German threat: " 'Thou art weighed in the balance and found wanting.' And do not suppose that this is the end. This is only the beginning of the reckoning. This is only the first sip, the first foretaste of a bitter cup which will be proferred to us year by year unless by a supreme recovery of moral health and martial vigor, we rise again and take our stand as in the olden time."

Just as the world planners want America to disarm its nuclear weapons, they want individual Americans to be disarmed as well. However, Americans should remember what was said in "olden times," when James Madison proclaimed in *The Federalist Papers*: "*Americans need never fear their government because of the advantage of being armed, which the Americans possess over the people of almost every other nation.*" And in *An Examination Into the Leading Principles of the Federal Constitu-*

tion (1787), Noah Webster pronounced: *"Before a standing army can rule, the people must be disarmed, as they are in almost every kingdom in Europe. The Supreme power in America cannot enforce unjust laws by the sword, because the whole body of the people are armed, and constitute a force superior to any band of regular troops that can be, on any pretense, raised in the United States."*

Thirdly, never underestimate the cunning of the world planners. In that regard, one should be wary of the Constitutional Convention (Con-Con) movement, as it could provide them with the vehicle to create a new U.S. Constitution in which we as individuals and as a nation no longer have our sovereignty or any of our cherished rights, instead coming under the authority of the dictatorial rulers of the New World Order.

Constance Cumbey has written in *The Hidden Dangers of the Rainbow*, *"The New Age movement's leadership is proposing to implement all the systems set forth in Revelation, chapter 13: they have called for the abolishment of a cash monetary system; they openly propose to give every world resident a number and require the usage of this number in all financial trans-actions of any sort; they plan to institute a 'New World Order' which will be a synthesis between the U.S.S.R. ('feet like a bear'), Great Britain ('spoke like a lion'), and the United States ('like unto a leopard'* [always changing its spots, from freedom to the coming tyranny]*), also featuring the ten nation Common Market nations of Europe ('ten horns'), and a worldwide government or 'planetary guidance system'; the system they propose to implement is **identical** in belief systems and cosmology to the Nazi system of Adolfus Hitler (the beast that was dead* *and came back to life — Naziism)!"* The beast that was dead and came back to life could also refer to the supposedly currently dying communism.

The coming time about which "Revelation" is referring is that of the Antichrist, who will be ushered in with a New Age pantheism to rule the "New World Order." In that regard, over a hundred years ago Reverend P. Huchedé, professor of theology at the Grand Seminary of Laval, France, wrote *History of the Antichrist* (1884) in which he prognosticated: *"But it does not suffice to destroy; it is absolutely necessary to build up again. The world cannot subsist long in a vacuum. It must have a religion; it must have a philosophy; it must have an authority. Revolution will furnish all these. Instead of the reasonable and supernatural religion of Jesus Christ,* **Revolution will preach Pantheism.**"

More recently in this regard, former leading New Ager Randall Baer who converted to Christianity revealed in *Inside the New Age Nightmare* (he mysteriously died the week that his book was to be released in 1989): *"This agenda is nothing less than the complete revolutionizing of the very foundations of not only America but the entire world. Such a plan calls for the total restructuring of planetary civilization into an enlightened One-World Federation in which national boundaries and sovereignty are secondary, and 'planetary citizenship' in the 'global village' is the order of the day. This . . . is to offer a world in desperate need, a grand solution to profound global problems. Apparent world peace and unprecedented opportunities for 'actualizing the human god-potential' (i.e. New Age higher consciousness) are to be unveiled. Herein lies the Antichrist's last temptation, offered to all the world."* Perhaps relevant here is the news item in the March 1, 1992 *New York Times* which related that Javier Perez de Cuellar (former U.N. secretary general) on March 1 became co-chairman (with former Xerox chairman Sol Linowitz) of the Inter-American Dialogue. The organization's president, Richard Feinberg, said on February 27 that de Cuellar would be involved in a new project "redefining sovereignty" that would *"consider the increasingly active roles of international organizations, non-governmental groups, and national governments in promoting economic integration and reducing social inequities in the region, a new trend in an area where national sovereignties were once jealously guarded."*

Shortly before this book was being written, it was learned that supposedly a symbol and seal are being developed for the New World Order. The symbol for the seal will be in three parts and made of gold, black, coral, diamonds, rubies, and emeralds. An announcement will be made regarding this in the not-too-distant future (for more information, see the front page of the National Research Institute *Trumpet*, September 1991). The announcement of the symbol and seal may not indicate that a world government as such has been formed, but so as not to greatly alarm the public the announcement may simply indicate that an organization is being formed to promote a "sea change" (note the recent increased usage of this term) toward the objectives of the New World Order. Many world political and religious leaders will applaud this action as an effort to bring about peace and justice, harmony, and cooperation among the peoples of the world. Unfortunately, the public reaction may be that foretold by H.G. Wells in *The Shape of Things to Come* where he wrote that although World Government *"had been plainly coming for some years, although it had been endlessly feared and murmured against, it found no opposition prepared anywhere."*

We would do well to remember President Abraham Lincoln's Proclamation of March 30, 1863, part of which said: *"We have been the recipients of the choicest bounties of Heaven. We have been preserved, these many years, in peace and prosperity. We have grown in numbers, wealth, and power as no other nation has ever grown. But we have forgotten God. We have forgotten the gracious hand which preserved us in peace, and multiplied and enriched and strengthened us; and we have vainly imagined, in the deceitfulness of our hearts, that all these blessings were produced by some superior wisdom and virtue of our own. Intoxicated with unbroken success, we have become too self-sufficient to feel the necessity of redeeming and preserving grace, too proud to pray to God that made us! It behooves us, then, to humble ourselves before the offended Power, to confess our national sins, and to pray for clemency and forgiveness."*

For those readers who care enough to want to help preserve our nation's sovereignty, it is imperative to act *now*. If you would like to say "No" to the New World Order internationaliism and to the increasing New Age and secular attacks on the biblical values upon which our nation was founded, there are five important, positive actions you can take. First, pray daily to God, our Father in heaven, for his protection and for the gifts of discerning wisdom, moral strength, and faithful perseverance in His service. Secondly, read or reread the *Constitution of the United States* with the *Bill of Rights*, and encourage the younger generation to do likewise. Regrettably, a 1987 nationwide survey *"found that only fifty-four percent knew the purpose of the original document* [the Constitution of the United States] *and fifty-nine percent could not identify the purpose of the Bill of Rights."* Thirdly, whenever there is an attack on biblical values (whether in the press, media, or other areas), respond immediately by letter or other appropriate means to editors, advertisers, sponsors, or others. Fourthly, widely distribute pamphlets published by America's Future (P.O. Box 1625, Milford, PA 18337-2625), especially this writer's pamphlet, "The New World Order: A Chronology and Critique." Fifthly, ask your senators and congressmen to sponsor and support a resolution proclaiming the year 1992 as the "Year of National Hymn." "National Hymn" is the name of the tune in your hymnal for the song, "God of Our Fathers." The lyrics to "God of Our Fathers" were written in 1876 for the centennial Fourth of July, and the tune of the same sang, "National Hymn," was chosen for the centennial celebration of the adoption of our U.S. Constitution. If Congress can pass all sorts of trivial resolutions year after year, then surely with December 1991 the bicentennial of the effective date of our Bill of Rights, it would not be too much to ask of them to proclaim 1992, the "Year of National Hymn." Rather than become "One nàtion, under the New Age New World Order," please help our country remain, as our Pledge of Allegiance for decades has proclaimed, *"One nation, under God."*

Remember, as Edmund Burke said in *Thoughts On the Cause of the Present Discontents* (April 23, 1770): *"When bad men combine, the good must associate; else they will fall one by one, an unpitied sacrifice in a contemptible struggle.* "It is absolutely essential that each one of us prayerfully and peacefully does that which is necessary to resist the principalities and powers driving our nation and all others toward the New Age New World Order.

Postscript

As this book is going to press, Mikhail Gorbachev has resigned as president of the now defunct U.S.S.R. However, do not be surprised if in the future, like the symbolic "phoenix rising from the ashes," he returns to world dominance in some official capacity. Don't forget that in his December 7, 1988 speech to the U.N. General Assembly, he remarked: *"The world economy is becoming a single entity outside of which no state can develop,"* and he called for *"creating an altogether new mechanism for the furtherance of the world economy . . . a new structure of the international division of labor . . . a new type of industrial progress in accordance with the interests of all peoples and states. . . . Further progress is now possible only through a quest for universal consensus in the movement toward a new world order."*

This is similar to a statement by the secretary general of the World Constitution and Parliament Association quoted in the May/June 1985 edition of that organization's publication, *Across Frontiers*: *"To escape from this trap* [recycling loans] *requires a truly New World Economic Order, which includes a new world financial and credit system based upon productive capacity and a single world monetary system. The introduction of such vast changes cannot be done by negotiations one-by-one among sovereign nations, but requires collective action by non-aligned and debtor countries within the framework of a new global system of finances mandated under a world constitution. By organized and collective action within the context of an emerging world parliament and world federation, the demand for acceptance of the new world economic order becomes possible.*"

Before the U.S. turns over more authority to the U.N. however, it should also be remembered that only a few days before Gorbachev's December 7, 1988 U.N. address advocating a "new world order," that organization showed its true colors. In a December 22, 1988 editorial, the *Pittsburgh Press* related that in November by a vote of 100 yes, 8 no, and 15 abstentions *"the Third World communist bloc rammed through a resolution favoring its so-called New World Information and Communications Order, or NWICO, to justify censorship and restrictions on press freedom where they exist and to try to spread those big-brother practices from unfree countries to the free world."*

Despite this attitude on the part of a majority of U.N. members, on January 31, 1992, President Bush joined other heads of government at the U.N. Security Council to press the U.N., according to the *Los Angeles Times* (February 1), *"to abandon its hallowed tradition of non-interference in the internal affairs of countries . . .* [declaring] *that the world community can no longer allow advancement of fundamental rights to stop at national borders."* In the same issue of the *Los Angeles Times*, staff writer Doyle McManus explained that the fifteen members of the Security Council *"proclaimed a rough outline for a new world order run partly through the United Nations, most of the initiatives coming from countries other than the United States."* McManus then related that one U.S.

official told him that President Bush welcomed the assertiveness of his allies *"because it strengthens the communal nature of the U.N. We're even willing to sacrifice some of our national interest — in the short-term sense — to make that work."*

In Gorbachev's *New York Times* syndicated article in the May 4, 1992 *Denver Post*, declared that *"now we have the chance to move toward a . . . human world order* (remember *Toward a Human World Order* by Gerald and Patricia Mische of Global Education Associates). Gorbachev then referred to "the demons of nationalism" and said, *"Even the United States itself is not immune from the dangers of nationalism. If America is 'always right,' . . . then the drive will never get under way to create a new world order based on international law, equality, and mutual respect, freedom of choice and the balance of interests. . . . The war in the Persian Gulf and its outcome may argue that America's calling is to be the noble sheriff, able to punish scoundrels in any corner of the planet. Actually, the Persian Gulf war showed just the opposite: the new role of the United Nations as a mighty instrument in the hands of the world community. . . . America must also make a constructive contribution to the effort of the United Nations to strengthen international law and order and to solve global problems."*

Warning Americans about entrusting the U.N. with too much authority and about financially "propping up" individuals like Gorbachev all in the name of maintaining stability in the world, Phyllis Schlafly, in "Reaganism vs. the New World Order" (*The Phyllis Schlafly Report*, January 1992), related: *"This peculiar passion for stability is indicated by the rumor, no doubt apocryphal, that one of the upper floors in the State Department has a room called the Shrine, and every day Secretary James Baker and emissaries from President Bush and the secretary of commerce gather there to pay homage. When this Shrine was supposedly installed a year ago, Mikhail Gorbachev was one of its High Priests and Saddam Hussein was the Devil to be exorcised. The United Nations was the 'mecca' toward which all faces turned, and all the incantations ended with the holy response: 'New World Order.' There was no problem in passing the collection plate to support missionaries for this new religion. The multinationals and international bankers are quite willing to donate petty change to win converts to the religion of Stability because they are betting that the bread they put on the waters will come back to them a thousandfold in taxpayer subsidies for their 'sales' to nonpaying 'customers' in Russia. . . . It's beginning to look as though the New World Order means the American taxpayers assuming the burden of propping up and financing whatever boundaries, corrupt regimes, and deadbeats the international bankers and multinational corporations want."* In this regard, the international bankers and heads of multinational corporations today are not really different from the Rockefellers, Morgans, and Carnegies at the turn of the last century who were financially supporting the furtherance of Marxism (see cartoon). In the same issue of *The Phyllis Schlafly Report*, she warned in "Will the U.N. Dictate the New World Order?" that the United Nations Covenant on Civil and Political Rights (supported by President Bush and ratified by the U.S. Senate on April 2, 1992) would *"imperil existing American rights by using treaty-law . . . [to] override provisions of our Constitution . . .*

subject us to supervision by busybody bureaucrats in the United Nations, and diminish our national sovereignty."

The phrase "religion of Stability" is not all that farfetched, as those supporting patriotic nationalism rather than the "New World Order" will in all likelihood be accused of "undermining stability" in the world. Note the use of the word "instability" in the following quotation from Paul Lewis' article, "As the U.N.'s Armies Grow, the Talk Is of Preventing War" (*New York Times*, March 1, 1992): *"In its summit declaration the Security Council widened its definition of what constitutes a threat to peace and security in today's world, saying this now includes 'proliferation of all weapons of mass destruction' as well as 'non-military sources of instability in the economic, social, humanitarian, and ecological fields.' Such language seems to cover just about anything that could go wrong in the present-day world. So a more politically intrusive United Nations may be the real price the world must pay if it wants fewer conflicts and smaller peacekeeping bills in the future."* While Lawrence Freedman in "Order and Disorder In the New World" (*Foreign Affairs*, Vol. 71, No. 1, 1992) did judge that *"these attempts to make stability the central strategic value of the new age are doomed to continual disappointment,"* he also noted that *"the United Nations will be taking a more active and important role in global management. . . . Despite the mockery and cynicism to which this slogan ('new world order') has been subjected, it seems as if it will last."* In the same issue of *Foreign Affairs*, the journal's editor, William Hyland, wrote "The Case for Pragmatism," supporting the movement toward a "New World Order" and bemoaning those calling for a "new nationalism."

It has been those government elitists who have desired "stability" and "pragmatism" at all costs who have not diligently pursued the issue of American POWs and MIAs. In "An Examination of U.S. Policy Toward POW/MIAs" by the U.S. Senate Committee on Foreign Relations Republican Staff (May 23, 1991), previously classified government documents are used to show that after the First and Second World Wars as well as after the Korean and Vietnam Wars, the American government simply abandoned many soldiers who were POWs and MIAs to live the life of slaves in communist countries (for a copy of the document, call (202) 224-3941, the U.S. Senate).

After the Vietnam War, the Institute for World Order (now the World Policy Institute) with board members C. Douglas Dillon, William Sloane Coffin, Jr., Father Theodore Hesburgh, and pollster Daniel Yankelovich among others, had a letter (signed by president Saul Mendlovitz) sent out on November 24, 1976 explaining that through its Lodi Project, one of its objectives during the period 1976 to 1980 would be *"to create by 1980 a situation within the United States which will encourage a significant number of senatorial and congressional candidates, as well as at least one presidential candidate, to make world order a central theme of their campaigns."* It was in 1980 that globalist George Bush challenged Ronald Reagan for the presidency.

As a former American ambassador to the United Nations, President Bush adopted the position after the Iraqi invasion of Kuwait that his *"administration would like to make the United Nations a cornerstone of its plans to construct a New World Order."* This is what *Time* magazine said on September 17, 1990. And in Peter

LaLonde's *One World Under Antichrist: Globalism, Seducing Spirits, and the Secrets of the New World Order* (1991), he related that *"as former American ambassador to the United Nations Jeanne Kirkpatrick notes, one of the underlying goals in Bush's handling of the entire crisis was to show the world how a reinvigorated United Nations could serve as a global policeman in the New World Order"* (*Jewish Press*, December 7, 1990).

Relevant to Gorbachev's possible return to prominence, it is ironic that on December 29 and 30, 1991, ABC television broadcast the movie *Spartacus* (coincidentally the code name of Illuminati founder Adam Weishaupt) in which Crassus feints a withdrawal from leadership only to have his archrival warn that this is simply Crassus' plot to "rise from the ashes" in that time of disorder, and Crassus' plan to rule the Roman Empire indeed succeeds as he uses terms such as "new order" and "destiny."

In the meantime today, eleven of the "republics" of the former Soviet Union are forming the Commonwealth of Independent States, with Russian president Boris Yeltsin the leading figure. He has indicated that membership for his country in NATO is a "long-term political aim" designed to help create an international security system "from Vancouver to Vladivostok," words like those of James Baker in Berlin on June 18, 1991, referring to a Euro-Atlantic community. Yeltsin in Rome on December 20, 1991 continued: *"It is not a question of five or six years but significantly more, when there are no nuclear weapons. By that time, the weapons will have been destroyed, and integration will have been completed not just in Europe but beyond its borders."* One should remember here that Yeltsin was sponsored earlier on a visit to the U.S. by the Esalen Institute, and Robert Lindsey's front-page *New York Times* (September 29, 1986) article said, *"Many in the field regarded Esalen as the mother church of New Age ideas."* One should also bear in mind that the breakup of the Soviet Union into eleven new states will mean quite a few more votes for them in the U.N. General Assembly. Likewise of note is the fact that despite Russia's dire economic condition, Yeltsin has ordered a ninety percent pay raise for soldiers, intelligence, and security personnel (the new Russian Ministry of Security is based on the old Russian Interior Ministry and the KGB, which according to Stephen Knight's *The Brotherhood* has infiltrated Freemasonry).

Also concerning nuclear weapons, the evening before Yeltsin's statement in Rome, the Bush Administration confirmed it had decided to lift sanctions (effective date February 3, 1992) on the sale of U.S. satellite parts and high-speed computers to China in order to meet the Chinese condition set for its willingness to abide by the international agreement that restricts the export of missiles, according to the *Los Angeles Times*. Many might consider this succumbing to blackmail by authoritarian rulers, but support for such rulers is not rare. According to Christopher Whalen's "Editorial Commentary" in *Barron's* (July 22, 1991), *"A hard look at the distribution of the U.N. Development Program's $1.5 billion annual budget makes plain that helping authoritarian governments preserve the status quo figures first in its priorities."* This has been under William Draper III, former head of the Export-Import Bank and a close friend of President Bush, who when vice-president recommended Draper to head the U.N.D.P.

Just as this book was going to press at the end of 1991, another book titled *Plausible Denial* by Mark Lane was being released. Lane quotes the forewoman of the jury in a U.S. district court as stating that the jury unanimously concluded on February 6, 1985 that *"the CIA had indeed killed President Kennedy."* The author refers to a *New York Times* April 25, 1966 report that JFK had told one of the highest officials in his Administration that because of the Bay of Pigs disaster, Kennedy wanted *"to splinter the CIA in a thousand pieces and scatter it to the winds."* He fired Allen Dulles as head of the CIA, but President Lyndon Johnson (a Mason) appointed Dulles to the Warren Commission investigating the assassination of Kennedy. Four days after JFK's death, LBJ signed National Security Action Memorandum 273 reversing Kennedy's NSAM 263 which ordered the immediate withdrawal of one thousand "military advisors" from Vietnam, with a timetable for withdrawal of all U.S. personnel. L. Fletcher Prouty, former chief of the Office of Special Operations in charge of all military support of the clandestine operations of the CIA, stated that *"when Kennedy signed NSAM 263, he signed . . . his own death warrant."* And according to the *Washington Post* (December 13, 1977), three years after the Warren Commission report was issued claiming Lee Harvey Oswald acted alone, LBJ said he felt the CIA had something to do with Kennedy's death. Mark Lane then goes on to say that George de Mohrenschildt was a CIA contract agent who brought Oswald to Dallas and arranged a job for him at the Texas School Book Depository. De Mohrenschildt was a wealthy white Russian oil man who had been charged earlier by the FBI with being a Nazi spy during

World War II, and was found killed just before he was to be questioned by the House Select Committee on Assassinations. Lane claims that in de Mohrenschildt's personal phone book was found, *"Bush, George H.W. (Poppy), 1412 W. Ohio, also Zapata Petroleum, Midland."* The author of *Plausible Denial* asserts that George Bush secretly began working for the CIA in 1960 or 1961 while CEO of Zapata Offshore Co. in Houston, and the CIA's secret code name for the invasion of Cuba was "Operation Zapata" with ships named "Barbara" and "Houston." In another new book, *Conspiracies, Cover-Ups, and Crimes: Political Manipulation and Mind Control In America* (1992), author Jonathan Vankin reminds the reader that John Hinckley, Sr. is a friend of President Bush, and that the president's son, Neil, was scheduled to have dinner with Scott Hinckley the evening of the same day his brother, John Hinckley, Jr., attempted to assassinate President Ronald Reagan on March 30, 1981.

Similar to the public's being misled for many years about President Kennedy's assassination, most Americans still believe President Franklin Delano Roosevelt's Administration was opposed to our entry into World War II prior to Pearl Harbor. However, Secretary of War (and a CFR founder) Henry Stimson's November 25, 1941 diary notes included: *"President Roosevelt brought up the event that we were likely to be attacked perhaps* [as soon as] *next Monday, for the Japanese are notorious for making an attack without warning, and the question was how we should maneuver them into the position of firing the first shot. . . ."* Was it mere coincidence that only four days before this, on November 21, Public Law 298 was approved, which authorized *"the sum of $50,000 to* *establish a national cemetery at Honolulu, Territory of Hawaii"* (the location of Pearl Harbor)?

Secretary Stimson actually wanted the U.S. to fire the first shot and was "relieved" when the Japanese attacked Pearl Harbor, noting in his diary on December 7 that *"this continued to be my dominant feeling in spite of the news of catastrophes which quickly developed."* Stimson as well as Harvey Bundy, George Harrison, and Robert Lovett who all worked for him, were all members of Skull and Bones, which according to an 1896 *New York Tribune* article *"is a branch of a university corps in Germany."* Stimson would initiate George Bush into this secret society in 1948. Lovett had been on the board of Union Pacific with Averell Harriman and was heavily involved with loans to Germany before the Second World War. He would later suggest that President Kennedy hire Dean Rusk, Douglas Dillon, and Robert McNamara (all CFR members, with McNamara later becoming president of the World Bank and a trustee of the Aspen Institute for Humanistic Studies, as well as on the board of directors of the World Future Society). And Lovett's father worked with the leading Houston law firm of Baker and Botts, the family firm of the current secretary of state, James Baker III. The usual story regarding George Bush's early business years is that he traveled to Texas "starting out on his own" in the oil business. Actually, Henry Neil Mallon of Dresser Industries (which helped build up the U.S.S.R.) helped the future president get a job, and Mallon along with George Bush's father (Prescott Sheldon Bush) and Edward Roland Noel Harriman were all members of Skull and Bones in 1917. The latter two joined Brown Brothers Harriman & Co., as did W. Averell Harriman who was a member of Skull and Bones in 1913. Many years later when George Bush was being sworn in as vice-president in 1987, rather than have the chief justice of the Supreme Court administer the oath, this was done by Mason Justice Potter Stewart (even though he was not well and had left the Supreme Court in 1981) who was a member of Skull and Bones in 1936.

It is interesting that toward the end of 1991 when Pat Buchanan decided to run for the presidency against George Bush, who was a member of Skull and Bones, the CFR, and worked for the CIA, Mr. Buchanan was criticized in a new book by William F. Buckley, Jr., who was a member of Skull and Bones, the CFR, and worked for the CIA (William Sloane Coffin, Jr., was likewise a member of Skull and Bones and worked for the CIA, as was William Bundy, who also was a CFR member). Is the motion picture, *The Brotherhood of the Bell*, with Glenn Ford relevant here?

One supporter of President Bush incorrectly accused Pat Buchanan of bordering on "facism" (when government regulates most or all private enterprise), when the fact of the matter is that there have been more new regulations implemented under the Bush Administration than under any other U.S. president. Buchanan's campaign theme is "America First," and he has also questioned President Bush's credibility, reminding voters of Bush's broken "read my lips" promise not to raise taxes. Christians might also remember that within hours of speaking at a Southern Baptist Convention, President Bush was asked about National Endowment for the Arts head John Frohnmayer, and in response the president said that he strongly supported him and thought he was doing a good

job. This was even though the NEA under Frohnmayer
funded blasphemous anti-Christian so-called "works of
art" with our tax dollars. Buchanan's "America First"
theme has been unfairly criticized as isolationist, when in
fact he does not say "America alone," but simply believes
our nation's interests should come first in all policy
decisions our government makes. After President Bush
said, *"I don't want to see this country go back to 'America
first,' "* Pat Buchanan noted that before the attack upon
Pearl Harbor, the head of the America First chapter at
Yale University was Gerald Ford and John F. Kennedy
contributed one hundred dollars to America First. Here
one would do well to remember the plan of Marx and
Engels to undermine nationalism, as they stated in their
1848 *Communist Manifesto*: *"In place of the old local and
national seclusion and self-sufficiency, we have intercourse
in every direction, universal interdependence of nations.
And as in material, so also in intellectual production. The
intellectual creations of individual nations become
common property. National one-sidedness and narrow-
mindedness become more and more impossible. . . ."*
And one might also remember that in the CFR's first
edition of *Foreign Affairs* (September 25, 1922), Charles
Eliot criticized those advocates of "America first" who
did not want to join the League of Nations (the first
attempt at a "New World Order," and President Wilson,
supporting the League, referred in a September 9, 1919
address in Minneapolis to its charter as *"the charter of the
new order of the world"*).

No doubt, "the new order of the world" would be a
racist and eugenic one because Charles Eliot (former
president of Harvard University) had been a vice-president

(along with Winston Churchill, Alexander Graham Bell, and Gifford Pinchot) of the First International Congress of Eugenics in 1912. This was the same year (1912), according to Allan Chase in *The Legacy of Malthus* (1977), that *"Governor Woodrow Wilson signed into law the brutal sterilization bill passed by the legislature* [but which] *the New Jersey Supreme Court found to be unconstitutional."* Chase then related that on January 14 of the next year, Mason Theodore Roosevelt, *"an old adherent of eugenics and racial superiority,"* wrote a letter stating: *"It is obvious that if in the future racial qualities are to be improved, the improving must be wrought mainly by favoring the fecundity of the worthy types and frowning on the fecundity of the unworthy types. At present, we do just the reverse. There is no check to the fecundity of those who are subnormal, both intellectually and morally, while the provident and thrifty tend to develop a cold selfishness, which makes them refuse to breed at all."* Then in a statement that sounds almost Hitlerian, Vice-President-elect Calvin Coolidge wrote in "Whose Country Is This?" (*Good Housekeeping*, February 1921): *"There are racial considerations too grave to be brushed aside for any sentimental reasons. Biological laws tell us that certain divergent people will not mix or blend. The Nordics propagate themselves successfully. With other races, the outcome shows deterioration on both sides. Quality of mind and body suggests that observance of ethnic law is as great a necessity to a nation as immigration law."*

Ten years later, Fabian socialist Arnold Toynbee in June 1931 delivered a speech to the Institute for the Study of International Affairs at Copenhagen in which he explained: "*We are at present working discreetly with all our might to wrest this mysterious force called sovereignty out of the clutches of the local nation states of the world. All the time we are denying with our lips what we are doing with our hands, because to impugn the sovereignty of the local nation states of the world is still a heresy for which a statesman or publicist can perhaps not quite be burned at the stake but certainly be ostracized and discredited.*" Then just before Hitler began the Second World War, Lola Maveric Lloyd and Rosika Schwimmer wrote *Chaos, War, or a New World Order?* (1938). And shortly after World War II, occultist Alice Bailey in *Problems of Humanity* (1947) claimed that "*humanity, as a whole, is of far greater importance than any one nation; it will be a new world order, built upon different principles to those in the past. . . . What we need above all to see — as a result of spiritual maturity — is the abolition of those two principles which have wrought so much evil in the world and which are summed up in two words: sovereignty and nationalism.*" The next year, Bailey had published *The Reappearance of the Christ* (not referring exclusively to Jesus) announcing a coming world religion. At the end of the next decade, Grenville Clark and Louis Sohn wrote *World Peace Through World Law* (1958) advocating turning the U.N. into a governing body for the world, and referring to world disarmament, a world police force, a world legislature, a world executive, a world judicial system, a World Development Authority, a global monetary system, and redistribution of the world's wealth. At the end of the next decade, Robert Kennedy wrote *To Seek a Newer World* (1967) in which he proclaimed that "*all of us will ultimately be judged . . . on the effort we have contributed to building a new world society."* And toward the end of the next decade, Mortimer Adler wrote *Philospher at Large* (1977), stating that *"the argument for world government is the indispensible condition of world peace can be boiled down to a single proposition: if local civil government is necessary for local civil peace, then world civil government is necessary for world civil peace."* Not too many years later, the (Willy) Brandt Commission (formally titled the Independent Commission on International Development Issues, and including Robert McNamara and Katherine Graham) recommended on February 9, 1983 that there be a supernational authority to regulate world commerce and industry, that there been an international currency, and that among other things there be an international police force under the U.N. Security Council.

This is relevant to Holly Sklar's edited volume, *Trilateralism: The Trilateral Commission and Elite Planning for World Management* (1980), in which she relates that trilateralists *"are determined to consolidate* **world economy** [and] . . . *in a 1973 memo on the Trilateral Policy Program that director Brzezinski recommended to study of 'Control Over Man's Development and Behavior' as a theme for later consideration. More specifically such a task force would undertake to study 'the social-education implications of the availability, especially in advanced societies, of new means of social control."* One should remember at this point that Aldous Huxley wrote in *Brave New World*: *"A really efficient totalitarian state would be one in which the all-powerful executive of political bosses and their army of managers control a* *population of slaves who do not have to be coerced, because they love their servitude. To make them love it is the task assigned, in present-day totalitarian states, to ministries of propaganda, newspaper editors and school teachers. . . ."* Sklar asserts that *"trilateralism is the current attempt by ruling elites to manage both dependence and democracy — at home and abroad,"* and one way to accomplish this is *"the debt leash can be pulled in tight — as part of an economic and political **destabilization** campaign — to strangle a rebellious nation into submission. . . . The goal of trilateral food policy, writes Dahlia Rudavsky, is to transform 'the basic human need for food into a source of economic gain and social control.' Indeed, economic gain and social control are inseparable goals of trilateralism."*

The year after Sklar's volume, Arthur S. Miller in *Democratic Dictatorship: The Emergent Constitution of Control* (1981) described a "new feudal order" controlled by elitists, and assessed that *"dictatorship will come — is coming — but with the acquiescence of the people, who subconsciously probably want it. The Grand Inquisitor likely was correct: People want material plenty and mysticism, not perfect freedom. Freedom is an intolerable burden. . . . The ideologist for this development is B.F. Skinner. The goal is 'predictable' man — a person who conceives of freedom in Hegelian terms. Americans are moving into a Skinnerian world, one in which they 'will no longer know, or care, whether they are being served or controlled, treated or punished, or whether they are volunteers or conscripts. The distinctions will have vanished' (Peter Schrag,* Mind Control, *1978)."*

Miller followed this work with *The Secret Constitu-*

tion and the Need for Constitutional Change (1987), expressing thanks to the Rockefeller Foundation for their help. In this book, he declares that *"a pervasive system of thought control exists in the United States. . . . The citizenry is indoctrinated by employment of the mass media and the system of public education, . . . people are told what to think **about**. . . . The old order is crumbling. . . . Nationalism should be seen as a dangerous social disease. . . . A new vision is required to plan and manage the future, a global vision that will transcend national boundaries and eliminate the poison of nationalistic 'solutions.' . . . A new constitution is necessary. . . . Americans really have no choice, for constitutional alteration will come whether or not it is liked or planned for. . . . Ours is the age of the planned society. . . . No other way is possible."* Three years later, after Iraq invaded Kuwait early in August 1990, the press reported that President Bush's national security advisor, Brent Scowcroft (who was, until he became national security advisor in 1989, co-chairman of the Aspen Institute for Humanistic Studies Strategy Group, which received a $200,000 grant from the Carnegie Corporation in 1988) suggested the term "New World Order" to the president for Bush's grand design to be used against Saddam Hussein. But is this really what happened? Look at the foreshadowing words, including the words "new world order," used by President Bush himself over six months earlier in a fund-raising speech in San Francisco on February 28, 1990: *"Time and again in this century, the political map of the world was transformed. And in each instance, a new world order came about through the advent of a new tyrant or the outbreak of a bloody global* *war, or its end."* This was nearly seven months *before* Saddam Hussein invaded Kuwait and the "New World Order" began! And what about the timing of President Bush's September 27, 1991 announcement regarding our large-scale unilateral reduction in nuclear weapons, which was just after World Goodwill (Lucis Trust) published its 1991, No. 3, newsletter titled "Shaping a New World Order," in which there was a section "Swords Into Plowshares" that described the May 1990 Disarmament Commission of the U.N.'s proposal for *"the reduction and final elimination of all nuclear stockpiles"*?

What a future non-nationalist world would be like in a political and economic sense was perhaps described by the youngest Milford in the TV movie *Amerika*, first aired February 15, 1987, when he spoke (in 1997) that, *"We are the voice of the New Generation. We are the voice of the New People. The destructive ways of the past are gone. We will replace them with our vision of the future. The Party will lead us to the New Age. There have been those who have tried to stop the New Age. They are the corrupt reminder of the past. They have tried to confuse us with the idea that the old America was a good country. We know that lie. History teaches us that lie. We are grateful to our Soviet brothers who saved the world from destruction and we can now join them in a World of Socialist Brotherhood. Everyone will go to school. Everyone will have a job. Everyone will be equal. No one will exploit or be exploited. And all those who oppose this wonderful vision will be crushed!"* The word "crush" here reminds one of the following entries for June 7 and June 12, 1895, in Vol. I of *The Complete Diaries of Theodore Herzle* (1960): *"I will bring to the Rothschilds . . . their historical mission. I shall gather all men of good will . . . and shall crush all those of ill will (this I shall say threateningly to the Rothschild Family Council). . . . The distribution of this new world will be handled equitably!"*

Just a few years after Herzl's pronouncements, H.G. Wells wrote *New Worlds for Old* (1908) using such phrases as "the finer order," "points of fire," "servants of the light," "the coming City of Mankind," and "the State (as) Over-Parent of children." He described the Fabians' development of administrative socialism characterized by increased taxation, an expansion of public education, public feeding of school children, taking over the food supply, and creation of a public health service. According to Wells, *"Socialism ceased to be an open revolution, and became a plot. Functions were to be shifted, quietly . . . from the representative to the official he appointed . . . a scientific bureaucracy appointed by representative bodies of diminishing activity and importance . . . the replacement of individual action by public organization"* could achieve socialism *"without popular support."*

One of the leading proponents of a new world order, the World Association for World Federation, has just changed its name to the World Federalist Movement with actor Peter Ustinov as its president. Also late in 1991, the World Federalist Association has just published *A New World Order*, including consideration of a full-fledged world government (CFR member and former congressman and presidential candidate John Anderson became WFA president in January 1992). Plans for a world government have been under way for some time, for example at Worldview '84 sponsored by the World Future Society in 1984 with master of ceremonies Congressman Bob Edgar, chairman of the Congressional Clearinghouse on the Future at that time. At Worldview '84, they spoke of transforming nation-states into a New World Order through "management by crisis," when at a "moment of critical instability," the nation-state system would collapse (perhaps due to debt) and networking groups would form a replacement society. This was reported by Peter LaLonde, who listed the following corporations as supporting both the World Future Society and the Trilateral Commission: Control Data, General Electric, General Motors, IBM, Weyerhaeuser, and Xerox. Concerning Weyerhaeuser, the father, Frederick Weyerhaeuser (a Trilateral Commission member) was a member of Skull and Bones. And regarding Xerox, its former chairman, David Kearns, is now chief deputy to Secretary of Education Lamar Alexander.

But how would a "moment of critical instability" occur so that it could be "managed"? You may have noticed in recent years that the press and media have been hyping controversies, trying to make "crises" out of them. Remember that in Saul Alinsky's *Rules for Radicals* mentioned earlier, he said that the radical organizer *"dedicated to changing the life of a particular community must first rub raw the resentments of the people of the community; fan the latent hostilities of many of the people to the point of overt expression. He must search out controversy and issues. . . . An organizer must stir up dissatisfaction and discontent. . . . He knows that all values are relative . . . truth to him is relative and changing."* Since God stands for absolute truth, it is not surprising that at the front of his book, Alinsky wrote: *"Lest we forget at least an over-the-shoulder acknowledg-*

ment to the very first radical . . . the first radical known to man who rebelled against the establishment and did it so effectively that he at least won his own kingdom — Lucifer."

Concerning "crises" and "instability," I cannot emphasize strongly enough the response of O'Brien in George Orwell's *1984* to Winston's assertion that a civilization founded upon fear and hatred and cruelty would disintegrate. O'Brien replied, "*Suppose that we quicken the tempo of human life.*" Orwell wrote this book in 1949, and beginning in the 1950s with "rock 'n roll," it seems that the pace of life steadily got faster. Whereas in the past, ideas or problems were discussed calmly and thoroughly, it now seems we are overwhelmed with one problem or crisis after another. This has caused increasing social instability, and it may not be accidental. If people feel they can no longer cope, they might be willing to turn over more authority to "Big Brother."

Relevant to both education and "crisis," the results of the 1991 SAT scores are now available, and the College Board's national report stated: "*The mean verbal score has declined for the fifth consecutive year to a new all-time low, two points below its previous low in 1980, 1981, and 1990.*" One reason perhaps for students' declining verbal skills is that many "progressive" educators today have bought the educational philosophy of John Dewey, who in his 1989 essay, "The Primary Education Fetish" attacked the teaching of reading in primary grades, saying, "*It does not follow that because this course was once wise it is so any longer. . . . The plea for the predominance of learning to read in early school life because of the great importance attaching to literature seems to be a perversion."* Similarly, Dewey's psychology teacher at Johns Hopkins University, G. Stanley Hall, proclaimed the benefits of illiteracy, stating that *"illiterates . . . escape much eye strain and mental excitement . . . and certain temptations."* More recently, a reporter wrote in "Reading Method Lets Pupils Guess" (*Washington Post*, November 26, 1986), *"The most controversial aspect of whole language is the de-emphasis on accuracy. . . . American Reading Council President Julia Palmer, an advocate of the approach, said it is acceptable if a young child reads the word house for home, or substitutes the word pony for horse. . . . 'Accuracy is not the name of the game.'"*

More important than "accuracy" concerning factual knowledge was the psychological manipulation of students, as G. Stanley Hall, Charles Judd, Edward Thorndike, and other "Deweyites" were directors of the Psychological Corporation founded in 1921. The corporation's president, J. McKeen Catell, wrote in "The Psychological Corporation" (*The Annals of the American Academy of Political and Social Science*, November 1923) that *"the Corporation is not so much concerned with arranging specific contracts for work by it or under its auspices, as in promoting the extension of applied psychology. . . . To get the best kind of people and to put them in the situations in which they will behave in the way best for themselves and for others, is more fundamental than any other enterprise of society. It is necessary to organize means by which this work can be accomplished. . . . Psychology is concerned with the causes of conduct and its control."*

About forty years later, I attended the first session of

the Governor's School of North Carolina, the first of its kind in the nation, about which *Time* (June 28, 1963) said, "*Four hundred of North's Carolina's most brilliant and creative high school students have been brought together for an intensive eight-week summer study program.*" On May 6, 1963, Prof. George Welsh of the Department of Psychology at the University of North Carolina at Chapel Hill wrote to the Psychological Corporation of New York indicating that at the Governor's School "*we are planning to administer an extensive test battery including measures of aptitude, interest, and personality.*" On May 10, Harold Seashore, director of the Corporation's test division, replied to Prof. Welsh and indicated that if he used their test, "*we would want a set of the cards filed with us, so that we can accumulate information on groups like this over the years.*" Welsh sent a memo to the Governor's School administrative staff indicating "*we can collect detailed information* [about family and so on] *later from those in whom we are seriously interested* [in attending the school]. " As students at the school, we were administered Terman's Concept Mastery Test and the Minnesota Multiphasic Personality Inventory (originally designed to assess personality characteristics related to psychiatric disability), both of which were published by the Psychological Corporation.

The results of the de-emphasis upon academic basics in schools can be seen in the *Blumenfeld Education Letter* (December 1991), in which Samuel Blumenfeld points out regarding verbal SAT scores that "*in 1972, 116,630 students scored between 600 and 800, the highest possible score, while 71,084 scored betwen 200 and 299 at the bottom of the scale. The total number of students who took the test in 1972 was 1,022,820. In 1991, the situation is exactly the reverse. The number of students achieving the highest score (600-800) had dropped precipitously to 74,836, and the number achieving the lowest score (200-299) had increased to over 134,600. The number of students who took the test in 1991 was 1,032,685. The dumbing down* [of American education] *has indeed taken place, and the figures are there to prove it."* Is this any wonder, when studies indicate that a typical eighth grader watches twenty-one and a half hours of television each week, compared with just five and a half hours on homework and two hours on reading?

For years, parents complained that something was wrong with American education, and that the academic basics were not being taught. "Progressive" educators denied there was anything wrong until parental outrage at falling test scores swept the nation, and then these educators began to promote "the new basics" which included not just the three "R's," but everything from dance to computer technology. This redefining of terms or their meaning is a favorite tactic of the professional education leadership. For example, in the early 1980s, they went along with the transfer of authority from Washington to the state level because they had their people in place at the state superintendent level across the nation, and the last thing they wanted was to be told what to do by newly elected conservatives and their appointees in Washington. As the 1980s and the 1990s witnessed a growing activism in every state by parents intent upon reforming education, one saw educational leaders begin to support "local accountability" and "site-based management." However, what they meant by these terms is that the authority of locally elected school boards directly answerable to the people would diminish, and greater control over education would be placed in the hands of "master" or "lead" teachers. These teachers would almost always be long-term members of the NEA, who believe that they as "professional educators" know how best to teach children. Therefore, rather than teaching a standard curriculum, they should have the autonomy to spend a week lecturing on "global warming," for example, if they think that is best.

Not long ago, on the national radio program "Phyllis Schlafly Live," a woman called in and asked why any teachers would not want to teach children the basics. She wanted to know where this attitude began. Actually, this attitude makes a great deal of sense if you are a change agent wanting to alter American society away from free enterprise capitalism and toward socialism. If you "dumb down" students so they cannot or do not want to read, then they will not know history and the negative results of socialism in the past. As George Santayana remarked, *"Those who cannot remember the past are condemned to repeat it."* Also, if you do not know basic math, then you will become more and more dependent upon government for your basic needs. Socialism also means emphasizing the group rather than the individual, and educational emphasis is placed upon students' relationships with others rather than upon academic basics. Similarly, there is a shift from individual rights under the Constitution to group rights.

Today, instead of properly instructing students how to read and solve math problems, a growing number of schools are now passing out free condoms, despite

Dr. Thomas Sowell's statement in *Forbes* (December 23, 1991) that *"condoms, as used by teenagers, have about a twenty percent failure rate — slightly higher than the failure rate in Russian roulette."* Dr. Sowell further remarked that before massive federally funded sex education programs entered American public school systems in the 1970s, teen pregnancies had been declining for more than a decade. However, after these programs were introduced, the pregnancy rate among 15- to 19-year-old females went from 68 per 1,000 in 1970 to 96 per 1,000 in 1980; and between 1970 and 1987, the number of abortions by teens increased by 250,000 even though the number of teens declined by 400,000. Despite these findings, two years later, in 1989, the Alan Guttmacher Institute (affiliated with Planned Parenthood) published *Risk and Responsibility: Teaching Sex Education in America's Schools* (funded by the Carnegie Corporation, New York Times Foundation, and Brush Foundation), which advocated more comprehensive sex education courses *"taught earlier than they are."*

Where did this "new morality" come from? Enlightening in that regard perhaps is *Five Lectures . . . on Moral Education* (1970), and in their "Introduction" to the book, Nancy and Theodore Sizer not only say they *"doubt the value of giving grades,"* but they also speak of *"the teacher who cares about a 'new world.' . . . The nineteenth-century teacher sermonized . . . but Christian sermonizing denies individual autonomy, which, with justice, lies at the heart of a new morality. . . . No longer can we list . . . objective moral 'truths' about the world and expect children to take them over intact. . . . Moral autonomy, the independent arrival at a conviction of one's own accountability toward one's fellow men, the rational and emotional acceptance of justice as the most proper atmosphere in which all individuals can flourish, including even one's secret self — this is the 'new morality' toward which we are to guide ourselves and other people. . . . Clearly the strict adherence to a 'code' is out of date. "* Remember here that today, Ted Sizer heads the Coalition of Essential Schools and the "Re:Learning" projects around the country, and he is touted by Secretary of Education Lamar Alexander.

Education will be globalist in the "New Age New World Order," a term I used and warned against at the end of the op-ed article, "Globalism' Tramples on American Values," in the Pulitzer Publishing Company's *St. Louis Post-Dispatch* on May 12, 1988.

Malachi Martin in *The Keys of This Blood* critically describes the transnationalists' goal that *"ideally the same textbooks should be used all over the world in both the hard sciences and the soft curricula. And sure enough, a concrete initiative in this direction has been under way for some years now, undertaken by Informatik, a Moscow-based educational organization, and the Carnegie Endowment Fund. . . . 'Good' will no longer be burdened with a moral or religious coloring. 'Good' will simply be synonymous with 'global.' Else, what's an education for? [But] educational changes will not be the half of it. The Transnationalist education formula is in essence one step in a drive to build a worldwide human infrastructure upon which an effectively working global economy can base itself with some security. The emphasis is on homogeneity of minds, on the creation and nourishing of a truly global mentality. . . . We must all become little*

Transnationalists." Then on the April 24, 1992 broadcast of Southwest Radio Church, when Rev. Noah Hutchings asked Malachi Martin if President Bush's reference to "a thousand points of light" is "New Age theology," Dr. Martin replied, *"Of course. Of course, it is . . . and the New Age will be the religion of the New World Order."* Both this statement and the one above from *The Keys of ¿ This Blood* fit well with the announcement in the March 1989 *Update* of the Association for Supervision and Curriculum Development, which was that *"effective citizens in the new age will be global citizens. . . . Intelligence for the new age will be global intelligence."*

In June 1990, a cross section of the educational community from seven countries was invited to Chicago to participate in a conference whose purpose was *"to explore the common vision for Holistic Education and establish guidelines and coordinating procedures for the dissemination of holistic principles. One outcome of that conference was the 'Chicago Statement on Education.' A movement has now taken form. . . . GATE is about people who have a vision for education transformed . . . about creating critical mass for change. . . ."*

Dorothy Maver, who was mentioned in chapter 20 and is on the Steering Committee of Global Alliance for Transforming Education (GATE), held a workshop on "Global Education — The Esoteric Connection" in Sydney, Australia, October 1990, in which she noted that *"the New Education is the science of 'Right Human Relations.' . . . Leaders in education from around the world are connecting in support of this project. . . . The big picture . . . is to present the framework at the* [1992] *Brazil Conference to Education Ministers around the globe and begin immediately to implement it in existing education systems. . . . We are told that when educators begin to speak of 'bridging,' that's when the New Education will come to light."* Dr. Maver plans also to teach a two-year course of study, "Planning the New Education," in Arlington, Texas, home of the Robert Muller School.

Facilitating the "Transnationalist" or "globalist" or "New Age" mentality have been the S-U-N (Spiritual Unity of Nations) conferences. In John Cotter's *A Study in Syncretism* is described how in May 1968, the S-U-N *"held an international conference of spiritual and esoteric organizations in Hove, Sussex, England. 1650 delegates attended, some coming from behind the Iron Curtain and even as far afield as Iceland. There is a S-U-N Center in Detroit, and groups in Chicago, Atlanta, Costa Mesa, California. . . . The Americans sponsored a large S-U-N conference in November 1968 to formulate 'a New Age world religion' to complement the New World Order of the Aquarian age,"* and later conferences were held in Detroit, Pretoria, and Bombay.

Likewise facilitating the "Transnationalist" or "globalist" or "New Age" mentality have been "intentional communities" like Findhorn, at which David Spangler was co-director from 1970 to 1973. Other "intentional communities" described as "awaiting a new dawn" are the Chinook Learning Center founded in 1972 in the state of Washington and committed to "building a new order of people," and the Sirius Community (in Massachusetts) founded by Corinne McLaughlin and Gordon Davidson who together wrote *The Builders of the Dawn* (1984). Sirius, High Wind Community (in Wisconsin), and Findhorn have developed a "new seed idea, the University of the Future" whereby students may obtain a full semester of undergraduate or graduate credit from the University of Wisconsin for an alternative "semester abroad" spending a month, living, working, and studying in each of these communities. Graduates of the "University of the Future" might go on to become members of the New Group of World Servers, whom Mary Bailey of Lucis Trust addressed in December 1983 at the Sagittarius Full Moon Festival in New York, saying that "... *the keynote for the disciple in Sagittarius: 'I see the goal, I reach that goal, and then see another' ... on the path of disciple-ship and to the path of initiation. ... The energy of Sagittarius ... [has] devoted humanitarian tendencies that can do much in the field of service ... and our capitol city, Washington, [is] ruled by Sagittarius."* Perhaps coincidentally, President Bush in his August 18, 1988, nomination acceptance speech emphasized "service" ("a thousand points of light") and said, *"I am a man who sees life in terms of missions — missions defined and missions completed."*

What is planned for the New Age New World Order in a religious sense regarding Christianity (including Catholicism) is also explained by Malachi Martin in *The Keys of This Blood* as perhaps best *"gleaned from the* Permanent Instruction *drawn up a few years after the Congress of Vienna, in 1819-20, by the French, Austrian, German, and Italian grand masters of the (Masonic) lodges: '. . . we must turn our attention to an ideal that has always been of concern to men aspiring to the regeneration of all mankind ... the liberation of the entire world and the establishment of the republic of brotherhood and world peace. ... Among the many remedies, there is one which we must never forget: . . . the total annihilation of Catholicism and even of Christianity. . . . What we must wait for is a pope suitable for our purposes. . . . Seek a pope fitting our description . . . make the younger, secular clergy, and even the religious, receptive to our doctrines. Within a few years, this same younger clergy will, of necessity, occupy responsible positions. . . . Some will be called upon to elect a future pope. This pope, like most of his contemporaries, will be influenced by those . . . humanitarian principles which we are now circulating. . . . 'The dream of the secret societies* [to have a pope as their ally] *will be made real for the very simple reason that it is founded on human passions. . . ."*

Pope Leo XIII was aware of the Masons' plans, and according to Paul Fisher's *Their God Is the Devil* (1991), Pope Leo on December 8, 1892, delivered the encyclical *Inimica Vis* to the bishops of Italy proclaiming that Masons *"wish to see the religion founded by God repudiated and all affairs, private as well as public, regulated by the principles of naturalism alone. . . ."* This encyclical was accompanied by another one, *Custodi Di Quella Fede*, to the people of Italy, which pronounced that *"by way of conspiracies, corruptions, and violence, Masonry has finally come to dominate Italy and even Rome. . . . Naturalism is substituted for Christianity; the worship of reason for the worship of faith. . . . Masonry has taken control of public schools; . . . confiscated the inheritance of public charity; and opens and maintains houses of vice."*

Concerning the Catholic Church in the U.S. today, the Sacrament of Baptism is now called the Sacrament of Initiation (at least for adults) but I believe Jesus was "baptized" by John the Baptist rather than "initiated." The *Mount Washington Press* (May 8, 1991) reported that a psychologist who is "worshipful master" of Mount Washington Masonic Lodge 642 (and a Rosicrucian) screens prospective priests for the Archdiocese of Cincinnati, Ohio. And regarding organizations supported by Masonry, Paul Fisher's research revealed that about eighty percent of the funding for the predecessor of Americans United for Separation of Church and State came from Masons.

Masons have been prominent in America from before the time of Charles Thompson (Mason who was secretary of the Continental Congress and who created the Great Seal of the United States) until after the time of Roscoe Pound (Masonic philosopher who was dean of the prestigious Harvard Law School and wrote *Lectures of the Philosophy of Freemasonry* in 1915). Similarly in Europe, prominent Masons included Solomon Meir Rothschild and the Adlers, the Russian anarchist Mikhail Bakunin, and Cecil Rhodes. Rhodes had been financially assisted by Rothschild banking interests (Lord Rothschild was involved with Rhodes' Round Table Group), and at Oxford University had been a pupil of John Ruskin who read Plato every day and believed in government by the elite who would control means of production and distribution (like the "philosopher-kings" of the French Revolution).

In Europe today, the European Community is supposed to be erasing all economic boundaries. In 1988, the head of the European Commission in Brussels, a French socialist named Jacques Delors, indicated that by 1998 *"no less than eighty percent of all Europe's micro-*

*economic legislation will come from Brussels rather than from the governments of the member countries. . . . The Delors Report eagerly anticipated imposing uniform economic policies on the member states. It cites 'the need for a **transfer of decision-making power** from member states to the Community' "* (*Forbes*, January 22, 1990). However, in the same year of 1988, Prime Minister Margaret Thatcher on September 20 at Bruges, Belgium, declared: *"We have not successfully rolled back the frontiers of the state in Britain only to see them reimposed at a European level with a European super-state exercising a new dominance from Brussels."* The arrogance of the European Community officials, though, can be seen today in a poster produced by the EC's Council for Cultural Cooperation. The poster shows a tower under construction which looks very much like the Tower of Babel as painted by sixteenth-century artist Pieter Bruegel, and the poster's legend states: "Europe: Many Tongues, One Voice."

Over twenty centuries after the Tower of Babel came the dawning of Christianity, and our present calendar began from that time with the system of dating from A.D. 1. However, this dating notation was challenged not long ago by a U.S. Catholic Bishops Committee, who decided to discontinue all references to A.D. (*anno Domini*, the year of the Lord) in favor of C.E.(Common Era) and B.C.E. (Before the Common Era). This ridiculous religiously objectionable decision is just one more indication that now is unfortunately the "dawning" of the New Age New World Order, which will reach its height under the Antichrist, who will claim that he will bring "peace" to the world. Daniel 8:25, however, shows that this great deceiver will be broken by Jesus, and remember when reading this verse that "craft" is another name for Masonry or Freemasonry:

> *"And through his policy also he shall cause craft to prosper in his hand; and he shall magnify himself in his heart, and by peace shall destroy many: he shall also stand up against the Prince of princes; but he shall be broken without hand."*

In a February 8, 1992 speech at the Catholic University of Milan, Cardinal Joseph Ratzinger criticized the "New World Order," recalling a book by Monsignor Robert Hugh Benson which was titled *Lord of the World* (1907). The Cardinal said it described a *"similar unified civilization and its power to destroy the spirit. . . . The anti-Christ is represented as the great carrier of peace in a similar new world order."* He warned that after the republication of Msgr. Benson's book in Germany in 1990, today this view is a *"real danger, which must be opposed."*

"The Lord of the World," according to Alice Bailey in *Initiation, Human and Solar* (Lucifer Publishing Co., 1922) was also *"the officiating agent* [for] *the focalization of influences and energies. . . . The organization of the Freemasons is a case in point. . . . At the head of certain occult groups, of the Freemasons of the world, and of the various great divisions of the church, and resident in many of the great nations will be found initiates or Masters. This work of the Masters is proceeding now, and all Their efforts are being bent toward bringing it to a successful consummation. . . . The process of initiation might therefore be regarded as one in which the different points of light (or human sparks) are stimulated, their radiance and temperature increased, and the sphere of influence of each light extended in radius."* Perhaps it is just a coincidence that in President Bush's August 18, 1988 nomination acceptance speech, he emphasized "a thousand points of light" and said the election was *"about philosophy. And I have one. At the bright center is the individual. And radiating out from him or her. . . ."*

Perhaps it is also just coincidental that one of President Bush's favorite expressions is "It wouldn't be prudent," and in Mason William Hutchinson's 1775 volume, *The Spirit of Masonry*, one reads that in the British Museum is an ancient beryl stone, which includes on it a star that *"seems to be used as a point"* (point of light?) *"only, but is an emblem of Prudence, the third emanation of the Basilidian divine person. . . . The emblem of Prudence is placed in the centre of the lodge, and is the first and most exalted object there: ever to be present to the eye of the Mason, that his heart may be attentive to her dictates, and steadfast in her laws; for Prudence is the rule of all the virtues. Prudence is the channel where self-approbation flows for ever. . . . A good Mason is a citizen of the world. . . . But as some members will be refractory in every society, your Hammer will likewise teach you how to use becoming discipline and correction toward such like offenders. If they will not submit to rule, you may strike off the excrescences of their swelling pride, till they sink into a modest deportment. Are they irregular in their practices? Your Hammer will instruct you to strike off each irregularity, and fit them to act a decent part on the stage of life. Do any affect things above their stations? Your Hammer will teach you to press them down to their proper level, that they may learn, in the school of discipline, that necessary knowledge — to be courteous"* (remember the Fabians remold the world with "hammer blows").

Increasing numbers of individuals are speaking out against the seemingly inexorable movement toward the New Age New World Order, but the problem is a lack of realization that organized opposition is the key. Those promoting the New Age New World Order pursue their objectives and basically ask their opponents, "What are you going to do about it?" This attitude covers all areas of life from education to religion. They do not mind if their opponents talk to each other about various concerns, or write books, or circulate newsletters, or anything similar. The only thing they fear is if their opposition forms a networking organization that will threaten their re-election to public offices, their teaching status, or their position of authority in any other area. Therefore, what must be done is to begin such an organization, so that the proponents of the New Age New World Order will know that whenever they try to diminish our national sovereignty or "clarify" our children's values, for example, they will be opposed by an organization which has the capability of removing them from public office or causing them to be removed from any other position of authority.

Otherwise, they will increasingly control our lives and the lives of our children. In Charlotte Iserbyt's *Back to Basics Reform Or . . . Skinnerian International Curriculum?* (1985), she describes *"the social engineers' continuing efforts, paid for with international, federal, state, and tax-exempt foundation funding, to manipulate and control Americans from birth to death using the educational system as the primary vehicle for bringing about planned social, political, and economic change."* And in Bettina Dobbs' February/March 1992 newsletter for Guardians of Education for Main, she predicts that *"children are to be held hostage by state agencies which will plaster them with 'At Risk' labels in order to direct them into various state regulated programs designed to clone 'consensus trained' brainwashed citizens for 'The New World Order.' Parents will be forced to cooperate and take parent retraining courses under threat of having the child(ren) removed from the home (and held hostage) under threat of possible charges of child abuse or educational neglect with court-ordered psychological counseling for parents. (Maine law, Title 20-A, Sec. 3273)"* C. Winsor Williams in the March 1992 edition of *Chronicle* verified that this threat applies to a number of other states in addition to Maine. Americans must wake up and act before it is too late to stop the New Age New World Order from gaining control over our lives and the lives of our progeny.

Lest one think there is no plan to control the population, it would be wise to reflect upon a speech delivered in Pittsburgh in March 1969. The speaker was Dr. Richard L. Day, national medical director of Planned Parenthood from 1965 to 1968, and according to Dr. Lawrence Dunegan, who was in attendance, Dr. Day announced that in terms of controlling population, *"Everything is in place, and nobody can stop us now. . . . This time we're going to do it right."* Dr. Dunegan recounted that Dr. Day pronounced the following things were planned: contraceptives would be dispensed at schools; abortion would become legal and paid for by tax dollars; homosexuality would be promoted as no longer to be considered abnormal behavior; hard-to-cure diseases would be created; cures for nearly all cancers had been developed, but were being hidden at the Rockefeller Institute so that the population wouldn't increase; a hard-to-detect means had been developed for inducing heart attacks (assassinations); drug (including school) addiction would be promoted so the unfit would die; euthanasia would be more accepted as the cost of medical care would intentionally be made burdensomely high; divorce would be made easier; I.D. badges would become more prevalent (eventually implanted under skin, and perhaps a transmitter in dental fillings); all salary payments and purchases would be conducted electronically by computer in one banking system; major world religions (especially Christianity) would have to change into a new world religion, and the churches will help bring it about; more airplanes and rail accidents, as well as building and bridge collapses, would occur to create an atmosphere of instability; terrorism would be used to make people demand international controls; and economic interdependence would help lessen national sovereignty, as people would become citizens of the world.

May God help and have mercy on us and our children in the years ahead.